Behind the Label

Behind the Label

Inequality in the Los Angeles Apparel Industry

Edna Bonacich and
Richard P. Appelbaum

with

Ku-Sup Chin
Melanie Myers
Gregory Scott
Goetz Wolff

UNIVERSITY OF CALIFORNIA PRESS

Berkeley / Los Angeles / London

University of California Press
Berkeley and Los Angeles, California

University of California Press, Ltd.
London, England

© 2000 by
The Regents of the University of California

Library of Congress Cataloging-in-Publication Data

Bonacich, Edna.
    Behind the label : inequality in the Los Angeles apparel
industry / Edna Bonacich, Richard P. Appelbaum.
        p. cm.

    Includes bibliographical references and index.
    ISBN 0-520-21769-1 (cloth : alk. paper)—ISBN 0-520-22506-6
    (pbk. : alk. paper)
    1. Clothing trade—California—Los Angeles. 2. Clothing
workers—California—Los Angeles. 3. Sweatshops—California—
Los Angeles. I. Appelbaum, Richard P. II. Title.

HD9940.U5 L712 2000
331.7'887'00979494—dc21   99-088415

Manufactured in the United States of America

08—07—06—05—04—03—02—01—00

10—9—8—7—6—5—4—3—2—1

The paper used in this publication meets the minimum requirements
of ANSI/NISO Z39.48-1992 (R 1997) (*Permanence of Paper*)

To the garment manufacturers and other powerful players connected with the apparel industry in Los Angeles, in the hope that they will see the need for social change. To the garment contractors, who occupy the uncomfortable middle in a highly charged situation, in the hope that they will find common cause with the workers. And to the garment workers of Los Angeles, in the hope that this book will help them empower themselves.

Contents

Figures and Tables

Figures

Tables

Preface

The growing disparity between rich and poor, in Los Angeles, in the United States, and in the world in general, is evident for all to see. In general, this divide is marked by a color line: The poor tend to be the dark-skinned peoples of the earth, the formerly colonized, some of whom have moved or been forcefully relocated to areas of the world now settled and ruled by people of European descent. The world's wealth is now controlled by giant, multinational corporations and financial institutions able to exercise inordinate power over the fate of most peoples. They operate on the principle that what is profitable for them benefits everyone else, a proposition that is patently false in practice.

As residents of southern California, the authors of this book are appalled by the growing social division of our society (and the world). We find this unconscionable. We reject the idea that immense wealth and power should be permitted to collect in the hands of a small class. We feel it is not permissible that vast numbers of people should be allowed to labor for the benefit of society and not receive their just reward. We find intolerable the growing divisions along race and class lines that lead people to view one another with hatred and suspicion.

Our goal in this book is to describe in detail the way in which race and class inequality is reproduced in one industry in one location. Although our topic is limited, we believe it is paradigmatic. This is an example of the way our social system works. We believe something is horribly wrong and we want to demonstrate how this has come about.

Despite the passionate judgment that has served as the spur to writing this volume, we have made every effort to be fair to everyone. We have listened to those with wealth and power and read what they have to say. We have done our best to understand the world from their point of view and to give their viewpoint a fair hearing. But ultimately, we have chosen sides with the workers. Along with a number of social philosophers, we believe that a society should be judged by its treatment of the people at the bottom of the system. Here the apparel industry in Los Angeles comes up sadly lacking.

Several studies, a few published and most not, have been conducted on aspects of the apparel industry in Los Angeles prior to this one. What is most striking about this literature is that it mirrors the polarization in the industry. There are, in a sense, two tales of the city: Authors focus either on the top end of the industry, telling the story of fashion and business development, or on the garment workers and contractors, recounting the oppression experienced by working women.

The two types of authors tend not to read each other and seem almost unaware of each other's existence. The division follows disciplinary lines. Generally, sociologists focus on the problems of immigrant and women workers; economists and business school people focus on the top end. The industry itself puts out voluminous materials, overwhelmingly about the upper end, while the union puts out reports about workers' problems. Government agencies publish reports from both points of view, depending on the department from which the report emanates. The press, too, sporadically covers both ends but tends to give much more space to the upper end in its business and fashion pages, with an occasional column devoted to labor. The recent case of Thai immigrants working as slave labor was a rare exception, generating press coverage of workers' issues for several weeks.

The literature, like the society, is divided between business and labor, and corresponds broadly to an ethnic division. These two literatures operate under completely different premises. The business side takes market capitalism for granted and focuses on ways to make the industry more competitive within this framework. It is concerned with developing technology, with promoting fashion, with finding solutions to problems faced by manufacturers and retailers in the conduct of their affairs. Labor is generally treated as a factor of production, whose productivity must be enhanced and whose cost must be minimized. This does not necessarily entail a callous disregard for human welfare; sometimes topics such as ergonomics, environmental concerns, more meaningful systems of work, compliance with labor law, elimination of illegal sweatshops, and so on are discussed. But the goal is to increase profits.

Much of the sociological literature, in contrast, starts by looking at the experiences of workers and focuses on the pain and harshness of their lives. Writers from this perspective tend not to believe that the market and profit system will create an equilibrium to the benefit of everyone. Instead, they see this system as producing winners and losers, and the people they study—women, people of color, low-wage workers—exemplify those who are hurt by the system. Students of labor also look at resistance on the part of the workers, examining unions and other individual and social efforts to counter oppression. They do not see the workers as simply victims but as people who react against their oppression. A recurring theme in this literature is the search for openings for social change. (See the Bibliographic Note for a more detailed review of the literature that has appeared on the apparel industry in Los Angeles.)

In our study we draw heavily on both the published and unpublished literature. Despite its abundance, there are gaping holes in the coverage. For example, no one has studied the social connections among the business leaders; no one has looked at the politics of the industry in Los Angeles and its connections with the city government; and no one has seriously considered the way in which the wealth generated by the industry is (mal)distributed. These will be among the contributions that this book tries to make: To turn a sociological perspective on the upper end of the industry, as well as to tie that analysis to the already rich literature on immigrant workers and contractors.

The text is divided into three sections after the Introduction. Part I, Capital, deals with the upper end of the industry. In Chapter 1 we examine the manufacturers, who are usually treated as synonymous with the industry. In Chapter 2 we look at global production, with special emphasis on the movement offshore by apparel manufacturers in Los Angeles. Changes in retailing and the power of giant retail chains are taken up in Chapter 3. In Chapter 4 we end the section with an analysis of the power elite in the apparel industry in Los Angeles, its composition and its social practices.

In Part II, Labor, our focus is switched to the sewing of garments. In Chapter 5 we describe the contracting system and the contractors who run it. In Chapter 6 we discuss the garment workers, examining who they are and the conditions under which they labor. Chapter 7, the third, and last chapter of this section, consists of an assessment of the way in which the considerable wealth generated by this industry is distributed among all the people who work in it.

In Part III, Fighting Back, we examine efforts to eliminate sweatshops in the Los Angeles apparel industry and describe strategies that have yet to be tried. The challenge is to find ways to improve conditions for garment workers while not driving the industry offshore. In Chapter 8 we examine government efforts to enforce basic labor law in this industry. In Chapter 9 we raise the question of empowerment for the workers and how it might be enhanced. In our conclusions, in Chapter 10, we turn to alternative possibilities, at the level of policy as well as public activism.

Our approach to this study was highly eclectic. We have used a variety of methods, including face-to-face interviews, telephone surveys, questionnaires, the perusal of trade newspapers and magazines, reviews of the materials of various organizations, attendance at meetings and events, and analysis of data derived from public and private sources. Because we have tried to cover many aspects of a very complex industry, we have had to use whatever method suited our need for particular information.

One problem that plagued this study is the fact that the apparel industry is continually changing. Bob Berg of the Textile Association of Los Angeles, who is in charge of putting out an annual directory of the industry, said: "Our directory is out of date one minute after it appears." Not only do the actors keep changing, but so also do the forces—economic, political, and social events—that impinge on them. For example, the passage of NAFTA had massive implications for the industry in Los Angeles. So did the 1992 Los Angeles uprising, the constant restructuring of retailing, local politics, and a rising tide of antiimmigrant sentiment. Strategies for coping with change create counterstrategies in a never-ending and unpredictable, lurching progression.

We have tried to capture some of this dynamism but must confess to an inability to keep up with it. We have been trying to photograph a moving target and could only keep up with parts of it at one time, while losing sight of other aspects. In some cases, data were collected at one point in time, and all we have is that particular snapshot. Data quickly get old. Moreover, the exigencies of publishing create a delay between the collecting of information and its appearance in public. Even though we tried to be as up-to-date as possible, this is, inevitably, a historical study of the apparel industry in Los Angeles during a particular period of time, from 1989 to 1998. Nevertheless, we hope that, even if some of our facts are old, the analysis of forces and relationships will still be current and useful.

We must also confess that such a huge and complex industry is impossible to study completely. No doubt we have ignored certain aspects of the industry and failed to introduce some important players. Some may be disappointed that we have not told their story or have not told it as they see it. Inevitably such a wide-ranging study is limited by the time, capacities, and connections of its authors. We are all too aware of its many shortcomings.

In this book we make some harsh judgments about people who were very friendly and helpful to us, especially those at the top end of the industry. They will surely be dismayed by our study and see it as yet another attack on a beleaguered industry. They already feel that they get unwarranted bad press, what with occasional exposés denouncing apparel as a sweat-shop industry. Although we certainly contribute to this image (for which we found ample justification), our intent is not a simple denunciation. Our purpose is to understand how the *system* works to produce class and race inequality and polarization. To the extent that we have written from a critical perspective, the target of the criticism is not any individual but a social system. The actions of individuals are typically highly constrained by the system in which they are actors; their choices are limited by the rules of the game, both formal and informal. As we see it, some decent and generous people are participants in a system that has very inhumane consequences. They obviously bear some responsibility for their partici-pation, but much more needs to be changed than their individual behavior. Most of those people are firm believers in the system (in part because they are the beneficiaries of it) and will experience a criticism of the system as a criticism of themselves and their most cherished beliefs. Nevertheless, we hope, probably in vain, that some will read what we have to say with an open mind, and will come to see more clearly the bigger picture in which they are involved.

Acknowledgments

The research for this book began as long ago as 1989. With the passage of almost ten years we have accumulated more debts of gratitude than we can mention or even remember. We present an abbreviated list and humbly apologize to anyone we may have forgotten.

We are very grateful to the Haynes Foundation for a grant to study this industry, as well as the University of California Pacific Rim Research Program. With intramural grants and a grant from the Ernesto Galarza Center at the University of California at Riverside, they enabled us to hire a number of research assistants who conducted particular aspects of the research. Christopher Arnold analyzed survey data and mapped the industry. Melanie Meyers co-authored a part of Chapter 2. Ku-Sup Chin conducted a survey of Korean contractors and co-authored a part of Chapter 5. Brad Christerson helped with analysis of spatial and statistical data. Peter Chua and Gilbert Garcia helped analyze 1990 census data. Jean Gilbert conducted a telephone survey of manufacturers and helped with some of the interviewing. Patricia Hanneman developed a complex data set combining lists of manufacturers and contractors and organized the telephone survey. Judi Kessler conducted a telephone survey of manufacturers in 1997 to ascertain the impact of NAFTA on the industry and carefully read the manuscript at various stages. Edward Park did in-depth interviews with Koreans in the industry. Gregory Scott conducted interviews with Latina garment workers and co-authored a part of Chapter 6. David Waller helped collect information on retailers and studied real estate ownership. Clare Weber explored Mexican production by firms in Los Angeles.

Other individuals expressed an interest in our study and sometimes made significant contributions. Farinaz Farshad investigated the factoring system that is used to finance the industry. Phillip Bonacich set up a preliminary network analysis of power players in the industry. Ralph Arbruster compiled information on offshore production and critically read the entire first draft of the manuscript, as did Carolina Bank. Goetz Wolff collaborated in an aspect of this project, and helped to co-author a part of Chapter 8.

University of California Press editor Stanley Holwitz supported this project enthusiastically from the moment we introduced him to it and provided us with three excellent external evaluators: Peter Dreier, Bob Ross, and Charles Tilly. Without their penetrating criticisms, this book would suffer from greater disorganization and lack of clarity. To all four we are very grateful.

Our editor from the University of California Press, Suzanne Knott, and copyeditor, Frances Bowles, have worked hard on this manuscript and made it much more readable than it otherwise would be. Even as we resisted changing too many of our own precious words, they managed to turn our turgid prose into English. We thank them most heartily.

We also owe a debt of gratitude to the hundreds of people connected with the apparel industry in Los Angeles, from the richest to the poorest, who let us interview them, hang out with them, and generally pester them for information. Without their cooperation, a study such as this would be impossible.

Last, we wish to thank our spouses, Phil and Karen, for their patience in dealing with our endless obsession with the garment industry. *Women's Wear Daily* became our oft-quoted bible, and the slightest tic in the industry had to be shared.

Although the task of writing this manuscript is over, the issues raised by it are not. We both intend to continue our commitment to the search for social justice in the apparel industry, both here and abroad. We earnestly hope that some of our readers will join us.

Introduction

The Return of the Sweatshop

... SO SHALL WE REAP.

Copyright, 1997, Paul Conrad. Distributed by *Los Angeles Times* Syndicate. Reprinted by permission.

> *The apparel industry is probably the hardest industry the United States Department of Labor has ever faced.*
>
> Gerald M. Hall[1]
> District Director
> U.S. Department of Labor

Where does the money from the sale of a $100 dress actually go? (See Figure 1.) The wholesale cost of a $100 dress made in the United States is about $50; half of the $100 sales price goes to the retailer. Of the $50 wholesale cost, 45 percent, or $22.50, is spent by the manufacturer on the fabric. Twenty-five percent, or $12.50, is profit and overhead for the manufacturer. The remaining 30 percent, or $15, goes to the con-

Retailer, $50

Manufacturer, $35
($22.50 for fabric)

Contractor, $15
(Workers, $6)

Source: Elizabeth Weiner and Dean Foust, "Why Made-in-America Is Back in Style," *Business Week,* 7 November 1988, pp. 116–18. Data from Kurt Salmon Associates, Inc.

Figure 1.   The Distribution of the Proceeds of a $100 Dress

tractor, and covers both the cost of direct labor and the contractor's other expenses, and profit. Only 6 percent, $6, goes to the person who actually sewed the garment. Furthermore, this individual was more than likely to have been paid by the number of sewing operations performed than by the hour and to have received no benefits of any kind.

Sweatshops have indeed returned to the United States. A phenomenon of the apparel industry considered long past is back, not as a minor aberration, but as a prominent way of doing business. Every once in a while, an especially dramatic story hits the news: an Orange County family is found sewing in their home, where a seven-year-old child works next to his mother. Thai workers in El Monte are found in an apartment complex, held against their will under conditions of semienslavement while earning subminimum wages. Kathie Lee Gifford, celebrity endorser of a Wal-Mart label, discovers that her line is being produced in sweatshops both offshore and in the United States and cries in shame on national television. The United States Department of Labor develops a program to make apparel manufacturers take responsibility for sweatshop violations. The President of the United States establishes the Apparel Industry Partnership to see if a solution can be found to the growth of sweatshops here and abroad. The nation is becoming aware that the scourge of sweatshops has returned.

Sweatshops first emerged in the United States apparel industry in the last decades of the nineteenth century with the development of the mass production of garments in New York City.[2] Immigrant workers, mainly young women, slaved for long hours over their sewing machines in cramped and unsanitary factories, for very low wages. Workers eventually rebelled. In 1909 a major strike by shirtwaist factory workers, sometimes called the uprising of the 20,000, was the first mass strike by women workers in the United States. (Shirtwaists, a style of women's blouse, were the first mass-produced fashion items.) It was followed by strikes in other sectors of the industry. In 1911 the infamous Triangle Shirtwaist factory fire in New York resulted in the deaths of 146 young garment workers, and provoked public outrage.[3] Organized, militant, and supported by an aroused public, the workers founded the garment unions and demanded contracts that would protect them against sweatshop production. New Deal legislation reinforced basic standards of labor for workers and protected their right to join or form independent unions. A combination of government protection and strong apparel unions helped to relegate garment sweatshops to the margins of the industry until the 1970s, when they began to reappear.

What exactly is a "sweatshop"? A sweatshop is usually defined as a factory or a homework operation that engages in multiple violations of the law, typically the non-payment of minimum or overtime wages and various violations of health and safety regulations. According to this definition, many of the garment factories in Los Angeles are sweatshops. In a sample survey conducted by the United States Department of Labor in January 1998, 61 percent of the garment firms in Los Angeles were found to be violating wage and hour regulations. Workers were underpaid by an estimated $73 million dollars per year.[4] Health and safety violations were not examined in that study, but in a survey completed in 1997, 96 percent of the firms were found to be in violation, 54 percent with deficiencies that could lead to serious injuries or death.

An emphasis merely on violations of the law fails to capture the full extent of what has been happening. In recent years the garment industry has been moving its production offshore to countries where workers earn much lower wages than are paid in the United States. In offshore production, some manufacturers may follow local laws, but the legal standard is so low that the workers, often including young teenagers, live in poverty, although they are working full time. The same problem arises in the United States. Even if a factory follows the letter of the law in every detail, workers may suffer abuse, job insecurity, and poverty. In 1990, according to the United States census, the average garment worker in Los Angeles made only $7,200, less than three-quarters of the poverty-level income for a family of three in that year. Thus we wish to broaden the definition of sweatshops to include factories that fail to pay a "living wage," meaning a wage that enables a family to support itself at a socially defined, decent standard of living.[5] We include in the concept of a living wage the idea that people should be able to afford decent housing, given the local housing market, and that a family should be covered by health insurance. If wages fail to cover these minima, and if families with working members still fall below the official poverty line, they are, we claim, working in sweatshops.

Why are sweatshops returning to the apparel industry a number of decades after they had more or less disappeared? Why have their numbers grown so rapidly, especially in the last two decades of the twentieth century? And why has Los Angeles,[6] in particular, become a center of garment sweatshops?

Global, Flexible Capitalism

The reemergence of apparel industry sweatshops is part of a much broader phenomenon, namely, the restructuring of global capitalism—a phenomenon we refer to as the new global capitalism. Starting in the 1970s, and accelerating rapidly especially in the 1980s and 1990s, the restructuring included a series of complex changes: a decline in the welfare state in most of the developed industrial countries; a growth in multinational corporations and an increase in global production; entry into manufacturing for export by many countries, among them some of the poorest in the world; a rise in world trade and intensification of competition; deindustrialization in the developed countries; a decrease in job security and an increase in part-time work; a rise in immigration from poorer countries to the richer ones; and renewed pressure on what remains of the welfare state.[7]

These changes are all interconnected, and it is difficult to establish a first cause. Combined, they are associated with an effort by capitalists, supported by national governments, to increase profits and push back the effects of egalitarian movements that emerged in the 1960s and 1970s and that achieved some redistributive policies. The new global capitalism is characterized by an effort to let the free market operate with a minimum of government interference. At the same time, nations are themselves promoting the hegemony of the free market and imposing it as a standard for the entire world.

Among policies that foster the free market are the elimination of trade barriers and the encouragement of international free trade, as exemplified by the North American Free Trade Agreement (NAFTA) and the World Trade Organization (WTO); the insistence by strong states on the rights of their corporations to invest abroad with a minimum of local regulation; and pressure by state-backed, world financial institutions on developing countries that they restructure their political economies so as to foster free markets. Internal policies associated with the disestablishment of the welfare state have included deregulation, the privatization of state functions, and the minimization of state interference in business practices. In the United States, for example, affirmative action, welfare, and other efforts to increase equality through state intervention have come under attack.

The new global capitalism is often touted for its so-called flexibility.[8] The decades of the 1980s and 1990s have been described as post-Fordist; i.e., we have moved beyond huge, mass-production plants making standardized products on the assembly line to a system in which smaller batches of specialized goods are made for an increasingly diverse consumer market. New systems of production, including contracting out the manufacture of specialized goods and services, and the ability to source goods and services wherever they can most efficiently be provided, enhance this flexibility. It is sometimes argued that the new, flexible production allows for more participation by the workers, by enabling them to develop several skills and encouraging them to use their initiative. Instead of repeating the same boring task, as did the workers on the Fordist assembly line, workers in the new factories may engage in more interesting, well-rounded activities. Critics have pointed out that, while some workers may benefit from the new, flexible production arrangements, others face increased job insecurity, more part-time and temporary work, a greater likelihood of working for subcontractors, and less opportunity for unionization. Flexibility for the employer may lead to the expansion of the contingent labor force, which must shift around to find short-term jobs as they arise.

One of the starkest areas of social change in the post–welfare state period has been the attack on organized labor. In the United States, for example, during the postwar period of the late 1940s and continuing until the 1960s, an accommodation was reached between industries and trade unions, whereby both sides accepted that the unions would help to eliminate industrial warfare under a "social contract." The tacit agreement was simple: In exchange for union-demanded wages and benefits, workers would cede control over industrial production to management. The cost of this arrangement would be paid for in the marketplace, through higher prices for goods, rather than in narrower profit margins. This arrangement particularly benefited workers in large, oligopolistic industries, where unions were strong and profits were substantial. The entire economy was seen to benefit from this arrangement because the workers would have enough expendable income to buy the products, thereby stimulating production, creating more jobs, and generating a spiraling prosperity. Even though unions were never popular with business, the major industries, including the apparel industry, came to accept them and accept the fact that they made an important contribution to the well-being of the economy at large.

This view of organized labor has collapsed. Business leaders in the United States now see unions as having pushed the price of American labor too high, thereby limiting the competitiveness of firms that maintain a workforce in this country. Firms in certain industries have increasingly moved offshore to seek out low-wage labor in less developed countries. Business owners and managers also see unions as irrelevant to the new flexible systems of production. Unions grew strong in response to the Fordist production regimes, but with more decentralized systems of production, they are viewed as rigid and impractical. Besides, argue the owners and managers, more engaged and multiskilled workers no longer need union protection, as they share in a commitment to the firm's goals. Unions interfere with a company's flexibility and therefore hurt everyone, including the firm's employees.

Organized labor has been weakened by various federal policies, among them, President Ronald Reagan's dismissal of the air traffic controllers, the appointment of antiunion members to the National Labor Relations Board, the acceptance of the right of firms to hire permanent replacements for strikers, the passage of NAFTA without adequate protections for workers in any of the three countries involved, and the encouragement of offshore contracting by special tariff provisions. The development of flexible production, with its contracting out and dispersion of production around the globe, has also served to undermine unions because it is much more difficult to organize workers in a decentralized system. As a result, the proportion of the workforce that is unionized has dropped, not only in the United States, but also in other industrial countries: in the United States from a high of 37 percent in 1946 to less than 15 percent of the total workforce in 1995, and only 11 percent of the private sector workforce.[9] These figures are much lower than for the rest of the industrial world.

Another significant aspect of the new global economy has been the rise of immigration from the less developed to the industrialized countries. Local economies have been disrupted by the arrival of multinational corporations, and many people see no alternative but to seek a means of survival elsewhere. The involvement of the more developed countries in the economies and governments of the Third World is not a new phenomenon, and it has long been associated with emigration. The countervailing movements of capital and labor in opposite directions have often been noted.[10]

What is new about the recent phase of global capitalism is the accelerated proletarianization of much of the world's remaining peasantry. Young women, in particular, have been drawn into the labor force to become the main workers in plants that engage in manufacturing for export. In many ways they are the ideal workforce, as they frequently lack the experience and alternatives that would enable them to demand higher wages and better treatment. The poor working conditions are exacerbated by political regimes, often supported by the United States, that have restricted the workers' ability to organize and demand change.

The increased exploitation of workers in the Third World has a mirror image in the movement of immigrant workers to the more developed countries. Immigrants come not only because of economic dislocations that arise, in part, from the presence of foreign capital in their homelands, but also because of political struggles that have ensued in connection with the Cold War and its aftermath. A paradox of the new global capitalism is that, although the right of capital to move freely is touted by the supporters of the free market, no such right is afforded labor. Immigration is restricted by state policies. One consequence has been the creation of so-called illegal workers, who are stripped of many basic legal rights. Immigrant workers, especially the undocumented, are more easily exploited than are native workers.

In sum, there has been a shift in the balance of power between capital and labor. Although the working class, including women and people of color, made important gains during the three postwar decades (from the late 1940s through the early 1970s), a backlash began developing in the 1970s and achieved full momentum by the 1980s. This backlash corresponds closely to the "great U-turn" in the United States and other capitalist economies, as a broadly shared postwar rise in living standards came to a halt.[11] Conservative governments in the United States and Europe have implemented policies that favor capital and the free market over labor and other disadvantaged groups. Even political parties that have traditionally supported the working class, such as the Democrats in the United States and the Labour Party in Britain, have shifted to the right.

The reappearance of sweatshops is a feature of the new global, flexible capitalism. The original sweatshops disappeared with the growth of unions and the development of the welfare state. Today, with both of those institutions weakened, markets have been able to drive down wages and reduce working conditions to substandard levels in many labor-intensive industries, such as electronics, toys, shoes, and sports equipment. Indeed, almost every manufacturing industry and some services are pressed to reduce labor costs by minimizing job stability, by contracting out, by using more contingent (part-time and temporary) workers, by reducing benefits, and by attacking unions. But the apparel industry is leading the way.

The Apparel Industry as a Paradigm

The very word *sweatshop* has its roots in the apparel industry. It is ironic that the apparel industry should be a leader in any trend since, as an old industry, it has remained backward in many areas. Significant advances have been made in certain aspects of production, notably computer-assisted design, computer-assisted grading and marking, and computerized cutting, and there have been innovations in sewing machine technology and in the organization of work flow, but the core production process, namely the sewing of garments, is still low-tech.[12] The primary unit of production continues to be a worker, usually a woman, sitting (or standing) at a sewing machine and sewing together pieces of limp cloth.

Garment production is labor intensive, and, unlike many other industries, it does not require much capital to get into the sewing business. Consequently, sewing factories proliferate and the industry is exceedingly competitive—probably more competitive than most. In some ways the apparel industry is the epitome of free market capitalism because the barriers to entry are so low. Less-developed countries take up apparel production as their first manufacturing industry in their efforts to industrialize. In the shift to global production and manufacturing for export, apparel has been in the vanguard. Clothing firms in the United States began to move production offshore to Asia as early as the late 1950s. Today apparel manufacturers in a number of developed countries are opening production facilities and employing workers in almost every country of the world. The result in the United States has been a rise in imports (see Figure 2), which started to grow in the 1960s and 1970s and grew at an explosive rate in the 1980s. In 1962 apparel imports totaled $301 million. They had tripled by the end of the decade, to $1.1 billion; increased another fivefold by 1980, to $5.5 billion; and nearly another fourfold by 1990, to $21.9 billion. By 1997, apparel imports totaled $42 billion; they are projected to exceed $50 billion in 1999. According to estimates by the American Apparel Manufacturers Association, imports accounted for 60 percent of the $101 billion wholesale apparel market.[13] Needless to say, this has greatly increased the level of competition within the industry, creating a pressure to lower wages in the United States garment industry to meet the low wages paid overseas. Global production is certainly expanding in other industries, but apparel is the most globalized industry of all.[14]

The United States is the largest consumer market for apparel in the world. One measure for comparing consumption that does not depend on relative prices is the average per-capita fiber consumption. In 1989–90 (the latest available figures), the average annual world consumption was 17.9 pounds per person. For the United States it was 57.3 pounds. Japan came second with 48.9 pounds per capita. Latin America consumed only 12.8 pounds per capita and Africa, 2.9. A primary target for exporting countries, the United States is by far the leading importer of apparel in the world.[15]

The return of sweatshops in the United States apparel industry can be partly, but not entirely, attributed to the dramatic rise in offshore production, and the concomitant increase in cheap imports. Much of the industry is driven by fashion, and sales of fashionable garments are highly volatile. The production of apparel is generally a risky business, which discourages heavy capital investment and limits the availability of capital for firms that want to expand or upgrade. The riskiness is augmented by time. Fashion can change quickly. Apparel manufacturers want to be sure that any demand is fully met, but must be wary of overproducing garments that may fall out of fashion. The industry needs to be especially

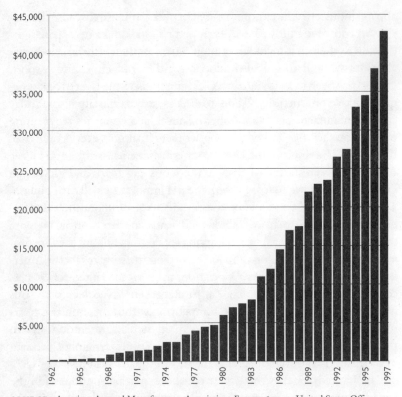

SOURCE: American Apparel Manufacturers Association, *Focus 1998,* p. 31; United States Office of Textiles and Apparel (OTEXA), Major Shipper's Report by Category, 9/1999 data; available at http://otexa.ita.doc.gov/msr/catv1.htm.

Figure 2.   Apparel Imports to the United States, 1962–1997 ($000,000)

sensitive to changes in consumer taste, to respond quickly to these shifts, and to cease production of dying trends in a timely manner.

Needless to say, the industry tries to mold the fickle consumers' tastes as much as possible, by heavy advertising, by producing fashion shows and magazines, and by publicizing the opinions of pundits who predict and help to determine the trends. Indeed, the industry has considerable internal variation in terms of susceptibility to the fashion dynamic. Some garments, considered to be basics, change only slowly. Basics include most underwear and sleepwear, T-shirts, sweatshirts and sweatpants, denim jeans, and men's shirts and pants. The areas of greatest fashion volatility include women's dresses, skirts and tops, women's bathing suits, and the broader area known as women's sportswear (casual clothing). Note that all the traditional basics also can include fashion lines. The Gap made a fortune by turning the basic T-shirt into a personal fashion statement. And denim jeans, when associated with the names of particular designers, have experienced the hot flash of fashion success.

Offshore production usually requires longer waiting times, thereby increasing the risk in making time-sensitive garments. Basics can be planned months in advance without much risk that the garments will go out of fashion. In the United States apparel industry, the production of basics has moved steadily offshore, and highly fashionable apparel is more likely to be made domestically. The distinction is likely to lessen with time as communication and transportation times decrease and as arrangements are made to produce garments in regions closer to their destination market. NAFTA, for example, has led to an enormous growth in Mexico's capacity to produce garments for the United States apparel industry. Because it is much closer to the United States than Asia is, some production has been shifted from Asia to Mexico; and it is possible that the production of more fashion-sensitive garments will also be shifted there. Their proximity also accounts for shifts to the Caribbean and Central America.

The fashion-sensitive sector of the industry is much more concentrated in women's wear than in men's wear, although this may be changing a little. Women in the United States spend twice as much on clothing as do men. The general difference between women's and men's wear has led to a segregation between the two sectors of the industry. For example, the major industry newspaper is called *Women's Wear Daily*. The two major sectors eventually produced two unions: the International Ladies' Garment Workers' Union (ILGWU), which organized workers in the women's sector, and the Amalgamated Clothing and Textile Workers Union (ACTWU), which organized workers in the textile industry and the men's wear sector. The two unions merged in 1995 into UNITE, the Union of Needletrades, Industrial and Textile Employees, probably less because of a convergence between the two types of garment production than because of the loss of membership that each was suffering.

The differences have also led to a divergence in production systems. Men's wear has generally been produced in larger, mass-production factories, women's wear in smaller, contracted-out production units. Typically, in the production of women's clothing, apparel manufacturers (companies known by the brand names) design and engineer the garments, buy the textiles, and wholesale the completed clothing. The actual production of the garment, the cutting, sewing, laundering, and finishing, is usually done by independent contractors. Most garment contractors are sewing contractors, and they typically receive cut goods that their employees sew. Most garment workers are employed in small, contracting factories, sewing garments for manufacturers, who typically employ several contractors. Contracting out extends at the margins to industrial homework, with a single woman sitting at her home sewing machine, making clothing for a firm that employs her.

The contracting out of apparel production can be seen as an instance of flexible production. It allows apparel manufacturers to deal with fluctuations in fashion and seasons by hiring contractors when they need them and letting them go when they do not. In this respect the apparel industry is at the cutting edge of the new global economy: It has used contracting out for decades and has developed this flexible production system to a fine art. Moreover, the contracting system has been extended to global production. Manufacturers not only employ local contractors, but also often conduct their offshore production through contracting rather than through the ownership of subsidiaries. The lack of fixed assets enables them to move production wherever they can get the best deal in terms of labor cost, taxes and tariffs, environmental regulation, or any other factor that influences the quality and cost of their products.

The virtue of the contracting system for the manufacturers is that they do not need to invest a cent in the factories that actually sew their clothes. Manufacturers engage in arm's-length transactions with their contractors, enabling them to avoid any long-term commitment to a particular contractor or location. The formal commitment lasts only as long as the particular job order. In practice, manufacturers may develop longer-term relationships with a core group of dependable contractors, attempting to ensure that they receive steady work. Nevertheless, the absence of firm ties provides maximum flexibility for manufacturers and the elimination of costly inefficiencies associated with having dependent subsidiaries. Contracting out enables manufacturers to hire only the labor they actually need.

The picture is not quite so rosy from the other side. Contractors, who in the United States and other advanced industrial countries, are often immigrants, must scramble to maintain steady work. And rather than employ a stable workforce, they pass the problems created by flexible production on to their workers. In the United States most garment workers are employed on a piece-work basis, so that they are paid only for the work they actually do. If the work is slow, they do not get paid. In offshore production, workers are more likely to receive an hourly wage rather than piece rate, but they are required to produce an arduous daily quota.

Their hours and quotas, like those of piece-rate workers, are determined by the shifting demands of their manufacturers; at the height of the season or if they are producing a hot fashion item, they are required to work long hours. During a lull, they are laid off and go unpaid.

It is out of such a system of contracting out that the sweatshop is born. What provides wonderful flexibility for the manufacturer provides unstable work, impoverishment, and often abusive conditions for the workers.[16] The idea that smaller factories, making specialized goods for an ever-changing market, means that workers are better trained and have more responsibility has not worked out for most garment workers. Instead, they continue to engage in Fordist-style, highly repetitive, boring tasks conducted at high speeds. But because they no longer work in large, centralized production facilities, it is much more difficult for them to join or form unions. In addition, the mobility of the industry makes the task of unionizing formidable because manufacturers can easily shift production away from contractors that show any signs of labor unrest. In sum, flexible production, at least in the apparel industry, has created a much more effective engine for exploiting workers than existed before the new era of global capitalism.

Another feature of the apparel industry that probably portends developments in other industries is the rapidly growing power of retailers in the new global economy, another consequence of the emphasis on increased flexibility. No longer selling to a mass market, retailers now expect to supply consumers with the variety that they want when they want it. Rather than carrying large quantities of inventory in standardized products, the retailers want to be able to order and reorder popular items on short notice. They cherry-pick from designers' and manufacturers' lines, order only the items that they want, and expect them to be delivered rapidly.

The power of retailers in the apparel industry is partly a product of the highly competitive character of the industry, which often gives them the upper hand in dealing with manufacturers. Retailers have also gained power by engaging in their own direct offshore sourcing. Recently, their power has been consolidated by a series of mergers; by 1996 the four largest retailers in the United States accounted for two-thirds of the total value of national apparel retail sales. Consolidation has increased the ability to demand more from manufacturers in terms of price and speed, demands that reverberate all the way down the system to the workers, who bear the brunt of lower wages and faster production.

The idea of fashion and of constantly changing products for specialized markets is spreading far beyond apparel to many other industries.[17] However, the very word "fashion" is deeply associated with the garment industry. It can be seen as the first industry that developed the notion of constantly changing styles. And as we have seen, its highly flexible production system is the most advanced of any industry.

We believe that the way apparel production is organized is a predictor of things to come in many industries and portends the expansion of the sweatshop. One can argue that in the return of the sweatshop we are witnessing a throwback to the earliest phases of the industrial revolution. But it is clear that what is going on is not only "old" but also very new. The apparel industry has managed to combine the latest ideas and technology for the rapid production and distribution of a highly diverse and continually changing product with the oppressive working conditions of the late nineteenth and early twentieth centuries, now coordinated over a global space. Consumers of clothing have never had it so good; the women and men huddled over sewing machines in foreign countries or immigrant enclaves suffer the consequences.

In Figure 3 the chief features of the apparel industry and the forces that are leading to the reemergence of sweatshops are summarized. Briefly, the forces are these. Apparel is a fashion-based, seasonal business and is, therefore, highly risky and competitive (1). It is also a low-tech, labor-intensive industry, particularly at the level of production, with low capital requirements and an ease of entry that encourage competitiveness (2). The unpredictability of the industry leads manufacturers to externalize their risk by contracting out the labor to enhance their flexibility (3). The ease of entry means that apparel production is usually the first industry chosen by countries seeking to industrialize (4). The availability of offshore garment factories with low-wage labor encourages United States apparel manufacturers to move some of their production to those facilities, leading to a rise in garment imports into the United States. Contracting out, both locally and abroad, also contributes to the competitive character of the industry (5 and 6).

The highly competitive nature of the apparel industry enables giant retailers to gain power over the manufacturers, a phenomenon that has increased as retailers have consolidated (7). In turn, the power and consolidation of the retailers adds to the competition between apparel manufacturers, who must jostle for favor with fewer and fewer buyers (8).

The movement of the apparel industry offshore, which is partly encouraged by United States trade and investment policies, combines with interventions by other industries (such as agribusiness) and neoliberal

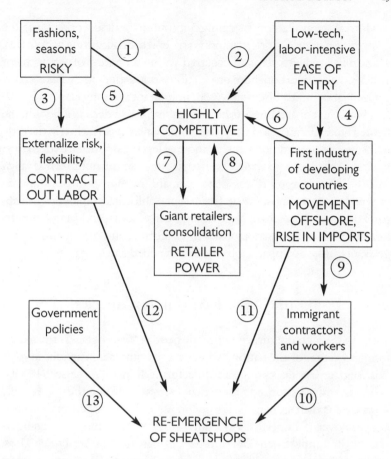

Figure 3. The Reemergence of Sweatshops in the United States Apparel Industry

government policies, to create severe economic dislocations among certain segments of the population, especially peasants, but also those in some urban occupations. Coupled with the impact of local wars, many with United States involvement, this dislocation results in a rise in immigration to the United States (9). Because of the low capital requirements for garment contracting, those immigrants with small amounts of capital or limited business experience enter the industry as entrepreneurs. Meanwhile, more impoverished immigrants become available to work in garment factories for low wages.

The reemergence of sweatshops is a product of the confluence of several forces: the availability of immigrant contractors and workers (10), the competition with low-priced imports (11), and the contracting system (12). These developments have all occurred within a context of government policies that support offshore production, contracting out, weakened organized labor, and a disenfranchised, immigrant working class (13).

The rise in apparel imports has inevitably led to a decline in jobs in the United States garment industry. Peak employment was reached in the early 1970s; since then, employment has more or less steadily decreased. In 1970 the industry employed 1,364,000 people. By 1980 the number had fallen to 1,264,000. In 1990 it was 1,036,000, and in 1997, 813,000. Between 1978 and 1998, in almost every state except California, employment in apparel declined. New York, New Jersey, Pennsylvania, and Massachusetts lost over half their apparel jobs.[18] In California, and mostly in Los Angeles, over 50,000 apparel jobs have been added since 1978.

Garment Production in Los Angeles

To the surprise of many people, Los Angeles is the manufacturing center of the nation, with 663,400 manufacturing jobs in 1997. Los Angeles has 5,900 more manufacturing jobs than the second city, Chicago, and over 200,000 more than Detroit, a distant third.[19] Equally surprising is the fact that the apparel industry is the largest manufacturing employer in Los Angeles County, with 122,500 employees enumerated by the Employment Development Department in April 1998. Thus, almost one out of five manufacturing employees in Los Angeles works in the apparel industry.

Los Angeles has felt the effects of global restructuring. Many high-paying union jobs in the automobile, tire, and aerospace industries have fled the region, while low-wage manufacturing jobs have multiplied. Among these low-wage industries, apparel "has been the lowest paying sector."[20] Nonetheless, Los Angeles is now the apparel manufacturing center of the United States. In Figure 4 apparel employment in the United States and in Los Angeles are compared. Los Angeles paralleled the United States decline during the early 1980s, but then broke away from the national pattern and continued to grow while the apparel industry employment nationwide continued to decline. The discrepancy is even clearer in Figure 5. More people are employed in the apparel industry in Los Angeles County than anywhere else in the nation, more than in New York, and far more than in any other center.

SOURCE: Goetz Wolff, "The Apparel Cluster: A Regional Growth Industry" (pamphlet prepared for the California College Fashion Symposium, Los Angeles, April 1997). Data from United States Bureau of Labor Statistics, Employment and Earnings Unadjusted, State and Area Unadjusted; available: http://stats.bls.gov/cgi-bin/srgate.
NOTE: Los Angeles accounts for 14 percent of the employment in the apparent industry in the United States.

Figure 4. Relative Growth in Apparel Employment, 1979–1997, Los Angeles and United States (1979 = 100)

Why has Los Angeles become such an important center of garment production? First, the city is a center of design and fashion. The entertainment industry is, through its movies, television, and music, but the most visible manifestation of the city's creation of style. Southern California represents a way of life that is idealized and emulated around the globe. The names Hollywood, California, Disneyland, and even Los Angeles itself conjure up images of fantasy, fun in the sun, the freedom of the western frontier, informality, rebellion, and the end of formal tradition. It is not surprising that Los Angeles attracts people from many different cultures. Los Angeles sells itself along with its products, and its products benefit from all the connotations of the place. The apparel industry finds a natural haven in Los Angeles in part because of the city's strong connections with fashion and style. The city produces style not only through the entertainment industry but also on its streets: The place creates fashion.

The apparel made in Los Angeles is overwhelmingly women's wear. In

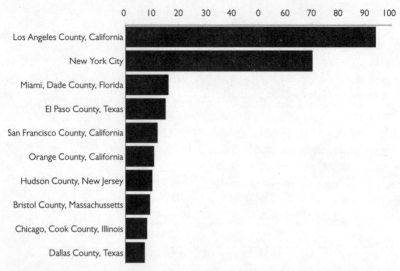

SOURCE: Goetz Wolff, "The Apparel Cluster: A Regional Growth Industry" (pamphlet prepared for the California College Fashion Symposium, Los Angeles, April 1997). Data from United States Department of Commerce, *County Business Patterns,* 1994. © Goetz Wolff.

Figure 5.   United States Counties with Highest Levels of Employment in the Apparel Sector (SIC 23), 1994 (000 employees)

1997 Goetz Wolff, using data from 1994 County Business Patterns, examined the various components of the local apparel industry to compare Los Angeles with the rest of the country. While 25 percent of the United States industry, excluding Los Angeles, was devoted to women's outerwear, 65 percent of the Los Angeles industry was so concentrated. Los Angeles accounts for about 10 percent of all apparel produced in the United States, but almost 25 percent of the women's outerwear.[21] Even in men's wear, Los Angeles tends to specialize in the fashion end, making hip-hop wear, or beach wear, or other garments for which the styles keep changing.

The fact that Los Angeles is also a major center for immigration, especially from Asia, Mexico, and Central America, combines with the industry's focus on fashion to create a location where the most "advanced" forms of flexible production are found. Los Angeles's apparel industry has spawned thousands of contractors who can produce small lots rapidly. In other words, the city's industry is primed for the production of fashion at cheap prices. Immigrants play a vital role in two aspects of the industry. They provide the workforce and the entrepreneurship to run the contracting shops. Many of the immigrant workers are undocumented, which means that they often lack the political wherewithal to resist exploitation. Meanwhile, antiimmigrant movements in California have made immigrants increasingly vulnerable and exacerbated their political disadvantage.

Los Angeles has a long antiunion tradition and has been a harbor for entrepreneurial activity that does not need to worry about union organizing. Many industries are less unionized in Los Angeles than they are in most other major cities in the country, including, importantly, New York and San Francisco. This adds to the attractiveness of Los Angeles as a center of flexible production. Without having to worry about a unionized work force, manufacturers and retailers can arrange production to their own maximal advantage, shifting all the risk to the contractors, and ultimately to the workers. Los Angeles can indeed be described as the "sweatshop capital of the United States."

The Race to the Bottom

The United States is growing more and more unequal, with increasing polarization along race and class lines. In Los Angeles the forces that are shaping inequality in the United States are more sharply focused. The city is characterized by immense wealth, on the one hand, and extreme poverty on the other.[22] A study by a committee of the California legislature found that, between 1989 and 1996, the number of very rich Angelinos, including those with annual incomes over $25 million, doubled, from 165 to 376 individuals, and that, from 1994 to 1996, the numbers of the very poor, those with annual incomes of less that $20,000, grew by 13.5 percent from 2.5 million to 2.9 million people. The authors conclude that there has been a hollowing out of the middle class and that the individuals and families hardest hit by the recession of the early 1990s have been slowest to benefit from the recovery, while the wealthy have benefited strongly.[23] Multimillionaires and even billionaires build mansions in the mountains and canyons and in rich communities such as Beverly Hills and Bel Air, while unemployment soars in the African-American community, and immigrant workers do almost all of the physical labor to eke out a bare survival for themselves and their children. The developments came to a dramatic climax in the so-called riots of April 1992, when all the bitterness of growing inequality in a land of plenty burst out in violent fury.[24]

The apparel industry shows these same extremes. It is an industry in which some people, such as retailers and manufacturers, managers and professionals, bankers and real estate owners, are able to acquire immense wealth. Others, most notably garment workers, are among the poorest, lowest-paid workers in the city. The industry is not only polarized along class lines, it also has a clear racial and ethnic structure and hierarchy. The wealthy at the top are almost all of European extraction. At the bottom, the workers are mainly Latino immigrants, especially from Mexico and Central America, and a minority are Asian immigrants. In the middle are the entrepreneurs who run the contracting shops that employ the workers, and who are mainly immigrants from Asia (and, to a lesser extent, from Mexico and Central America).

Even the phenomenon of Asian middlemen became an issue in the 1992 uprising, as stores owned by Koreans became the target of much of the angry violence. These stores, mainly mom-and-pop operations, came to be seen as the direct oppressors and drainers of African-American and Latino neighborhoods. The situation has parallels in the garment industry. Latino and Asian garment workers come into contact mainly with Asian contractors (among whom Korean immigrants are especially significant) and rarely meet the wealthy whites who are making most of the money generated by their labor.

We must emphasize that the apparel industry is not fundamentally different from other industries in the United States. They all operate on the same principles of private property and competition, and they all demonstrate the same propensity for an increasing accumulation of wealth at the top and growing racial oppression and exploitation at the bottom. Because the apparel industry is one of the worst, it offers a good example of how our society works and how the system produces and reproduces an intensifying polarization by class and race.

In recent years there has been a redistribution of wealth upward, and there is no immediate end in sight. The common justification for this redistribution is the belief that putting wealth in the hands of the rich will lead to greater productive investment, which should benefit everyone. This may sometimes be true, but an important result has been a greater ability by business owners to lower labor's share of the wealth that is produced.

The push for keeping labor costs low comes not only from individual firms or industries but also from the highest levels of finance and government. When wages appear to be climbing, the stock market drops. When unemployment drops, the fear of a tight labor market that will drive up wages has the same effect. The Federal Reserve Bank then raises interest rates in order to keep inflation in check; unemployment is maintained at a so-called acceptable level and wages stagnate.

These abstract economic concepts—the unemployment rate, inflation, and flexibility—have very human faces. A 5- or 6-percent unemployment rate may be good for the economy, but it is dreadful for the individuals and the communities that must endure it in practice. Similarly, the danger of inflation, which never seems to be associated with rising salaries for chief executive officers or excessively high profits, becomes a personal hardship when translated to mean that the earnings of a working family making minimum wage or less should be held where they are. And the much-touted flexibility, which creates a growing army of contingent workers who work in part-time or temporary jobs completely lacking job security, means that many people find it increasingly difficult to plan for any kind of future they can count on.

The problem is that our system has winners and losers, flesh and blood human beings, who enjoy the windfall benefits or suffer the fallout of policies that claim to be neutral and of benefit to all. How can one talk of a "healthy economy," a daily topic in our newspapers, when more workers are pushed into greater marginality and insecurity? Does the economy exist apart from the people who make up the entire society? Or is the economy really meant to be only for the benefit of the owners of securities and their managerial and professional assistants?

The Los Angeles apparel industry participates in this kind of perverted logic. On the one hand, the industry's leaders are embarrassed by the proliferation of sweatshops. They hate the image of being a sweatshop industry. Obviously it creates unfavorable public relations, as well as various governmental efforts to regulate the industry. It also runs counter to the socially liberal self-image held by many of the leaders themselves, who contribute large amounts of money to worthy causes, oppose racism, and often vote for Democratic Party candidates. Moreover, the growth of sweatshops can provoke movements by consumers, religious leaders, and others that call the industry's practices into question, threatening sales and profits. On the other hand, industry leaders fight with all their might to keep the cost of labor down. They fought against the rise in the minimum wage. They objected when the city of Los Angeles passed a living wage ordinance because, even though it did not affect them directly, they saw it as the first crack in the door toward rising wages.[25] They cheered when the state Industrial Wage Commission eliminated daily overtime rates payable after eight hours in favor of weekly overtime rates payable only after forty hours, which, of course, means that garment workers who work long days will be paid less. And they are ferociously antiunion, willing to spend millions of dollars fighting unionism rather than raising wages.

The possibility that sweatshops might be eliminated if the workers were paid more never gets raised, except in reference to the ever-present specter that higher wages would force otherwise well-intentioned manufacturers to source their production offshore. The industry justifies its position by claiming that it faces intense competition at every level and is always trying to cut costs to meet the competition. Consumers, it is argued, will not accept rising prices. It is really all their fault: Consumers want cheap clothes, and the industry must give them what they want.

In fact, as we saw in that $100 dress, labor's share of the cost of most garments is a small fraction of the price on the sales tag. The greatest portion goes to profits and executive and professional compensation at the top. Yet cost cutting is never aimed at the executives or professionals or company profits. All the pressures to cut costs fall on the poor, relatively powerless workers at the bottom of the system.

The strongly individualistic ideology of the United States, fueled during the past two decades by conservative attacks on big (i.e., "socialistic") government and the "irresponsible poor," runs counter to the portrait we have drawn. In the prevailing view, low-wage jobs are regarded as stepping stones to upward mobility. Workers are presumably free to change their jobs if they do not like the ones they are in; after all, as one industry leader told us, no one is holding a gun to their heads. Immigrants are so much better off here than they were in their homelands that they are grateful for the jobs the industry offers them. Through hard work one can work one's way up the ladder and become a millionaire. Wealth does not depend on the impoverishment and exploitation of others; it is self-generated by the person with a good idea and an entrepreneurial drive to succeed. The United States is a land of opportunity for everyone, and while there may occasionally be a little injustice, things are far better here than they are anywhere else in the world.

In this book we challenge many of these assumptions. We do not mean to imply that hard work cannot pay off, that talent and entrepreneurial drive are irrelevant to success, or that immigrants do not benefit in some ways from their move. But we do not believe that such opportunities justify a situation in which vast wealth is accumulated at the cost of creating poverty. We believe that the apparel industry, as presently constituted, is exploitative at its core. We also believe that a better understanding of its dynamics is necessary if the industry is to preserve what is good while eliminating what is so destructive.

The World According to Nike.

Jeff Danziger, © *The Christian Science Monitor.*

Garment manufacturers may, as individuals, have an interest in undercutting their competition by lowering their prices and their costs, but they also have a contradictory, collective interest in maintaining their consumer market. The polarization of the population into rich and poor, a polarization that extends beyond the United States to the rest of the world, creates a stratified market. As poor people only can afford cheap clothing, discounters flourish, and the middle level of the market is threatened. The growth of discounters, which attracts not only impoverished buyers but also some of the middle-class consumers, creates a new level of pressure on wages: the lower the final price of the garment, the cheaper its cost of production must be. Wages and consumer prices spiral down together at the lower end.

Not all apparel manufacturers are caught up in a race to the bottom. Some maintain high prices through developing a recognizable brand name and by selling an image. Such companies can be highly profitable as they benefit from the depressed wages of garment workers while selling their goods to the upper end of the market.

A major contradiction sits at the heart of a system that manages to treat workers as though they are merely producers, whose cost must be kept to a bare minimum, and not as consumers, whose wages could be spent on consumer goods. To a certain extent, the world can be divided into impoverished producers, who cannot afford to purchase what they produce, and well-off consumers, who do not engage in production themselves, but this social division cannot last. As globalization accelerates, it brings millions of low-wage workers around the world into direct competition with their counterparts in formerly high-wage countries. This competition undermines the principal market for the very goods that are being produced. Endearing anecdotes notwithstanding, very few Chinese workers earning $25 a month are likely to pay $100 for a pair of athletic shoes or jeans, however prestigious the label. And whatever the long-term economic effects, the class and racial polarization that results from the present system is destructive to society as a whole.

In this industry we have, on the one hand, owners, managers, and professionals, who have considerable control over the workers, a control not only over the means of livelihood but also over the very presence of workers, especially undocumented immigrants, in this country. On the other hand, we have workers who are unusually vulnerable to the whim of their employers. They can be fired without cause and are likely to face the loss of a job and sometimes even deportation if they should complain or attempt to improve their circumstances.

One might argue that, where the balance of power is so inequable, part of the government's role is to protect workers against flagrant abuse. In reality, the two groups have very different degrees of access to the government. Owners, managers, and professionals in the apparel industry have all the normal levels of access through their voting power, and those who are wealthy have even better access. They make campaign contributions and employ lobbyists; some of them can call the governor on the phone if they are unhappy about something; they can threaten to leave the jurisdiction, taking their jobs and taxes with them. This gives them a clout that leads governments to pay special attention to their demands.

Garment workers have little or no access to governmental institutions. The undocumented, of course, live in fear of the government, and even those with proper immigration papers rarely are in a position to vote, because they are new immigrants or lack a knowledge of English. This reality affects the Latino immigrant population in general. For example, about 40 percent of the population of Los Angeles is now Latino, but they make up less than 15 percent of the electorate. An affluent, mainly white community elects and governs a poor, largely minority community. This situation is gradually changing as Latinos gain electoral strength, but for garment workers as a class access to governmental institutions is still more limited than it is for the Latino community at large. The imbalance of power in the workplace is exacerbated by the underlying imbalance of political power.

In many ways southern California resembles the old South, where African Americans were also a disenfranchised population. In the South, the major marker for disempowerment was race. In Los Angeles, it is a combination of race and immigration status. Immigration status alone marks off a segment of the population as unprotected by the basic laws of the land, but the effect is exacerbated by race because, of all undocumented immigrants, Latinos carry a special burden as the target of anti-immigrant movements. The racism of the system in southern California is more subtle than that in the South because it is hidden under a layer of legalese. In southern California, the combination of race and immigrant status is used to create a workforce without rights. Employers are the major beneficiaries of undocumented immigration from Mexico and Central America. They have under their control a highly exploitable workforce. They can pay illegally low wages and get away with it. The gross imbalance of power leads to a kind of corruption that very few are able to withstand.

PART I

Capital

CHAPTER 1

Manufacturers

© 1995, *Washington Post* Writers Group. Reprinted with permission.

Manufacturers are the key to the apparel industry. They are the creators and owners of "labels," the brands by which firms are identified. They occupy a central position of creativity and power, making many of the major decisions that affect the lives of those who work for them. Yet all but the largest and best-known manufacturers are becoming beholden to the retailers, who, as we shall see in Chapter 3, increasingly call the shots in apparel production and merchandising.

In this chapter we begin by describing how apparel manufacturing works and then turn to a description of those manufacturers who dominate the industry in Los Angeles. Given that there are possibly 2,000 apparel manufacturers in Los Angeles County, most of our coverage will necessarily be limited to the largest firms.[1] Still, as those firms account for most apparel sales, we believe that our coverage accurately captures the nature of the most important firms in the region.

What Is a Manufacturer?

Paradoxically, most garment manufacturers in Los Angeles do not manufacture clothing. They design the clothing that appears under their label, purchase the necessary textiles, arrange for production, and wholesale the finished goods to retailers. But the actual manufacturing, the sewing of garments, is done by independent contractors. Most manufacturers in Los Angeles neither own nor operate their own factories. This intentionally confusing system serves the important function of diffusing legal and moral responsibility for working conditions: Manufacturers can reap the benefits that come from designing and marketing clothing, without having to dirty their hands in its actual manufacture.

This was not always the case. At one time a significant proportion of manufacturing in Los Angeles was done in-house, the manufacturers employing their own workers to make clothing in their own factories. Today few do, in part because of a decline in the more stable men's sector and the dominance of the fashion-sensitive women's sector in Los Angeles. In New York City, where women's wear is less dominant, more manufacturers do produce in-house, and the term *manufacturer* is reserved for them; the term *jobber* is used for apparel firms that rely entirely on independent contractors to sew their garments. In Los Angeles the use of independent contractors for apparel fabrication is, however, so common that such fine terminological distinctions are not made, leaving the term *manufacturer* to describe all firms that design clothing destined to be sold wholesale to retailers, even if all the work is contracted out.

If manufacturers are principally designers, they vary enormously in the degree to which they perform that function. Some manufacturers are consistently innovative; others equally consistently "knock off" (or copy) other firms' designs. Most firms fall somewhere in between. Some manufacturers also engage in licensing, arranging for another company to produce a line under their own brand names. For example, a manufacturer of garments for young adults (juniors, in the language of the industry) may want to put out a children's line and will arrange with a children's wear manufacturer to serve as a licensee for such a line. The licensee pays the licensor a royalty for the use of the name.

Los Angeles apparel manufacturers specialize in fashion-oriented apparel, made in response to orders from retailers. Manufacturers develop their lines for a particular season. The line, termed a *collection,* consists of a coordinated mix of garments that go together to provide a particular "look."[2] They make samples of each item in the collection and display them, either at shows or in showrooms, their own or a rented showroom in one of Los Angeles' downtown marts, such as the CaliforniaMart and the New Mart. Samples are also sometimes displayed in a showroom (typically in a mart) rented by a representative who shows a series of lines.

Manufacturers may also show their lines in shows and showrooms in other locations around the country. In some cases, very powerful retailers, such as Wal-Mart Stores Inc., insist that manufacturers bring their lines to *them* (in this case, to Fayetteville, Arkansas).

Retail buyers examine the lines and place orders for the items they want. The manufacturers then arrange for the production of those items in the quantities requested. At one time, according to some manufacturers, retailers would order the whole collection. That is seldom the case today; retailers go through and cherry-pick the items they want. As a result, some manufacturers now no longer design entire collections, but rather develop lines that focus on specific items. Unlike the collection, such manufacturing tends to be narrow but deep, resulting in inventories that are larger but less varied. Such niche manufacturing thus typically involves the designing of a handful of basic yet fashion-sensitive items; one designer termed them "fashion basics."[3] The movement from collection to niche-market manufacturing illustrates a trend in the apparel industry: The classic wholesaler, or branded manufacturer, is being squeezed by giant retailers.[4]

Firms used to produce lines for two seasons a year. Then, as the market became more fragmented, and retailers demanded more change over the course of a year, the number of seasons began to grow. Firms began producing for five or six seasons a year: Fall 1, Fall 2, Holiday, Cruise, Spring, and Summer. Today, many fashion-oriented firms change their lines monthly, in an effort to supply retailers continuously with fresh, movable products.

In this system of making goods in response to retailers' orders, most manufacturers do not carry much inventory. Contracting arrangements, which are set up once the orders have been placed, provide manufacturers with considerable flexibility, allowing them to respond only to orders that have actually been placed. The system also shifts the burden of uncertainty to the contractor and his workers, who never know whether future orders will be forthcoming.

There are manufacturers who do not follow the general pattern. At the upper end of the industry, a few large, well-known manufacturers operate their own retail outlets, just as a few well-known apparel retailers manufacture almost all of their own garments. In Los Angeles, Guess? Inc. and BCBG Max Azria are examples of the former: By operating their own retail stores, typically in malls, they are able to sell part of their product directly to the consumer.[5] (They wholesale their garments through retailers as well.) Gap, Inc. in San Francisco is an example of the latter, a retailer that manufacturers its own lines of clothing, which are sold in Gap stores throughout the world.[6] The convergence of retailer and manufacturer in a single firm is a logical outcome of competitive pressures in the industry, because it effectively eliminates one major layer of profit taking. Although most manufacturers lack the know-how and capital to become retailers, many retailers are moving into manufacturing. Most department and specialty stores now have their own private labels of store-brand lines, designed and produced to their specifications by independent manufacturers.[7] Several once-prominent Los Angeles apparel manufacturers have shifted to private-label production for retailers, because it provides a secure source of income; some, for example, the Tarrant Apparel Group, now specialize in private label and make nothing else. Occasionally the retailers even employ their own designers, eliminating the manufacturer as an unnecessary middleman. A good deal of private-label apparel is produced overseas, especially in Asia, but some retailers have some of their private-label clothing made domestically.

At the lower end of the industry, some manufacturers wholesale their garments at discounted value directly to the public, bypassing retailing altogether. This is typically done in pseudowholesaling locations such as Santee Alley in the downtown garment district of Los Angeles, where discounted goods and knock-off labels can be had at bargain basement prices. The two extremes tend to sell in different markets, but there has probably been some erosion of the fashion sector, as cheaper producers are able to compete with them and offer discounts even to middle-class consumers.

Apparel manufacturing is an ideal start-up industry: It has relatively low capital requirements for entry, and because the labor is contracted out, it is relatively easy, at least in comparison with other industries, to break into garment manufacturing. Until fairly recently, large amounts of capital were not a prerequisite.[8] There are fabled examples of people with good design ideas starting their firms out of their garages and building them up to highly successful businesses. The promise of going literally from rags to riches continues to attract newcomers to the industry, particularly would-be entrepreneurs fueled by success stories such as those of Robin Piccone and Mossimo Giannuli, who began in a garage.[9] But today's vaunted success story can become tomorrow's failure. A firm is only as successful as its last season, and most do not have the capital to withstand many failures. Nevertheless, the apparel industry is still a stronghold of small business. Many small manufacturers have entered the industry, most to fail, some to survive, and a handful to regenerate the myths of success.

One typical way of becoming a garment manufacturer in Los Angeles is to work for an established firm for a while, develop a design idea of one's own, and then to break off and set up one's own company. The effect of this continual splitting off has been the creation of a complex network of personal relationships in the industry. Even though firms are in serious competition with one another and are therefore highly secretive, they nonetheless share overlapping histories that result in a great deal of insider knowledge. This pattern, reminiscent of an occasionally dysfunctional family unified through intermarriage, divorce, and remarriage, is more likely to characterize the old, largely Jewish, establishment.

Raising Capital

When apparel firms need to raise outside capital, either for new ventures or for business expansion they sometimes turn to commercial banks. Some commercial banks have long been associated with the garment industry in Los Angeles. Union Bank, for example, was founded by a sheepherder, Kaspare Cohn, in 1914; Cohn's flock provided wool for the emerging needle trades industry in Los Angeles. Union Bank has been a major source of financing for the industry ever since; significantly, one of its branches today shares a plaza with the CaliforniaMart.[10] Commercial banks are likely to work with well-established firms, typically those that have been in business for a while and have a reasonable net worth. They make standard business loans for equipment and other capital costs. Because of the volatility and risk of the industry, bank loans may, however, be hard to get, especially for smaller and upstart companies.[11]

Another source of capital is the sale of shares in the company to the public. The vast majority of apparel companies in Los Angeles are privately held, but a few are publicly held, at least in part, among them Guess? Inc., Jalate, Ltd. Inc., Sirena Apparel Group, Tarrant Apparel Group, and Yes! Several apparel firms had disappointing results after going public. For example, Guess raised $126 million in August 1996 but it experienced a sharp drop in the value of its stock, which declined from an initial high of $18 a share to lows in the $3- to $5-a-share range.[12] In late 1998, Jalate agreed to remove its stock from the American Stock Exchange because it had too few stockholders.[13]

Factoring is the most common form of financing in the apparel industry and, although factors have tried to expand into other industries, apparel and textile companies remain their most important clients. The most common form is advance nonrecourse factoring. *Advance* means that the factor advances funds to the manufacturer upon receipt of sales invoices showing that a retailer, whose credit has been approved, has placed an order. *Nonrecourse* means that the factor accepts the consequences of nonpayment by the retailer. In this, the factor provides the manufacturer with accounts receivable insurance, guaranteeing the creditworthiness of the customer (the retailer). The factor usually advances 80 percent of the value of the receivables and receives in return a commission of about 1 percent, for accepting the credit risk and for performing a number of related services, and interest, for making the advance, paid usually at a rate of between 1 and 3 percent above the prime lending rate.[14]

The great advantage of factoring is that it gives manufacturers cash right away to plow back into production. The manufacturer farms out the work of credit checking and collecting receivables, as well as assuming the risk of nonpayment. Of course, if a manufacturer exposes himself to too many high-risk retailers, he will cease to be able to raise capital in this way.[15]

Most factors are multibillion-dollar institutions, frequently part of multinational commercial banks.[16] There was a merger movement among factors in 1994, when four leading factors merged into two. BNY Financial Corporation, the factoring arm of the Bank of New York, acquired BancBoston Financial, the factoring arm of the Bank of Boston. The CIT Group/Commercial Services, owned by Dai-Ichi Kangyo Limited, and Chemical Banking Corporation, bought Barclay's Commercial, to create two "megafactors." In 1996, nationwide, factors did $63.8 billion worth of business. The largest factors were the CIT Group, BNY Financial Corporation, NationsBanc Commercial corporation, Heller Financial Inc., and Republic Business Credit Corporation.[17] In 1992, when we studied the 184 largest apparel manufacturing firms, 78 percent used factors, the most frequently used being Republic (twenty-nine firms), Heller (twenty), NationsBanc (fifteen), Congress (fourteen), BNY Financial (eleven), Barclay's (ten), and CIT (six).[18]

A Brief History

Although clothing manufacturing began in the 1850s in California, production in Los Angeles did not surpass that in San Francisco until the First World War. The rapid growth of southern California during the first half of this century created a strong local market for clothing, fueling the growth of the local industry. Between 1900 and 1910, the population of Los Angeles County doubled; it doubled again by 1920, and again by 1930. By 1940 there were 2.3 million Angelinos to buy clothing,[19] and sixteen local buying offices had emerged to help connect retailers up with local manufacturers. Only six years later there were eighty-four.[20]

The emergence of Hollywood during the 1920s meant that the legend Made in California would soon have national appeal. Charles S. Goodman, writing in 1948,[21] noted that "the burgeoning of the motion picture industry following World War I produced a nationwide interest in Hollywood styles which was quickly and expertly capitalized upon by the state's apparel industry." Hollywood stars and designers were daring in their styles, and movies provided a particularly good means of influencing fashion trends. Los Angeles became a style center that represented glamour, creativity, innovation, and casual informality. California, and especially southern California, meant beaches and outdoor living, a lifestyle that did not have to pay attention to the more rigid dress conventions of Europe and the eastern seaboard. Instead, people could live and dress as they pleased. These characteristics combined to create what was promoted as the California Look, a description of casual, yet fashionable, moderately priced sportswear, especially for young women, and including jeans, swimwear, beachwear, activewear, and light dresses, mainly for spring and summer. The high-fashion end of the industry still tends to be located in New York and Europe; the mass production of staple items is found, in the United States, in the South or, overseas, in Asia or Mexico and the Caribbean. Los Angeles thus occupies a particular niche in the nation's apparel industry, although almost every type of garment can be found there. Although it is now a half century since Goodman described the Los Angeles apparel industry, his words still ring true today.

Sportswear attracts most buyers to Los Angeles. This includes not only active sportswear, such as play togs and swim suits, but less formal types of outerwear generally. For women, this comprises the more sporty dresses and suits, skirts, and slacks; for men, it includes the sport shirt and various types of "leisure" coats and jackets. In recent years, the market has achieved attention because of its wider use of colors. . . . Though all of these items did not originate in California, they gained widest American acceptance there. This acceptance has been an outgrowth of the California way of life, which is generally more informal than that in other parts of the United States since there is a greater emphasis on out-of-door activities. California apparel is, consequently, noted for utility and casualness as well as for color (pp. 28–29).

By the 1940s, the image of California was so well established that even clothing designed in New York City occasionally boasted colorful patterns, sporty style, and the label "California"—a practice upheld as legal because, at least in the view of the courts, the word *California* referred to "a type of garment rather than a place of origin." The glamour of the name had advertising value, while the colorfulness of the garments made them attractive for window displays as prestige merchandise. Made in California quickly came to be associated with a casual, warm-weather lifestyle, one freed from the stodgy customs of the east coast. Buyers looking for heavy winter coats, furs, formal suits, or haute couture would have to go elsewhere.

Significantly, one of the first important apparel sectors in southern California was women's swimwear, a sector that remains important today. Movie stars such as Esther Williams modeled locally produced swimwear, contributing to its national popularity. Even though their styles were not as daring as the swimsuits sported on *Baywatch,* the Los Angeles designer Rudi Gernreich did pioneer the topless bathing suit. Some of the original swimwear firms in Los Angeles, such as Catalina and Cole of California (now owned by the giant Authentic Fitness Corporation), still enjoy prominence, alongside more recent arrivals such as Apparel Ventures Inc. (makers of the Sassafras, La Blanca, Too Hot Brazil, Citrus, Sessa, and Elizabeth Stewart brands), Beach Patrol Inc. (Daffy, Jag, and Rebel Beach), and Sirena Apparel Group (the licensee for Anne Klein, Liz Claiborne, Rose Marie Reid, Hang Ten, and others). Along with swimwear came denim jeans, a garment associated with the western frontier and the challenging of urban conventions. Major manufacturers in Los Angeles that specialize in denim today include Guess (the largest apparel manufacturer in the region), Michael Caruso and Co., Inc. (makers of Bongo), Revatex, Inc. (makers of JNCO), Lucky Brand Dungarees, Paris Blues Inc., Steel Sportswear Inc. (makers of Steel Jeans), and Z Cavaricci Inc.; a number of less specialized manufacturers also have denim lines. Several firms in Los Angeles also specialize in women's dresses and sportswear, particularly for young women looking for stylish contemporary clothing, among them ABS USA, BCBG Max Azria (which now owns Francine Browner, Inc. and Hervé Léger), Bisou Bisou, California Fashion Industries (makers of Carole Little), Chorus Line Inc., Jalate Ltd., Inc., Harkham Industries (makers of Jonathan Martin), Karen Kane, Inc., Rabbit Rabbit Rabbit, Rampage Clothing Company, Wild Rose, and Lola, Inc. (makers of XOXO).

Today, the California Look depends not only on images from Hollywood, but also on an awareness of the latest tastes among the young, fashion-conscious residents of the city. Designers haunt the beaches, high schools, and clubs in search of inspiration—a new "look" that can be marketed to give a handful of manufacturers the momentary advantage that comes from identifying and creating a temporary market niche.

Other features have contributed to the growing importance of Los Angeles as an apparel center: It is a source of inexpensive immigrant labor; it is itself a major market for the goods that are produced, meaning that manufacturers can provide quick turnaround for local retail outlets; and, as a major city, it provides myriad business services that are vital to the industry—banks and other sources of financing, advertising agencies, law and accounting firms, retail buying offices, fashion schools, sewing schools, and technical colleges, all within reach of the downtown garment district. With all the firms related to the industry clustered together in a single location, a substantial cumulative effect results. The downtown geographical focus has been strengthened in recent years, receiving considerable impetus from the construction of the CaliforniaMart, located on the corner of Main and Ninth Streets.[22]

The garment industry is central to the Los Angeles economy and has emerged as the largest manufacturing employer in the county. Apparel employment overtook electronic equipment in 1988, instruments and related products two years later, and transportation equipment (which includes aircraft and parts, missiles and spacecraft, and instruments and related parts) in 1994. In 1983 apparel accounted for 8 percent of all manufacturing employment; by 1997 its share had more than doubled, to 18 percent. In fact, by April 1998, the apparel industry was running close behind the movie production industry, with apparel officially employing 122,500 persons, in comparison with movie production's 138,500.

The Manufacturers in Los Angeles

Obtaining an accurate picture of the apparel manufacturing firms in Los Angeles is virtually impossible. In fact, merely estimating their numbers can be a daunting task. Most publicly available data do not draw the crucial distinction between contractors and manufacturers.[23] For this section, we combined various data sources to provide a broad overview of the approximately 1,500 apparel manufacturers in operation in the early 1990s.[24] One reason for the difficulty in getting a clear picture is that the scene is constantly changing. Although the two oldest firms in our database were founded in 1878, half were less than ten years old at the time of our study (1992), and two-thirds were founded in 1980 or later.[25] We have no way of estimating the number of firms that went out of business in recent years, but the relative youth of most firms suggests that very few age gracefully or live to old age.

VOLUME

According to the Los Angeles Economic Development Corporation, the garment and textile industries today account for as much as 10 percent ($28 billion) of Los Angeles County's $282 billion economy.[26] The economic importance of the industry is especially impressive in light of the fact that most of the firms are oriented toward the middle and lower segments of the market and thus depend on volume to generate their revenues. Nearly half (45 percent) of the 817 firms reported their production was intended for the low-end, "popular" market, slightly more than one-third (39 percent) characterized themselves as moderate in price, and the rest (16 percent) were oriented toward more upscale ("better") designs.[27] The industry in Los Angeles focuses especially on women's outerwear; two-thirds of the local manufacturers design for this market. In comparison, of all the firms in the rest of the United States industry, excluding Los Angeles, only one quarter did.

The firms in our data bank produced a total wholesale volume of $8.7 billion in 1992, averaging $6.9 million per firm.[28] Most of these firms were extremely small by industry standards: one-third had annual sales of less than $1 million, three-quarters, less than $5 million annually, and well over four-fifths, less than $10 million. At the other extreme, the approximately one hundred firms each with annual sales exceeding $20 million accounted for almost two-thirds of the wholesale value produced by all 1,500 manufacturers.

Most manufacturing firms in Los Angeles employed relatively few people directly. (Bear in mind that, in manufacturing, direct employment usually excludes sewing machine operators, who comprise the bulk of the workforce in this industry, because sewing is contracted out.) Employees include design and administrative personnel, secretarial and clerical staff, and the sales force, as well as some workers who make samples, cut fabric, and operate warehouses. We estimate that in the early 1990s, if we exclude contracted sewing, approximately 43,000 people worked directly for Los Angeles garment manufacturers, averaging about thirty persons per firm.[29] Yet fully half of this employment was found in only eighty-two larger manufacturers, each with 100 or more employees. Half of all Los Angeles manufacturers employed fewer than ten people, and two-thirds employed fewer than twenty. Despite the prominence of a few big-name firms with universal brand-name recognition, the vast majority of manufacturers are small operations with low annual sales and high mortality.

LOCATION

Garment manufacturers are found throughout Los Angeles County, although half of all firms are found in three downtown areas we have labeled the "garment district," the "growth region," and the "expansion district."[30] These geographic patterns strongly suggest the importance for manufacturers of a central location with ready access to cutting services, sewing factories, the showrooms at the CaliforniaMart, and the range of services and facilities that are relatively concentrated.

The official downtown Los Angeles garment district (now renamed the Fashion District), as designated in the city's land-use plans, comprises fifty-six city blocks bounded by Seventh Street to the north, the Santa Monica Freeway to the south, Broadway to the west, and San Pedro Street to the east (see Figure 6).[31] At its center lies the CaliforniaMart. At the time of our study, the downtown garment district was home to two out of every five manufacturers in Los Angeles County (41 percent). The district is characterized, in part, by eight- to twelve-story buildings, mainly constructed during the 1930s, and many in need of repair. These buildings house countless small contracting factories, buying offices that provide services for the country's principal retailers, fabric providers, and numerous other providers of apparel-related goods and services.

The industry has been spreading in a southern and eastern direction, into the adjacent "growth region," which in 1992 was home to about 5 percent of all manufacturers in the county. This region includes the city of Vernon, two miles southeast of Los Angeles, as well as some surrounding areas.[32] Vernon, with a tiny residential population of 150 and a workforce of 45,000, is noted for being a city dedicated to industry.[33] Because it has almost no residents, Vernon's budget can be devoted entirely to luring industries by offering lower business licensing fees and less governmental regulation than does neighboring Los Angeles. Property values are much lower and the cost of leasing factory space is about 75 percent less than it is in Los Angeles. Larger facilities are available there, along with better parking and less traffic. In sum, Vernon serves as a business-friendly enclave within easy reach of the Los Angeles garment district. At the end of 1996 Vernon listed 200 apparel firms among its 1,100 businesses, including some of the largest, such as BCBG Max

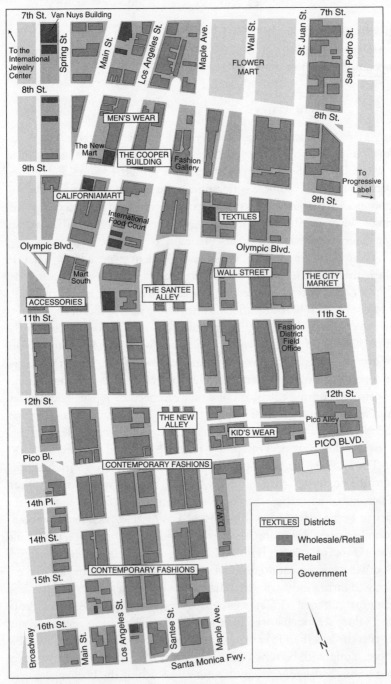

Source: The Potentia Group, "Downtown Los Angeles Development Map," Los Angeles, California.

Figure 6. The Fashion District, Los Angeles

Azria, Chorus Line, David Dart, Inc, Leon Max, Inc, Lucky Brand Dungarees, Rabbit Rabbit Rabbit, Lola, Inc., and Z Cavaricci.[34] Three percent of manufacturers are found in what we have termed the "expanded district," where the industry has spilled over further afield to parts of East Los Angeles, El Monte, the City of Commerce, and the City of Industry.

Depending on their location, the manufacturing firms vary considerably in size, whether size is measured by average sales or by number of employees. The traditional garment district has an enormous concentration of relatively small firms, in terms of both average annual sales ($6.1 million) and employment (32.1 employees), figures that are typical of the City of Los Angeles as a whole, which accounts for three-fifths of all firms in the county.[35] Although the neighboring growth region has barely one-seventh as many firms, its firms are on average three times as large in terms of both annual sales ($23.8 million) and employment (108.2 employees). As a consequence, the growth region accounts for nearly half (43 percent) as much in total sales as the garment district itself does ($1.6 billion versus $3.7 billion). It is clear that the principal site of manufacturing is shifting away from the congested downtown to neighboring areas that can offer more space and better value and amenities. The expanded district displays a similar pattern, although on a reduced scale: Its small number of firms are on average approximately twice the size of those in the garment district. Apparel manufacturers in the Cities of Commerce and Industry had average annual sales of $22 million and $24.8 million, respectively, although the number of companies was fairly small.

ETHNICITY

In the words of one major Los Angeles manufacturer, "the industry has always been ethnic"[36]—both nationally and in Los Angeles. In the first decades of this century, garment manufacturers were mainly European, and usually Jewish. This was true in New York City, which was the center of the garment industry, as well as in the nascent industry in Los Angeles, where apparel manufacturing was initially developed by Jewish transplants from the east coast, and soon linked to another southern California industry with an important Jewish presence, the movie industry.[37] The ethnic composition of the industry nationally has changed somewhat over the years; today the principal manufacturers include giant corporations without ethnic identities. In Los Angeles, however, smaller, family-owned firms still abound, and Jewish manufacturers dominate the industry. Although they compromise only a fifth of the 1,269 manufacturers for which we have sales data, they account for nearly half (46 percent) of total sales. Jewish-owned firms averaged $16.1 million in sales in 1992, more than twice the industry average of $6.9 million. European Americans (excluding those who are Jewish) comprise nearly half of all manufacturers (49 percent), but account for only a third of total sales. Their 1992 sales averaged $4.8 million, slightly below the industry average. Other ethnic groups play marginal manufacturing roles in Los Angeles. There are sixty-seven Chinese-owned firms (5 percent of all firms), forty-six Korean-owned firms (3 percent), and forty-nine Latino firms (4 percent). Significantly, Korean- and Chinese-owned firms tend to be much larger than Latino-owned firms are: Average 1992 sales for Korean- and Chinese-owned firms slightly exceeded $6 million; Latino-owned firms averaged only $1.4 million.

Our method for establishing ethnicity, coding surnames,[38] did not allow us to distinguish African-American apparel manufacturers. However, there have been a number of successful African-American manufacturers. One firm that rocketed to stardom, only to come crashing down after expanding too quickly (a not-uncommon story irrespective of ethnicity) was Cross Colours, maker of hip-hop clothes for young men.[39] Karl Kani, a designer who had been a partner in Cross Colours, now has his own $69 million designer jeans company. Karl Kani Infinity was the twenty-fifth-largest African-American–owned company in 1996.[40] Another prominent African-American manufacturer is Clotee McAfee, producer of school uniforms. Part of her goal is to train young African Americans in computer skills associated with the apparel business.[41]

The growth of Korean apparel manufacturing is also not adequately captured in our data. Larry Jacobs of the accounting firm Stonefield Josephson reports on a transformation that is occuring along Ninth Street and down San Pedro Street. In a big, three-story building on San Pedro Street, he said, "I discovered a whole apparel district within an apparel district. The level of human intensity was enormous. People were moving quickly between the different stores. I discovered that these were not ordinary stores but more like showrooms for apparel manufacturers! The predominant language spoken was Korean. These manufacturers sold all kinds of apparel at what appeared to be extraordinarily good prices and were offering goods directly off the retail sales floor, or for more substantial quantities, were offering five- to seven-day delivery. . . . No sales commissions, no factoring fees, no disputes, just cash and carry. This apparel center within the apparel center was complete with its own bank,

Korean, of course."[42] The buyers were mainly small retailers and a few national discounters and off-price retailers.

The ethnic distribution of the industry undoubtedly reflects the historical development of the industry, which, as we have noted, originated with Jewish manufacturers who have increasingly relied on Asian contractors for their labor. Some of the latter subsequently moved into manufacturing, and are now found in the middle tier. In the meantime, only a small number of the Latino contractors have gained entry into the lower rungs of manufacturing.

Ethnic differences are associated with a degree of geographic distribution as well. Jewish manufacturers tend to be found either in the downtown garment district (45 percent) or dispersed outside the three primary garment zones altogether (40 percent). Korean manufacturers are heavily concentrated in the downtown garment district (57 percent) and the adjacent growth region (11 percent), locations where Korean contractors also tend to be heavily concentrated (see Chapter 5). This geographical clustering enables Korean manufacturers to place orders with Korean contractors who are simply down the street or on the next block. Conversely, Latino manufacturers tend to be widely dispersed. Seventy-two percent are found outside the three primary zones, a pattern that parallels that of Latino contractors. In an industry where manufacturing and contracting are separate functions, ethnic ties provide an important avenue of informal communication and coordination and results in an ethnically constructed use of space, as firms of the same ethnicity tend to locate near one another.

The Big Players

To gain a more detailed understanding of the larger manufacturers, we conducted a telephone survey of all those whose annual sales volumes exceeded $10 million, successfully reaching 184 of 255 (or 72 percent) of such firms. The survey was conducted during the summer of 1992.[43] This group of larger manufacturers generated combined sales in 1991 of $6.2 billion, averaging $34.1 million per firm, or five times that of the average Los Angeles manufacturer. Together, the larger firms accounted for 72 percent of the total combined sales ($8.7 billion) of the 1,269 apparel manufacturers for whom we have sales data. The portrait we paint of these larger manufacturers is, therefore, in one sense a portrait of the industry as a whole: It includes the lion's share of production and sales, and therefore of contracting and labor employment as well. (In contrast, as many as 1,100 firms each with annual sales under $10 million comprise the underbelly of the industry, and include start-up firms, mom-and-pop manufacturers, cash-and-carry companies, and fly-by-night operations of various sorts. The vast majority of those firms have annual sales of well under $1 million and employ very few people.

CHARACTERISTICS

Even at the top of the industry all firms are not equal. Three-quarters of the 184 larger firms reported annual sales of less than $30 million, and more than half (55 percent) had sales under $20 million. At the other extreme, the twenty-five largest firms (with annual sales of $60 million or more) accounted for $3 billion in combined sales, averaging $121.8 million each. This represents nearly half of the total sales of the 184 larger manufacturers, and more than a third (35 percent) of the 1,269 apparel manufacturers for whom we have sales data.

Clearly at the top of the list in 1992 were four firms with combined sales of nearly $1.2 billion: Guess? Inc. ($575 million); California Fashion Industries, makers of Carole Little ($200 million); Paul Davril Inc., makers of Introspect ($200 million); and Cherokee Inc. ($194 million). Guess alone directly employed 1,200 people at the time of our study. One indicator of the rapid shift in fortunes of the apparel industry is the fate of Cherokee, which was the fourth-largest manufacturer in Los Angeles in 1992. Cherokee filed for bankruptcy in 1994, citing poor sales and excessive debt acquired during a leveraged buyout in 1989. In 1997 the company posted revenues of only $8.7 million, derived entirely from licensing its label to other manufacturers and retailers, including Target.[44] (By 1997, the principal manufacturers in Los Angeles were, in order of sales volume: Guess, Rampage, Tarrant Apparel Group, Chorus Line, the Carole Little label manufactured by California Fashion Industries, Podell Industries Inc., makers of Laundry by Shelli Segal, and BCBG Max Azria.)[45]

That the volatile women's and children's wear sector dominates the Los Angeles apparel industry was shown in our survey. Among the larger firms surveyed, 80 percent produced predominantly for this sector. Moreover, those companies tended to be somewhat larger than average, accounting for 85 percent of the sales of the larger firms.

Three-quarters of the larger firms manufactured for the lower to middle price ranges, 43 percent classifying their principal target as the "moderate" market, 25 percent, as the "popular" market, and 7 percent falling somewhere between those two categories. Conversely, only 19 percent manufactured for the "better" market, with another 5 percent falling between "better" and "moderate." Only 1 percent manufactured "couture" (fashionable, custom-made clothing).

Seventy percent of the larger firms reported doing some private-label production, and 17 percent reported that they were licensed to make apparel for other companies. Ninety percent sold their goods in department stores and specialty stores; 55 percent reported engaging in mass-market sales. Half of all the firms reported doing some exporting, 22 percent to Mexico, 36 percent to Canada, and 13 percent to Asia, but only three reported that exports accounted for more than 10 percent of their sales. At least in 1992, manufacturers in Los Angeles designed primarily for the domestic market.

Most manufacturers in Los Angeles contract out to specialized firms for the cutting of fabric; they then ship the cut fabric to their sewing contractors. Nineteen percent of the larger manufacturers reported doing all their fabric cutting in-house, 60 percent did none, 21 percent did both. Of the 146 manufacturers that used outside cutting contractors, the average number used was three.

Only 17 percent of the manufacturers reported doing any in-house sewing of garments at all: 9 percent did "some," 2 percent did "more than half," and 6 percent did "all." Among the 171 manufacturers who reported using at least some outside contractors for sewing, 62 percent relied exclusively on domestic contractors, 31 percent on offshore production, and the remaining 7 percent on both. (See Chapter 2 for further discussion of offshore production.) Among those manufacturers who contracted locally, the average number of sewing contractors used was nineteen. About a quarter of all firms reported using only five or fewer sewing contractors; three firms used 100 or more. All told, these larger manufacturers reported using approximately 2,900 sewing contractors, some of whom probably overlap because contractors often sew for more than one manufacturer. One industry insider estimated that as few as fifteen manufacturing firms control four-fifths of the contractor base in southern California, which means that they have an enormous amount of control over the factories that provide contracted labor.[46]

Among the 182 larger manufacturers for which we have data on both ethnicity and sales, nearly half (45 percent) are Jewish, and about a third (35 percent) are European American, but not Jewish. There are also eight Chinese, four Korean, and nine "other" Asian manufacturers in this se-

Table 1. *Annual Sales of Larger Apparel Manufacturers, by Ethnicity of Owner*

Ethnic Group	Average Sales ($ millions)	Total Sales ($ millions)	Combined Sales (Percentage of Total)
Jewish-Americans (n=82)	$42.5	$3,485.0	56.1
Koreans (n=4)	39.3	$157.2	2.5
Chinese (n=8)	37.1	$296.8	4.8
European (n=64)	26.9	$1,721.6	27.7
Other (n=15)	25.3	$379.5	6.1
Other Asians (n=9)	19.4	$174.6	2.8
All manufacturers (n=182)	$34.1	$6,214.7	100.0

NOTE: Missing data = 2.

lect group. The ethnicity of fifteen (8 percent) could not be identified. As Table 1 indicates (and as discussed earlier), the companies of Jewish manufacturers are the largest, even among this manufacturing elite. Their combined sales account for more than half (56 percent) of total sales for this group, while the sales of the other European Americans account for little more than a quarter (28 percent), and that of all other ethnic groups combined, only 16 percent. It is clear that, despite the influx of Chinese and Koreans into manufacturing, the industry remains dominated by Jewish Americans and other European Americans at the top end. Interestingly, there were no manufacturers with Spanish surnames among the larger firms we were able to interview in 1992. If the industry does indeed provide an entrée into the business world, this had not yet, apparently, benefited Latinos, despite, as we shall see in Chapter 6, their overwhelming dominance as workers.

Koreans have been the most successful ethnic group in pursuing the entrepreneurial route into manufacturing, although the more successful among them are those who arrived in Los Angeles with manufacturing know-how and financial resources. Those who came directly from South Korea arrived with a strong desire to get ahead; they were classic immigrant entrepreneurs, some of whom began as garment workers and wound up owning factories (see Chapter 5). A second stream of Korean immigrants originated in Brazil, where they had already established themselves as the mainstay of that country's thriving garment industry. Although many Korean-born Angelinos already owned garment factories, they tended to regard their work in the apparel industry as a necessary evil, a somewhat undignified first step towards the American dream.

Brazilian-Korean immigrants, in contrast, had long roots in the industry, and tended to value the work itself. Today they constitute the core of the Korean garment community.[47]

Yet the experience of even the more successful Korean immigrants shows the difficulties of crossing the divide from labor to capital. Koreans in Los Angeles may have moved from factory floor to the owner's office, and some have indeed made it into the ranks of the manufacturers. But those who have been truly successful are few indeed. We have already noted that in 1992 there were a mere forty-six Korean manufacturers in Los Angeles (out of a total of nearly 1,300); only four had annual sales exceeding $10 million. Today there may be several more, but they are not the giants of the industry.

Firms in Profile

In order to put some flesh on the names and numbers, we offer brief profiles of a handful of prominent apparel manufacturers in Los Angeles. Theirs is a risky undertaking: Today's success story is tomorrow's goat, the victim of overexpansion, bad business decisions, unwise buyouts, and fashion's unforgiving fickleness. The attraction of apparel manufacturing is that it holds the promise of moving literally from rags to riches; yet the return route can be equally quick. Any cheerful tales we tell today may well have had unhappy endings by the time this book goes to press. In fact, the principal lesson to be drawn from the following examples is that talent, hard work, and aggressive business practices are seldom sufficient to assure long-term success.

There are numerous examples of firms whose fortunes changed overnight, both for the better and for the worse. We have already mentioned Cherokee, Inc., which went from a $200-million company at the time of our original research in 1992 to a bankrupt licensing operation with only $9 million in revenues five years later. Or consider the fate of Rampage Clothing Co., founded for $30,000 in 1983 by the twenty-two-year-old Larry Hansel. Rampage grew by as much as a third a year, acquiring the Judy's chain of junior apparel stores, engaging in private-label production for Mervyn's, and grossing nearly $200 million in 1993. One industry insider could not find enough superlatives to describe Hansel, whom he characterized as "a California contemporary man. He never sees any ceiling, any limits. He's got imagination and the guts to go with it. He's building an empire, and he's building it faster and bigger than most people do, and it's sound."[48] Hansel's seemingly sound empire came crashing down and Rampage filed for bankruptcy protection in 1997, the victim of acquiring nearly $100 million in debt during its expansion.[49] This story was all too familiar to B.U.M. International, whose sales peaked at $175 million in 1991 before the company went bankrupt five years later, the victim of an unwise merger and move into retailing and an inability to rescue itself by moving into licensing.[50]

YES CLOTHING COMPANY

The story of Yes Clothing Co., makers of Yes! brand clothing, is especially illustrative of the changing fortunes of the apparel business in Los Angeles, featuring as it does several prominent members of the apparel community. At the time of our original research in 1991 and 1992, Yes! was flying high. The owners, George Randall and Moshe Tsabag, had acquired the company from its founder, Harry Berman, in 1985, taken the company public, and found a ready market for their pioneering use of a slinky, sexy cotton and spandex knit for young women's clothing.[51] When we interviewed Randall in 1991 and 1992, he raved about his company's fortunes, which he attributed to hard work and a positive attitude, epitomized in the name Yes! (with its distinctive exclamation point). The company was in the process of moving from its cramped headquarters on Seventeenth Street, where "I grew from $8 million to $40 million in five years," to a 76,000-square-foot facility on West Washington Boulevard. Randall was bullish on the move, forecasting between $80 and $90 million in business at his new location: "I'm sorry," he told us, "life is easy."[52]

Life turned out, however, to be not so easy for his growing company. In 1991, Randall's enthusiasm was easy to understand: In that year Yes! had posted gross profits of nearly $10 million on sales of $36 million, for a hefty return of 29 percent. Although sales had grown slightly by 1993, the following year business turned sour. In 1994 sales dropped to $28 million, and in November of that year, Randall and Tsabag signed an agreement to sell their holdings to Georges Marciano, the founder and former chairman of a competitor, Guess. In January 1995 Marciano acquired 80 percent of the company's stock. Randall, Tsabag, and their board of directors were out. Marciano immediately put his stamp on the company, shifting its focus from cotton-spandex knit and cotton jersey to a stronger emphasis on denim (Guess's specialty) and twill. Marciano's reborn Yes! also licensed a number of designs and trademarks from Marble Sportswear, a company he controlled. These strategies proved to be disastrous. Between 1995 and 1996 Yes! sales plummeted and the company lost $1.5 million. As noted in the company's 1997 financial statement: "In fiscal 1996, net sales decreased by $21,029,000 (73.5 percent) to $7,551,000 due to a lack of market acceptance of the Company's then marketing and design direction. . . . Gross profit as a percentage of net sales decreased significantly (to minus 20.0 percent) in fiscal 1996 from 11.8 percent in fiscal 1995 due to a number of factors, including decreased sales volume, increased materials costs and markdown of inventory as a result of poor sales and an excessive inventory level."[53]

By June 1996 Marciano himself was out, selling his 3.5 million shares of stock for a penny a share. (One year earlier the stock was valued at $3.5 million.) The new owner (Guy Anthome) returned to the more traditional fabrics (cotton and spandex knit, cotton jersey, and denim) that had worked prior to Marciano's short-lived tenure. He also reintroduced the Yes! label as a mass-market line, terminated the licenses Marciano had acquired from his own Marble Sportswear, and began licensing Yes's own lines of apparel. Unfortunately, this strategy did not prove successful either. Although a modest profit was reported for 1997, sales for the year were only $3.4 million, and in January 1998 Yes! filed for bankruptcy protection. George Randall's once-proud company, a rising star in the Los Angeles apparel world, was no longer a player.

CALIFORNIA FASHION INDUSTRIES

California Fashion Industries, which makes clothes for the Carole Little label, has enjoyed consistent success, although this firm's good fortune has been marred by a seemingly made-for-Hollywood series of misfortunes as well. The company, founded in 1974 by Carole Little and her then-husband, Leonard Rabinowitz, aims at the "sophisticated career woman"; its clothes "show an attitude—in their design, fabric, bright palette—that is breezier than much of women's clothing offered in the same price range."[54] According to one analyst, the company is but a step away from breaking into the ranks of world-class designers, a step that, because the top tier of United States women's clothing designers is still found in New York City, is hampered by the very California mystique that underlies its appeal. Carole Little's rising fortunes suffered a reversal during the 1992 uprisings, when the torching and looting of the company's downtown headquarters caused millions of dollars in losses. Yet even in that year, Carole Little rebounded, posting revenues in excess of $200 million. Significantly, when the company threatened to leave smoldering Los Angeles, the city responded by providing assistance for the move to its current location.[55] In 1995, the most recent year for which we have data, the company reportedly enjoyed gross sales of $375.1 million, an increase of nearly a third over the previous year.[56] Perhaps encouraged by that performance, two years later Little and Rabinowitz sold half of their company in order to finance and produce the film *Anaconda*.[57]

Between 1993 and 1995 Carole Little was plagued with a series of murders and attempted murders that, some believe, were connected to the company's decision to change contractors. In response to a warning from the California Department of Labor to stop doing business with sweatshops that violated labor laws, the company informed its contractors in July 1993 that it planned to shift some orders to new contractors in the United States and to foreign factories. Later that year one of the company's contractors was killed as he drove away from his factory in Glendale; the Carole Little executive responsible for placing orders in United States factories survived two murder attempts, a shot fired into her car and a bomb set off at her home (she subsequently left the company); another executive and his wife were shot and wounded in 1994; the company's vice president and director of manufacturing was shot to death in his truck in late December of that year; and Carole Little's comptroller suffered the same fate five months later. Eventually someone was accused and convicted of killing the contractor, but the rest of the crimes remained unsolved.[58]

BCBG MAX AZRIA

Another major, and rapidly growing manufacturer of contemporary clothing is BCBG, which was launched by Max Azria in 1989. Born in Tunis, Azria was raised in Paris, where he made blue jeans for twenty years. The name BCBG stands for *bon chic, bon genre,* French slang for "good style, good attitude." The company's style and attitude paid off; sales were reportedly $160 million in 1997, its clothing made by local contractors. By that time BCBG owned forty retail outlets and had acquired Francine Browner, Inc., a designer of young women's contemporary clothing. It had begun licensing swimwear and eyewear and held its first runway show in New York City. In recognition of his accomplishments, in 1996 Azria won the California Designer of the Year award given by the CaliforniaMart.[59]

JALATE LTD., INC.

Another important, newer Los Angeles manufacturer, Jalate Ltd., Inc. makes moderately priced knit and woven sportswear and
dresses for women and clothing for children that hangs in more than 600
stores nationwide. Its products "are intended to appeal primarily to the
fashion-conscious young woman who desires to continually upgrade her
wardrobe on a limited clothing allowance," and to "youthfully figured
women of all ages who desire the youthful styling and value pricing of the
Company's products."[60] In 1996 the firm also bought a 40 percent share
in Airshop, a startup clothing catalogue company whose colorful website, geared toward teenage girls, sells "ultra funkadelic fashions." Jalate
also does private-label design for the Dillard's, Victoria's Secret, and Limited Express stores. Its budget-minded marketing strategy is based on the
belief that "the importance of brand awareness in general has diminished
and that consumers have come to view value pricing as increasingly important," leading the company to emphasize "basic designs, which are less
costly to manufacture than [are] more detailed high fashion styles." Jalate's
sportswear items retail for between $15 and $25; its dresses for between
$30 and $40.

Unlike most manufacturers in Los Angeles, Jalate does all of its cutting and about 10 percent of its sewing in-house, by means of a joint-
venture agreement with an affiliate of its largest sewing contractor. This
unusual arrangement enables the manufacturer to exert greater control
over costs, quality, and turnaround time for some of its larger customers
by dedicating a portion of production to their immediate needs. For the
remainder of its domestic production, Jalate prides itself on using only
local contractors. In 1997 it reported using twelve local contractors, of
which five filled most of its orders. The firm's rationale for using local
contracted labor for the bulk of its products provides a concise statement
of the advantages of this strategy for manufacturers. "The rapid response
to a customer's needs permitted by contract manufacturing, as well as the
Company's policy of manufacturing products based primarily on orders,
enables the Company and its customers to reduce the costs and risks of
making early commitments for fabric and piece goods and maintaining
finished goods inventory, including the risk of fashion obsolescence."[61]
In other words, contracting reduces Jalate's costs, while shifting the risks
to its contractors and their workers. Such advantages of domestic contracting notwithstanding, increased competition and price pressure compelled Jalate to move some production to the Philippines, Hong Kong,

and China in 1994. The firm's reliance on offshore production nearly doubled between 1996 and 1997, amounting to about a fifth of the value of its total production in the latter year.

Between 1993 and 1995 Jalate's sales nearly doubled, growing to $71 million. In the following year, however, it discontinued two of its divisions, and by 1997 the company's revenues had dropped to $51 million. In that year Jalate reported a net loss of $4.5 million, along with technical defaults on some bank loans and factoring agreements, problems that were resolved when its lenders waived demands for compliance in early 1998.[62]

TARRANT APPAREL GROUP

The Tarrant Apparel Group offers an example of another type of manufacturing business, one engaged exclusively in private-label production. Tarrant, a publicly traded company, specializes in providing casual clothing to some twenty specialty retail and mass-merchandise chains. Its moderately priced clothing includes jeanswear (denim garments), casual pants, T-shirts, shorts, blouses, shirts, dresses, leggings, and jackets. The firm took on private-label production in 1988, and has prospered ever since. With nearly three-quarters of its goods going to affiliates of the Limited (Limited stores, Limited Express, Lane Bryant, Lerner New York), Tarrant posted sales of $260 million in 1997, making it one of the largest firms in Los Angeles.[63] Between 1993 and 1997, Tarrant's sales grew by more than 15 percent a year, with annual gross profits regularly exceeding 15 percent. Future growth seems assured, particularly with Tarrant's recent acquisition of Marshall Gobuty International and MGI International, private-label firms that design and manufacture men's and boys' clothing for such national retailers as J. C. Penney. The acquisition is projected to boost sales in 1998 to more than $320 million.[64] In June 1998, Tarrant stock split two-for-one, reflecting the company's good fortunes.[65]

Tarrant has historically had most of its clothing made by independent contractors in Hong Kong and China, and maintains an office in Hong Kong to oversee its Asian operations. In 1997, however, the company shifted a sizable amount of production to Mexico and Central America, where it planned to expand the production of its basic denim and twill products; it opened negotiations to acquire a denim mill in Puebla, Mexico, where it had begun to construct a twill plant. As of 1997, 61 percent of the firm's clothing was imported from Hong Kong and China, 12 percent from elsewhere in East Asia, 11 percent from Mexico, and 15 percent was made in the United States.

GUESS? INC.

Our last profile is of the largest apparel manufacturer in Los Angeles, Guess?, Inc., with 1997 sales of $515 million.[66] Guess was founded in December 1981, when the four Marciano brothers, Georges, Maurice, Paul, and Armand, produced their first twenty four pairs of pants.[67] The Algerian-born Marcianos came to Los Angeles from France, where they had already established themselves in the apparel business. Georges Marciano excelled in designing tight-fitting, European-style jeans, which quickly became a huge success in the American market. The company's ability to turn ordinary denim into a widely recognized sex symbol was spurred by the creative advertising ideas of Paul Marciano, whose suggestive photography created a sultry mood in which the jeans themselves often appeared to be an afterthought. Claudia Schiffer, today one of the world's most successful (and wealthiest) models, achieved fame and fortune through advertising campaigns for Guess. The company soon expanded from jeans production into other lines of clothing, developed an extensive licensing program, and even opened its own line of Guess stores. It grew to become one of the most profitable apparel manufacturers, with some of the highest paid executives, in the nation (figures are presented in Chapter 7).

Guess's rise to prominence has not always been smooth. In 1983, in an effort to raise badly needed capital for their fledgling company, the Marcianos sold a 51-percent interest to the Nakash brothers of Jordache Enterprises, a jeans producer in New York, for $5 million. When Guess's sales exploded a few years later, the Marcianos launched a long and costly legal battle with Jordache to get their company back. The battle, which in an article in *Fortune Magazine* was characterized as "one of the bloodiest, most maniacal corporate battles of the 1980s,"[68] lasted six and a half years and reportedly cost both sides $80 million in legal fees. The Marcianos eventually won, gaining complete ownership of Guess for $70 million.[69] When a settlement was eventually reached in 1990, the Marcianos announced that they had reached it themselves, and therefore no longer needed the services of Marshall B. Grossman, the attorney who had argued their interests for the previous five years. Grossman sued Guess for the $10 million bonus he had been promised, and in 1994 a panel of the Los Angeles County Bar Association awarded Grossman and his partners $17 million in legal fees, plus interest, for a total of $23.1 million.[70]

In August 1993, Georges Marciano, then chief executive officer and chairman of Guess, left the company, selling his 40-percent share to his three brothers for $220 million. Georges then acquired the ailing Yes Clothing Company, whose fate under his leadership we have already discussed. There was some litigation between the brothers over trademark usage,[71] but by the time of this writing Guess had other issues to preoccupy it, including an IPO that was not as successful as expected, a union organizing drive and consumer boycott, and a 7-percent slump in sales, which the firm attributed to both increased competition and "aggressive campaigns against the Company by [the labor union] UNITE."[72] Guess is also noteworthy for being the first United States apparel company to sign an agreement with the United States Department of Labor to monitor its own contractors, an agreement we discuss in more detail in Chapter 8.

The manufacturers constitute an important segment of the apparel industry in Los Angeles. To many outsiders, they define the industry, and all the other actors are appendages and dependents. They certainly make many of the important decisions that affect other participants in the industry, including the majority, those who actually sew the garments. Among such decisions is the determination of where to locate production. Should the manufacturers make use of some of the thousands of factories available in Los Angeles, or should they move their production offshore, to take advantage of lower-wage labor there? It is to this vital question that we now turn.

CHAPTER 2
Offshore Production

In January 1997, Guess? Inc., the largest apparel manufacturer in Los Angeles, announced that it was moving 40 percent of its production to Mexico.[1] That same month, the California State Employment Development Department reported that apparel employment had grown in Los Angeles County by more than 6 percent over the past year, continuing a pattern of growth over the past few decades. How are we to understand these contradictory facts? Is Los Angeles an exception to the general pattern throughout the United States of erosion of employment in the apparel industry? Or is it, too, succumbing to the lure of lower wages offshore, especially in nearby Mexico, now that the North American Free Trade Agreement (NAFTA) has eased restrictions on imports from that country—and will entirely eliminate them by 2004?

There are some indications that the industry in Los Angeles has a special vitality, as shown in its exceptional pattern of employment growth in comparison with substantial decline in the United States as a whole. Most jobs have been lost in the northeast. No other state besides California shows robust employment growth, and southern California accounts for four-fifths of the California apparel industry. But despite the continuing growth of apparel-related employment in Los Angeles, the region faces an uncertain future.

There are compelling reasons for design and marketing to remain in the region, but not necessarily for assembly. Throughout the world today, there is a global race to the bottom for labor-intensive production as capital seeks out the cheapest possible workers. For southern California's apparel industry, the temptations are obvious. Mexico, now unfettered thanks to NAFTA, provides workers at a tenth the cost of those in Los Angeles. Moreover, even though Mexico has strong labor laws, enforcement is even more lax than it is in California. Perhaps more importantly, labor abuses in Mexico are more likely to be undetected than they are in Los Angeles: Few independent unions are organizing workers there, few muckraking journalists are eager to expose sweatshops, and few citizens' groups are scrutinizing the industry.

The Growth of Global Production

Beginning with the move from the relatively high-wage, unionized northeast to the low-wage, nonunionized south in the 1920s and 1930s, United States apparel manufacturers have for a long time relocated production in search of cheaper labor.[2] The movement offshore did not begin, however, until well after World War II. In 1956 offshore sourcing was pioneered in the menswear industry in Los Angeles, when Ben Kurtzman, the owner of Sportclothes Ltd., then a leading manufacturer of inexpensive suits "for the people who live between New York City and Los Angeles," began sourcing in Japan.[3] In the 1950s and 1960s governments in East Asian countries such as Hong Kong, Taiwan, and Korea, with financial and technical assistance from United States aid programs, encouraged the growth and expansion of textile and garment production. By the early 1970s the three countries were running massive trade surpluses in those goods and had greatly surpassed Japan in apparel exports.[4] By the end of the decade nearly three-quarters of all United States apparel imports came from East Asia.[5]

The shift accelerated in the 1980s, leading to a massive increase in imports. These imports have not increased because other countries have decided to produce clothing for the United States market; they consist of goods made by United States companies overseas. Both retailers and manufacturers have become significant importers of garments that are produced more cheaply in developing countries around the globe. This has created a rift in the industry: Those who produce locally find themselves in competition with the importers. In 1987 the United States had already become the world's leading apparel importer, accounting for 27 percent of global imports in clothing.[6] Between 1988 and 1992 United States imports of clothing grew by 50 percent, to $30.5 billion; in 1992, 92.4 percent of all clothing imports were from the developing economies.[7]

By now United States apparel manufacturers, scouring the globe for the cheapest labor they could find, were followed by retailers seeking offshore production of their own private-label lines. In 1991 Greater China (Hong Kong, Taiwan, and the People's Republic of China) accounted for 40 percent of United States apparel imports.[8] By the early 1990s the apparel export industries in Thailand and Indonesia had surpassed the $3 billion mark, and India, Sri Lanka, and Malaysia topped $1 billion in apparel exports.[9] By this time manufacturers in the garment business in the United States, Hong Kong, and South Korea made it clear that such far-flung sites as Vietnam, Guatemala, Burma, North Korea, and Mongolia were either targets of planned investment in export-oriented garment factories or had already gone on line.

Since the passage and implementation of NAFTA in 1994, Mexico has surpassed Hong Kong and approaches China in terms of the dollar value of combined textile and apparel exports to the United States. As recently as 1990, United States imports of textiles and apparel from Mexico totaled only $678 million, in comparison with $3.8 billion from Hong Kong and $3.6 billion from China. By 1997, United States apparel and textile imports from Mexico, 40 percent higher than they had been in the previous year, had grown to $5.9 billion, far greater than imports from Hong Kong ($4 billion) and approximating imports from China ($6 billion).[10]

Since the early 1960s, when garment imports and exports were roughly in balance, the trade deficit in apparel and related textiles has grown at an increasing rate, more than doubling in each of the past three decades. By 1996 imports exceeded exports by nearly $40 billion.[11] In that year, imports comprised more than half (57 percent) of wholesale apparel consumption in the United States.[12]

The push by United States companies to produce abroad found a welcome in many developing countries that were seeking to industrialize. Garment production is relatively labor intensive, requiring little start-up capital. It is, thus, one of the first industries that newly industrializing countries enter. They welcome the orders from United States firms, which boost their exports. In exchange, they offer the United States companies a docile and controlled labor force, typically composed of very young women. The offer may be backed by the creation of special export processing zones and, frequently, by repressive regimes that provide guarantees against labor unrest.

Offshore apparel production is usually the result of arm's-length transactions. Rarely do garment firms establish manufacturing subsidiaries abroad. Instead they contract with independent firms to produce the goods to their specifications. The offshore contractors fall into two broad categories: what is called full-package production (sometimes called Original Equipment Manufacturing, or OEM), for which the contractor takes complete charge of the entire production from the purchase of textiles to the completion of garments, and offshore assembly plants (or *maquiladoras* as they are called in Latin America) that assemble cut cloth and provide only the labor for sewing. This latter category is often called 807 production, after the paragraphs in the United States tariff regulations that allow the reimport of goods assembled offshore with a tariff charge only on the value added, that is, the cost of labor.[13]

The flood of imports led to attempts by segments of the domestic apparel industry to regulate the flow of trade. Although world trade during the postwar period was to have been liberalized under the 1947 General Agreement on Tariffs and Trade (GATT), textile and apparel trade was never entirely included. As textile and apparel trade with Japan grew during the 1950s, for example, a number of so-called voluntary export restraints, the result of pressures by the United States textile and apparel industry, restricted United States imports of selected categories of goods from Japan. European countries followed suit, fearing Japanese penetration into their traditionally strong textile and apparel industries. The restraints imposed on Japan did not affect the growing imports from other Asian countries, such as Hong Kong; moreover, European restrictions were seen by United States trade officials as violations of GATT. Accordingly, a more comprehensive approach to regulating global trade in apparel and textiles was sought. The Multifiber Arrangement (MFA), reached in 1974,[14] provided for bilateral agreements between trading nations that would regulate trade in apparel and textiles. Its principal vehicle was an elaborate quota system, whereby each country established im-

port quotas for detailed categories of goods from each major trading partner (for example, the United States might allow 300,000 women's wool
sweaters from Hong Kong in a given year).[15] Subsequent versions of the
MFA became increasingly restrictive as global textile and apparel trade
exploded during the 1970s and 1980s. Nonetheless, imports to the United
States have continued to grow steadily. In fact, one of the effects of quotas has been to disperse apparel production throughout the world, as
United States companies have sought new sources of production in countries where quotas are unfilled or even nonexistent.[16]

United States firms, supported by the United States government, began to use *maquiladoras* in the Caribbean, Mexico, and Central America,
as a way of gaining access to "their own" cheap labor. Special programs,
such as those for 807 production, were created, in part, to make offshore
production easier in the Western Hemisphere in order to compete with
the rising Asian tigers. The Caribbean Basin Initiative, enacted in 1983 to
eliminate tariffs on most Caribbean exports to the United States, did not
initially apply to textiles and apparel. In 1986 such exemptions were provided in the 807A ("super 807") provisions, which liberalized quotas for
apparel assembled in the Caribbean from fabric made and cut in the United
States.

But by far the most important trade agreement affecting textiles and
apparel has been NAFTA, which calls for the complete elimination of all
tariffs on industrial products traded between the United States, Canada,
and Mexico within ten years of the treaty's implementation, which occurred on 1 January 1994.[17] The treaty immediately removed barriers on
about 20 percent of United States textiles and apparel exports to Mexico,
with most of the remaining tariffs scheduled to be eliminated by the turn
of the century. (Prior to NAFTA, Mexican tariffs were 20 percent on apparel and 15 percent on textiles.) In order to qualify under NAFTA rules,
clothing must be made from North American yarn that has been spun into
fabric in North America.

At the time of this writing the Clinton administration was making efforts, in the face of some opposition, to extend NAFTA to other countries, and was also attempting to pass legislation liberalizing trade (and
offshore production) in Africa. Moreover, under GATT international trade
is to be deregulated and the entire protective quota system for apparel
imports dismantled. The World Trade Organization, which emerged out
of GATT, is now overseeing this dismantling; under current provisions
(adopted in 1994 as a result of the so-called Uruguay Round), quotas under the MFA will be eliminated within ten years and textile and apparel
trade will then be governed by the trade rules for other sectors.[18]

Offshore Production
(Profiles of Four Large Firms)

Los Angeles is the gateway for apparel imports from Asia and Mexico. Each year, billions of dollars worth of clothing comes in through the ports of Los Angeles and Long Beach, loaded in containers and piled high on ships. Los Angeles is also conveniently close to Mexico; precut goods are easily driven across the border to be sewn in Mexican factories. Los Angeles is thus situated at a global crossroads, so the transfer of the industry offshore is not logistically difficult. (In speaking of the apparel industry moving offshore, we are referring only to production.) The apparel firms that are based in Los Angeles are likely to maintain their headquarters and design facilities there because, as Brent Klopp, the senior vice president for production planning for Bugle Boy Industries, commented in 1991, "we see ourselves as merchandise managers rather than manufacturers. We have 700 factories throughout the world, including Taiwan, Hong Kong, China, the Philippines, Indonesia, Korea, Singapore, Malaysia, Pakistan, Bangladesh, Sri Lanka, Mexico, Honduras, the Dominican Republic, Turkey, and, to a limited extent, Guatemala. We are looking at Oman and Dubai for future production. In the United States we use factories in Los Angeles and the Carolinas. Five years ago [1986] we only produced in Taiwan. Now it represents 18 percent of our production. China is 22 percent. Mexico and Central America are six percent, while Los Angeles accounts for one percent."[19]

BUGLE BOY INDUSTRIES

Bugle Boy, one of the region's largest firms and a well-known manufacturer of young men's clothing, represents one end of the import continuum. At the time of this interview, Bugle Boy had nearly all of its clothing made in Taiwan, China, and elsewhere in Asia and claimed to be the number one receiver of containers in the Port of Long Beach. Bugle Boy initially produced in Taiwan because the company's founder and chief executive officer, Bill Mow, had strong personal ties in that country, where he was born. The firm has since diversified geographically, and its reasons provide some understanding of the considerations that go into a firm's sourcing decisions. According to Klopp, Bugle Boy initially began spreading its operations to obtain a larger quota to raise the ceiling on the number of garments it could import, but there were other reasons as well. "When we go into a country, we don't want to dominate. We just want to get a piece of the action. Given our volume, we could distort the economy, and would find ourselves competing against ourselves. You also avoid risk by spreading around, for example, fluctuations in exchange rates, political upheavals and national disasters. We never have production in Bangladesh during June and July because of the monsoon season. And it is important to know what is going on politically."

Bugle Boy evaluates each country in terms of what is called its needle capability. Can it make fancy pants or basic pants? "Asia," said Klopp, "is flexible," that is, capable of making a variety of products. "The rest of the world is a cookie cutter," meaning that, "outside of Asia, if you ask for a small change in the product, labor costs can shoot up from $1 to $5. Mexico and Central America, as well as the Europeans, suffer from being too mechanical. They are too automated and can't be flexible. Mexico and Honduras have had too many joint ventures with the United States. They are not being trained to do flexible work." Despite these reservations concerning Mexico, by 1998 Bugle Boy's production in that country had increased five-fold during the previous three years, to 15 million units.[20]

CHAUVIN INTERNATIONAL LTD.

Another manufacturer with almost all of its production offshore in the mid-1990s was Chauvin International Ltd., a $100-million company that made the once-popular label B.U.M. Equipment. (The firm went bankrupt in April 1996, and has since moved to Rhode Island.[21]) The garments were what is called fashion basics, namely, T-shirts and sweatshirts, and they were made offshore and then dyed, screen-printed, embroidered, and otherwise finished in Los Angeles. According to the production manager, Jeff Richards, whom we interviewed in 1994:

We have everything cut and sewn overseas by contractors. It is all CMT [Cut-Make-Trim: the garments made in their entirety, from cutting through assembly]. We only buy finished garments. A tiny percent of our production is done domestically, less than one percent. We use buying agents overseas and work through them, though we are involved in the selection of the factories they use. In the past, 60 to 70 percent of our production was in Hong Kong, but now it is down to 30 percent. We also have agents in India. What we do locally is finishing. We bring in the sewn garment and have it dyed, printed, and embroidered locally. This finishing comes to 30 to 35 percent of the total production cost. Producing in Asia is definitely slower than producing locally. You need a 90- to 120-day lead time. We try to allow for even more time than that. The truth is, the quality is much higher for imports. We have had low success with United States–made goods.

Los Angeles offers numerous finishing establishments, including several hundred local dye houses, but Richards predicted that local finishing was doomed, because the cost was not competitive with that in low-wage countries. "It costs 25 cents per 1,000 stitches to embroider [the company logo] here. In India it costs 6 to 8 cents. That means if you have a 10,000-stitch embroidery, you have a $1.80 per garment difference. Finishing abroad requires increasing the lead time by 30 to 60 days. The technology is moving overseas. We get some of our production from Israel. They couldn't embroider finished goods, so they came here, bought the appropriate equipment, and now can do it."[22]

CHORUS LINE, INC.

At the other end of the continuum, Chorus Line, Inc., one of the well-established and venerable manufacturers of fashionable junior dresses and sportswear in Los Angeles, had long prided itself in producing virtually all of its garments in southern California. According to the senior vice president, Gene Light (whom we interviewed in 1994), all that began to change in the early 1990s. "We have been in business for almost twenty years. For seventeen of them, everything was produced domestically, and by that I mean in southern California. About three years ago we started looking into Mexico, under the 807 program. Last year we began dabbling in the Pacific Rim. Now we have set our projections for 1995. We have six divisions, each with somewhat different plans. Some will increase their work in Mexico, and some in the Orient."[23]

By 1995, Chorus Line was planning to have as much as a quarter of its production done offshore, including between 5 and 10 percent in Mexico and much of the rest in such low-wage Asian countries as the Philippines, Indonesia, Sri Lanka, Dubai, and possibly Bangladesh. Light reported that the firm was shifting its production offshore for several reasons.

One is that we are increasing our volume and we can't increase it here because of price. The price pressure is coming from the retailers. If we remained in the United States we would have no growth pattern. We wouldn't be competitive any more. The retailers are vicious. They come to us and say they want to buy a garment for $10. We say we can't make it for $10. They say they can get it from so and so for $10, and so and so is making it in north China. Here the minimum wage is $4.25 an hour. How can you compete with $2.50 a day? A second reason for moving offshore is that the government and the state are becoming zealots in invoking the labor laws. They are invoking 1938 labor laws and using them to put the onus on the manufacturer because they don't have the money to enforce the laws. You should realize that we don't endorse child labor or nonpayment of minimum wage. But we have our own business to run. Our position is: If we continue to face pressure, we will move offshore or to Mexico.

Production offshore is not without its costs, especially in Chorus Line's fashion-sensitive market niche. Longer lead times and higher transportation costs increase the risks, requiring the firm to carry more inventory that might not be sold. As a result, Chorus Line is more inclined to go with tried-and-true styles that have proved successful over the years. Nonetheless, Light predicted that Chorus Line will end up producing half of its goods offshore, although half would still be made locally because retailers were demanding ever quicker delivery from the time of ordering. If Asia had a four-month cycle and Mexico a two-month cycle, orders could be turned around in Los Angeles in a single month. Light observed that "so long as the stores need a quick turn, a large segment of the industry will remain in Los Angeles." Even so, "if we are forced to move everything to Mexico, we will." This prediction appears to be coming true: By early 1997, Chorus Line had shifted 70 percent of its production to Mexico, the rest remaining in Los Angeles. According to Barry Sacks, the chairman and chief executive officer, because of tough price competition, the company had no choice.[24]

CALIFORNIA FASHION INDUSTRIES (CAROLE LITTLE)

In 1994 we also interviewed Kenneth Martin, the production manager of Carole Little, the principal label of one of the largest manufacturers of fashionable women's clothing in Los Angeles. At that time, nine months after NAFTA went into effect, the firm employed between 1,100 and 1,200 workers in-house, including designers, product engineers, sample makers, and distribution workers. "The garment industry," said Martin, "does have a future here, but the government needs to give the industry a break, on workers' comp[ensation], and to offer tax breaks and incentives, because this industry employs a lot of people, especially those who don't have much education. I think we may see a short-term exodus, but we're also likely to see fluctuations. Some firms will come back after they discover that they face problems with cycle time, quality, and control. Many are looking at Mexico right now, and some may try it out for a while. The industry will always be here, I think. But you can't take that for granted."

At the time of this interview, in September 1994, the firm was increasing its production in Asia, because much of its work required labor-intensive beading and hand embroidery, which was too costly to do domestically. The company was already importing up to half of its clothing from Asia and was planning to increase that figure to two-thirds. Less than 15 percent of the work was being done in Mexico but, with the passage of NAFTA, said Martin, "we are looking to expand our [Mexican] production if we can develop quality production in Mexico. We tried using the Dominican Republic for a few months and we are looking at Guatemala, Costa Rica, and Honduras. We've also looked at Colombia. These places have a problem of logistics. Delivery takes ten days to two weeks, and even air freight provides poor service. Producing there makes more sense for the east coast than for us. We've been in Mexico for four years. Our hope is to reverse the percentages, so that 10 to 15 percent will be produced in the United States and the remainder in Mexico. We are planning to complete this shift in five years. We recognize that, when you get out of Los Angeles, you need to assign more managers to oversee production. There are many more experienced sewing machine operators here."[25]

In sum, four of the largest apparel manufacturers in Los Angeles rely on offshore production for at least some of their contracting. With the passage of NAFTA, more and more firms are looking south, rather than across the Pacific. NAFTA offers the advantages of proximity, low wages, and fewer trade restrictions.

The Consequences of NAFTA

In our 1992 survey of the 184 largest apparel manufacturers in Los Angeles (see Chapter 1), about 30 percent (fifty-six firms) reported that they were producing offshore. Only 25 percent of the firms doing offshore sourcing (fourteen firms) reported that all of their production was done offfshore. Thirty-one firms (17 percent of the total) reported sourcing from Mexico. Yet many manufacturers expressed concern that NAFTA, which was implemented in 1994, would harm local production. The opinion of Mitch Glass, the vice president for production of Cherokee, Inc, is typical of sentiments expressed before NAFTA's passage. "If they open the border with Mexico, the immigrants will go away and so will the contractors. The government needs to work out a special deal for this industry like they have in agriculture. NAFTA will kill the local industry. Only the high-priced fashion items will stay, Los Angeles will become a ghost town. Five years from now we will be in Mexico. I am opposed to NAFTA; it isn't fair to the contractors in Los Angeles. They can't compete. The industry will definitely move to Mexico, but at a cost in terms of start up, training, quality, supply of materials, trim, and zippers. I've been looking at shops in Mexico. I saw fabulous textile goods being made there. I'm thinking of cutting there, and have looked at eight or nine sewing shops near Mexico City."[26]

In late 1997 and early 1998, using our list of 184 large companies, Judi Kessler reinterviewed sixty-seven firms, and found that now about 75 percent were having some of their production done in Mexico. Most expected to increase their Mexican production in the future.[27] Kessler also found that about 25 percent of the firms interviewed were sending production to Asia and other countries, suggesting that they were developing global sourcing strategies. She concluded that the companies moving to Mexico tend to be larger or to be engaged in high-volume, private-label production. Smaller firms, she reported, lacked the financial and personnel resources to move as easily as the bigger companies can.

The movement of the apparel industry to Mexico predates the passage of NAFTA. Between 1989 and 1993, apparel imports from Mexico to the United States grew at an annual rate of about 30 percent, increasing from about $535 million in 1989 to $1.3 billion in 1993. After NAFTA passed, the rate of growth of apparel imports from Mexico jumped to 45 percent per year. The value of these imports grew from $1.8 billion in 1994 to $5.2 billion in 1997, just three years after NAFTA took effect. These statistics in themselves do not prove that the Los Angeles appparel industry is shifting its production to Mexico. Some of the growth in Mexican exports could be accounted for because companies (in Los Angeles and elsewhere) that are already engaged in offshore sourcing are moving some of their Asian and Caribbean production to Mexico. Nevertheless, the statistics do reveal the rise in importance of Mexico as a source of garments produced for the United States market.

Melanie Myers, the co-author of this chapter, conducted in-depth interviews with ten firms, including two suppliers of apparel inputs such as textiles, five apparel manufacturers, one manufacturer of a related product, one sewing contractor, and one industrial laundry. She received tours of these factories and was able to get a clear picture of the impact of NAFTA upon them. Two high-end manufacturers reported feeling no effects of NAFTA, positive or negative; others were clearly enthusiastic or discouraged.

The owner of one of the supply firms reported that, unless he receives some sort of low-interest financing, he would close his operation in Los Angeles and move to Mexico within the next six months. He had already purchased a building in Mexico and was preparing to move all of his production down there. Moving to Mexico would reduce his labor costs from about $80 a day per person to about $5 a day per person. In addition, in Mexico he could purchase cheaper supplies, face less regulation, and pay lower taxes. Even if this firm receives financial assistance from the city, it will still open its Mexican facility, but will retain the more technologically advanced production in Los Angeles, keeping some jobs here.

The sewing contractor was one of the larger of such firms, with over 200 employees. The owner reported that her business had been hit hard by NAFTA. The company's principal manufacturer, a private-label producer for J. C. Penney and Wal-Mart, used to supplement in-house sewing by employing seventeen contractors around the Los Angeles area. Now that manufacturer has moved most of its production to Mexico and employs only two remaining local contractors. The manufacturer suggested to the contractor that she, too, move her business down to Mexico but she did not want to do that and was planning to close down in May 1999. The manufacturer will, however, continue to use its other local contractor for quick-turn production.

The vice president of a large manufacturer with annual revenues of about $150 million and about 325 employees stated that the need to be located in or around the garment district for production work has been declining over the past ten years. Until five years ago, this manufacturer sourced all of his production in Los Angeles. Now every year the percentage sent abroad rises. Retailers, he feels, are placing contradictory demands on apparel manufacturers. On the one hand, they require prices that can be met only by offshore production. On the other hand, they require quick turnover for certain products, which generally means local production. This firm is a licensee for a local design establishment and needs to remain close to the design teams, so its headquarters, at least, will remain in the greater Los Angeles area.

The industrial laundry, which is also a dye-house, employed around one hundred workers. The owner reported that many laundries previously based in Los Angeles have already moved to Mexico. She stated that, although labor costs are much lower, transportation, time lags, and quality of work continue to be problems in Mexican production. Moreover, water is scarcer than it is in California and the quality is different. For these reasons, dye-houses, as distinguished from laundries, are unlikely to leave Los Angeles. Moreover, dye-houses need to be close to the de-

signers. Laundries tend to locate close to the sewing contractors, so follow them as they move. The firm has opened a laundry in Mexico, but
still retains a laundry and dye-house in Los Angeles.

Not all of the stories were as bleak as these. One major manufacturer,
with $120 million in annual sales, had a sourcing plan that included local
and offshore production. This company has a large inside shop that employs six hundred people and uses the latest technology. It also employs
between thirty and seventy local contractors, owns a factory in Mexico,
and employs contractors there, in Central America, and in China. The president felt that NAFTA has been good for business, allowing the company
to combine sourcing strategies.

These interviews suggest that apparel firms have mixed responses to
NAFTA. Some firms, especially small contractors competing in the moderate market, have been harmed by competition from low-wage areas offshore. Other firms, particularly large manufacturers, welcome the opportunity to have freer access to those same low-wage areas. The interviews
suggest that a firm's sensitivity to NAFTA is, in part, a function of its
size, the type of market it produces for, and other industry-specific factors, such as the need to be near designers or the need to retain some local employment for quick-turn production.

Until recently, the southern California apparel industry has appeared
to live a charmed life. Running counter to the rest of the nation, employment in the industry increased every year, despite the obvious fact
that individual firms were moving some of their production to Mexico.
Then in 1998, for the first year since 1993, the number of apparel and textile jobs in the County of Los Angeles fell, from 111,900 at the end of
1997 to 110,000 a year later, according to statistics provided by the Employment Development Department. This represents a drop of less than
2 percent, after years of more or less steady growth. Nevertheless, it could
signal the beginning of the end. Ted Gibson, the chief economist at the
California Department of Finance, saw no cause for alarm, but Joe Rodriguez, the executive director of the Garment Contractors Association
said, "For a while, we've been able to hold our own. But maybe NAFTA
has finally caught up with us."[28]

GUESS? INC. MOVES TO MEXICO

In January 1997 Maurice Marciano, the chairman and chief
executive officer of Guess? Inc., announced that the quantity of Guess
garments sewn in Los Angeles would drop from 75 percent in August 1997

to 35 percent by February 1998. Because Guess is the largest apparel manufacturer in the Los Angeles area and had previously boasted that 90 percent of its production was in Los Angeles, Marciano's announcement gave a special urgency to the debates about the effect of NAFTA on production in Los Angeles.

Some blamed the move on stepped-up enforcement efforts. For example, a prominent local apparel attorney, Richard Reinis, who heads the Compliance Alliance, a group of firms that polices its contractors for compliance with minimum wage and overtime laws, explained the Guess move as partly the result of "tremendous pressure from a very effective Department of Labor Wage and Hour division. It's causing a sea change in an industry that has operated virtually untouched for sixty years."[29] In response to the move, Bernard Lax, then the president of the Coalition of Apparel Industries of California, commented that price was not as much of an issue as was liability related to labor law enforcement. "They have created a bad environment in California," he said.[30]

Others blamed the exodus of Guess on the fact that it had been targeted by UNITE, the garment industry union, for an organizing campaign. "For the most part, manufacturers and contractors believe UNITE is one of the biggest threats to the apparel community in L.A.," stated an article in *California Apparel News*.[31] Some feared that unionization would drive up the cost of labor, pushing production offshore. Although Marciano had stated that the shift was mainly "a commercial decision," to "stay competitive" and "lower costs," it was widely believed in the industry that there were other reasons for the firm's decision: UNITE's efforts to spotlight the firm's use of sweatshops in Los Angeles and embarrassing state and federal investigations of the firm's practices. Guess was the first company in the United States to be targeted by the Department of Labor to develop a compliance agreement, earning it a short-lived place on the department's Trendsetter List, until investigations in late 1996 led to the company's being removed from the list and placed on "probation." Marciano's emphasis on the economic reasons for the move were partly the result of legal considerations: UNITE had filed a complaint with the National Labor Relations Board, claiming that Guess was moving to Mexico in order to evade unionization.[32] Such a move would be illegal under the terms of a settlement agreement that Guess had just signed with the NLRB, which included a provision that the company would not intimidate unionizing workers by threatening to move to Mexico rather than allow its workers to join a union.[33]

Guess had already begun to move some production to Asia in 1993, but none to Mexico because it felt that Mexican factories could not deliver the quality required. According to Marciano, since the passage of NAFTA, Mexican factories had invested in automated equipment, and many of Guess's competitors were already moving there.[34] He therefore announced a production shift of several million units a year with a whole-sale value of between $300 and $325 million. Marciano claimed that Guess would save between $1.50 and $2 per garment by sending cut fabric to sewing plants in Mexico, Peru, and Chile.

Although it is beyond the scope of this book to examine working con-ditions in apparel factories outside the United States, we can offer a few comments on one location to which Guess? Inc. moved production, namely Tehuacán, Mexico, which is fast becoming a center of denim pro-duction for manufacturers in Los Angeles and elsewhere. A city with an exploding population of some 300,000 people, Tehuacán is a few hours' drive southeast of Mexico City. It is the second-largest city in Puebla, in an impoverished region populated mainly by indigenous peoples who pro-vide a large and hungry source of labor. Tehuacán's estimated 400 sewing factories[35] reportedly sew and stone wash jeans for such major labels as Polo, Lee, Bugle Boy, Cherokee, and Levi's, and for Guess, since it de-cided to move out of Los Angeles.

In February 1998 a delegation of human rights observers, one of the authors (Rich Appelbaum) among them,[36] heard evidence from local work-ers of many forms of exploitation and mistreatment in the factories, and of a pervasive atmosphere of fear. For example, guards at one of the fac-tories pulled guns on local human rights workers who were attempting to interview workers on a public sidewalk outside one of the larger factories a few days before the delegation's arrival. Wages ranged from $25 to $50 (United States) for a forty-eight to sixty-hour workweek, with forced (and unpaid) overtime often required to meet production quotas. Sometimes overtime involved all-night shifts, with workers prevented by security guards from leaving the factories. Minors as young as thirteen years of age were reported to be working alongside adults under unsafe conditions that sometimes resulted in accidents. The enormous, prosperous-looking, and frequently windowless factories (surrounded by high walls and locked gates) stood in stark contrast to the sprawling *colonias,* where workers lived in make-shift, dirt-floor shacks, typically without access to running water, electricity, sewage, schools, or other basic urban amenities. The final re-port stated, "What the delegation found in Tehuacán, Mexico, is that worker rights are not respected and codes of conduct are not enforced; instead they are subordinated to the global search for cheap labor. Humane treatment of *maquiladora* workers and respect for their rights are traded off for the mass production of on-time and high-quality clothing."[37]

Tehuacán provides cheap labor far from the eyes of union organizers, muckraking journalists, and antisweatshop activists. Its location far from the United States border, in a rural, semifeudal area, helps to assure that it remains largely out of view. It typifies the opportunities available to United States manufacturers in the wake of NAFTA, opportunities that seem to force a choice between exploitation at home and exploitation abroad.

Who Will Stay—and Who Will Leave?

Is Guess's departure indeed the beginning of the end, the start of NAFTA's "giant sucking sound," that Ross Perot predicted? Jack Kyser, the director of research for the Economic Development Corporation in Los Angeles County, clearly thought so. Saying that Guess's move "could be the thing that turns the tide," Kyser suggested that other apparel makers might conclude that, if Guess were satisfied with Mexican production, why shouldn't they be? The *Los Angeles Times* article containing Kyser's observations continued: "Typical of the trend is J. Michelle of California, a women's sportswear and dressmaker, which says it has shifted about half of its production to Mexico since December 1995. Richard Tan, the company's president, said that Mexico has long offered low labor costs but that the difficulties of doing business kept him away. But now that Mexican contractors have improved production quality and delivery time, he said, it has become an attractive place to do business. 'The bottom line is prices. If I don't go to Mexico, I won't get the business, because I've got to be competitive,' Tan said."[38]

The doomsayers looked at the statistics on the continued growth in local apparel industry employment and, quite simply, didn't believe them. For example, the day following Guess's announcement, the *Wall Street Journal* reported Richard Reinis's estimate that 50,000 apparel jobs had been lost in Los Angeles between mid-1995 and early 1997, even though official statistics were later to show an increase of some 9,000 jobs during that same period. Reinis based his figures on the fact that three members of the Compliance Alliance (L'Koral Industries, Toni Blair of California, and Little Laura of California) had shifted production to Mexico.[39] Bernard Lax also disbelieved the official figures. He claimed that more than 20,000 jobs had been lost in Los Angeles County from September 1996 to February 1997 and that as many as 40,000 jobs would disappear in 1997.[40] Economists at the University of California at Los Angeles were somewhat more circumspect; although they did not claim that jobs had been hemorrhaging to Mexico, they did worry that the industry had added only 1,000 new jobs in 1996, instead of the 11,000 it had added in each of 1994 and 1995.[41]

How is it possible to reconcile official statistics showing a growing industry, with the insiders' belief that it is in a state of imminent collapse? According to Bernard Lax, the increase in official employment was an artifact of enhanced enforcement efforts, which "brought companies that were operating underground onto the books, generating misleadingly strong numbers."[42] Others argued that, while the major firms were leaving, smaller firms were expanding to take up the slack.

For most manufacturers Mexico remains a mixed blessing for production. In our interviews, manufacturers complained about poor quality, unpredictability, bribery, excessive bureaucratic red tape, late deliveries, and hijacked shipments of goods. "In Mexico, the border patrol charges to let your goods pass. This happens as you move from one province to the next, each one having different rules."[43] Labor accounts for only about 12 percent of the wholesale cost of making a garment, and savings on labor can be offset by the other costs of doing business in Mexico. Goetz Wolff, a professor of Urban Planning at the University of California at Los Angeles, and expert on the apparel industry, concurred. "There are going to be significant amounts of production remaining here," he said. "The low wage in Mexico is not as low as it appears—once you start looking at the other costs involved."[44] After interviewing a number of manufacturers and other persons knowledgeable about the industry, Larry Kanter concluded that a massive move to Mexico was unlikely. "Frustrated by high local labor costs and encouraged by the North American Free Trade Agreement, L.A. clothing manufacturer Tony Podell decided two years ago to try his luck in Tijuana. He located a large factory and began hiring Mexican crews to produce some less expensive lines of shirts, dresses and pants. 'I've yet to make a profit,' said Podell, whose Podell Industries Inc. makes high-end women's wear. 'I've found very few large factories down there that can produce consistently.' Podell makes the Laundry by Shelli Segal label."[45]

These sentiments were echoed by Jeff Mowdy, the production manager for Francine Browner, Inc., one of the ten largest manufacturers in Los Angeles, with annual sales of $100 million. In August 1996, when we interviewed Mowdy, 90 percent of the firm's production was domestic, with the remainder done in Mexico. Although Mowdy complained about the costs of the compliance programs required by the Department of Labor and of the difficulty of finding legitimate shops, his experience with

Mexico was not encouraging: "We don't produce in Mexico because of NAFTA. We began talking about moving there before NAFTA passed. We went there solely because of price points [lower costs]. We contracted in Tijuana. Typically you start at the border and move inland, where the better production is done. It's been a nightmare and now we are moving back to the U.S. It's worth doing stuff there if you have a big volume because they can do it cheaply. But we don't do programs [large volumes of unchanging styles that can be mass-produced], and the learning curve there is very different from here. In order to succeed in Mexico you have to have your own shop. But then you have to be able to feed it. And you can't keep changing the styles because of the slow learning curve. I hate doing work there."[46]

Gus Leonard, the production manager for Paul Davril, Inc., a firm whose products included licensed men's and boy's wear for brands such as Bugle Boy and Guess, expressed similar sentiments. "We don't produce in Mexico. I'm now looking at Ecuador, Honduras, Guatemala, and Costa Rica. There is a problem with Mexico. The factories don't have middle management. So if the owner is out of town, or having a two-hour lunch, you can't get decisions made quickly enough. There is a sense of arrogance among Mexican producers. They have the attitude: 'You can't just come into my place and tell me how to run things.' You need to have your own people living there and working for you. If I used Mexico I'd have to send someone to live there. This hasn't only happened to us, but to other companies as well. NAFTA hasn't improved it."[47]

Ilse Metchek, the executive director of the California Fashion Association (the major organization of manufacturers), argues that small firms cannot afford to shift production out of Los Angeles. She estimates that nine out of ten apparel firms are too small to move, and that these firms employ most of the region's garment contractors and workers. "They can't afford to make 100,000 [items] at a clip, which is what is required to go to Mexico. You can't do small runs of high fashion [in Mexico]—and that's what the majority of the firms here do."[48] Metchek's viewpoint is supported by Mark Lesser, the president and a co-owner of Wearable Integrity Inc., a smaller company that makes women's casual dresses under the Barbara Lesser label. He pointed out that companies with sales between $1 million and $40 million would have a hard time moving textiles and garments back and forth across the border, especially if they are dealing in small quantities.

Some of the confusion in these contradictory predictions stems from sectoral differences. Certain types of clothing are more easily manufactured in Mexico than are others. According to Tony Podell, "You can make T-shirts for Kmart or Wal-Mart [in Mexico], but for our product you just can't do it."[49] Marcus Sphatt, the owner of Bebop Clothing, a company that opened a new facility in January 1997 near Tecate, Mexico, where it will eventually employ 1,000 workers, and will be able to do cutting, sewing, washing, and finishing, says that his company will maintain fashion production in California and source basics from Mexico. Turnaround times in Mexico, he said, range from eight to ten weeks, compared with four to five weeks in California.[50] Obviously, this is a factor that helps to keep the production of fashion local.

Lonnie Kane, the president of Karen Kane Co., Inc., a producer of expensive, fashionable women's wear, does not plan to move to Mexico. High-end companies with shorter runs rely on the contracting base in Los Angeles; it is the manufacturers of high-volume junior, moderate, and budget clothing that, he said, are prime candidates for Mexico.[51]

Writing in the *Los Angeles Times,* business analyst Joel Kotkin drew similar conclusions. He argued that companies such as City Girl, Inc., concentrated in the fashion end, want to stay in Los Angeles because of the skilled labor base, the textile suppliers, the design community, and the large number of contracting firms that enable quick turnarounds. "The large-scale economics," he wrote, "that drive larger producers of relatively standardized goods to Mexico often turn out to be unsuitable for smaller, specialized producers. As L.A. manufacturers learned in the 1970s and '80s with respect to production in Asia, the delays and lead times associated with outsourcing, not to mention quality control, often prevent firms from seizing the initiative on fast-changing fashions. A product sewn in Mexico, for example, can take up to six weeks to return to the states, compared with a turnaround as quick as two weeks in Los Angeles."[52]

There is a pattern in these and similar comments made by experts and manufacturers. The consensus seems to be that the production of basics, for which there are big runs of the same line and styles do not constantly change, are likely to leave Los Angeles. The smaller companies and those that specialize in fashion, for which runs are short and styles constantly changing, will remain. These companies need a quick turnaround, and they need the smaller factories characteristic of the industry in Los Angeles. Joe Rodriguez, the executive director of the Garment Contractors Association in southern California, summarized the situation. "We are the last holdouts because of the niche market we're in. We do work nobody else wants to do—low-volume fashion stuff, small, unmanageable lots with an ungodly mix of styles."[53]

The Attractions of Los Angeles

Although it is evident that apparel firms will increasingly shift production to Mexico, so far at least, employment has remained high and has shown only a minor downturn. Something is keeping the industry in Los Angeles. What are the factors that lead apparel companies to continue to source at least some of their production locally?

One obvious factor is the availability of low-wage, immigrant labor. Yet, if that were the only reason for the success of Los Angeles as an apparel center, the local industry would clearly be doomed, because much cheaper labor is available just across the border. Other regions of the country also have low-wage, immigrant labor pools, yet have experienced a decline in apparel production.

Two other factors help to account for the presence of a thriving garment industry in Los Angeles. The first is the region's national (indeed, global) cultural significance, which helps assure a ready market for what have been called its "cultural products." The second is the existence of a well-developed infrastructure that provides exceptional support for the apparel industry. In Chapter 8 we consider a third factor, the efforts of local government to keep the industry from leaving.

"CULTURAL PRODUCTS"

Allen Scott and David Rigby of the Geography Department at the University of California at Los Angeles have proposed that the synergy within the apparel industry in Los Angeles extends to a larger complex of what they call "cultural-products industries."[54] They see a propensity in Los Angeles for industries to specialize in the creation of cultural products: apparel, textiles, furniture, printing and publishing, leather products, prerecorded records and tapes, jewelry, toys and sporting goods, advertising, motion picture production and distribution, entertainers, and architectural services. These industries produce "small batches of output for specialized market niches and [their] competitive strategy typically entails constant product differentiation and/or significant levels of customization."[55]

Involved in so-called hyperinnovation, which tends to be associated with small, labor-intensive firms, these industries produce high-quality, constantly changing goods and benefit from an identification with a particular place, the goods being associated with the locale. The mystique of the location of origin adds to the value of the goods, which assume in the popular imagination the reputation of the place and its characteristics. The words "California" and "Los Angeles" conjure up images of sun and surf, of people who are wealthy and glamorous, of Beverly Hills and the beach. Cultural-products industries both benefit from these images and help to create and maintain them.[56] The movie and music industries help to define Los Angeles and at the same time benefit from being associated with the city. Similarly, the fashion industry has helped to define an "L.A. style," and that style is, in turn, a product of preexisting, and constantly evolving images of Los Angeles.[57]

The fashion and entertainment industries provide synergy for each other. The annual Academy Awards demonstrate this vividly, as the stars showcase the work of prominent fashion designers. The movies and television employ fashion designers, some of whom are part of the Los Angeles fashion industry, and whose work sometimes creates new consumer tastes. Moreover, at a social level, fashion and entertainment often intersect. Both *Women's Wear Daily* and *California Apparel News* report on the rich and famous, the people from both industries who attend social events and are seen. Both industries produce wealthy celebrities who comprise an important sector of the glitterati of Los Angeles.

IT ALL COMES TOGETHER HERE

Once an industry becomes established in a region, a critical mass is achieved, after which numerous supporting components of the industry provide a crucial infrastructure for further development. The industry becomes self-sustaining; future growth becomes a self-fulfilling prophecy. Economic geographers refer to such regions as industrial districts and to the results of geographic concentration as agglomeration effects.

A large body of literature suggests that successful industries are more likely to thrive in geographical areas that have firms, factories, supporting infrastructure, and specialized labor markets.[58] Geographically dense industrial concentrations minimize the cost of doing business by providing proximity to markets, the ability to acquire goods and services quickly, lower transportation and communications costs, access to suppliers, and in general the rapid exchange of information and knowledge. A strong support infrastructure—business services, training schools, and research and development facilities—can also benefit competitive firms. Such geographical concentrations can reinforce personal contacts that may be rooted in family connections, ethnic ties, and other long-standing connections and give rise to social networks that provide informal economic relationships with a structure. The ability to have face-to-face, handshake connections is especially important in industries that are based largely on trust and personal knowledge. Geographical concentration also tends to intensify competition, motivating the participants to outshine one another, thereby improving the quality of the goods.[59]

The apparel industry in Los Angeles provides a textbook example of the benefits of concentration because everything one needs to "make it all happen" is close at hand. Sidney Morse, a former owner and director of the CaliforniaMart, maintains that a downtown location is crucial for the industry because "we're an information business—the faster and better the information the more significant the sale."[60] Los Angeles is a generator of fashion: Designers the world over watch the kids there to spot the latest trends. Los Angeles also boasts numerous textile converters, companies that specialize in altering fabric by dyeing and printing it, creating the colorful, fashionable, sometimes fanciful garments for which Los Angeles is known. In addition to design and fabric, every other need of apparel manufacturers can be found within a few miles of the downtown garment district: financial, accounting, and legal services; zippers, bindings, threads, sewing machines, and other supplies and equipment; schools that provide training in everything from design to machine operation; and more than a thousand manufacturers' showrooms hosting a year-round stream of buyers. In addition, Los Angeles itself, consuming the very fashion that it generates, is a major market for clothing.

To illustrate how these elements work together to provide its unique vitality, we will describe briefly three important components of the apparel industry in Los Angeles: the CaliforniaMart, various business services, and schools that train fashion designers and would-be manufacturers.

The CaliforniaMart. The CaliforniaMart, in the center of the garment district on Ninth Street between Los Angeles and Main Streets, was built by Harvey and Barney Morse. The Morse brothers moved to Los Angeles from New York City, getting their start as manufacturers of women's lingerie. During the 1950s, according to Harvey Morse's son, David, buyers would come to Los Angeles with their checkbooks in hand, yet wind up spending days wandering throughout the sprawling Los Angeles basin in a sometimes futile search for suitable manufacturers. The Morse brothers saw an opportunity, figuring that they could actually "create a marketplace to capture more buyers' dollars."[61] They acquired the land in 1952, opened the first Mart building in 1964, the second two years later, and the third in 1973. Barney Morse's son, Sidney, emphasized the entrepreneurial nature of this venture: "No government financing, tax incentives, nothing. My father and my uncle did this by their balls."[62] The

Mart was envisioned as providing one-stop shopping for buyers who came to Los Angeles to view the samples of California manufacturers, along with those of other United States and even international firms.

Today the Mart's buildings contain more than three million square feet of space, devoted primarily to some fifteen hundred showrooms representing more than ten thousand collections. Showrooms are staffed by either independent manufacturers or independent representatives who receive commissions for showing lines for manufacturers who do not want to maintain a showroom themselves. The Mart also provides travel programs, apparel-related directories, meeting rooms, event management, shows and conferences, a print shop, a fashion office responsible for producing fashion shows, and a department that organizes trade shows, not to mention a food court and underground parking. It houses buying offices, trade associations, major trade publications, and libraries. Unlike apparel marts in other cities, the CaliforniaMart, because of its proximity to the country's largest concentration of manufacturers and contractors, has buyers visiting year-round, rather than only in response to periodic trade shows. Buyers are also attracted by the Mart's many special events: Each year it produces more than fifty fashion shows and twenty specialty markets for particular types of apparel.[63]

All told, an estimated one hundred thousand buyers were visiting the Mart annually around 1990, when the facility was reportedly running at nearly full occupancy and plans were being laid to construct another building specializing in men's wear.[64] At that time the Mart claimed to generate over $8.5 billion in annual wholesale sales and was the largest apparel mart in the United States.[65] Those halcyon days were not to last. By the early 1990s, ownership and management of the Mart had passed down to Harvey Morse's son and daughter, David Morse and Susan Morse-Lebow, and Barney Morse's son, Sidney. The brother, sister, and cousin shared responsibilities on an informal basis, although over time each came to specialize, David in leasing, Susan in finance, and Sidney in overall operations. By 1992 the Mart was experiencing financial and administrative difficulties, caused partly by a downturn in the economy and partly by an overall weakening of the position of the independent manufacturer in the face of consolidation among retailers. Increased price competition from discount stores such as Price Club and Wal-Mart and private-label production by large retailers were squeezing the manufacturers who comprised the Mart's tenant base. By the mid-1990s, according to the Mart's owners, occupancy had declined to between 80 and 85 percent. The tenants were also displeased with rising rents and declining service, which many attributed to the debt service incurred in 1987 when the property had been refinanced by Equitable Life Assurance and the owners had taken $250 million in cash out of their property. Rising rents and space reconfigurations that were done without their consent contributed to the tenants' revolt, which is described in Chapter 4.

In response to these difficulties, Sidney Morse, who had given up full-time duties in 1990, assumed full control.[66] Morse attributed the Mart's financial difficulties not only to the changes in retailing mentioned above, but also to such misguided government policies as the maintenance of high interest rates, which he viewed as squeezing out credit for small business.[67] Under these unfavorable conditions, the Mart's owners were drawing the conclusion that devoting a valuable piece of downtown real estate exclusively to manufacturers' showrooms might not be its best possible use. Alternative uses, including office space for other industries and increased cash-and-carry operations,[68] were all under consideration.

Business Services. Within a short walk from the California-Mart is a host of business services such as banks, factors, lawyers, buying offices, and accountants who specialize in apparel manufacturing. For example, Union Bank shares a long history with the industry, as well as a plaza with the CaliforniaMart. In the immediate vicinity there are several buying offices, companies that arrange purchases (or place orders directly) for retailers, thereby providing an important link between retailers and manufacturers.

There are approximately fifteen Certified Public Accountants (CPAs) in Los Angeles who specialize in apparel manufacturing, although fewer than a half dozen dominate the industry.[69] A brief discussion of their role will illustrate the importance of nearby business services to the industry. Marty Josephson, a partner in Stonefield Josephson, one of the leading apparel accounting firms, reported to us that the firm's average client did between $15 and $20 million in annual sales, the largest, $200 million, and that Stonefield Josephson provided some specialized services for even larger firms. He told us that the CPAs sometimes serve as the chief financial officers for manufacturing firms, providing them with a wide array of financial services that most manufacturers could not otherwise afford, among them, the preparation of financial statements and tax returns, the provision of compliance checks and other audits, accounting for inventory flow, reconciling factor accounts and business ledgers, forecasting, and advising on long-term planning. The very largest firms are more likely to have their own accounting and financial services; the very smallest are likely to be too risky to be taken on as clients by the principal CPAs in the garment industry.[70]

The fact that the CPA is independent of the firm helps to assure the manufacturer's creditworthiness. A particular CPA typically manages the books of many competing manufacturers, providing an important cross-cutting linkage in the industry. For example, one of the largest apparel accounting firms in Los Angeles, Moss Adams, in 1992 managed the accounts of more than 200 apparel firms nationwide, half of whom were in Los Angeles County; Stonefield Josephson had 100 clients in apparel.[71] The relationship between the manufacturing firm and its CPA is extremely close. The fact that the CPAs have access to the books of competing firms means that confidentiality, and trust, are key attributes of this relationship.

Schools. Los Angeles County is home to several colleges and universities that prepare students in fashion design and other aspects of the apparel business. These schools are significant for continually producing new generations of designers, many of whom enter the local apparel industry. The schools also train people in the various aspects of running apparel firms, from both a technical and a business point of view. In recent years, they have worked closely with city and other public agencies to help promote the image of Los Angeles as a major design center.[72]

The four major apparel-related schools in Los Angeles are the Fashion Institute of Design and Merchandising, Otis College of Art and Design, and California Design College, which are private, and Los Angeles Trade-Technical College, a public school that is part of the statewide community college system. The American College of the Applied Arts and Woodbury University are smaller private schools.[73]

The Fashion Institute of Design and Merchandising was founded in 1969. This school offers an associate of arts degree in fashion design, interior design, merchandise marketing, and apparel manufacturing management. Its principal campus is in the garment district, and there are branch campuses in San Francisco, Orange County, and San Diego. The institute is a significant force in the apparel industry in Los Angeles, and its founder and owner, Tonian Hohberg, is extremely influential. The school links its programs to the entertainment industry by providing programs that combine fashion and entertainment, another example of the synergy generated by being located in Los Angeles. Karen Kane is one of the school's graduates.

Otis College of Art and Design offers a four-year degree in fine arts. It has close connections to many industry leaders. California Design College, which graduates about 100 students a year, specializes in computer-aided design, and is expanding its curriculum to cover advanced professional fashion design and manufacturing.

Los Angeles Trade-Technical College provides technical training and apprenticeship in fashion design for those willing to settle for hours of technical classes in plain, concrete-block buildings located in the industrial downtown. Among the school's better-known graduates are Carole Little, Karl Logan, Robin Piccone, Dorothy Schoelen of Platinum Clothing Co., Inc., and Sue Wong. As with other design programs, the emphasis is strictly practical: Classroom education is shunned in favor of a hands-on approach to learning the specifics of apparel manufacture, from sewing to fabric selection, from advanced design to merchandising. As part of the statewide community college system, Trade-Tech is able to offer an inexpensive, two-year associate of arts degree. For California residents, fees run a few hundred dollars a year; the private schools are much more expensive. The college provides aspiring designers who could never afford the more upscale schools with an opportunity to find jobs with local manufacturers, even if the starting rung is as patternmaker rather than designer. About half of its thousand students attend daytime classes full-time; the remaining half are older, working students who attend evening and Saturday classes.[74]

Several public community colleges, including Trade-Tech, make up the California College Fashion Consortium.[75] Offering training in various aspects of the apparel industry, these schools throughout California ensure that talent can be recruited by the industry irrespective of class background. Once they graduate, alumni form a network that helps to recruit the next generation of graduates.

The Los Angeles apparel industry faces a critical dilemma. On the one hand, much of the industry wants to retain production here for all the reasons cited above. On the other hand, the intense competition and the fragmentation generated by the contracting system tend to produce illegal and abusive sweatshops. The fact that government agencies have cracked down on sweatshops drives some industry leaders to recoil at what they define as government overregulation and an antibusiness climate, developments that drive them, they maintain, to move offshore. This threat is credible because labor costs are even lower in countries such as Mexico and China. Each firm's decision to move puts greater pressure on its competitors to move as well. And the lower the wages they find offshore, the more will be the pressure on local firms to lower their own wage bills, increasing the number and proportion of sweatshops in Los Angeles.

Some will argue that this movement ultimately benefits everyone. Countries such as Mexico will develop economically and wages there will gradually rise, as has happened in the newly industrializing countries of East Asia. Meanwhile, consumers in the industrial economies benefit from ever-lower prices and fashionable garments become accessible to everyone. But the argument can equally be made that the movement offshore ratchets down wages in the industrial world, while the workers in poor countries find that they must operate under regimes in which their efforts to raise wages are crushed. Instead of benefiting, the workers lose.[76] Meanwhile, industry profits and executive salaries remain high, reflecting the fact that businesses are able to use offshore production to take most of the gains for themselves.

Lowered wages for workers cause problems down the line. The less workers make the less they can buy, leaving apparel manufacturers to chase fewer consumer dollars. How can NAFTA hope to increase United States exports to Mexico if Mexican wages are too low to sustain an increase in consumption at least equivalent to that lost from United States workers who are no longer employed as a result of capital flight? The rich winners in the system can only buy so many clothes; they cannot sustain a mass market. By continually trying to push labor costs ever lower, the apparel industry kills the goose that lays its golden egg. Meanwhile, the industry's threats to move offshore in the face of overregulation by the Department of Labor and other government agencies puts it in the unconscionable position of appearing to condone the exploitation of an oppressed workforce, both here and abroad. No fancy words about entry-level jobs providing immigrants with a toehold on the first rung of a ladder that is supposed to lead inevitably into the middle class can veil the ever-lower wages that characterize the industry.

For now, we can expect that the production of basics, namely, garments that do not reflect rapid changes in fashion and that can be produced in bulk for the continual replenishment of a predictable market, will gradually find a way to Mexico and elsewhere. But the part of the apparel industry that generates cultural products is likely to remain, and to keep growing, as new firms with innovative ideas keep emerging. It is possible that the continued growth in employment statistics already reflects this reality, that is, even as the industry loses one sector, another continues to grow and pick up the slack.

CHAPTER 3
Retailers

Retailing is central to the apparel industry. This may seem a truism because all manufactured products must be sold to consumers primarily through retail outlets. In the apparel industry, however, retailing takes on unusual significance because of the role that retailers play in determining what will be produced, and because of the changing balance of power between apparel retailers and manufacturers.

Unlike apparel manufacturing, where locality is significant, retailing tends to occur at a national level. Put another way, although apparel manufacturers in Los Angeles may have their headquarters there, and managing their designing, planning, merchandising, and sometimes their sewing there, they do not produce exclusively for a local market. Their clothing is made for the United States as a whole. The national character of the retail market is mirrored in the national (indeed, transnational) character of retail establishments. There are numerous tiny boutiques that sell only to local consumers, but the vast majority of apparel retailing is done by national chain stores. It makes little difference that Wal-Mart Stores Inc. is headquartered in Fayetteville, Arkansas, or May Department Stores Co. in St. Louis: These are national chains with global aspirations. Even predominantly regional chains, such as Dillard's, Inc. (in the Southeast) and Dayton-Hudson Corp. (in the Midwest and California) would become truly national if they only could. Despite minor regional variations in clothing styles, the United States is a national apparel market.

The distinction between local manufacturing and national retailing has important implications for the relative power of these two components of the apparel industry: Unlike manufacturers, retailers have the economic and organizational clout to reach a national and even global marketplace. Most manufacturers do not have this breadth of reach, and so are at the mercy of retailers to provide it for them. This makes the vast majority of clothing manufacturers beholden to the retailers that carry their lines.

The Retail Revolution

Retailing in the United States has been undergoing a rapid evolution. In the early 1970s there were three large national chains, about

three dozen big-city department stores with branches, myriad independent (some of them mom-and-pop) specialty stores in cities and towns of all sizes, and a few mail-order catalogue houses.[1] Department stores were the most influential; discount stores were still looked down upon by the industry and consumers, although there was a growing number of regional discount chains. This structure supported relatively easy access for new apparel manufacturers. It did not take much to get started — a sample line, some creativity, a good idea, $100,000 in financing, and some specialty stores willing to sell the product.[2]

Since that time, retailing has undergone two major convulsions. In the first phase, which occurred in the late 1970s and early 1980s, the department stores grew into national chains with immense power. This phase was described as the retail revolution by Barry Bluestone and his co-authors,[3] who draw a parallel between corporate concentration in retailing and the earlier growth of concentration in such industries as steel and automobiles. In the second phase, which occurred in the late 1980s and early 1990s, retailers were subject to a wave of mergers and acquisitions, widespread bankruptcies, and ultimately consolidation into considerably fewer entities.

After World War II, a new middle class of professionals and managers emerged in the United States and, along with more prosperous blue-collar workers, began moving out of the cities and into suburbs. Large downtown department stores such as Macy's followed them, setting up suburban branches, and mass merchandisers, such as Sears Roebuck & Co. and J. C. Penney Co. increased their branches. Combined with an expansion of consumer credit and a widening of product lines, suburbanization led to a retail revolution, in which stores became concentrated and competition increased.[4] By the end of the 1970s, considerable consolidation had occurred in retailing, which, in a somewhat arbitrary categorization, could be described as having five principal sectors: independent department stores, specialty stores, department-store chains and mass merchandisers, discount department-store chains, and national holding companies.[5]

THE INDEPENDENT DEPARTMENT STORE

The independent department store, a mainstay of small-town America's Main Street, was already an endangered species by the early 1980s. It had come under siege in part because of the changing character of United States consumers. Department stores (along with some mass merchandisers) had catered to middle-class, single-income, suburban families, in which the mother, as the chief buyer for the entire family, valued the convenience of one-stop shopping.[6] By the late 1970s and early 1980s, women were entering the labor force in increasing numbers. Not only did this provide them with more disposable income to spend on clothing, but also their clothing needs changed with their new occupations, and they no longer had the time to shop for the whole family. Meanwhile, the social movements of the 1960s had created a demand for fashion designed specifically for, and even by, teenagers' fashion. Specialty stores emerged to cater to this important market niche. At the same time, the United States experienced a widening divide between rich and poor. Although people of various income levels were attracted to the discount department-store chains, specialty stores also catered to the increasing income differences. Some stores specialized in wealthy customers, some catered to the poor.

SPECIALTY STORES

Specialty stores, which predate World War II, tended to sell a narrow range of full-priced, high-quality merchandise—for example, expensive clothing and related items for middle- and upper middle-income shoppers. Initially, most specialty stores were small shops and boutiques, although specialty-store chains soon emerged. (Nordstrom Inc., Limited Inc., and Gap Inc. are prominent contemporary examples.) Because they emphasize service to customers, specialty stores tended to be labor intensive, the staff employed full time, and payrolls taking as much as 25 percent of sales. (In other forms of American retailing, according to retail mythology, sales is merely the first rung on the entrepreneurial ladder. As is fondly recounted in retail circles, John W. Nordstrom launched his retail career in 1901 by selling $12.50 worth of shoes from his newly opened shoe shop in Seattle.[7]) Initially most specialty stores were located in the downtown area of cities; during the 1970s they were increasingly moving

to suburban shopping malls, where they benefited from their proximity
the department stores that served as mall anchors. Their chief form of advertising was their front window display, attracting drop-in shoppers.

DEPARTMENT-STORE CHAINS
AND MASS MERCHANDISERS

Department-store chains developed after World War II,
growing out of old, family-owned, central-city department stores. The
mass merchandisers were older, having become established at the turn of
the century and then growing after World War I. However, they shared
several characteristics. They both provided a full line of goods and services including home furnishings, housewares, appliances, and other
goods unrelated to apparel. They tried to appeal to consumers with a wide
range of incomes. And they grew by opening branches that were clones
of themselves, the central management retaining control over investment
decisions. The large chains relied on mass-market advertising rather than
on sales personnel to sell their products. Subsequent changes in the system of buying and the development of electronic data interchange to control inventory and accounting made an experienced sales staff superfluous.
Full-time jobs became part-time, dead-end work for young people and
minorities, and the share of revenues going to payroll dropped to between
12 and 14 percent. Chains and mass merchandisers were thus able to un-
derprice the independent department stores.

DISCOUNT DEPARTMENT-STORE CHAINS

The discounters rose to prominence in the mid-1960s, sur-
passing in sales volume the department-store chains and the mass merchandisers. They tended to be located in the suburbs, where land and
construction costs were cheaper than they were in more urbanized areas.
Because they economized on overhead costs, discounters were able to
offer cut-rate prices, typically to suburban consumers (rather than to poor
people, who still tended to shop downtown). Like the department-store
chains, the discounters had centralized management, and grew by opening branch offices. They, too, used advertising and electronic data interchange as a substitute for labor, and achieved even lower payroll costs
than did department-store chains—sometimes as low as 6 or 7 percent
of revenues. By the end of the 1970s, K-mart was the leader among the
discounters.

The growth of discount chains was aided by the repeal of fair-trade legislation, which had been enacted by the federal government during the depression and subsequently adopted in many states. Fair-trade legislation gave suppliers the right to specify minimum retail prices and prohibited discounters from carrying brand names. After a retailer won a court case against Louisiana's fair-trade law in 1952, other states began to repeal theirs. By the end of the 1970s discounters, no longer forced to carry unknown labels, could compete head-on with other types of retailers.

NATIONAL HOLDING COMPANIES

As their name implies, holding companies emerged as huge retail conglomerations of regional department-store chains. They originally began after World War II as downtown department stores and then grew by acquiring regional department-store chains. By the early 1980s, the four largest national holding companies were Federated Department Stores, Inc., Allied Stores Corporation, May Department Stores Company, and Dayton-Hudson Corporation. Holding companies permitted their subsidiaries to maintain their own identities and management and sell brand-name products rather than their own store label. The member stores usually provided extensive customer service, so payrolls ranged between 16 and 20 percent of sales in most full-price department stores to as much as 25 percent in the higher-priced stores such as Bloomingdale's. Still, even those stores were hiring more part-time, unskilled sales personnel, especially as the holding companies moved into the discount chain-store business. The discount specialty shops still carried high-quality merchandise, but cut costs by offering less personalized service. They were units within the large discount department-store chains, and some became parts of holding companies. (For example, in 1977 Dayton-Hudson operated fifty-nine Target Discount outlets along with thirty-one full-service department stores and some specialty stores.) Individual specialty stores could not afford electronic data processing, but specialty-store chains were able to introduce it.

MERGERS, ACQUISITIONS, AND BANKRUPTCIES

Although by the early 1980s retailing was becoming increasingly concentrated and organized along corporate lines, it was still fiercely competitive. Most chains believed that they needed to grow or die and opened more branches around the country. Between 1970 and 1990, for example, the number of shopping centers in the United States grew from 10,000 to 37,000, resulting in too many retail stores searching for too few customers.[8] The mass merchandisers and department-store chains, which had been the major powers in the industry, found themselves increasingly squeezed, on the one hand, by discounters, which offered lower prices for high-quality goods, and, on the other, by specialty stores, which offered service and a narrower, more clearly defined range of products.

As a consequence, in the late 1980s retailing underwent a major merger movement that sent reverberations throughout the apparel industry. A large number of well-publicized mergers and leveraged buyouts consolidated retailing into a shrinking number of giants. The consolidations exacerbated the woes of department stores, which were already being buffeted by competition from specialty stores, discounters, and shopping malls, where the specialty stores replicated many of the departments in department stores. Department stores were also frequently saddled with complex, overstaffed bureaucratic management structures, such as regional distribution centers with their own administrative infrastructure, a condition that was only exacerbated by the mergers and acquisitions.

Then, by the early 1990s, a number of the newly consolidated retail giants, squeezed between the debt they had acquired to finance their mergers and the retail recession, began to file for bankruptcy protection. A few interlocking cases will illustrate the dizzying shakeup in ownership that occurred as long-established retail giants gobbled one another up with a ferocity that completely transformed the retail landscape.

In January 1986, the top management of Macy's, using $3.7 billion in debt financing, took over the company.[9] Now privately held and in an expansive mode, Macy's proceeded to open a bidding war with Campeau Corporation, the Canadian real-estate firm that, in 1986, had acquired the Allied Stores Corporation.[10] Macy's reportedly offered $6.1 billion in an unsuccessful effort to prevent Campeau from acquiring control of Federated Department Stores, a giant retail holding chain, in a hostile takeover. Campeau used high-interest junk bonds to leverage its $6.7 billion takeover, saddling its acquisition, now a holding company for Federated Department Stores and Allied Stores Corporation, with excessive debt. To raise cash, Campeau then sold Bullock's, Bullock's Wilshire, and I. Magnin to Macy's for $1.1 billion, thereby significantly enhancing Macy's presence in California.

Such costly trading was eventually to push both Macy's and Federated into bankruptcy and result in their eventual merger. Macy's, now saddled with debt of its own, initially sought to cut costs by centralizing its buying and advertising departments, resulting in a merchandise mix that seemed to ignore regional tastes in favor of a single, bland selection.[11] Whatever the aesthetics of this reorganization, it proved to be fiscally wanting. Macy's filed for bankruptcy protection in 1992, leaving 20,000 suppliers with between $150 and $250 million in bills that would be eventually paid off at only a fraction of their value. A number of manufacturers in Los Angeles were adversely affected, particularly the smaller and more marginal ones, who were forced to seek other outlets as Macy's closed stores and cut back on orders. Ed Finkelstein, the man who had initiated Macy's adventures by leading the original leveraged buy-out, retired, most likely under pressure.

Federated, which had acquired far more debt than Macy's had, filed for bankruptcy protection two years earlier, in 1990, reporting a debt of more than $8 billion.[12] The company reorganized and significantly reduced its costs by centralizing its buying operations across all of its divisions. Federated emerged from bankruptcy in 1992 as a new public company, Federated Department Stores, Inc. The new company turned out to be as hungry as the old one. It pulled Macy's (now split into Macy's East and Macy's West) out of bankruptcy by purchasing it in late 1994. Its appetite still not sated, the following year Federated acquired the eighty-two-store Broadway chain, which was owned by Carter Hawley Hale Stores Inc. of Los Angeles and included the Broadway, Emporium, and Weinstock department stores.[13] In 1987, Carter Hawley Hale had faced a hostile takeover from The Limited and taken on $1.4 billion in debt to counter the bid. Carter Hawley Hale then put three of its most successful specialty stores (Neiman Marcus, Bergdorf Goodman, and Contempo Casuals) into a separate public company controlled by General Cinema Corporation, leaving the parent firm with the fading Broadway department stores. Finding itself in trouble, Carter Haley Hale then sold its Thalheimer's Division to May Department Stores in 1990 and eventually filed for bankruptcy the following year. Federated's acquisition of the Broadway chain was a profitable transaction for all involved: Merrill Lynch, the financial adviser to Broadway Stores, reportedly made a $3-million fee on the sale; a second adviser, Salomon Brothers, made $1 million.[14] (David Dworkin, the president and chief executive officer of Broadway, was reported to have received $5 million in severance pay.[15])

As of mid-1998, Federated, operating 400 department stores and more than 160 specialty stores in thirty-six states, boasted of being "the nation's largest operator of department stores located in all major regions of the United States."[16] It had 115,000 employees, and sales in 1997 of nearly $16 billion. The holding company's retailers at that time included Macy's

East, Macy's West, Rich's, Lazarus, the Bon Marché, Burdines, Bloomingdale's, Stern's, and Goldsmith's, as well as more than 120 Aeropostale
specialty clothing stores and Bloomingdale's by Mail, a national mail-
order catalogue company. As part of its consolidation, Federated folded
the Broadway, Bullock's, and Jordan Marsh stores into its Macy's or
Bloomingdale's divisions and sold off its specialty stores.[17]

In a third saga of consolidation, the British financier Sir James Gold-
smith attempted, in late 1989, a $22-billion hostile takeover of B.A.T.
(British American Tobacco) Industries, a conglomerate based in London.
To combat the attempt, B.A.T. was forced to sell its United States retail
operations, including Saks Fifth Avenue and Marshall Field and Company. The former was sold to Investcorp Bank, a company based in
Bahrain, for $1.5 billion; the latter, for $1.04 billion, to Dayton-Hudson
Corporation, which already operated 657 stores in thirty-three states.[18]
This was the second time in a decade that the ownership of Marshall Field
had changed, B.A.T. having bought the retailer in 1982, when it was first
publicly traded. Because these transactions strained an already debt-rid-
den Dayton-Hudson, the company cut costs by consolidating its legal and
buying staffs.

These changes in ownership contributed to a significant increase in the
concentration of retailing in the United States. More than 77,000 retail
stores went out of business between 1991 and 1996; the failure rate among
apparel outlets was two-thirds higher than the overall national retail failure rate.[19] Retail bankruptcies continued into 1998, though perhaps their
rate was slowing. In 1995, nine chains with liabilities exceeding $70 mil-
lion went bankrupt. The number declined to four in 1996, three in 1997
(but a major chain, Montgomery Ward, was among their number), and
two as of mid-year, 1998.[20]

The shakeout led to the following ownerships: May Department
Stores Company owns Lord & Taylor, Hecht's, Strawbridge's, Foley's,
Robinsons-May, Filene's, Kaufmann's, Famous-Barr/L. S. Ayres/The
Jones Store, and Meier & Frank. Federated owns Bloomingdale's, the Bon
Marché, Burdines, Goldsmith's, Lazarus, Macy's East (including the for-
mer Abraham and Strauss, and Jordan Marsh), Macy's West (including
the former Bullock's, Broadway Stores, Emporium, and Weinstock's),
Rich's, and Stern's.

Yet, even though May and Federated may have emerged as the two
largest department-store chains in the country, department stores (in
which apparel, particularly women's apparel, typically accounts for 65 percent of total sales) face an even more formidable foe: More and more con-

Table 2. *The Largest United States Retailers Compared with the Largest
          Department-Store Holding Companies (Fiscal year ending January 1998)*

Discount and Department-Store Chains	Annual Sales ($ 000,000)	Employees	Sales Growth (% annual)
Wal-Mart Stores Inc.	$117,958	825,000	12.5
Sears Roebuck & Co.	$41,296	334,000	8.0
K-Mart Corporation	$32,183	261,000	2.4
Dayton-Hudson Corp.	$27,757	230,000	9.4
Total	$219,194	1,650,000	
Department-Store Holding Companies			
Federated Department Stores Inc.	$15,668	114,700	2.9
May Department Stores Co.	$12,685	116,000	5.7
Total	$28,353	230,700	

SOURCE: Hoover's On-Line Company Capsules (http://www.hoovers.com/) (data only).

sumers are buying clothing from stores such as Wal-Mart, Sears, K-mart,
J. C. Penney, and Target.[21] By mid-1998, Wal-Mart's annual sales had
reached nearly $118 billion, and K-mart's, $32 billion; together, they out-
sold all department stores combined. The four largest United States retailers, the discounters Wal-Mart and K-mart, and the department-store
chains Sears and Dayton-Hudson (which operates Target and Mervyn's),
accounted for more than $219 billion in sales, approximately two-thirds
of the United States total, and employed 1.7 million people (see Table 2).

The overwhelming domination of the market by a handful of enormous retailers signals the completion of the retail revolution in apparel.
No longer controlled by its principal manufacturers, apparel retailing is
now clearly driven by large retail buyers.[22] The retailers that were doing
well in mid-1999 were the discounters at one end of the economic spec-
trum and the higher-end department stores at the other.[23] By the next mil-
lennium, according to Kurt Salmon Associates, a team of industry analysts, retailers who are not solidly entrenched in one of three niches,
offering a high level of service, low prices, or unique merchandise, are unlikely to survive.[24] The national developments have dramatically changed
the department store line-up in southern California as well. Federated Department Stores is becoming the dominant retailer, setting up a potential
conflict with the other major department-store chain in the region,
Robinsons-May, which is owned by the country's "number three upmar-
ket department store operator (after Dayton-Hudson and Federated)."[25]

Some members of the apparel establishment in Los Angeles have been critical of these changes. David Morse, the former managing partner of the CaliforniaMart, complained that "Wal-Mart has been a big success, but they have killed Main Street. And they have squeezed out the middleman. Walton is seen as a hero by many, but I see him as having destroyed American business. Sam Walton is raping the land, changing the character of cities."[26] In 1992 Stanley Hirsh, a former manufacturer, owner of real estate downtown, and one of the most powerful and influential "garmentos" in Los Angeles offered a characteristically colorful commentary on the then-recent changes in apparel retailing:

The department stores fucked up, and they're eating it now. The shlubs from Harvard Business School raped the industry, trying to make more money for the CEOs. Take Bullock's, once the epitome of a good department store. Bullock's used to be the best store in Los Angeles. They had a 40 percent markup. Then they chased out their customers, and offered higher CEO salaries. They kept offering sales: taking off, off, off from the price. The customers wised up and wouldn't buy at regular prices, and turned to the discounters. The customers no longer trust the department stores. The drop in sales is only partly because of the recession [in 1992]; customers have lost confidence because of this overly aggressive discounting in the department stores. Retailers used to deal exclusively with particular manufacturers. Now the retailers aren't loyal. And the manufacturers don't trust the retailers.[27]

Mona Danford, a partner in the Los Angeles buying office, Directives West, commented that the retailers were no longer merchants, but "money people," who destroyed retailing with their leveraged buyouts. "I've never been through an era like this one. There is a big shakedown. The strong will survive. We are seeing the dominance of specialty stores, chain stores, and new discounters. There are always new ideas. This a creative industry and clothes are a necessity. But this is a unique period. I've been in the business for thirty-six years and I've never seen department stores dropping like this, and it's not over yet. You can't look like your competitors. Everyone looks the same. Stores can't all have the same customer focus, but many of them carry the same merchandise. Part of the problem with the department stores is that they became boring."[28]

The Price Makers

Consolidation among retailers is contributing to the decline (and, in the views of some industry analysts, eventual demise) of smaller, innovative manufacturers, who are ill equipped to deal with the retail giants.[29] With few exceptions the large retailers are price makers: They set the price, and most apparel manufacturers are forced to accept. Sammy Lee, the vice president of Contempo Casuals, was especially candid in describing how retailers set the prices and control their suppliers. Contempo Casuals, at the time of our interview in 1993 a subsidiary of the Neiman Marcus Group, was a specialty-store chain based in southern California and with 280 stores in thirty-three states. It has a large private-label program. According to Lee, retailers know how many minutes it takes to sew a particular garment and calculate, on the basis of the minimum wage, how much they need to pay per garment in order to cover it. For large orders, however, retailers can simply cut back the price they are willing to pay, forcing the contractor to pay less than the legal minimum wage. In Lee's calculus, "the pressure goes right down the line. Pricing starts from the retailer and moves down. It doesn't start from the bottom, from the real costs of making the garment. The retailer can always go down the street and find someone who can make it for less. The manufacturers and contractors are stuck. Everyone down the line is squeezed."[30]

Consolidation has had other effects. Because fewer retailers are making the key buying decisions, they are more likely to select the wares of fewer firms; concentration among retailers seems likely to lead to concentration among manufacturers. For example, when Macy's bought Bullock's, manufacturers in Los Angeles who had previously sold to both of those stores now dealt with only one buyer; those who had supplied Bullock's alone sometimes found themselves cut out altogether. Consolidated buying also tends to benefit larger apparel manufacturers at the expense of smaller ones. For example, retailers are demanding that apparel manufacturers have electronic data interchange, which until recently only larger companies could afford.[31]

For the same reasons, consolidation has also led to a convergence of style, particularly for inexpensive and moderately priced clothing. Because of their increasing concentration and economic power, the large retail chains and mass merchandisers, if they buy independently designed items at all, are now able to go to all but the largest manufacturers and cherry-pick the items they think are most likely to sell, rather than buying entire collections. In fact, moderately priced brand names are becoming more important, even among discounters and mass merchandisers. Both Sears and J. C. Penney have shifted from providing basics to providing their own private-label fashion items, and Wal-Mart is aggressively expanding its branded apparel offerings, including private-label and manufacturer brands. Wal-Mart has even added Catalina, an old, established southern Californian swimwear firm, now owned by Authentic Fitness Corporation, to its inventory.[32]

Because retailers often occupy valuable urban real estate, the issue of land use also weighs heavily in their decisions. Real estate ownership plays an important role in the ability to leverage debt and therefore can drive a firm's ability to play the mergers-and-acquisitions game.[33] In fact, some stores were spun off in the restructuring and consolidation process more for their real estate value than for their merchandising potential. Urban real estate is costly and, therefore, figures in the retailer's profit-and-loss calculations. According to one apparel industry consultant in Los Angeles, "What drives the retail business now is gross profit [in] dollars per square foot, or how quickly you can turn over the product relative to your markup. You have so many weeks' supply in the store, and you calculate what percent[age] sold this week."[34] The implications are important: Because department stores turn the goods over more slowly than discounters do, they need a higher markup, which places them in an unfavorable competitive position in the face of the growing market power of discounters and other mass-merchandise retailers.

Department stores have come up with a number of strategies to cut costs.[35] One way is to rely increasingly on imports, because their low cost permits a higher markup. Another is private-label production, which enables department stores to cash in on the glamour of their names and save money by eliminating the manufacturer. However, as we noted above, even the discounters are now developing their own private-label brands. As we were told by the director of retail relations at CaliforniaMart: "If they can establish a reputation, there is no reason why Price Club cannot play the same game as Macy's and sell private label too. People know they are getting quality for their dollar. It doesn't have to be upscale stores. It's confidence."[36]

Another way to reduce costs is to turn over smaller inventories more rapidly. Inventories are costly for two reasons: They tie up storage space (and hence costly real estate) and they may go unsold. The latter possibility can be especially worrisome in the fashion industry, where markets are volatile and unpredictable. If a store can increase the turnover of goods per square foot, it uses its valuable space more profitably and is able to move new goods to the floor before they become unfashionable. The multiplication of seasons beyond nature's four is a direct result of retailers' need to bring fresh inventory into their stores regularly. There is a constant pressure to increase the number of seasons, a pressure that is felt directly by apparel manufacturers, who are asked to produce smaller lots of distinctive clothing more frequently during the year. Some manufacturers told us that they are now changing their lines every month, with minor seasons between the major ones; a few are even designing and developing new products continuously. For example, The Gap, based in San Francisco, changes the look of its stores every six to eight weeks. Jim Cunningham, The Gap's vice president for Offshore Sourcing (and whose office is in Hong Kong) is responsible for this accomplishment. "I can't miss a beat," he says. "The fashion package, the particular look, is in the store; it sells; it's over. The stops between cash register and factory are shorter. The key is control. The best retailers will be the ones who respond the quickest, the best. We are on a treadmill that doesn't stop often."[37]

Quick turnover is facilitated by the development of computerized quick-response systems.

Large investments in scanning, distribution automation, satellite communication, and more sophisticated buying, merchandising, and labor-scheduling technologies have driven down operating costs. . . . Through advances in computer-assisted scanning, on-line receiving, merchandise tracking, and labor management, retail firms are able to reduce dollars tied up in inventory and shorten the lead time during which merchandise is moved into the store. . . . Managers are examining every aspect of the distribution pipeline— from fiber to fabric producers, from apparel manufacturers to the store—to devise ways to shorten the distribution cycle. Successful retailing demands sophisticated planning and technology, so that decisions can be made on the basis of information rather than intuition of the next hot fashion trend.[38]

Improvements in the efficiency of distribution centers and transportation fleets have included investments in automated conveyer systems and high-tech scheduling of truckers, which has helped to eliminate errors and waiting time. The most impressive aspect of the shift to quick-response systems has been the rise in investment in computer telecommunications technology, with which the giant retailers can keep track of sales daily and even hourly. Point-of-sale scanning enables retailers to respond quickly to consumer demand. Electronic data interchange (EDI) takes this a step further by transmitting this information to vendors and automatically reordering items that are selling well. In some cases, delivery time has been cut from four weeks to three days. Thus, $250 billion-worth of products were reportedly exchanged using EDI in 1998.[39] A decade ago, the American Apparel Manufacturers Association boldly predicted that "the days of mass production to serve mass markets with stable products and predictable growth are gone. . . . [Retailers] are buying closer to seasons, and resist backorders. They are operating with leaner inventories, and seek faster turns. They are using new electronic technology to improve their market intelligence and respond quickly to sales. All of these changes translate into increased pressure upon manufacturers to supply the right product at the right place and at the right time. Few of today's apparel plants are able to meet these new market conditions."[40]

The explosive growth of direct ordering on the World Wide Web has greatly accelerated this process. An increasing amount of EDI is now done via the Internet, vastly reducing its cost. Whereas a manufacturer must contribute as much as $50,000 to add a trading partner to its EDI network, comparable systems, in which manufacturers fill out purchase orders from retailers on the Web, cost as little as $1,000 to start with, a price that opens up the technology to even the smallest firms.[41] The new technologies also greatly facilitate direct on-line ordering by the consumer, who can go to a merchant's webpage and place a custom-made order for a particular item. This approach was pioneered for book sales (by Amazon.com and Barnes and Noble) and computers (by Dell and Gateway) and is finding its way into apparel sales as well. In 1997 nearly $100 million in apparel and footwear sales were done on the Web, an amount that is predicted to increase fivefold in the next four years.[42]

How these technological changes will affect the future of apparel retailing remains to be seen. Business analysts triumphantly tout the emergence of a new, frictionless capitalism in which "mass customization" finally makes the consumer all powerful.[43] In reality it seems likely, however, that the hand of the largest, most powerful retailers will be greatly strengthened. Wal-Mart, for example, now *requires* its suppliers to assume the cost of warehousing and delivery and make just-in-time deliveries of exactly the quantity of goods that are likely to sell.[44] Although the new technologies may enable some retailers to survive in an increasingly competitive environment, that does not mean that their suppliers will survive as well. The retailers, so much bigger and more economically powerful, can dictate terms to most apparel manufacturers, except for those with the strongest brand names. As a result, manufacturers feel squeezed. According to an accountant, "Retailers are buying less, buying closer to the dates they want the goods, and demanding shorter delivery times. Retailers have such strength that they can drive the prices down and that makes it difficult for the manufacturer to make money."[45]

Apparel retailers typically set their prices through a practice known in the industry as "keystoning," which means setting a price by doubling the wholesale cost. Many retailers use a policy known as keystone plus or minus, by which they double the price and then add or subtract a couple of dollars.[46] Thus the markup by the retailer from the manufacturer's price will typically be 100 percent or more. The retail markup has been rising in recent years, especially among department stores, which are trying to match the profits of discounters and specialty stores. Yet, because department stores are under increasing price competition, they are simultaneously under pressure to lower their retail prices. In the mid-1990s, for example, only 20 percent of all department store merchandise was sold at full price.[47]

Retailers have responded by squeezing the manufacturer ever harder. Apparel manufacturers in Los Angeles constantly complain that the prices they receive for goods has not increased in a decade or longer, despite a 35 percent increase in the minimum wage in California between September 1996 and March 1998 and other rising costs. Apart from holding the line on wholesale prices, retailers use a variety of devices to squeeze manufacturers further, including price concessions, charge-backs, and markdown money.

Price concessions are discounts that retailers negotiate with manufacturers before placing their orders for clothing. Giant retailers are able to exact price concessions because of their relative economic power and because of the intense competition between manufacturers. When large orders are at stake, manufacturers vie with one another to obtain them. We heard that manufacturers will do favors for store buyers, such as getting them Dodgers' tickets or taking them to restaurants, in order to encourage a purchase order. There are several types of discount, including trade discounts (to buyers of a certain category), quantity discounts (for bulk purchases), and cash discounts (for prompt payment of the invoice). The latter are especially profitable for the retailer. For a typical cash discount, the manufacturer might offer the retailer 2 percent off the list price if the bill is paid within ten days after the invoice date (rather than the standard thirty days).[48] Manufacturers in Los Angeles complained to us that, even though retailers would sometimes insist on a discount, they would then fail to honor the agreement, and manufacturers were in no position to bargain if they wanted business in the future.

Charge-backs are penalties the retailer imposes on the manufacturer when the order does not precisely meet specifications. Charge-backs thus occur at the point of delivery and may be as much as 10 percent of the wholesale price. Retailers claim charge-backs when clothing arrives that is not "floor-ready." It might be packed in the wrong type of box, hung on the wrong kind of hanger, or be tagged improperly. Manufacturers regard charge-backs as a thinly disguised effort by retailers to make money "at the loading dock instead of inside the store." Charge-backs reportedly occur for the most trivial reasons. One irate manufacturer complained that "we were charged $150 for putting a piece of tissue paper in a carton." This same manufacturer stated that the biggest retailers are the most difficult to work with: "The people who rape us most are the largest companies."[49] Ellen Bradley, a principal with the Los Angeles branch of the Frederick Atkins buying office, which is based in New York, described the practice.

The retailer tries to pass the risk back to the manufacturer. Nobody buys to stay anymore. They try to pass back unsold goods. They engage in very unreasonable charge-backs and buybacks, and the bigger stores are the worst offenders. Part of the reason is that they are all computerized so it is more important to follow the rules. For example, it matters whether the invoice is on the inside or outside of the box. They have a legitimate reason for complaining, but not necessarily for charging money for the offense. They will charge $40, $50, $60 for an offense. This can add up. Dillard's has seven divisions, and let's say you ship 20 to 30 cartons to each of them and get charged $50 per carton. That adds up to a lot of money. The stores deny that they engage in charge-backs to make money. They say the charges are just to get the point across, especially when they are dealing with small, California companies. They are trying to impress them with the importance of correct packaging.[50]

Smaller manufacturers are more likely to have difficulty meeting the complex demands of large retailers, each one of whom has a different set of specifications, some running to shipping and packing guides the size of telephone books.

Markdown money is a type of rebate imposed by the retailer on a manufacturer to partially recoup the retailer's losses on unsold goods, or goods for which prices have been slashed in closeout sales. They have become increasingly common as retailers rely on promotional markdowns and special sales to turn their goods over more rapidly, and the retailers are now powerful enough to pass the costs on to manufacturers, who must pay the markdown money in order to assure future orders.[51] Markdowns not only cut into manufacturers' profits, but also devalue their brand names. As consumers look for more sales, retailers shift to more private-label goods, and the smaller manufacturers are hurt. Smart shoppers are likely to hold out for sales or to shift to discounters and price clubs. Promotional price-cutting may thus have a short-term benefit but, in the long run, creates persistent problems. For this reason, stores such as Sears and Dillard long ago shifted to everyday low prices to escape from the extremes of occasional full-price transactions and constant discounting.

The prevalence of price concessions, charge-backs, and markdown money reveals the retailers' dominance. "If," said Sammy Lee of Contempo Casuals, "you are using a domestic resource [a manufacturer or contractor] and they are one day late, you can cancel the order. Even if they are not late, but the goods aren't selling, you can still control them. That's because the retailer has lots of power. If a resource is doing 30 percent of their production with us, they have to give in to our demands. We can ask for markdown money. He will do what he has to do. The manufacturer is often engaged in trying to cover his overhead to break even. They only make money when the market rises and they hit a wave. Otherwise they are just trying to ride it out. It is hard to make money in this industry because the retailers control everything. The retailer doesn't want to bear any risk, so they do everything to pass it on to the manufacturer."[52]

Buying Offices

The relationship between retailers and manufacturers is often handled by intermediaries, such as sales representatives. One important institution that straddles the relationship between the two major actors is the buying office. Buying offices are firms that arrange purchases for a wide variety of retailers, particularly when they are shopping for branded apparel. The offices act as the retailer's representative through the production process, visiting with manufacturers, looking over their samples, and following up on slow orders.

Buying offices may represent entire small specialty stores or a couple of departments of the larger department stores. When buyers from the stores visit Los Angeles, the buying office will arrange their itinerary, tell them which showrooms in CaliforniaMart to visit, make hotel arrangements, and escort them on buying visits. They also keep tabs on the latest designs, new talent, and trends. "We are," said the head of one major buying office, "consultants to retail. We sell information." Such information includes market overviews, the identification of important items to buy, help with planning, and market research in the form of weekly or monthly retail reports on trends in Los Angeles and elsewhere (including Europe), on fashion forums, and on new resources.[53] Some buying offices shop the local stores in an effort to get a complete picture of the most recent fashions that are being made in Los Angeles.[54] Barbara Fields, the head of the buying office that bears her name, told us: "We work with every L.A. manufacturer and have comprehensive knowledge of all of them. We recommend to our clients who is good and who isn't. We are paid for telling our clients who is the best, given what they need. We critique what is happening with the L.A. manufacturers. We are like movie critics. We help provide them with information on what they are looking for, including delivery, quality, price, and gut feelings. Everyone has the same items. You have to know who is reliable, who will deliver."[55]

One of the roles of the buying offices is to find fresh new designers who will add variety to goods provided by the major labels, especially in the juniors and contemporary markets, in which California is known for its innovation. Major retailers may still shop in New York City for most of their goods, but they come to Los Angeles for currently fashionable ideas and looks, because, said Mona Danford, the owner of Directives West, "Trends typically start here first. They also stop here first. You can use what is happening here to monitor what will happen in the rest of the country. Something that is already dead here will still be continuing in the Midwest, but you can predict that it will die. Retailers come here not just for the markets, but to shop the stores to see what the California customer is buying."[56]

Some buying offices have an agreement with the retailers they represent, enabling them to write orders directly to manufacturers. This arrangement may extend to the buyers' working with manufacturers to create private-label products for their clients. "The store can initiate [private-label production] by asking for something, like junior cotton shirts. Or we can see a void in their offering and suggest a line to them. We meet with the stores in a workshop meeting. We compare sourcing options, price the product around, in the Orient, Los Angeles, etc. Then we work with the vendors to develop the product. We have started to try to work directly with contractors, getting rid of the middleman. But this is difficult because we aren't equipped to know enough about production."[57]

The buying offices thus serve as a conduit for getting retailers to be aware of what is going on in the industry in California. There were more than twenty buying offices in Los Angeles at the time of our research; the largest ones included Arkin, Atkins, Barbara Fields, and Directives West. There is some specialization among these firms; for example, some focus on large sizes, or on off-price goods (such as close-outs, irregular items, and store returns). Not all retailers use buying offices; high-priced boutiques, for example, may buy directly from Europe. And, with some exceptions (such as that of Atkins, mentioned above), the retailers' private-label purchases generally do not fall under their jurisdiction, because private-label production typically results from a direct relationship between retailers and manufacturers (and sometimes even contractors). Buying offices typically do not deal with basics. They are oriented toward the discovery and shaping of fashion; indeed, the most powerful buying offices tell manufacturers what they should be making.

The larger buying offices represent major retailers and receive substantial compensation for their services, sometimes as a percentage of sales, sometimes in the form of a monthly fee. When we asked Barbara Fields what she provided for a former $25,000-a-month account (which she had just lost to a competing buying office), she replied, "Blood. We set up a separate staff of three people just for them." In 1992 Frederick Atkins had a client base of about fifty major department stores; Directives West handled Carter Hawley Hale, Federated, Sears, and Wal-Mart; Arkin handled some ninety stores, including the May Company, and Barbara Fields focused on some 250 specialty stores, including Nordstrom and Mervyn's. The combined buying power of the retail client base of these four offices approached $200 billion. Buying offices thus provide an important crosscutting connection between manufacturers and retailers, and as a result exert a great deal of influence in the industry. They are often "in killing competition" with one another. According to Barbara Fields, "Not only do we not cooperate with each other; we don't even speak to one another."[58] The fact that they often recommend the same manufacturers to a large number of competing retailers "is even more of a problem than you think," said Ellen Bradley of Atkins, "because we help to create private-label product. We try to avoid having clients with stores in the same trading area, but now some of them overlap in the same malls. We try to offer different labels to different stores but, in reality, there are only small differences. We are basically offering the same product under different labels and hope the customer makes a distinction."[59]

The owners and leaders of the buying offices are an important part of the power elite of the industry in Los Angeles. For example, Ruth Bregman, the head of the Arkin buying office and subsequent founder of her own office, Bregman and Associates, remained a major figure in the Los Angeles industry virtually until the moment of her death at the age of eighty. For a quarter century she was a driving force behind the Cedars-Sinai Hospital Fashion Industry Guild charity fund-raising organization, which twice made her woman of the year and then named an outpatient unit for children with HIV-AIDS and other diseases the Bregman Clinic. When we interviewed her in 1992, her wall was festooned with the many honors she had received throughout her career, including awards from the City of Hope Merchants Club and Millionaires Club, Israel Bonds, the American Jewish Committee, Mayor Bradley's Committee, and the State of Israel's Jerusalem Award; she has been honored by the city, county, and state as woman of the year. Many of these awards were for fund-raising and other philanthropic activities.[60]

New Forms of Retailing

The greater economic power of retailing over manufacturing has meant that the manufacturing function is increasingly being absorbed into retailing. Of especial interest are those retailers who become manufacturers through private-label production, and the efforts by manufacturers to resist being reduced to the role of designers for large retailers.

PRIVATE LABEL

A significant trend in retailing is the expansion of sales of private-label merchandise. Retailers selling goods under their own store label can bypass the manufacturer altogether. This practice is not confined to apparel, but it is a large and growing trend in the industry. The Gap, based in San Francisco, epitomizes the successful retailer-as-manufacturer. The company designs its own private-label clothing, manufactures it in 1,200 independently owned factories around the world, and then sells the clothing in 2,200 stores.[61] According to Jim Cunningham, a vice president of the company, "Retailers are more sophisticated, capable of design and manufacturing as well as selling, which enables them to control all aspects of the production process, minimizing risk."[62]

The Limited Inc. was the first major United States retailer to contract out for its own manufacturing. Other retailers such as The Gap quickly followed suit, as did mail-order companies such as L. L. Bean. Soon the large department-store chains moved into private-label production, as did discounters such as Wal-Mart. Department stores and specialty stores can use their store name as their private-label brand, but often they develop special names for their private-label goods. For example, J. C. Penney uses the name Arizona for its private-label jeans. Sometimes the private-label brand names are based on a celebrity endorser, such as the Kathie Lee brand sold by Wal-Mart, or the Jaclyn Smith products sold by J. C. Penney.

Private label has been growing dramatically for the obvious reason that it is more profitable to the retailers. In 1998, private-label merchandise accounted for 32 percent, $29.3 billion, of the sales of women's apparel in the United States.[63] By expanding their private-label merchandise, retailers can avoid paying a premium for the brand name of a manufacturer, especially if they can develop a strong identity for their own label. In some cases they are even able to avoid using manufacturers entirely by maintaining their own design staff and dealing directly with contractors. More typically, however, retailers employ established manufacturers to make their private-label goods.[64] The manufacturers may make a special line for the retailer, or may take their own products and alter them slightly for the retailer, a practice that enables them to avoid having the private-label goods, which generally sell at lower prices, compete directly with their branded goods. High-end manufacturers producing for low-end retailers may use a different name, so as not to cheapen the value of the principal label. Still, Mona Danford of Directives West told us, "when Liz produces under a private label for Wal-Mart, the customers will be made to know that it is Liz Claiborne."

In the view of some industry insiders, only the most successful, well-known brand names in Los Angeles will survive. The rest will be pushed into private-label manufacturing for retailers. One of the larger manufacturers in Los Angeles, the Tarrant Apparel Group, engages exclusively in private-label production. Even well-known manufacturers do private-label production on the side, in the interests of a stable source of income. The production of private-label goods for retailers is very common among Los Angeles manufacturers.[65] According to a local manufacturer, "these specialty chains know their customers so well, and are so successful in drawing customers in, . . . it is easy to go private label. They now have customer allegiance, so customers are not put off by the brand label. And their overhead is sufficiently low so they can spend some money on the product development necessary to develop private label. What's happening now is that the classic vision of the wholesaler, the branded manufacturer, is being squeezed out of existence. A Levi Strauss can survive, because it is viewed as more than a brand of apparel. It is like Coke. But there are precious few of these. You are going to see less and less of this, because it is harder and harder for entrepreneurs to get into business."[66]

Yet even Levi Strauss & Co. may not be immune to competition from private-label production. Between 1990 and 1997, the lucrative jeans market has seen the share of private-label jeans grow from 16 percent to 25 percent.[67] At the same time, Levi's share of the men's denim pants market, the biggest sector of the jeans market, dropped from 48 percent to

26 percent.[68] Although much of the success of those companies selling private-label jeans can be attributed to the phenomenal growth of the Gap, whose sales in 1997 of $6.5 billion reflect an average annual growth rate exceeding 20 percent over the past ten years,[69] J. C. Penney's private-label Arizona brand has also made significant inroads and now does a billion dollars in sales.[70] One formerly successful manufacturer in Los Angeles told us how private-label retailers had effectively driven him out of apparel manufacturing. "So much has gone private label that there are fewer opportunities for independent label manufacturers. The retailers now hire designers and contract with them directly, creating less need for companies that provide, and charge for, value-added. Retail has gone narrow and deep, with fewer suppliers. This will continue for the next decade or so. The result is a greater risk in growth, with less return on investment; the fewer surviving manufacturers are increasingly played off against one another. The retailers have gone direct. They test from the manufacturers, then produce their own private label."[71]

THE COUNTERREVOLUTION

Manufacturers in Los Angeles have countered the growing power of retailers by attempting to gain greater control over their own retailing. One obvious route has been to set up their own retail stores as Guess, Rampage, BCBG, and XOXO have done. Their experience suggests that only the largest of manufacturers are likely to move successfully into retailing and that the route can be costly and dangerous. Rampage, for example, bought a financially troubled retail chain called Judy's and attempted to remake the chain in its own image. This effort failed, driving Rampage into bankruptcy. Bugle Boy, which is based in Simi Valley and is one of southern California's largest clothing manufacturers (with sales in 1997 of approximately $500 million), has opened some 160 stores in factory outlet malls that enable it to display a much wider range of its products than would be possible in a department store.[72] Guess, the largest manufacturer in Los Angeles, in mid-1998 had eighty-four retail boutiques in malls around the country. The firm also sold through some 270 international stores operated by licensees and distributors.[73] These stores not only provided Guess with the additional profits that could be obtained by bypassing the retailer, but also helped Guess to develop its image by controlling its own retail environment. The stores attempt to create an atmosphere, almost like a Hollywood set, in which the consumer can develop the fantasy identity that Guess attempts to generate.

Another way that manufacturers have sought to exercise more control over retailing is by developing their own "shops" within department stores. Major labels are allocated floor space, which they then configure to their best advantage (subject, of course, to the control of the store itself). In the women's section of Robinsons-May, for example, Carole Little will occupy one area, Liz Claiborne another. This arrangement does not give control over retailing to the manufacturer, but it does allow the manufacturer to have more influence over aspects of the retailing process. The manufacturer can arrange the layout of its products, give special instruction to sales personnel, and help ensure that the customer recognizes the brand name by collecting all its products together in one place. The "shop in a store" makes a department store look more like a series of boutiques owned by brand-name manufacturers who happen to be sharing the same space. In reality, of course, the economics are unchanged; the manufacturers are not renting the space to sell their wares. But the impression that they are somewhat independent of the store enhances the power of their brand, to the benefit of both manufacturer and retailer. Needless to say, only successful brands are able to set up such arrangements. They need to have a proven track record for the store to dedicate space to them in this manner. Presumably as major brands rise and fall, they gain and lose such a space advantage.

Clearly retailing has an enormous influence over the apparel industry, and the industry in Los Angeles is no exception. The fact that apparel retailing has been undergoing such profound changes in recent decades has had important reverberations for apparel manufacturing. Retailers have merged, gone bankrupt, and merged some more. Meanwhile, discounters have grown and undercut the market. Intense competition among the retailers has killed off some of the players, but has still left too many stores competing for too few consumer dollars. The number of competing retail giants has diminished, but they are still opening new stores in an effort to beat out their major rivals. We have not seen the end of these retailer wars, and the story of their effect on apparel manufacturing in southern California is not yet complete, if it ever will be.

Many analysts of the industry place the origins of the trends we have been describing with the changing consumer. Standard and Poor's, for example, devotes seven pages of a report (published in 1995) on textiles and apparel to an analysis of the changing demographics of consumers and their accompanying changes in attitude.[74] Today's consumers are seen as more cost-conscious, more willing to shop for the best price, more aware that sales and promotions will inevitably come and that they need not pay full price, more eager for comfortable clothes, and less susceptible to fashion. Price pressure is thus laid at the feet of the consumer, rather than on such factors as the intense competition among retailers because too many stores are chasing too few consumers.

Consumer psychology notwithstanding, however, the restructuring of the United States (and the world) economy is affecting consumers' choices. As companies become more global, downsize, or contract out—actions reportedly taken in the name of lowering prices to consumers who are shopping more discriminately—they increase the insecurity of their employees while contributing to a decline in real wages. But, of course, the consumers are also employees and, as their jobs deteriorate, they are forced to watch prices more carefully. Holding consumers responsible for lowering prices helps justify a harsher relationship with employees, but in turn, undermines the very market that the retailers are trying to reach. This strategy may not be unreasonable for the owners and managers of giant retail establishments, because profits and executive salaries keep going up. But the long-term consequences of such an approach are ominous for the consumer and, therefore, for the industry itself.

CHAPTER 4
The Power Elite

For years it appeared that the apparel industry in Los Angeles lacked a coordinated leadership. Unlike industries that are consolidated around a few major companies, the apparel industry is still competitive and fragmented. Turnover is high, new firms emerge, and old ones disappear. Most of the industry is privately owned, enabling firms to be secretive about their practices. Industry leaders and observers bemoan the fact that apparel manufacturers are unable to develop a joint strategy of industry protection and promotion. Nevertheless, there has always been a group of power players who share a common ideology, socialize together, and have been able to persuade governmental agencies to respond to their concerns. This group is not a formal organization, but we refer to its constituents as members because they operate as an informal club. The winners in this industry are rich, and they act in a coordinated way to protect their wealth. Individual participants come and go, but the group as a whole continues.

The apparel industry is not unique in having a power elite. Indeed, the elites of some other industries are far more prominent, wealthy, and politically powerful. The leaders of the apparel industry in Los Angeles do not sit at the centers of city power. They are poorly represented on the Central City Association, which is probably the most influential organization in the downtown area. The association's major members include banks, transnational corporations, real estate developers, and giant law and accounting firms; these corporations deal in billions of dollars, while the apparel industry deals in millions. As an entrepreneurial industry whose largest firms are relatively small, and perhaps as a mainly Jewish industry, apparel operates at the fringes of power. Its leaders often complain that the industry is ignored and does not get the respect it deserves. Nevertheless, within the industry itself, power is wielded and wealth is accumulated by a relatively small group. To ensure its own wealth and privilege, this group does what it can to exert influence in its favor.[1] (It must be noted that much of the research for this chapter was done in 1992, so is somewhat dated, although we do focus on individuals and organizations who are presently important.)

The apparel elite is composed of two broad segments: business owners

DILBERT reprinted by permission of United Feature Syndicate, Inc.

and salaried managers and professionals.[2] In both segments, only the wealthiest and most successful make it into the elite. Business owners include apparel manufacturers, owners of buying offices, and owners of apparel-related real estate. Managers include high-level executives of the larger manufacturing firms and financial institutions (such as Union Bank), real estate operations (such as CaliforniaMart), and educational institutions (for example, the Fashion Institute of Design and Merchandising). Professionals include successful designers, lawyers, accountants, and consultants who specialize in the industry.

These members of the power elite make money in somewhat different ways. The owners make profit and rent; the managers and professionals are paid salaries. These sources of income overlap, however, at the upper end, when manufacturers serve as their own executives and pay themselves a salary or when managers and professionals are able to purchase stock in their companies.

Prominent real estate owners are among the most influential members of the power elite. Stanley Hirsh is repeatedly cited as *the* key figure in the Los Angeles apparel power elite. He owns extensive real estate in the fashion district, he is a manufacturer, and he is the only apparel-related business owner who has served in city government, as head of the Community Redevelopment Agency. Annette and Jack Needleman are the largest downtown property owners. Their ubiquitous Anjac Fashion Buildings, with the name emblazoned in multistory-high letters on the buildings' exterior, house many of the garment district's factories. Arthur Gerry and Jack Lumer also own extensive property downtown. In 1992, Bruce Corbin of Union Bank estimated that the Needlemans were worth about $250 million, Hirsh over $100 million, and Gerry between $75 and $100 million.[3] The properties of those three owners housed more than a third of all tenants in the downtown garment district. The

Needlemans' properties alone accounted for 20.1 percent, Hirsh's, 9.2 percent, and Gerry's, 6.4 percent.[4]

The chief executive officer of CaliforniaMart is also always a power player, although in 1994, during the time of our research, the ownership changed hands from its founders, the Morse family, to the Equitable Life Assurance Society. Equitable first appointed Maurice "Corky" Newman as chief executive officer and, when he left in 1997 to be become chief executive officer of Sirena, a large swimwear firm, Equitable appointed Susan Scheimann to succeed him. All of the directors have been members of the power elite at one time or another.

Major manufacturers change over time, but some of the important people have included Maurice, Paul, and Armand Marciano of Guess? Inc., Doug Arbetman of Sirena Apparel Group, Max Azria of AZ3 Inc., Larry Hansel of Rampage Retailing, Inc., Barry Sacks of Chorus Line Corporation, and Robert Margolis and Jay Kester, originally of Cherokee, Inc. Ruth Bregman, who ran and then owned a buying office until her death in February 1998, was a very influential member.

Professional members of the power elite include lawyers such as Stanley Levy, who served as general counsel for Guess from 1992 through 1996 and joined the Fashion Industry Group of the powerful law firm, Manatt, Phelps, and Phillips in February 1998, and Richard Reinis, of Reinis and Reinis, who organized the Compliance Alliance, which is discussed in Chapter 8. Influential accountants include representatives from specialized accounting firms with several apparel clients, such as Moss Adams and Stonefield Josephson. Other professionals who would qualify as members include Tonian Hohberg, the president of the Fashion Institute of Design and Merchandising, Sharon Tate, the dean of academic affairs at Los Angeles Trade-Technical College, and Bruce Corbin, the regional vice president of Union Bank and a specialist in the apparel industry.

Some individuals, themselves without the wealth and status to exert power directly, serve as spokespeople, among them, Ilse Metchek, the executive director of the California Fashion Association, and Marianne Giblin, of the Downtown Property Owners Association, an organization of real estate owners. Various experts and commentators may also fall into this group. For example, Joel Kotkin, senior fellow at the Pepperdine Institute for Public Policy and research fellow at the libertarian Reason Foundation, frequently articulates the industry's interests as a contributing editor to the opinion section of the *Los Angeles Times*. Jack Kyser, the chief economist with the Los Angeles Economic Development Corporation, often serves as a semiofficial voice when expert opinion is sought. People in these roles give public legitimacy to the views held by most members of the power elite.

No consensus list of so-called power players exists and if such a list could be contrived, it could not easily be kept up to date. Nor can we assert that all the members of the power elite agree with one another. As in any group of diverse and changing people, they vary in their ideas and behavior. Nevertheless, we believe there are detectable patterns in their social organization, their ideology, and their political involvement.

Industry Organizations

The most overt form of coordination occurs through formal organizations such as the Coalition of Apparel Industries in California, the Apparel Industry Roundtable, the California Fashion Association, and the Downtown Property Owners Association. When we began studying the industry in 1989, only the Coalition of Apparel Industries was in existence. It gradually declined in influence, however, and in April 1998 merged into the California Fashion Association,[5] which, by 1998, had clearly become the major organization of the Los Angeles apparel industry.

THE COALITION OF APPAREL INDUSTRIES IN CALIFORNIA

A membership organization ostensibly of manufacturers, contractors, and members of service-related industries, the Coalition of Apparel Industries in California was much more of a manufacturers' than a contractors' organization, although the Garment Contractors Association was a member. Before its demise, the president was Bernard Lax, who had been the owner of a knitwear company, Louis Bernard Inc. The CAIC's main purpose was to influence legislation and state policy in favor of the apparel industry. It maintained lobbyists in Sacramento and Washington, D.C., kept its members informed of the latest legislative initiatives, and tried to encourage them to put pressure on officials as needed.

In a brochure soliciting applications for membership, the CAIC listed as accomplishments the organization's opposition to a bill raising unemployment benefits and to a joint liability bill that would have held apparel manufacturers responsible for their contractors' violations of labor standards; a decrease in sweeps by the Immigration and Naturalization

Service of apparel plants, and an extension of the cutoff date for amnesty applications by another year; opposition to more stringent legislation on the flammability of children's clothes; the introduction of amendments to the state registration law, limiting the penalties and provisions under which garments may be confiscated; and opposition to an increase in the state minimum wage. The general thrust of these actions is evident: to prevent the government from raising labor costs and holding manufacturers responsible for violations of labor standards in contracting shops. Interesting in this list is the CAIC's position on immigration. Because the industry has relied heavily on undocumented immigrants, the CAIC found itself supporting certain immigrants' rights.

THE APPAREL INDUSTRY ROUNDTABLE

The Apparel Industry Roundtable was convened in 1993 by Barry Sedlik, the manager of the Southern California Edison Company's Business Retention Group. Edison, which has a strong self-interest in keeping its business customers in southern California, sought to help them revitalize their industries. Edison worked with a number of industries, but the only lasting effort involved apparel. The initial purpose was to help develop a coherent strategy for the industry's development. The organization did succeed in bringing together leaders of preexisting organizations such as the CAIC, the Garment Contractors Association, Rebuild L.A., and the California State Trade and Commerce Agency but did not succeed in attracting a core group of manufacturers who would commit resources to the organization, because, reportedly, they doubted that it would be worth their time and energy.

Their skepticism proved to be well founded. The roundtable generated several working groups, but only one survived, the Apparel Roundtable Educational Consortia, led by Sharon Tate, the dean of academic affairs at Los Angeles Trade-Technical College, and consisting of representatives of a number of apparel schools, leaders of the CAIC and the California Fashion Association, leaders of the various contractors' associations, a few government officials, and a few representatives of individual apparel-related firms.

The roundtable began its series of monthly meetings with brainstorming sessions to determine the key issues facing the industry, and invited experts to discuss solutions. It then held a workshop on the issue of compliance with labor law, inviting officials of the state and federal Labor Departments to address manufacturers and contractors. By 1997 the roundtable was working principally to upgrade technology and training in the industry. (See page 251).

THE DOWNTOWN PROPERTY OWNERS ASSOCIATION

Landlords in the garment district have their own organization, the Downtown Property Owners Association (DPOA). Although not confined to owners of apparel-related property, it was created by them and they provided the primary leadership. The DPOA was founded in 1993, partly in response to the riots in Los Angeles in 1992 and the resulting perception that downtown Los Angeles was dangerous, and partly to halt the deterioration of the garment district, where the presence of homeless people, dirt, and graffiti were deterring visits by store buyers. The earthquake in 1994 added to these woes. The owners of buildings with showrooms in the downtown area, including Stanley Hirsh (owner of the Cooper Building) and Sidney Morse (owner of the California-Mart), were especially threatened because their assets were diminished by their physical location in the district.[6] They wished to make the district more attractive to their tenants and assure the buyers that Los Angeles was a desirable place to visit.

The first goal of the DPOA was to clean up the area and improve security. In July 1993 the organization launched a three-month pilot project called "Clean and Safe," receiving a grant from the city of $75,000 (consisting of $50,000 from the city council and $25,000 from the Community Redevelopment Agency), and another $155,095 in donations from landlords in the garment district. The DPOA hired security guards to form a bicycle patrol, and contracted crews from Chrysalis, a homeless agency, to pick up trash and paint over graffiti. The project was renewed for another three months, receiving an additional $75,000 from the city, but property owners came up with only $80,000 themselves in the second quarter. The voluntary funding was based on an assessment depending on front footage and rental values. The largest contributor was CaliforniaMart, which paid $20,229 per quarter.

The DPOA also successfully lobbied in Sacramento for the passage of legislation that would permit localities to create a Business Improvement District (BID) to funnel public funds into efforts to improve business. The Los Angeles Fashion District BID, put together by the DPOA and seeded by a $150,000 federal Community Development Block Grant, took effect in August 1995. It was the second BID in California to be established under the new state law. In a press release announcing its establishment, the DPOA stated that the BID area, extending to fifty-six blocks, generated $16.5 billion a year and employed more than 100,000 people. Members of the BID advisory board appointed by the city council in spring 1995 included Ruth Bregman, then of Arkin/California, a buying office, the downtown property owners Richard Gerry and Stanley Hirsh, and Corky Newman, the chief executive officer of the CaliforniaMart.

The Fashion District BID gave the programs run by the DPOA a sounder financial footing derived from tax assessments backed by the city. The BID pumped $6 million-worth of improvements into the garment district over the next three years. One of its major accomplishments was, in partnership with Chrysalis, to get a homeless assistance grant of $300,000 for three years from the United States Department of Housing and Urban Development.[7] It also changed the name of the garment district to the more up-scale Fashion District, established a Street Beautification Banner Campaign, and posted signs to publicize the district.[8] These efforts received the strong endorsement of Mayor Richard Riordan.

The DPOA has conflicting attitudes toward the poor and the homeless. On the one hand, worried about the image of Los Angeles in the eyes of store buyers, especially in light of riots, earthquake, urban blight, and crime, it is very concerned about the squalid effect of panhandlers and homeless people on the streets of the garment district. At some level it would, no doubt, like to remove the homeless altogether. But this inclination would have been counter to the beliefs of its more liberal members, including its key leader, Stanley Hirsh. We have not questioned Mr. Hirsh directly about this issue, but imagine that he devoted some effort to finding a more humane way to deal with the problem. Working with Chrysalis and employing homeless people in the clean-up effort was one result. Going after the Housing and Urban Development grant was another. This concern with social issues is reflected in the tendency of the apparel industry power elite to support the Democratic Party and to be active in raising money for charities.

THE CALIFORNIA FASHION ASSOCIATION

The California Fashion Association (CFA) grew out of the New Fashion Industry Roundtable, convened in February 1995 by the city's Office of Economic Development in hopes of promoting local industrial development.[9] Although the goals of this effort were very similar to Edison's goals for its roundtable, a major difference was the ability of the mayor's office to use its prestige to get the influential members of

Table 3. *Participants in the New Fashion Industry Roundtable, 16 February 1995*

George Akers	Executive vice president of operations, O Wear
Veronica Becerra	Operations manager, ANJAC Inc.
Bruce Entner	Manager and vice president, New Mart
Debbie Esparza	Executive director, Business Expansion Network, University of Southern California
Marianne Giblin	Associate director, Downtown Property Owners Association
Stanley Hirsh	Owner, Mercantile Center
Tonian Hohberg	President, Fashion Institute of Design and Merchandising
Gary Jue	Director for public relations, American Chinese Garment Contractors Association
Mike Kim	Senior vice president, Korean-American Garment Industry Association
Bernard Lax	President, Coalition of Apparel Industries of California
Carole Little	Co-chairman, Carole Little, Inc.
Maurice Marciano	Chief executive officer, Guess? Inc.
Clotee McAfee	Chief executive officer, Clotee, Inc.
Ilse Metchek	President, Image Makers
Cathy Morales	Vice president, David Dart, Inc.
Bill Mow	Chief executive officer, Bugle Boy Industries
Corky Newman	President, CaliforniaMart
Joseph Rodriguez	Executive director, Garment Contractors Association
Bjarne Schmidt	General manager, Continental Colors/Garment Industry Laundry
Barry Sedlik	Manager, Business Retention Group, Southern California Edison Company
Sharon Tate	Dean of Academic Affairs, Los Angeles Trade-Technical College
Robert Walter	President, Apparel Contractors Alliance of California
Kenneth Wengrod	Chief operating officer, Rampage Clothing Co.

the industry to attend. The participants are listed in Table 3. There was a larger number of invited observers, including the authors. The list includes many of the leaders and participants of the Edison effort, including the convenor, Barry Sedlik, and Sharon Tate from Trade-Tech. Riordan also drew in the chief executive officers of several major manufacturers, including Bugle Boy, Carole Little, David Dart, Guess, and Rampage. Moreover, major real estate owners were part of this new organization, in particular the CaliforniaMart, the New Mart, Anjac Fashion Buildings (owned by Annette and Jack Needleman), Stanley Hirsh, and the Downtown Property Owners Association.

Out of this meeting emerged two organizations: the Mayor's Technology Task Force, which folded into the Educational Consortia, and the California Fashion Association, or CFA. The CFA was a nonprofit association, whose purpose was described, in 1995, in its mission statement as "the first statewide forum for the fashion industry. Members include manufacturers, their suppliers, [representatives from] the financial and professional services, and [staff members of] applied educational institutions. Our purpose is to foster industry networking and information for compliance with labor law, international trade, and technological advancement; developing a positive image for our industry. The California Fashion Association will focus on the promotion of global recognition for the 'Created in California' image."

The issue of image was obviously of great concern. An ad in *Women's Wear Daily* states: "The California Fashion Association responds to *every negative issue* thrown at the apparel industry . . . and is making a major impact on the media as well as city, state, and federal officials. The Association's mission is to change the general perception of our industry and reverse the trend for additional regulation and oversight."[10] According to Lonnie Kane (of the manufacturer Karen Kane Co.), who was the first chairman of the CFA, "we are very interested in changing the image of the apparel industry in California. Obviously it's getting battered. Everyone thinks it is a disgusting situation . . . and it paints a black eye on an industry that is trying to clean itself up."[11]

The CFA also aimed to develop guidelines to help manufacturers and contractors comply with labor laws and to help upgrade the industry with new technology and training. "If," said Kane, "we can train companies to use the newest equipment and . . . show them how cost-effective it can be, we will make a big advance in getting rid of the old sweatshop image."[12] The CFA also has the goal of acting "as a liaison between city, state, and federal agencies."[13]

By April 1998, the CFA's 150 members included a large number of major manufacturers, industry suppliers (including the Textile Association of Los Angeles), banks and factors that service the industry, apparel law and accounting firms, buying offices, schools (such as the Fashion Institute of Design and Merchandising, the Apparel Technology and Research Center at California Polytechnic in Pomona, and the Fashion Center at Los Angeles Trade-Technical College), compliance firms and organizations, the Downtown Property Owners Association, and the Garment Contractors Association. Here, in a nutshell, is the power elite.

Charities

Members of the apparel industry are known for their generosity to public causes. Indeed, some charities have explicitly acknowledged this by creating suborganizations expressly for people from the apparel industry. Thus Cedars-Sinai Medical Center has a Fashion Industries Guild, a group of people who raise contributions to the hospital from the apparel industry. At the time of our study, the City of Hope hospital had two apparel-related groups: the Merchants Club, composed of manufacturers, and the Professions and Finance Association, which, although not formally composed of apparel industry professionals and finance people was, in practice, dominated by them. The two groups have since merged into the Apparel Industries Chapter. The United Jewish Fund, which serves as the fund-raising branch of the Jewish Federation Council in Los Angeles, has a Fashion Division within its Business and Professions Division.[14] Israel Bonds also has a Fashion Industry Group. The Fashion Industry Council for AIDS has been an important fund raiser for AIDS-related research and treatment. One charity, Save-a-Life, even raises money for needy members of the apparel industry itself.

In addition to their manifest purpose of raising money for worthy causes, these charities also provide a community for industry leaders. They meet at charitable events, they attend planning meetings, and they have overlapping memberships in several charities. We cannot say that business is conducted at these events, but participation in the charities creates a reputation for an individual and sets the stage for later business transactions. People come to be known in the industry through their participation in the charities, and that can have an indirect benefit for their businesses.

The system of charities seems to be heavily influenced by the fact that many of the leaders of this industry are Jewish. Thus, several of the charities have a Jewish or Israeli focus, calling upon a tradition of charitable giving that has existed for years in the Jewish community in the United States. Although others certainly participate in these charities, one wonders whether the charitable organizations would disappear if the dominant manufacturers were no longer Jewish.

FASHION DIVISION, UNITED JEWISH FUND

The United Jewish Fund (UJF), a subsidiary of the Jewish Federation Council of Greater Los Angeles, in 1998 reported raising approximately $40 million each year for a variety of causes in Los Angeles, Israel, and throughout the world.[15]

We interviewed Tracy Baum, the director of the Business and Professions Division, in 1992. He was accompanied by Judy Fischer, a previous director, and Karen Schetina, who was then in charge of the new Israeli Division.[16] At the time of our interview, about 600 Jewish apparel industry people contributed to the UJF. The organization's Cabinet, which met monthly, consisted of about fifty people who "give generously, and generously of their time . . . helping to raise money, as well as contributing themselves." Between fifteen and twenty-five showed up at the meetings, for which there was a core group of between eight and ten people. Stanley Hirsh, who was described as "larger than life for our Federation," played a lead role; "they usually don't come unless Stanley calls the meeting."

"Apparel and real estate people," according to Baum, Fischer, and Schetina, "are very generous. They make the most money and get hit the hardest when things go wrong. They are deal makers. You can make a deal with a deal maker, just like you can sell a salesman. They are suckers for a shpiel. They have heart."

FASHION INDUSTRIES GUILD, CEDARS-SINAI MEDICAL CENTER

The largest nonprofit health care facility west of New York, Cedars-Sinai Medical Center also undertakes training and research.[17] The establishment began as the Kaspare Cohn Hospital, named for the man who, in 1914, founded the Union Bank in the garment industry in Los Angeles. By 1992 Cedars-Sinai was raising over $900 million a year. One branch of its massive fund-raising system consisted of thirty-two support groups, which together raised between $4.5 and $5 million a year; the Fashion Industries Guild was one of them. The Guild, founded in 1956 by the Morse family, which then owned the CaliforniaMart, was the only support group that was formed around a single industry. By 1992 the Guild had raised over $8 million. Its major fund-raising effort is an annual black-tie dinner dance that honors a leading member of the apparel industry. Money is raised both by the sales of tickets to the event and by the publication of a book, in which individuals and firms pay for advertisements congratulating the person honored. In 1992 the guest of honor was Jonathan Bernstein, a partner of Stanley Hirsh, with whom he owned Alex Colman, Inc., manufacturer of the labels A. C. Sport, Elizabeth Stewart, and Stewart Sport. The previous year the guests of honor had been Robert Margolis and Jay Kester, who were, at the time, the board chairman and chief executive officer, and the executive vice president, respectively, of Cherokee.

We presume that the advertisements in these books serve multiple functions. The money paid constitutes a charitable donation, but also it buys advertising for one's company and enhances one's image as a generous philanthropist, which probably does not hurt one's business dealings. It proclaims that one is rich enough to be able to support this kind of charity, which signifies that one's business must be doing well. It repays obligations to the guest of honor and incurs new ones from him. And, it declares one's membership in this community. Charitable giving may be an end in itself, but there is plenty of opportunity to display one's philanthropy publicly.

The dinner dance for Jonathan Bernstein was held at the Regent Beverly Wilshire Hotel on 10 October 1992. Co-chaired by Ruth Bregman, of the Arkin/California buying office, and Enid Goldman, of Monarch Knit and Sports Wear, Inc., the dinner cost $250 per person or $5,000 for a table; the Guild's events are not for the person in the street. About 700 people were expected to come, and about $300,000 was raised. When we expressed a desire to attend this unaffordable (to us) event, Susan Morse-Lebow (the daughter of one of the founders of CaliforniaMart, Barney Morse, and at that time responsible for the Mart's financial operations) graciously invited us to be her guests. Attending the dance proved to be one of the high points of this research.

The thought of a formal event hosted by the fashion industry was daunting in itself, as neither author is known for a sense of style. For Richard the solution was simple—a rented tuxedo. Edna felt compelled to venture into previously unknown territory, the formal dress section of an upscale department store. After anxiously picking her way through racks of thousand-dollar dresses, she settled on what someone at the dance later characterized as a light dress. Costing under $300, the dress was still an extravagance by her previous standards. Indeed, amidst the beads, embroidery, and spangles that adorned the formal gowns of women who shape the country's fashion, *light* proved to be an understatement.

Thus formally if not quite properly attired, we hoped to mingle freely with the guests, and we were not disappointed, even though a number of the industry's central figures did not attend. Our host, Susan Morse-Lebow, said she recognized only about half of the people by sight and a quarter by name. Among the people we recognized were Stanley Hirsh, Mitchell Glass of Cherokee, Barry Sacks of Chorus Line, and Larry Hansel of Rampage. Although the crowd was heavily Jewish, there were also a significant number of African Americans, many of them employees of Jonathan Bernstein's A. C. Sports Company. Bernstein reportedly paid as much as $15,000 for sixty people to attend; his workers had only good things to say about him and the company.

The evening went smoothly, although Edna did cause a few eyebrows to be raised when she pulled a pad and pencil out of her purse in order to take notes on our dinner conversation with the Morses. We were especially interested in the speeches for and by Mr. Bernstein. One important point he made—and attributed to his mentor, Stanley Hirsh—was: "Charity isn't only giving money—it's giving time." Bernstein received a plaque from the city, presented by Barbara Yaraslavsky, the wife of Zev Yaraslavsky, a city councilman, to commemorate his dedicated service. We thoroughly enjoyed our evening of dinner, dancing, and schmoozing, our single foray into the high society of the Los Angeles apparel industry.

CITY OF HOPE

The City of Hope was founded in 1913, prompted by the death of a garment worker from tuberculosis on the streets of the garment district. The fact that the worker died simply because he could not afford health care led a group of garment industry people, workers as well as manufacturers, to form the Jewish Relief Fund, with an initial capitalization of $1,200. The fund bought a few acres of land in Duarte, twenty-five miles northeast of Los Angeles, and opened a tuberculosis sanitarium. From those humble beginnings, City of Hope has grown to be one of the largest research hospitals in the country, working on cancer, Alzheimer's disease, AIDS, and several other major diseases.[18]

The offices of the City of Hope are located in an Anjac building, prompting us to inquire of hospital staff whether the Needlemans provided a special deal on the rent. Although we did not receive a direct answer, we were told that "Jack Needleman is a big supporter of City of Hope and of every charity in town. He is very special."[19] At the time of our study, City of Hope had 450 fund-raising auxiliaries nationwide, with between 150 and 160 in Los Angeles. Two of the Los Angeles auxiliaries were heavily supported by the apparel industry: the Merchants Club and the Professions and Finance Association.

The Merchants Club, which began in 1933, included garment manufacturers, button and zipper makers, manufacturers' representatives (salespeople), and "other Jews in the *schmatte* business."[20] City of Hope is no longer a Jewish hospital, but the Merchants Club remains heavily Jewish, as was the husband of its matriarch, Lee Graff, of Graff Californiawear. (Lee herself is Italian.) In 1992 the Merchants Club had about 170 dues-paying members, with a core of between 30 and 40 activists. The

City of Hope raised about $54 million in donations every year, out of total revenues of $235 million (the rest came from patients, insurance, and research grants). In 1992 the Merchants Club raised $2.85 million, making it among the top three fund-raising auxiliaries in the country. Several of its members have served on the hospital board.[21]

The Professions and Finance Association (PFA) consisted mainly of lawyers, bankers, factors, and accountants, two-thirds of whom were connected with the apparel industry. In 1972 the PFA branched away from the Merchants Club, which focused more on manufacturers and was primarily a social club. PFA members, according to the director, Karen Paull, "use their charitable work to conduct business. They are not just friends, but use this as an opportunity to network." The PFA had 400 members, of whom between 100 and 150 were active, and raised a half million dollars in 1993. Most of its members were Jewish; among those who were not, Bruce Corbin, of Union Bank, had been active for many years. Paull went on to comment, "these charities are mainly a Caucasian thing. There isn't much giving in the Asian and Iranian communities. They don't have a tradition. The Christians do and so do the Jews. But it's starting with other groups. The Jews are not as wealthy as the rich Christians, but they work hard at fund raising. They don't have the fortunes of the Annenbergs, Chandlers, and Gettys. But they have friends and know how to raise money. The newer immigrants don't know the American system of raising money. They have to be taught. The Japanese are just learning."[22]

The PFA also had an annual, black-tie dinner dance, held at the Beverly Hilton on November 20. In 1993 they honored Robert S. Marx, the president and co-chief executive officer of the apparel manufacturer Gilda Marx, Inc. and son of Gummo Marx of the Marx brothers. We did not attend this event.

Although each charity had its own core group of activists, some individuals participated in several charities. In many of the offices of the members of the power elite whom we interviewed, the walls were covered with plaques acknowledging contribution to various charities or showing recognition from the city. For example, Jonathan Bernstein, honored by the Fashion Industries Guild of Cedars-Sinai in 1992, had been president of the Guild for three years and chairman of its board of directors for two. He had served as divisional chair of the Apparel Industry Cabinet of the United Jewish Fund for three years. He had been chair of the Israel Bonds Fashion Industry Group. He had been active in the Pediatric AIDS Foundation, the AIDS Project Los Angeles, and the City of Hope. And he had been active with Mayor Bradley's Fashion Advisory Committee.

Sidney Morse, a former managing partner of the CaliforniaMart, had been on California Hospital's PACE Advisory Board, co-chairman of the Los Angeles County Museum of Art's textile and costume renovation project, executive secretary of Guardians of the Jewish Home for the Aged, on the board of directors of the Jewish Home for the Aged and the real estate committee of the Wilshire Blvd. Temple, president of the Fashion Industries Guild of Cedars-Sinai and of the Barney Morse Lodge of the B'Nai B'rith, on the board of directors of the California Fashion Creators,[23] vice chairman of the United Jewish Fund and chairman of its Business and Professions Division, on the board of directors of the Los Angeles Theater Center, and active in other organizations. Among other honors, Morse received the Humanitarian Award given by the National Conference of Christians and Jews and the Lion of Judah Award given by the State of Israel.

Ideology

We believe, that, in spite of differences among individuals, loose generalizations can be made about the beliefs of the power elite as a whole. These generalizations result from many conversations with members of this leadership, perusal of their public statements and reports on their positions in the press, and observation of their actions in the political arena.

The ideology of the apparel power elite can be seen as a system of thought, common to all privileged classes, that justifies their wealth and privilege. Inequality, especially the extremes of inequality witnessed in this industry, requires some justification. Not only does the individual need to find a way to feel at peace with his or her special good fortune when others live so poorly, but also one needs to be able to justify that inequality to others. This is a problem that confronts United States business leaders in general, and they have developed an elaborate rationale in the form of beliefs about the benefits to all of the free market. The apparel power elite accepts this ideology, but its members put their particular stamp on it in the face of their own circumstances.

LIBERAL IDEOLOGY, EXPLOITATIVE PRACTICES

Many of the leaders of the apparel industry in Los Angeles have historically been members of the Democratic Party, and many still are, although their numbers may be waning. They are part of the up-scale, Los Angeles Westside, liberal establishment. This affiliation, which is typical of the Jewish community, is contradictory in that it combines participation in a ruthlessly competitive industry with a strong commitment to social justice and a general (although weakening) belief in the welfare state. Despite their socially liberal leanings, industry leaders complain bitterly about the antipathy toward business in California and in the city of Los Angeles, and about the Democratic control of the State Assembly, which they see as unsympathetic to business interests. Still, despite a propensity to rethink their traditional loyalty to the Democrats, at least some of the key leaders, such as Stanley Hirsh, remain staunchly committed to the party. At the same time, a turn toward the Republican Party can be detected among others, as they experience frustration with state regulation of the economy. For example, Sidney Morse told us that he had been active in Republican politics and was a former member of the Republican State Committee, even though "the industry overall tends to be Democratic."[24]

The apparel industry power elite is faced with a dilemma. Seen by much of the public as being responsible for sweatshops, both in the United States and abroad, its members feel attacked as vicious exploiters. Yet they want to think of themselves as moral people and not as exploiters. Their generosity to charities demonstrates this concern. They want to be seen, not as ruthlessly pursuing their own economic interests at the expense of others, but as contributors to the community, as giving back because they are fortunate enough to have done well and become rich. This desire to be seen as benefactors rather than exploiters rubs up against the harsh realities of the low wages and poor working conditions in the industry. Industry leaders thus have to engage in some ideological juggling to deal with the dissonance between their values and their practices.

The first line of defense is to deny that they have anything at all to do with sweatshops. They blame sweatshops on others, such as Korean immigrants, and refuse to acknowledge any shared responsibility. Some simply deny that sweatshops exist to any significant extent, claiming that they were invented to stir up trouble. According to this view, the left-leaning press gleefully picks up the stories, sensationalizes the issues, and generalizes the practices of a few "bad apples" to the majority of perfectly reputable and legal firms. This is the California Fashion Association's main response to the "image" problem it is continually battling.

A classic example of the dilemma was posed by the exhibition at the

Smithsonian Institution, *Between a Rock and a Hard Place: A History of American Sweatshops, 1820–Present,* which opened in April 1998 in Washington, D.C. The exhibit highlighted the El Monte "slave-shop," a notorious garment factory in Los Angeles where seventy-two Thai immigrants were discovered in 1995 to be working as virtual prisoners, some claiming to have been held in semislavery for as long as seven years.[25] The California Fashion Association firmly opposed the exhibit, unsuccessfully attempting to derail it completely, and the executive director, Ilse Metchek, pulled no punches in her opposition. "In painting the entire apparel manufacturing community as a 'sweatshop enterprise,' it amounts to a diatribe against the industry. It insinuates that our industry prospers through the systematic abuse of our labor force . . . a concept that couldn't be further from the truth[26] . . . We'd give them our full 100 percent support if they want to talk about the contributions the American fashion industry has had on the world and the opportunities it has given to immigrants and the undereducated.[27] . . . The Smithsonian is taking a political position by focusing on sweatshop conditions rather than the apparel industry's broader contributions to American life and commerce. . . . We cannot stand idly by. We want to turn this exhibit into another *Enola Gay.*"[28]

(In one of the more strained analogies we encountered in our research, Metchek was referring to the cancellation, in the face of protests by veterans' groups, of a Smithsonian exhibit that proposed to commemorate the dropping of the atomic bomb on Hiroshima.) The National Retail Federation, too, initially opposed the exhibition, but changed its position.[29] Apparently the Smithsonian was induced to make some changes, including the removal of former Labor Secretary Robert Reich as a narrator for a video on the El Monte case and the addition of an advertisement boosting the industry.[30]

On the one hand, the apparel elite do not want to be seen as exploiters, but on the other hand, they do everything in their power to keep labor costs down to the bare minimum. They fought against the rise in the minimum wage, and cheered when the state of California got rid of the eight-hour-day provision for the payment of overtime, limiting overtime premiums to hours worked over and above forty per week. Metchek (of the CFA) and spokespeople for the Downtown Property Owners Association were outspoken antagonists of the city's living wage ordinance, by which it was proposed that all firms receiving city contracts, tax breaks, or other benefits, must pay their workers a so-called living wage that would bring families up to the federally defined poverty level.[31]

THE BOOTSTRAP MYTH

Apart from simple denial, many of the powerful people in the apparel industry rationalize extreme inequality by the belief that the industry is an engine of upward mobility. Theirs is a bootstrap ideology. They have mythologized the American Dream, seeing the United States as a land of opportunity, especially for new immigrants. In fact, they see the garment industry as one of the last bastions of this opportunity, given its relatively low-capital entry requirements. Over and over they repeated the idea that this is an entrepreneurial industry, where anyone can make it. Sidney Morse, then director of the CaliforniaMart, declared, "I'm for immigration. I think this is the greatest country in the world. I love it. You can make it here. So whether it's Jews coming over in the early 1900s, Vietnamese after the Vietnam War, Mexicans and Haitians now, I think it's great, it's super. If you have to take an entry level job, fine. We're here to help you make it. Can the Mexicans make it? Absolutely. The Jews came in the early 1900s, worked in factories, became contractors, then manufacturers. Koreans the same. Latinos will repeat this."[32]

Stanley Hirsh echoed this sentiment, recounting the story of "Josie," a former seamstress in one of his factories who now reportedly owns her own factory and has put two children through college. Hirsh blames the union (UNITE) for what he regards as the unfair image of sweatshops that pervades the industry. "We'll never get rid of that image," he said, "but it isn't true. We provide entry-level jobs for women, for Mexican women. These women have no other options: they can either do this or become dish washers. Working in a garment factory requires learning some skills. Maybe they are being taken advantage of, but they have a choice. No one is holding a gun to their heads. They come in at minimum wage, get some training, and can then put their children through college. It's the great American Dream."[33]

"If people work in bad conditions, that's deplorable," said Jonathan Bernstein. "But why do they do it? Because they need work. Few of those on welfare apply for jobs. If you want a job and want to work, and want an income to feed your family, there is tons you can do, like driving a cab and work for the city and many other things. I'm not saying there are enough jobs for full employment, but there are many that go unfilled. Just look in *California Apparel News* and count the ads that run continuously. They are always looking for people."[34] In the same interview, Bernstein offered some opinions about the corrupting effect of welfare that are widely shared in the industry, beliefs that welfare destroys the incen-

tive to work and get ahead. In this view, African Americans were generally seen as the prime victims of the welfare system, a fact that accounted
for their underrepresentation as workers in the industry. Bernstein dis-
missed the argument that undocumented immigrants were taking jobs
from United States citizens, primarily African Americans. "You keep hearing that illegals are taking work away from local people. I can show you
factory after factory with ads for employment, but those on welfare won't
come in and apply for them. People are blaming the people who *want* to
work. Few of those on welfare apply for jobs."

Few in the industry articulated the bootstrap philosophy better than
George Randall, the aggressive former chief executive office of Yes! Corporation. As the name suggests, Randall had an unwavering belief that,
with a positive attitude and hard work, anyone can be successful. He frequently cited his own experience—he dropped out of high school to join
the merchant marines and survived a Chinese prisoner of war camp during the Korean War—as proof. "I am a product of sweatshops, I created
them, I love them. Sweatshops kept families together, and they still do.
My wife put her kids in a cardboard box next to her in a sweatshop; now
she runs a $20 million business. You have to choose to be downtrodden.
Hard work, choice, that's the key. Anyone can make it; there are no ex-
cuses. I work twenty-four hours a day, seven days a week. But I also play
hard. Choice—don't ever forget about it. Everything else is bullshit."[35]

Rather than simply making an assertion about opportunities for upward mobility, the industry went on the offensive in 1998 to try to prove
it through a survey. Organized by the nonprofit Los Angeles Manufacturing Networks Initiative, and endorsed by the California Fashion Association, the project was planned as a survey of more than 500 manufacturers and about 200 contractors. Linda Wong, the director, said, "We
want to demonstrate to public agencies and elected officials and others
that there are career paths in the apparel industries above and beyond
sewing machine operators."[36] Jack Kyser, the chief economist of the Los
Angeles Economic Development Corporation, commented, "The truth
is many of the jobs in the apparel industry pay well. The salary scale ranges
from $20,000 to more than $100,000 annually, from patternmakers to
production managers, according to a 1996 study by Rebuild L.A. The
majority of jobs are indeed lower paying. The first rung on the ladder
isn't always easy, but opportunities for advancement do exist."[37] Or, Ilse
Metchek suggests, "ask any contractor where she started."[38]

We did ask just this question, and found that, although some contractors might have worked their way up from the factory floor, Metchek's
question is the wrong one to ask. Some contractors began as workers, but

this does not mean that sewing machine operators, of which there are more than 100,000 in Los Angeles, have any real prospects of becoming factory owners, much less manufacturers. Such opportunities may have existed for Jewish immigrants in the early decades of the twentieth century, and they may even exist for some Korean immigrants who, arriving with a college education and access to capital, want to learn the industry from the bottom up. The prospects for an undocumented Mexican immigrant in the late 1990s seem much bleaker. Nevertheless, a belief in upward mobility helps the wealthy businessman feel more comfortable about the chasm of inequality that separates him from the garment workers.

ANTIUNIONISM

Consonant with their ideology, and with their determination to keep labor costs to a minimum, members of the power elite hold a deep-seated opposition to the labor movement. They will do anything to prevent the unionization of their workers. Indeed, many garment manufacturers moved to Los Angeles from the east coast in order to escape unionization. Although some of them deny that they oppose unions, they engage in every imaginable form of union bashing and union busting when faced with a real organizing drive. For instance, the ILGWU (International Ladies' Garment Workers' Union) in 1995 helped workers organize a strike against a contractor named Good Times/Song of California. Members of the Apparel Industry Roundtable were uniformly supportive of the contractor and opposed to the union. After a protracted strike, the contractor decided to go out of business rather than deal with the union. At one roundtable meeting industry leaders commented on the tragedy this was for the workers, blaming the union for the workers' losing their jobs. After listening quietly for some time, one of the authors of this book (Bonacich) raised the possibility that the contractor did not have to go out of business but could, in fact, have signed a contract with the union. This statement was greeted with stunned silence, followed by arguments from all quarters that such a resolution was unthinkable. From that moment onward, she was treated as a pariah in the group.

The Smithsonian exhibit on American sweatshops brought out the antiunion sentiments of the industry in full force. At a meeting of the California Fashion Association, Jose Millan, the California Labor Commissioner, urged the industry to support the exhibit, adding that, "if the local industry does not step forward, the union could point to the silence of the industry and use it as a rallying cry." In response, Joe Rodriguez, of the Garment Contractors Association, said: "Sharing a platform with the union and giving them undue recognition and credibility is something I do not want to get involved with." The manufacturer Lonnie Kane is reported to have taken a similar stance, and Bernard Lax of the Coalition of Apparel Industries of California said: "It would be better for the industry to take a proactive approach. You take the wind out of the union's sails and they will have nothing to say."[39]

One of the most stridently antiunion spokesmen is Joel Kotkin, a frequent commentator in the press on the apparel industry. Commenting on UNITE's campaign to organize the workers of Guess? Inc., Kotkin wrote that "ultimately the current union campaign, while doing little to improve working conditions for garment workers, may unwittingly serve to break the back of an industry that has been one of the key routes of upward mobility for immigrant entrepreneurs and workers. The miracle that is the Los Angeles garment industry—where Farsi, Spanish, Arabic, Chinese, Korean, and Hebrew are heard as often as English—could end up a nightmare, with tens of thousands of workers thrown into the streets."[40]

In an interview Kotkin stated unambiguously that "the garment industry has no future as a unionized industry." He criticized Stu Silverstein, a reporter for the *Los Angeles Times,* for being a union front, and assumed that Robert Reich, then the Labor Secretary, was merely a mouthpiece for the AFL-CIO. As the grandson of a cutter, who later established his own garment manufacturing firm in New York, Kotkin clearly feels that he has the credentials to attack the union and any efforts by workers to organize themselves. His solution to the problem of sweatshops, like that of so many other industry leaders and analysts, is that the industry must fix its image.[41]

Another prominent antiunion spokesman is Stan Levy, previously general counsel for Guess? Inc., and chairman of the Labor Committee of the California Fashion Association. (It is noteworthy that the Labor Committee does not have a single representative, either worker or union official, of labor on it.) Levy, who is also a rabbi of a Jewish Renewal congregation, wrote an article entitled "Prophets and Profits: The Search for Jewish Ethics in Business and Labor," for *Sh'ma.*[42] Levy contended in the article that UNITE does not have the interests of garment workers at heart, and that the people who really care for labor are the business owners.

Political Clout

The power elite of the apparel industry has access to politicians and political administrators in a way that garment workers clearly do not. When they are dissatisfied, when they want change, when they seek to influence policy, they can readily contact people in positions of political power and have their concerns attended to. For example, in its advertisements, the California Fashion Association claims that:

> CFA members met with Sacramento legislators, Governor Wilson, Senators Lockyer, Calderon, Johnson, Solis and Speaker Bustamante, and Labor Commissioner Jose Millan.

> We met with our federal representatives in Washington, D.C. and L.A.; Senators Feinstein [and] Boxer, [and Representatives] Shadegg, Waxman, Sherman, Royball-Allard.

> And city politicians including Richard Alatorre and Mayor Riordan.

In July 1997, the Association joined a delegation to Washington, D.C., that met with Secretary of Labor Alexis Herman and Senator Dianne Feinstein and were able to hold an impromptu meeting with House Speaker Newt Gingrich. Among other topics, they expressed concern that the Department of Labor's enforcement methods were "unnecessarily placing at risk a number of well-paying entry-level jobs."[43]

Having political influence is, in part, rooted in campaign contributions. Some of the leaders in the apparel industry in Los Angeles have been generous contributors. They give to city, state, and national political campaigns. We do not want to suggest that contributing to a campaign buys favors in any direct sense; there is no necessary quid pro quo. A campaign contributor cannot ensure that his case will be favorably viewed in proportion to the amount of money he gave. Still, contributing money does get one a foot in the door. A generous contributor can call a political representative and at least expect his interests to be listened to, even if he isn't guaranteed a favorable vote. We made no systematic attempt to collect information about campaign contributions and most of the information we did acquire was collected in the earlier phases of our research. Certainly more research is warranted on this topic. Nevertheless, we present what we did find out.

Stanley Hirsh is one of the largest campaign contributors in Los Angeles, especially to the Democratic Party and its candidates. He has given generously to national as well as local politicians. In a front-page article in the *Los Angeles Times* it was stated:

When Democratic Senator John Kerry of Massachusetts needed money for his 1990 reelection campaign, a friend asked Studio City, California, garment manufacturer Stanley Hirsh to put on a fund-raiser. When Republican George

Bush met with a small group of Los Angeles movers and shakers at the Four Seasons Hotel during his 1988 presidential campaign, Hirsh was there. . . . Hirsh is one of the financial magnets who draws politicians from all over the United States to Los Angeles, particularly the Westside and the Hollywood Hills. He is a major campaign contributor—"a $1,000 hit"—in a city loaded with wealthy, activist givers . . . "We have a book at the house that my wife keeps with records of annual votes by candidates that we follow," said Hirsh, a Democrat. "A lot of it is how they vote on Israel, a lot of it is a liberal democratic bent and whether they are pro-choice.[44]

The *Los Angeles Times* did an analysis of 1989–90 federal campaign contributions for the direct support of candidates in four congressional districts, using the records of the Federal Election Commission. Hirsh was the top contributor, giving $70,600. His wife, Anita, contributed another $28,250. Hirsh was one of twenty-three Californians who violated the federal campaign contribution limit of $25,000 in 1991 by giving $28,300. Anita joined him on this list with a contribution of $26,500. Hirsh also exceeded the limit in 1990.[45] It is no surprise that he is a frequent member of a talley, the Hall of Fame, kept by the *California Apparel News,* which, in 1993, described Hirsh: "A forty-five year apparel veteran, Hirsh has been the voice of the garment industry at City Council meetings for several years. His activism was recognized in July when he was appointed to the board of commissioners of the Community Redevelopment Agency. Charged with enhancing the garment industry's image, he is the only apparel manufacturer and property owner (most notably of the Cooper Building) to hold a city government post."[46] Hirsh was appointed to the Community Redevelopment Agency by Mayor Bradley, and subsequently became chairman.

In 1992 William Mow, the founder and chief executive officer of Bugle Boy, contributed $63,350, earning him the distinction of being at the top of a list of Californians who exceeded the limit.[47] At the state level, Guess? Inc. contributed $145,000 to John Garamendi, the California insurance commissioner and, later, Democratic gubernatorial candidate between 1991 and 1994. This made Guess Garamendi's second largest contributor. According to the *Los Angeles Times,*

It was as insurance commissioner that Garamendi met one of his biggest benefactors, Maurice Marciano, chairman of Guess? Inc of Los Angeles. Marciano was distressed at the runaway cost of workers' compensation. Concluding that he was a victim of fraudulent claims by some employees, Marciano met with Garamendi in 1991. Garamendi, who has authority to investigate workers' compensation fraud, formed an antifraud unit. Now, Marciano said, his workers' compensation costs have been cut by half, and he gives Garamendi much of the credit. . . . Marciano has shown his appreciation. Since 1991, Guess? has donated $95,000 to Garamendi. When Garamendi asked for more money last year, Marciano wrote out a check for $50,000. It is a loan. If he loses the primary, Garamendi must repay it. If he wins the primary, Marciano said, he will convert it to a donation.[48]

Guess also gave $170,000 (the largest single contribution to any politician in the state in 1992) to the campaign of Gil Garcetti, who was running for Los Angeles district attorney.[49] In 1994, for legislation that was signed by the governor, Pete Wilson, Guess drafted language that changed the status of counterfeiting from a misdemeanor to a felony. With the passage of the "three strikes you're out" rule, deputy district attorneys were reluctant to view counterfeiting as a genuine felony and were not pressing charges. It was reported that Mr. Clark, a deputy district attorney, was contacted by Stan Levy, who was the in-house counsel at Guess:

Clark admits he's spent time with Guess? attorneys, working out mutual strategy against counterfeiters. "Stan Levy was the one who sort of took my hand and said, 'Here's what you have to do', " Clark says. . . . In fact, it is unlikely that the district attorney would prosecute any of the cases without Guess? Guess? investigators do all the legwork, from drafting affidavits for [Los Angeles Police Department] officers to obtain search warrants, to rounding up witnesses for the prosecution. Guess? even stores the seized goods for free. "We're having the private sector do our work for us," one law-enforcement official laments. . . . Once the Guess? cases come into the [deputy attorney]'s office for criminal filings, "The word is you just rubber-stamp them," says one deputy familiar with the cases. Guess?, it seems is not content with the present intimate relationship. It has pressed recently to create a special unit with the district attorney's office dedicated to counterfeit prosecution. Funded by: Guess?[50]

In March 1996, Clark was carrying a caseload of sixteen counterfeit cases, three of which involved Guess.[51]

Guess also contributed $25,000 to the campaign for Proposition 226 in 1998, an initiative that tried to prevent unions from giving campaign contributions without polling their members. It is widely believed that it was aimed at crippling the ability of the labor movement to have a voice in California politics. The proposition was voted down.

A member of the Los Angeles city council gave us her assessment of how influence is exerted by the garment landlords. "There is a campaign contribution limit of $500. What people like Hirsh do to bypass this limit is to serve as fund-raisers. They speak to their friends. They promise the candidate that they will raise $20,000. Landlords can raise money from their tenants by asking them to contribute $100 to a campaign as part of the cost of doing business. They use established relationships. A person like Hirsh gives to charities and is probably active in his temple. He is known as a good person and has established a broad network. He can call on loyalty to get his network to give."[52]

Apart from campaign contributions, powerful members of the apparel industry could also exercise clout over politics in a more global sense. By being rich and powerful, by being part of a major industry in the city, they have an ability to gain the attention of political officials, even when they have not given them any money. Threats to relocate out of Los Angeles or California bring the quick attention of politicians. The California Fashion Association and the Downtown Property Owners Association both received substantial support from the city. In general, they are able to exert political influence on a number of different issues. The development of the Broadway Trade Center and expansion of the garment district, and the tenants' revolt at the CaliforniaMart furnish two examples.

ZONING WARS

In 1991 a proposal was put forward to change an old, unoccupied building owned by the May Company on Broadway into a center of garment manufacturing that would house 600 businesses and 7,000 workers. The problem was that the building fell a little to the west of the garment district, in an area not zoned for apparel manufacturing. The proposal was put forward by Art Snyder, who had been a member of the city council and who represented two men who wanted to buy the building and convert it. The proposal was strongly opposed by some of the landlords, especially Hirsh and Gerry, who maintained that the district needed a coherent location. It was, however, clear to many of the people we interviewed that personal interest was also at stake: Landlords in the garment district would suffer intensified competition if the Broadway Trade Center were developed. Given that their buildings were not full, a result, in part, of the recession, these landlords did not want to lose more tenants.

The city council split on the issue, with a majority supporting the expansion and conversion of the May Company building. One city councilman, Joel Wachs, opposed the proposal, a position appreciated by Hirsh, who later became Wachs's campaign finance chairman in his losing bid to become mayor. Another council member, Ruth Galanter, received campaign donations of $500 each from Stan and Anita Hirsh, but she voted in favor of the project. "Stanley Hirsh doesn't speak to me now," she told us, "because, not only did I vote against him; I spoke out loudly about it."[53] Because Galanter's district did not cover the garment district, Hirsh's interests were not that important to her. The mayor, Tom Bradley, eventually vetoed the project, reportedly because of the influence of key garment-district landlords.[54]

In August 1992, Mayor Bradley and a councilmember, Rita Walters, proposed an expansion of the garment district west to Olive Street. They acknowledged that hundreds of garment shops were occupying office buildings along a one-mile stretch of Spring Street, in buildings that had once housed bankers, attorneys, and real estate agents, but were now filled with garment plants, often without the proper permits. The proposal aimed almost to double the existing 2,300-acre district, while requiring new safety policies for workers and buildings there, including a limit of one sewing machine per 100 square feet, the acquisition of five-year renewable conditional-use permits, the provision of adequate parking for employees, and compliance with city health, fire, and building regulations.[55] The illegal expansion of garment factories had occurred while the Ninth District was represented by Gilbert Lindsay, who rarely opposed plans to open garment shops in vacated buildings because he felt that the empty buildings attracted criminal activity. He did not enforce compliance with city codes because he felt that the shops gave life to the area. As might be expected, garment district landlords objected. "Stanley Hirsh, who owns several buildings in the garment district, objected to the mayor's proposal. 'I don't hear a solution, I hear absolution for violators,' Hirsh said. 'I'm shocked because there was no consultation on these issues. The problem is we don't have enough police, firefighters, or anything else to spread the garment district out.' "[56] We do not know what happened to this proposal, but suspect it died, in part because the garment-factory owners themselves had no interest in complying with the stringent conditions about spacing.

A TENANTS' REVOLT

In the early 1990s, some of the tenants of the California-Mart threatened to move out of the Mart and out of downtown. The tenants, it should be recalled, are wholesalers of clothing who run showrooms that buyers for retailers visit and where they place orders. The Mart has two major types of tenants: manufacturers' corporate showrooms and independent showrooms that are run by tenants who show and sell several lines.

The tenants' principal grievance concerned rent. Their rent of between $2.85 and $3.40 per square foot was higher than their sales could sustain. Moreover, given that southern California was suffering from a recession, real estate prices had plummeted, and (according to Langdon Reider Strategic Real Estate Services, a firm that specializes in tenants' issues) the Mart's rents were out of line with downtown real estate prices. As a monopoly of sorts, the Mart could set its rents on a noncompetitive basis. Of course, the tenants did not simply pay for the space. They also benefited from (and were charged for) a variety of promotional schemes orchestrated by the Mart owners valued at $3 million in 1992.

The tenants complained that the Mart's promotional efforts were inadequate and they objected to the rising number of cash-and-carry operations in the Mart (retailers who displayed premade goods, generally low in quality and price, that they sold in bulk to buyers). This system damaged the wholesalers, who required time to arrange for the production of ordered garments. Sidney Morse had invited the cash-and-carry merchants in because the building had too high a vacancy rate.[57] Leonard guessed that they occupied as much as 20 percent of the space. The cash-and-carry problem was not limited to the Mart itself. Such operations were sprouting up in the surrounding neighborhood as well. "Much to the chagrin of garment wholesalers, the neighborhood [around the Mart] has been transformed into an ethnic bazaar, enlivened by Korean, Chinese, and Latin American entrepreneurs. . . . The wholesalers feel besieged."[58]

Another grievance of the tenants, one over which Morse had little control, was the location of the Mart. Tenants complained that buyers hated to come to Los Angeles. They hadn't liked the city even before the riots, but now they were afraid to come. The garment district faced many problems. It was run down, dirty, had many homeless people, suffered from crime, lacked adequate public transportation, was congested, and had costly parking. Buyers could choose to go elsewhere, to Atlanta or Dallas, for example. They could not perhaps, avoid New York, as the fashion center of the nation, however uncomfortable it might be, but many could avoid Los Angeles.

Underlying these grievances lay two issues. First, the changes in the industry, particularly the concentration in retailing, the rise in discount stores, and the decline in department stores, were putting a squeeze on the old system of wholesaling. According to Harry Barnard, an analyst of the industry, "Retail buyers no longer work like shoppers with a million dollars." Often stores went directly to vendors to arrange production, reducing buyers to the status of "merchandise-flow directors" who merely worked out the shipping and delivery. And many buyers made the sales representatives come to them.[59] In sum, the very concept of a wholesale apparel mart was under attack, or at least declining seriously.

Second, the equity loan taken out by the Mart's owners in 1987, when they cashed out for $250 million at the height of the real estate boom in Los Angeles, had come back to haunt them. As Joshua Leonard put it, the owners treated the Mart as a "cash cow." Although the economy had slowed and real estate values in southern California plummeted, the Mart's owners were still saddled with paying the mortgage. In the view of many of their tenants, this was what induced them to fill the building with cash-and-carry operations and to charge high rents. Needless to say, the tenants felt resentful.

In April 1992, two weeks before the riots, some of the tenants, led by Jeffrey Krinsky, formed an association, officially called the 110 E. 9th Street Tenants Association. Krinsky was assisted by Joshua Leonard, a certified public accountant with Langdon Reider.[60] Tenants' associations had already formed in the Dallas and Atlanta marts, and had won concessions. The association consisted predominantly of the owners of independent showrooms; the manufacturers, who owned the corporate showrooms with the bigger brand names, tended to stay out of the fray. Although the initial goal of the association was to get lower rents and better conditions, the members also saw an opportunity to break their leases and relocate out of downtown. Sid Morse would not deal with the association; he would not even recognize it. Instead, he negotiated rent reduction deals with individual tenants. In Morse's view, the Mart's hefty rents reflected the equally hefty costs of the services it provided; in his words, "we are not an office building. We are a piece of real estate with a major business attached to it."[61]

"If," said Leonard, "we had been able to come to an agreement with Sidney, as a union, [Langdon Reider] would have received a commission. But Sidney won't deal with unions. He is following the book on how to avoid a union, but as a result he has antagonized many of his tenants." Leonard told us that, following the individual negotiations, Morse dropped the rent as much as 30 or 40 percent (to between $2.00 and $2.40 per square foot), reduced parking costs by 20 percent, and lowered assessments for operating costs. Langdon Reider made no money from its efforts, despite achieving this gain for the tenants, but the firm continued pushing for relocation which, if successful, would bring it a commission.

The tenants' association issued a request for proposals in 1992, resulting in three detailed proposals for new marts by two of the most prominent developers in Los Angeles. Several sites were considered, including

Fashion City in Hawthorne, the Water Garden in Santa Monica, Wilshire Place near the museums, and the Hughes Aircraft site. The mayor, Tom Bradley, called an emergency meeting when he and the Community Redevelopment Agency received a copy of the request for proposals.[62] According to Jack Lumer, about fifteen people attended the meeting, including a representative from the police department, and the landlords Stanley Hirsh, Jack Needleman, Arthur Gerry, Sid Morse, and Lumer himself. Out of this came a joint public and private effort to improve the garment district. The landlords donated $7,500 for the purchase of nine bicycles and police uniforms for a police bicycle patrol, to be headquartered in the Mart and cover the thirty-block area east of Broadway between Pico and Seventh Streets. It was also decided to close off some alleys to provide more security for the loading and unloading of trucks. These efforts were supported by the Central City Association, which contributed $8,000 toward hiring homeless workers and others to assist in the cleanup.[63]

As the time for voting on the proposals for a new mart drew near, Mayor Bradley held a press conference to publicize the cleanup and law-enforcement efforts and the reduction in rents and parking fees that had begun in the summer.[64] Nevertheless, in December 1992, the tenants voted to move to the Water Garden, a project developed by Jerry Snyder of J. H. Snyder Co.[65] Then nearly a year went by and financing for the project was not secured. Meanwhile, Comstock, Crosser, and Hickey, the company from Manhattan Beach that planned to develop the site in Hawthorne, submitted an improved bid.[66] That site was sponsored in part by Mission Land Co., the land-development subsidiary of the giant electric utility company, Southern California Edison, which owned the land on which the project would be built. Edison stood to benefit by supplying electrical power to the new facility.[67] Given that Edison was also sponsoring the Apparel Industry Roundtable to promote the industry in Los Angeles, the utility found itself in an awkward situation. After embarrassing revelations, Edison withdrew from the project.

The city became involved again. According to a report in *Women's Wear Daily*, "The CaliforniaMart and Los Angeles city officials were not about to stand by and do nothing. Within two weeks of his swearing-in, Mayor Richard Riordan of Los Angeles met at the Mart with industry heavyweights including executives from B.U.M Equipment, Yes! Clothing, Karen Kane, the Textile Association of Los Angeles, the Fashion Institute of Design and Merchandising, and Mart general partner Sidney Morse. The discussion included ways to improve security and downtown parking."[68]

On 17 November 1993, CaliforniaMart officials announced that they

had defaulted on their $250-million loan from Equitable, and were at-
tempting to restructure the mortgage. Commercial real estate values had
dropped by between 30 and 50 percent. "Almost all [landlords who had
their] commercial real estate refinanced in 1988–1989 got loans at 80 percent of the appraised value. . . . They have seen the property markets substantially decline since then, and today the value of the property is generally less than the amount of the loan."[69]

In the end the tenants' movement fizzled, possibly because it had
achieved the desired rent reductions. Had it succeeded in moving the tenants out of downtown, both the Morses and Equitable would have suffered a substantial loss. According to Joshua Leonard, the Mart property
was worth about $300 million, or between $200 and $250 per square foot.
If the tenants had moved, the value of the building would have dropped
drastically. The City of Los Angeles would also have been seriously affected both directly (by the reduction of taxes) and indirectly (by untold
damage to the garment district and all that it attracted). According to a
report in the *Los Angeles Business Journal,* "Cal Mart is a key factor in downtown L.A.'s economy. It attracts 100,000 wholesale buyers a year to downtown, and they tend to stay at local hotels and dine in nearby eateries.
More that 8,000 people are employed in the Cal Mart building. Moreover, Cal Mart anchors a part of downtown—the Ninth-and-Spring-
streets area—that is troubled, faltering between being merely seedy or declining into an urban netherworld of hopelessness, vice, and crime."[70]
Note that the Downtown Property Owners Association was formed, in
part, as a reaction to the CaliforniaMart tenants' revolt, as well as to other
contemporaneous events. Helping the association was another way in
which the city government involved itself in solving the problems of the
apparel industry in Los Angeles.

Because of their wealth and power, apparel industry leaders are able to
gain access to the political process in a way that is unavailable to the masses
of garment workers. While they are not a particularly powerful segment
of the business class, they nevertheless are immensely powerful relative
to the poor immigrants whom they employ. Workers not only lack access
to power, they also lack the means to shape public debate in a way that
might change the system of apparel production altogether. This power
discrepancy plays an important role in perpetuating inequality in the industry. And it helps to explain how sweatshops flourish in the midst of
affluence.

PART II
Labor

CHAPTER 5
Contractors

THE APPAREL INDUSTRY MOVES TO END SWEATSHOPS

Reprinted by permission of *Fort Worth Star-Telegram*.

Almost all of the actual production of garments in Los Angeles occurs in contracting shops. Apparel manufacturers, many of whom at one time made their garments in-house, now almost invariably contract out for labor to thousands of small factories spread out across southern California. Most engage in garment assembly or sewing. A smaller number perform other functions, such as cutting, laundering, or finishing. A few manufacturers cut the garments in-house and use contractors for the remainder of the production, but generally, all the labor-intensive elements of production are contracted out. It is at the contracting level that sweatshops have reemerged and are flourishing.

Several people writing about garment contracting have considered it to be an example of ethnic or immigrant entrepreneurship. The ability of immigrants to form their own small businesses and achieve some upward mobility has been praised, sometimes with a hidden or not so hidden message that other minorities ought to emulate the methods of these entrepreneurs as a way of escaping poverty. Garment contracting is interpreted as a positive example, a success story for immigrants in their pursuit of assimilation and wealth.[1]

The question of how and why members of particular ethnic groups are more able than others are to get into this line of business is certainly of interest to us, but we do not view the phenomenon through the same rose-tinted lenses. Rather than use the theoretical framework of ethnic entrepreneurship, we prefer to view these businesses as an example of the phenomenon of middleman minorities; we view garment contracting in terms of its function for the apparel industry as a whole. Contracting is explained not primarily as a product of entrepreneurial immigrants, but as a business that responds to the demands of the industry. Contractors serve as middlemen between manufacturers and workers, helping to control labor on behalf of the manufacturers. That such a position requires entrepreneurial assets is undeniable, but those assets cannot in themselves explain the peculiar niche occupied by garment contractors, nor the various forms of social hostility that swirl around them.

The Contracting System

The contracting system provides at least five major benefits to apparel manufacturers, which is probably why it evolved: It externalizes risk, it lowers the cost of labor, it enables manufacturers to evade moral as well as legal responsibility for violations of labor laws, and it helps to thwart unionization. These benefits have implications for the way contracting is organized.

EXTERNALIZING RISK

Employed only when they are needed, contractors do not have long-term contracts with manufacturers. This enables the manufacturer to expand and contract his production with seasonal shifts in demand or with the popularity of his styles. If he needs to increase production, he increases the number of contractors he works with. If he needs to decrease production, he stops sending work to some contractors.

Manufacturers are thus surrounded by layers of contractors: those whom they use most regularly and those to whom they turn only when they need to expand production. At times the expansion occurs through subcontracting: The contractor himself arranges for the extra production capacity with another contractor. Because of the instability of the work, most contractors, unless they are extremely close to one economically strong manufacturer, try to work for more than one manufacturer. The contractor must juggle the schedules of a number of manufacturers to maintain a more or less steady flow of production through the factory.

Ultimately, the externalization of risk by the manufacturers is passed on to the workers by the contractors. If the flow of work slows down, they lay off some of their workers. If work picks up, they hire more people. Workers in contracting shops have no job security, and often suffer from continual, forced mobility from one job to the next. The contracting system means that the real employers of the garment workers, the manufacturers, do not have to bear responsibility for the workers' employment or unemployment. The workers become disposable factors of production to be used only when needed. The risks of instability of work associated with apparel are thus borne by the workers and the contractors, not by the manufacturers.

LOWERING THE COST OF LABOR

Apparel manufacturers think of contracting as labor. To them, the cost of contracting is the same as the cost of labor. Contracting out the labor lowers labor costs because several so-called independent contractors compete for the work by underbidding one another. Each attempts to offer the manufacturer a better deal than the next guy can, bidding down the price of labor. Manufacturers themselves use this competition to keep labor costs as low as possible. They will present a contractor with a low price on a take-it-or-leave-it basis, claiming that another contractor down the street will always do the work for less.

Offshore production is merely another form of contracting. The typically lower cost of labor among offshore contractors can be used by manufacturers to pressure local contractors to lower their prices. The possibility of resorting to ever cheaper labor sources around the globe serves as a constant threat to local contractors to cut their costs to the barest minimum.

EVADING MORAL RESPONSIBILITY

Manufacturers claim that they have no responsibility for the conditions in the factories and that, if laws are violated in those factories, it is solely the fault of the contractors, who have chosen to break the law. We argue that the assertion that contractors are completely independent entities is fallacious.

First of all, the manufacturer never gives up title to the clothing that is being sewn by the contractors. The goods always belong to the manufacturer. They are not sold to the contractor. The manufacturer is only buying a service—the provision of labor. The contractors are essentially labor contractors for the manufacturers.

Second, the manufacturers maintain considerable oversight over the activities that go on in the contracting shops. They send quality-control inspectors constantly, sometimes daily. They oversee all aspects of production and demand that the work be redone if it does not meet their specifications. Essentially, they manage the production. The contractor has only to employ the workers and keep them working to the satisfaction of the manufacturer; he disciplines the workforce for the manufacturer.

Third, contractors lack true independence because they are unable to bargain effectively over the amount they are paid. Although the legal assumption is that the contract between manufacturer and contractor is freely undertaken by two equal, negotiating parties, in fact most manufacturers have much more power in the relationship than do the contractors. The contractor is usually offered a nonnegotiable price because the manufacturer threatens to take the work elsewhere if he will not accept that price. The low prices paid by the manufacturers to the contractors set the stage for violations of labor standards in this industry.

EVADING LEGAL RESPONSIBILITY

Manufacturers are very careful to preserve their separation from the contractors because they do not want to be held legally responsible for violations of labor standards. They do not want to be seen as joint employers, and industry leaders have fought fiercely against any efforts to define them as such. This evasion of responsibility is demonstrated on the standard order form (the so-called Adams Form) used by manufacturers for placing work orders with garment contractors. Several items printed on the back of the form deal with the issue of legal responsibility:

5. Contractor acknowledges that it is an independent contractor and not an employee of MANUFACTURER, and that it is contractor's sole responsibility to comply with all City, County, State and Federal laws applicable to employers. Contractor expressly represents that

all persons who perform work for the contractor under this agreement are solely employees of the contractor and not employees of the MANUFACTURER.

9. In the event that contractor is found to be in violation of any City, County, State or Federal law, contractor agrees to indemnify, hold harmless, and defend MANUFACTURER from any liability that may be imposed on MANUFACTURER as a result of such violation.

14. Contractor agrees to indemnify, hold harmless, and defend MANUFACTURER from any liability that may be imposed on MANUFACTURER arising out of any claim made by an employee of contractor against the MANUFACTURER.

The repeated and emphasized language shows how important maintaining this distance is to the manufacturer. We believe that the avoidance of legal responsibility for labor standards is a major reason for the proliferation of contracting in apparel manufacturing, and helps to explain the return of sweatshops in this industry. As we shall see, however, in Chapter 8, despite the efforts of manufacturers to draw a legal divide between themselves and the contractors, the United States Department of Labor has found a way to break through and force the manufacturers to take at least some responsibility.

THWARTING UNIONIZATION

A final advantage of the contracting system to manufacturers is that it inhibits union organizing. The contracting system could well have been designed as an antiunion device. The workers in any single contracting shop cannot win a meaningful union contract, even if 100 percent of them wants a union, because the manufacturer will simply remove his work from that shop and it will go out of business. Workers can win the battle, but they will surely lose the war. Contractors can truthfully tell their workers that, if they unionize, their shop will be boycotted by almost all manufacturers and will not receive the work it needs to remain in business. The contracting system enables manufacturers to distance themselves from any contracting shops that show any signs of labor trouble. This applies to the industry in Los Angeles, but also it extends offshore. If garment workers in another country show any signs of militancy, apparel manufacturers are likely to look for some new country, where the labor force is more docile or suppressed.[2]

Contracting occurs beneath a shroud of secrecy. Apparel manufacturers treat their lists of contractors, both here and abroad, as proprietary information that is unavailable to the public. Consequently, workers who are employed by the same manufacturers cannot easily locate their fellow workers in other branches of the same production system. Usually, they have no idea how many workers are employed by a particular manufacturer, and would not begin to know how to find them. The workforce is fragmented, not only in terms of location, but also at the most fundamental level of being aware of one another's existence. This secrecy is a tremendous shield against union organizing. Needless to say, manufacturers fight with all their might against the removal of this shield.

Because manufacturers keep shifting their work depending on seasons, styles, demand, and other factors, they may maintain a core group of stable contractors, but can shift production continuously at the periphery. Thus, not only do workers in the same production system not know one another, but also their membership in that production system may keep changing. On top of that, a particular contracting factory is likely to make garments for more than one label, so any one worker may be a member of a number of production systems simultaneously. One can see the difficulties of organizing in such an unstable environment.

Unionized workers are more expensive. The contractor does not generate enough surplus to afford much of an increase to the workers, even if they should win a struggle with him. The real profit centers of the industry are the manufacturers and retailers.[3] A manufacturer may be able to afford a union contract that would drive a contractor out of business. But manufacturers fight against the notion that they are joint employers, not only because they do not want to be held legally liable for contractor violations, but also because they do not want to pay for a union contract. They want to keep the contractors at arm's length, maintaining the fiction that they are completely independent businesses, as a shield against the claim that they should pay union wages to the people who actually sew their clothes. In sum, the contracting system is of great advantage to apparel manufacturers for one underlying reason: it maintains a low-wage labor force. No better system has yet been devised to keep workers fragmented and powerless.

Middleman Minorities

In some places the ethnicity of garment contractors and the workers they employ is the same. For example, in New York and San

Francisco, Chinese contractors employ Chinese workers; in England, Pakistani contractors employ Pakistani garment workers; in the Netherlands, Turkish contractors employ Turkish workers. Shared ethnicity permits paternalistic relationships to develop that partly mute or mask exploitation. For example, owners may allow female employees the flexibility to leave early and pick up their children from school. They may work alongside their employees, even helping workers to establish themselves as entrepreneurs in their own contracting shops. Of course, ethnic homogeneity does not guarantee paternalistic treatment: in the Thai slave shop in El Monte, contractors and workers alike were from Thailand.

The apparel industry in Los Angeles takes a different ethnic form: Asians comprise the largest group of contractors operating the largest factories and most garment workers are Latino.[4] This ethnic difference creates a particular dynamic. The contractors play the role of a middleman minority, outsiders to a hierarchical social system and serving as go-betweens, enabling the elites to avoid direct contact with the dominated classes or racial groups.[5] Jews in Eastern Europe, Chinese in Southeast Asia, and Indians in South and East Africa are typically groups targeted by both sides as foreigners or strangers. The elites find them very useful for doing their dirty work and serving as shock absorbers, but are willing to discard them if social tension rises. Koreans in Los Angeles clearly played this kind of role in setting up shops in the poor, racially oppressed neighborhoods of Los Angeles. They also bore the brunt of the civil unrest in 1992, when a disproportionate number of Korean stores were burned and looted. Police failed to provide them with adequate protection, perhaps because they were a racially distinctive group. Had rioters attacked white-owned businesses, one wonders whether the protection would have been more animated.[6]

The garment industry in Los Angeles appears to present a classic middleman minority situation. Largely white-owned manufacturers employ primarily Asian contractors to control and exploit Latino labor. The contractors thus serve as a buffer for the manufacturers. This would be true even if the contractors were not of a distinctive ethnicity. That they are is an advantage to the manufacturers, who can frame the conflict in racial or ethnic terms, blaming the contractors for ethnically stereotyped characteristics. Manufacturers will often blame sweatshops on "the Asians" or "the Koreans," who, it is claimed, do not know the law, or come from a culture where disobeying the law is rampant, or are harsh people who treat workers badly. This kind of argument enables the manufacturers to distance themselves still further from violations of labor standards and to reinforce their claim that they cannot be held responsible for sweat-shop conditions.[7]

The ethnic differences between the contractors and workers discourage paternalism in apparel factories in Los Angeles. Contracting shops are typically run on very businesslike principles. The noneconomic values that can intrude when a contractor employs people from his own community, and when he is likely to be judged by that community for how he treats his employees, are for the most part absent. Not only do most contractors not belong to the same ethnic community as their workers do, but also they often do not even speak the same language. The social distance between them is immense, and contributes to the workers' sense of maltreatment and exploitation. Meanwhile, most workers never see the manufacturer, and have only the vaguest sense of who he or she might be. The person workers deal with every day is the contractor, who is the immediate source of oppression and therefore most likely to be hated. Among Latino garment workers, anti-Asian sentiments are rampant. Contractors are referred to generically as *chinos* or *koreanos,* and are described in very disparaging terms.

It is easy to see the benefit of such a regime to the manufacturers. The Asian contractors receive all the blame for a system that oppresses Latino garment workers to benefit largely Anglo- and Jewish-owned companies. The manufacturers keep their hands clean by never directly oppressing the workers; they let their Asian contractors do their dirty work for them. Should workers in a particular factory rise up against their boss, the manufacturer will abandon him without any misgivings.

Garment Contractors in Los Angeles

Studying contractors is made difficult by the fact that the distinction between manufacturers and contractors is rarely drawn in any of the available official data. They are usually lumped together under a single designation, making it almost impossible to assess the number of either.[8] For example, in a report issued in May 1998, the United States Department of Labor stated that there are 2,000 manufacturers and 5,100 production shops (i.e., contractors) in Los Angeles.[9] Apparently the latter figure came from a newspaper article that cited statistics obtained from the state of California Employment Development Department (EDD).[10] However, the EDD figure, which was for 1996, covered all the apparel firms enumerated in the county, including both manufacturers and contractors. If there are truly 2,000 manufacturers, which is questionable, then there were only 3,100 contractors in 1996. Of course, EDD is unable to count the extensive but unknowable underground contractor economy.

The Department of Labor used state registration lists[11] to draw a sample of contractors. They found 5,648 garment firms registered in January 1998 in Los Angeles, Orange, Ventura, Riverside, and San Bernardino Counties. However, about 5,100 (90 percent) were located in Los Angeles County. In verifying their random sample of 129 firms, they found that 59 were out of business or not engaged in manufacturing, an ominous statistic suggesting a very high turnover. Of the remaining seventy firms, sixty-five were contractors and five were manufacturers, suggesting that about 90 percent of registered firms are contractors rather than manufacturers. This leads us to an estimate that there are about 4,500 registered contractors in Los Angeles.

Regardless of the statistics, there seems little doubt that the number of contractors is growing. According to EDD, the number of apparel firms (manufacturers and contractors) in Los Angeles County grew from 3,669 in 1990, to 4,425 in 1993, and to 5,070 in 1996. Moreover, the state Labor Commissioner, Jose Millan, reported that the state was receiving between thirty-five and sixty new applications for apparel registration per month, most of them from southern California. Millan did think that some of the increase came from previously unrecorded underground factories that were driven to become legitimate by increased enforcement efforts, but he did not deny that many of the new registrants must be new companies.[12]

Another source, *County Business Patterns,*[13] lists 4,238 firms in SIC 23[14] in 1996, the latest available year. Contractors are not distinguished from manufacturers, but these data are helpful in providing firm size as measured by number of employees. In 1996, 69 percent of the enumerated apparel firms had between 1 and 19 employees, 26 percent had between 20 and 99, 5 percent had between 100 and 499, and 0.3 percent had 500 or more. We cannot estimate the average size accurately from such data, but it is evident that most garment firms, including contractors, are *small* businesses. In its sample study the Department of Labor found that the average contractor's shop employed thirty-three people in 1998.

In 1991 we created our own data set of contractors, based mainly on state licenses. The state maintains an up-to-date list of these registered businesses, sometimes coding them to indicate whether they are manufacturers, contractors, or other kinds of enterprise, and including their addresses and the names of their owners. We combined these data with information from several other sources, including membership lists of contractors' associations, and the small number of contractors covered by Dun & Bradstreet. We came up with a data set of 3,629 garment contractors in Los Angeles County in 1991, which we then used to analyze the ethnicity and geographical location of contractors.[15] We sought to establish the ethnicity of owners by using a computer to match the names in our data set with a dictionary of ethnic names.[16] Zip codes were used to establish location. Together these two pieces of information give us a portrait of who runs the garment contracting shops and where they are concentrated. No doubt a significant number of underground contractors escaped our attention. Moreover, the data were compiled in 1991, so changes have certainly occurred since then. Nevertheless, we present our findings as a snapshot of at least licensed contractors at that time.

ETHNICITY

Garment contracting is almost exclusively the province of immigrants, who find the business attractive because its capital requirements are relatively low, affording a point of entry for those who aspire to the American Dream of entrepreneurial success. According to John Y. Cho, the general manager of the Korean-American Garment Industry Association in 1993, it cost between $30,000 and $50,000 to start a sewing factory with twenty or thirty machines.[17] Of course, it is possible to start a sewing operation in one's own home or garage for far less.

In Table 4 we present the results of our ethnic analysis. Although they come from all over the globe, in 1991 half (49.5 percent) of the contractors were Asian and nearly three out of ten (29.3 percent) were Latinos. Although Koreans account for only 23 percent of the contractors, Korean-owned factories are almost twice as large on average as are other factories, and therefore account for about half of the employment in the garment industry in Los Angeles.[18] Koreans have also shown the ability to branch out into other sectors of the industry. For example, as of 1994, there were 478 Korean jobbers (middlemen who sell irregular goods, end lots, and garments that are not sold through the regular channels) in downtown Los Angeles. There is also a Korean Garment Wholesalers Association. The Korean business community provides both backward links (supplies, machine rentals, and business services), and forward links (retail outlets and indoor swap meets) for Korean garment contractors. This level of vertical integration has no parallel in the other immigrant communities, though it used to be a feature of the old Jewish establishment.

Table 4. *Ethnic Background of Contractors in Los Angeles County*

Ethnicity	Number	Percentage
Asian	1,546	49.5
Korean	722	23.1
Vietnamese	342	11.0
Chinese	301	9.6
Other Asian	181	5.8
Latino	915	29.3
European-American	375	12.0
Jewish	96	3.1
Armenian	110	3.5
Other European	169	5.4
Other, unknown	286	9.2
Total	3,122	100.0

NOTE: Information on ethnicity missing for 497 contractors.

Despite the significant presence of immigrants, some contracting shops in Los Angeles are not owned by immigrants. We cannot establish their numbers from the owners' names, but they are likely to be European in origin and possibly include some of the Jewish and Armenian contractors, although those groups also have immigrant contractors among them. The second and third generation-owned contracting shops tend to be among the larger, most established contractors in the county, and are well represented in the Garment Contractors Association, which has few Asian members.

The growth in contracting has changed the geography of the industry. As manufacturers moved out of the downtown garment district so have contractors, for various reasons. Rents tend to be higher in downtown than they are in neighboring areas and downtown is older, with narrow and congested streets, parking and loading problems, and older buildings that have been subdivided into factories that are accessible only by outdated elevators. Nearby cities, such as Vernon, by way of contrast, offer industrial park facilities to apparel contractors. Of course, the garment district still remains attractive for its convenience, visibility, and access to a nearby workforce which is entirely dependent on the region's notoriously poor public transportation system.

Garment contracting has been expanding to the south and southeast toward Vernon, an incorporated city immediately adjacent to the garment district, and to the east in the El Monte and San Gabriel Valley areas, in what appear to be centers for Chinese, particularly Chinese-Vietnamese

Table 5.   *Geographic Distribution of Contractors by Ethnicity (Percentages)*

Ethnicity	Garment District	Growth Region	Expanded District	Other County Areas
Asian				
Korean	70.7	5.0	3.7	20.6
Vietnamese	16.1	1.8	36.0	46.1
Chinese	32.2	1.0	23.6	43.2
Other Asian	24.1	1.7	19.0	55.2
Total	45.7	3.1	16.4	34.7
Latino	28.7	8.9	8.5	53.9
European-American				
Armenian	13.6	0.0	0.9	85.5
Jewish	42.7	4.2	5.2	47.9
Other European	27.2	3.0	8.9	60.9
Total	27.2	2.4	5.6	64.8
Other, unknown	28.7	5.9	7.3	58.1
Total (percentage)	37.0	5.0	12.0	46.1
Total (number)	1,154	155	374	1,439

NOTE: The Garment District includes zip codes 90007, 90014, 90015, 90021, and 90079 (the California Mart; there are no contractors in this zip code). The Growth Region (so designated by the city) includes the adjacent zip codes, 90011 and 90058 (the City of Vernon). The Expanded District is our own designation of adjacent areas in which there is a high concentration of contractors; it includes zip codes 90023, 90031, and 91733 (the City of El Monte). Other County Areas covers the rest of Los Angeles County.

contractors. It has also been expanding south to Orange County, the location of Vietnamese-owned factories, though some Koreans have shifted there too.[19]

In Table 5 we present the ethnic distribution of contractors in various locations. We distinguish the official downtown city garment district from the officially designated adjacent growth region and an expanded district close to those two areas, the boundaries of which are described according to our own observations. The three areas together comprise the primary garment area, which is then distinguished from all other county areas. In 1991, there were garment contracting shops throughout Los Angeles County, with slightly more than half (54 percent) in the primary garment area. The garment district alone accounted for more than a third (37 percent) of all contracting factories in the county. Patterns of concentration differed significantly by ethnicity. Korean contractors were by far the most heavily concentrated, with 71 percent found in the garment district itself and 80 percent in the primary garment area. Jewish contractors were the second most concentrated of the major groups, with 43 percent in the garment district and nearly 50 percent outside the primary garment area. Armenians were the least concentrated, 90 percent of them outside the primary garment area, primarily in zip codes 91204, 90027, and 90029. Other Europeans and Latinos exhibited a similar geographical pattern, somewhat less dispersed than Armenian contractors were, but still with roughly only 25 percent to be found in the garment district, and about 60 percent outside the primary garment areas. About 33 percent of all Chinese contractors were located in the garment district, and 36 percent of the Vietnamese contractors were in the expanded district, with most of those (26 percent) in the City of El Monte.

Looked at another way, we found that 61 percent of all licensed factories in the downtown garment district were owned by Asians, significantly more than were in the county as a whole (50 percent). Koreans tended to be the most geographically concentrated ethnic group, accounting for 44 percent of all factories in the garment district (and only 23 percent of all factories in the county). Conversely, Latinos tended to be somewhat underrepresented among factory owners in the garment district (23 percent) relative to their representation in the county as a whole (29 percent), but were substantially overrepresented in the growth region, where they accounted for more than half (52 percent) of all factories. The Vietnamese, although accounting for only 5 percent of all garment district factories, accounted for 33 percent of those in the expanded district, three times their representation in the county as a whole (11 percent).

Contractors' Stories

We spoke to a number of contractors in the course of this research. In general, we found them to be frustrated and angry about their situation. Although these interviews were done a number of years ago, we doubt that their feelings have improved since then. The experiences of three, from three different ethnic groups, Latino, Korean, and Jewish, are instructive.

LUIS LOPEZ

At the time of our interview (4 October 1991), Luis Lopez's factory was located just west of downtown Los Angeles. The approximately 100 sewing machines were largely idle; his declining business supported fewer than fifty workers, mainly women from El Salvador and Mexico. Crammed into 12,000 square feet of floor space (which cost him $4,000 a month), he complained of falling prices, growing competition from Asia and Mexico, workers' compensation claims, and two equipment thefts in a single year.

Mr. Lopez's thirty-seven years in the business—ten years at this same location—had left him discouraged and disillusioned. Because of the intensity of competition among Los Angeles contractors, he told us he would "do anything" when it came to small-volume garment production, regardless of the nature of the task. His production output ranged from women's skirts to men's beachwear shorts. Partly out of desperation, he was also attempting to branch out. He proudly showed us a recently designed combination seat cushion and beverage-carrying case that, he hoped, would appeal to sports fans and college students, perhaps, he suggested, if sold through a university store.

Although Mr. Lopez once priced his services on actual production costs, he told us that today he is forced to take whatever the manufacturer offered him. "The manufacturer used to give you a garment and you would cost it out. Now the stores make the decision, take off the markup, fabric, and other costs, and the manufacturers tell the contractor the price. We either take it or leave it." To illustrate this point, he showed us a garment that retailed for between $32 and $34. The retailer paid the manufacturer $15.75, the manufacturer paid him $3.50, and he paid the five workers who jointly produced the garment a total of $1.25, or about 25¢ each. The remaining $2.25 covered his rent, utilities, equipment costs, thread, insurance, and other expenses. Anything left over was profit. Mr. Lopez was not doing well in this food chain, and within two years of our interview, had gone out of business.

YOUNG WASHINGTON

Young Washington, a Korean woman married to an African American, ran a jeans factory in the garment district. At the time of the interview (5 September 1989), she worked exclusively for Guess? Inc., employing forty workers, all Latinos. "There are too many contractors," she said. "When I first came, most of the contractors were Jewish. They got $10 per garment. Then the Koreans came and offered $9. Now the Chinese and Vietnamese are coming and they go for the low price. The minimum wage went up, but the price I get goes down. In 1984 I used to get $4.50 for a pair of jeans. In 1989 I get $4.10. Meanwhile, everything else has gone up, including thread. I came to America twenty years ago. I always worked hard. I come in at 6:30 in the morning and leave at 6:30 at night. I work on Saturdays until 3. I look at the stars when I come to work and I look at the stars when I go home. I feel we shouldn't work that hard. The Americans don't appreciate it. They feel we take away their business."

We asked if she had any problems with her employees. "If you have work," she replied, "you don't have enough employees. If you don't have work, you have too many. You are always off balance. You have to lay people off when work slows down, and you have to rehire them when it picks up. But they are poor people who need work in between, so it is hard to find them. The manufacturer doesn't give us much warning. They don't have a contract with us promising that they will give us so much work a month. They don't have any obligation."

JOEL AND HARRIET GOLD

When we interviewed them, 5 September 1989, the Golds owned a factory in an Anjac building in the garment district. Born in the United States, of parents who had been in the garment industry, the Golds complained bitterly about Asian contractors, claiming that they did not pay minimum wage, worked twenty-four hours a day, paid in cash, and so on. "They will make anything at any price. They work seven days a week." They complained that the labor laws are not enforced. For example, there is tons of homework. "Come here at 6 a.m.," said Joel Gold, "and you'll see workers bringing in their bundles of homework, to factories in this building. We were told by an inspector from the Labor Department, 'As a garment contractor, you can't afford to stay in business if you obey the law. But don't come crying to us if we catch you in violation.' It's sickening," he went on. "It's disgusting. I'm bursting with anger. Someone offered ten cents less than me and took all my work away. They are going seven days a week, twelve hours a day. Don't tell me they are paying time and a half."

Harriet saw the problems as originating with the takeovers and mergers at the retail level. The retailers then went to the manufacturers and asked for a 20 percent discount up front. "We get $5 for a skirt," she said. "Maybe it has $7 worth of fabric. The retailer sells it for $85. The contractor is the only point of flexibility in the system. Everyone steals from the contractor. They take it out of labor. There is no such thing as a legitimate price. The Orientals can do it because they don't pay taxes. The biggest companies, like Guess, pay a ridiculous amount. The minimum wage went up July 1, 1988. Guess lowered its prices right before that date so that they could claim they raised them when the minimum wage went up. It was a sham. People fight over nickels and dimes in this industry."

Korean Contractors

Because of their importance in the contracting community, Korean contractors have been the subject of a number of in-depth studies.[20] The first systematic study was a survey taken in 1979 by Hyung-Ki Jin, in which the importance of garment contracting to the Korean community was emphasized.[21] A second survey, conducted in 1989 by Darrel Hess, focused on the ethnic resources that Koreans were able to use to become entrepreneurs.[22] Hess discovered some interesting characteristics of Korean firms apart from their entrepreneurial success. For instance, he found that 40 percent of the surveyed contractors reported using homeworkers, some for specialized tasks.

Our survey, based on a random sample, was conducted by Ku-Sup Chin, in Korean, between September 1992 and April 1993.[23] The 100 Korean contractors surveyed were drawn from the 512 names on the membership list of the Korean-American Garment Industry Association and the Korean names on the state licensing registration list. The combined list yielded 942 different names although, given the high turnover among contractors, a substantial number of these was likely no longer in business. A sample was then drawn of 125 contractors. Thirteen of those were out of business or under different ownership; six refused to answer, and six failed to return the questionnaire. The survey, containing about 100 questions, took an hour to complete. All but three were conducted in the respondents' factories during two separate periods, between September and December 1992 and in March and April 1993.

The Korean contractors we surveyed, overwhelmingly originating in metropolitan areas of South Korea where they were well educated and middle class in origin, had averaged 11.6 years in the United States. Fifty-two percent reported having achieved four or more years of college education before emigrating from Korea, and 16.6 percent had bachelor of arts degrees from United States universities. Thirty-six percent had held white-collar jobs (as professionals, managers, or clerks) in Korea before emigrating, and 22 percent came as students. They also tended to be in their middle years at the time of interview, their average age 43.7 years. About 70 percent were Protestants, reflecting the strong inroads of the

Protestant evangelical movement both in South Korea and in the Los Angeles Korean community, as well as the important role played by church networking in entrepreneurship. Twenty-eight percent reported having been involved in the garment industry in Korea, and 66 percent reported working in the United States apparel industry before starting their own businesses.

Seventy percent owned the businesses in a sole proprietorship, 26 percent were incorporated; the remaining 4 percent were in partnerships. Their median annual sales were reported at around $500,000, with 10 percent reporting more than $1.5 million in sales. They reported having an average of fifty-seven sewing machines and fifty-four employees. About 10 percent owned their own buildings and roughly 10 percent rented from another Korean. Nearly 66 percent reported renting from a Jewish landlord, another instance of the cross-cutting ethnic relationships that prevail in this industry.

In 1991 most licensed Korean contractors were located in the downtown garment district, with some in adjacent areas. Rather more of our sample was in the geographically peripheral areas, and they tended to be in their own stand-alone buildings, to be more likely to do work for Anglo manufacturers (rather than for other Koreans), and to have their own manufacturing operations. They also tended to be the more stable contractors, somewhat larger in size, with a higher-paid and less mobile workforce. Tending to have long-term relationships with manufacturers, these contractors needed more space and a secure, stable labor supply. The more remote locations, along with the higher wages paid, tended, apparently, to discourage employee turnover. Moreover, such firms tended to be closer to Latino residential areas, an advantage in securing labor. They were also less likely to be subject to investigations by government agencies, and benefited from being in locations with less traffic and somewhat lower rents.

THEIR CHANGING WORKFORCE

In 1979, 43 percent of the workforce in these firms was Korean. By 1989, the Korean segment had declined to 11 percent, and by 1993, to less than 5 percent. Correspondingly, the proportion of Latino workers in Korean factories has grown from 56 percent to 95 percent. It appears that Korean garment workers have, by and large, been able to move out of this low-paying job. It seems safe to say that, for Koreans, working in a garment factory has been a way station on the way to a better job. Such has not, however, been the case for Latino immigrants. In part, these consequences can be traced to the disparity in the assets of the newly arrived immigrants.

Many Korean immigrants arrived with considerable education, and some came with capital to invest.[24] Employment as a garment worker can serve as a first stage of adaptation to this country, particularly for educated immigrants who know little English. Once they have acquired some English, they are able to move on to something better. One apparent route of upward mobility for Korean garment workers appears to have been to move into contracting themselves, as shown by the fact that two-thirds of the Korean contractors we interviewed had worked in a factory before opening their own businesses. They had learned the business before investing their capital. These patterns of mobility, it should be noted, may differ by gender. Whereas some Korean women have become successful garment contractors in their own right, other immigrant women have found themselves stuck in homework or lower paying jobs. Many of the Latino immigrants come to the United States from rural backgrounds, and with little formal education. For most, lacking the economic resources of Korean immigrants, the idea of having enough capital to invest in one's own factory is a distant dream.

The Korean contractors in our survey reported a preference for Latino workers. Forty-seven percent stated that wages that were paid to Koreans were too high, and 39 percent noted difficulties in finding Koreans willing to work in garment factories. Latino workers were viewed as plentiful and cheap. They were also viewed as culturally docile and obedient. As one contractor put it: "If Mexican workers were not available, many Korean contractors would have had to close their factories a long time ago." Koreans reported feeling less obligation toward Latino workers, especially when it was necessary to lay off workers. Of course, this is a two-way street: Latino workers also feel less obligation to their Korean employers, and may shift jobs looking for a better situation. One can see in these attitudes, and in the shift from Korean to Latino workers, the emergence of the middleman minority role for Korean contractors.

Another interesting shift in the workforce of Korean contractors concerns gender. In 1979 Jin found that women made up an average of 73 percent of the workforce. In 1989, Hess found that this figure had dropped to 59 percent. In our survey, we found that, on average, women comprised 46 percent of the workers in the factories. (The rising numbers of male garment workers, in general, will be discussed in Chapter 6.) Some Korean contractors reported a preference for male workers who were less likely to miss work because of child care and other domestic responsibilities. Korean contractors believed that most factory work can be done by either men or women, with the exception of ironing, a male specialty, and trimming, a female task.

The middleman minority position of Korean contractors contributes to ethnic stereotyping and often open hostility. Korean contractors sometimes speak of Latino workers as disloyal, opportunistic, irresponsible, and lazy in comparison with Korean workers. "The Latino boys are not like the Korean workers. They don't care about the deadlines. Although I beg them to work hard, they turn a deaf ear to my request. Even when a lot of work is left unfinished, they go home earlier on their own, or even move to other firms without notice. It makes my blood boil. I think they are irresponsible." Korean contractors, who reported an average turnover rate of 44 percent, view their Latino workers as lacking the solidarity and commitment that characterizes Korean workers, but at the same time, as more uncomplaining and docile. The Latino workers, in turn, view their Korean employers as harsh, rigid, and exploitative. Korean contractors do sometimes express sympathy for their workers' difficulties as impoverished, uneducated, and largely undocumented immigrants, but say that they have to deal harshly with workers if they hope to survive in this business. One of the contractors whom we interviewed described being caught between manufacturers' pressures and workers' expectations. "Once my boys [the workers] mastered the pattern, they were able to produce more garments within a given time, and earn more. When we tried to take a reorder, however, the manufacturer demanded to reduce the production price since we got used to the style. I had to cut down the piece rates of the workers.[25] It caused a lot of problems. My boys always got mad at this. They demanded the initial price. Some quit, but the majority remained. One of the workers reported it to the Labor Department."

Another source of antagonism results from short delivery deadlines and pressures from manufacturers for strict quality control. The threat of lost contracts, the return of poor-quality items, or fines for failure to meet delivery deadlines were all cited as reasons for pressing workers to speed up their work. A further difficulty arises from disputes over payment. One contractor reported that his workers resented being told not to cash their Friday checks until the following week, because he himself was being paid tardily by his manufacturers. According to the contractors, workers also often dispute the amount of their paychecks, claiming they are not being paid for all the work they have done.

Despite the underlying antagonisms, Korean contractors report that, at least on the surface, the factory environment is friendly. For example, 54 percent reported that their Latino workers were "somewhat" or "very" favorable in their attitudes toward management; only 11 percent viewed their workers as "somewhat" or "very" hostile. Reasons cited for such amicable relationships included the undocumented status of many workers, which might place them at risk of deportation if they openly expressed hostility, and the low level of unionization in the industry. It could also simply result from misperceptions on the part of the Korean contractors, or unwillingness to reveal problems to the interviewer. The owners seem to recognize that antagonism is a structural feature of their relations with their workers, but they apparently regard it as latent at present.

Given the stresses of the middleman minority role, one might wonder why anyone would take it on. Part of the reason probably lies in a lack of satisfactory alternatives. Korean immigrants with professional degrees are unable to practice their professions because of their limited English or lack of local accreditation. Moreover, ambitious immigrants who want to improve their economic condition would rather not work for someone else, preferring self-employment even though it may be risky. In addition, Koreans, facing generalized racial discrimination, find their upward mobility limited. Running a garment factory, like running a grocery or liquor store in the ghetto or barrio, is often a way of making the best of a bad situation.

THEIR INCOMES

The reported median income of Korean contractors at the time of our survey was roughly $50,000 per year. Only 9 percent reported making under $30,000; fully 40 percent made more than $70,000. Twenty-nine percent reported making over $100,000 a year, and 8 percent reporting annual earnings exceeding $200,000.[26] It seems clear that at least within the Korean community, the promise of substantial earnings through contracting is not unrealistic. This undoubtedly helps to explain the willingness of well-educated Korean immigrants to put in long hours running factories. Garment contracting, despite its hardships and uncertainties, appears to be a fairly profitable activity for immigrant entrepreneurs. Given that 50 percent of the firms reported opening during the past four years and 75 percent within the past decade, the high reported incomes are especially striking. Another indication of economic success is that 70 percent of the contractors we interviewed owned their own homes, and 63 percent had moved from Koreatown to the suburbs. Of course, we should note that we interviewed only those contractors who had survived. Many may have failed and lost their savings. Furthermore, we have no information about the income of contractors from other ethnic groups.

As middlemen, Korean contractors obviously do not make nearly as much money as do manufacturers and retailers. Nevertheless, they do receive a significant cut of the wealth that is generated by this industry. Unlike garment workers, they are able to send their children to good schools and universities, and achieve a solid middle-class status for their families by the second generation. The Korean contractors we interviewed reported paying their workers an average of between $200 and $250 a week which, although slightly above minimum wage, was still below the poverty line for a four-person family. To judge from the contractors' reports, which most likely overstate their workers' earnings and understate their own, median earnings for Korean contractors were around six times as much as their workers' earnings were. It is worth reporting that Chin and Sarmiento surveyed sixty-five workers in these same factories; they reported an average pay of only $2.95 per hour and 70 percent earned below the minimum wage.[27]

THEIR TIES TO KOREAN MANUFACTURERS

To avoid the skyrocketing costs of workers' compensation, as well as to secure steady work in the face of seasonal and other fluctuations, Korean contractors reported turning increasingly to Korean manufacturers, who are concentrated in the informal sector, largely unregulated by the state. They were more tolerant of using undocumented workers, lax about requiring workers' compensation, and less concerned about violations of health, safety, and other regulations in the factories. Most importantly, perhaps, they were willing to do business in cash and avoid both records and taxes: The contractor is paid by the manufacturer in cash and, in turn, pays his workers in cash. (The Korean term is *hyungum pakchigi,* or "cash-based.") Thirty-three percent of the surveyed contractors reported working only for manufacturers who were not Korean, 29 percent worked exclusively for Koreans. The remainder (38 percent) worked for both. Nearly half of all contractors reported that more than 80 percent of their total production was with Korean manufacturers. It seems clear that this ethnic tie represents an increasingly important part of Korean contracting.

What we see here is the emergence in the early 1990s of a somewhat separate Korean subeconomy of garment production.[28] Centered around the Santee Alley area in the garment district, this subeconomy is producing goods very cheaply, on a cash-and-carry basis, a phenomenon that greatly upsets the established industry. Many industry leaders claim that it is this sector that is responsible for the reemergence of sweatshops in the apparel industry, but, as sweatshops have also been linked with some of the most established labels in the country, blaming "the Koreans" will not suffice as an explanation. A shift toward the creation of a Korean subeconomy removes Korean contractors from one aspect of the middleman minority position. Fewer of the profits of their role as controllers of the garment labor force are siphoned off by the Anglo-Jewish establishment as the Koreans keep the profits in their own community. The other side of the middleman role remains intact however: Korean contractors continue to play a part in controlling Latino immigrant workers.

Politics

Garment contractors in Los Angeles have established a number of organizations along ethnic lines, including the Garment Contractors Association, the American Chinese Garment Contractors Association, and the Korean-American Garment Industry Association. These three organizations have joined the Northern California Chinese Garment Contractors Association to form the Apparel Contractors Alliance of California. These organizations act separately and together to protect the interests of their members.

Joe Rodriguez, the executive director of the Garment Contractors Association (GCA), kindly put us on the mailing list to receive its monthly newsletter, which contains information about the activities of the group and reveals the political orientation and interests of its members. Ku-Sup Chin was able to use information from interviews and articles in the Korean press to develop a composite portrait of the opinions of Korean contractor. We cannot claim that all garment contractors would agree with every position that is expressed by members of the GCA and the Korean-American Garment Industry Association, but we believe they do give us a good indication of the positions that contractors are likely to endorse.

GLOBALIZATION

The GCA opposes the expansion of the North American Free Trade Agreement (NAFTA) and the extension of NAFTA principles to the Caribbean nations, referred to as CBI parity. For example, in the August/September 1997 issue of the *GCA Newsletter,* Joe Rodriguez reported that, "thanks to the vigilance and independent thinking of many GCA members who did not blindly follow the advice given by so-called friendly associations that are in fact unduly influenced by importers, and who made the effort to join us in communicating our concerns to key legislators, Congress did not append the CBI Parity initiative to the recently ratified Budget Bill. . . . Importers were joined by retailers and others in making their pitch to Congress that they represented the U.S. apparel industry. . . . Key members of Congress found out that indeed the importer-dominated groups did not represent the *entire* industry." On the expansion of NAFTA, in the same issue, Rodriguez comments, "Apparently our esteemed leaders believe NAFTA has not done enough harm to our domestic apparel manufacturing industry." This opposition to more liberal trade policies is perfectly reasonable for domestic contractors in direct competition with offshore contractors who have access to much cheaper labor. Their position does, however, put the GCA on the same side of the NAFTA debate as organized labor.

Rodriguez also believes that the industry in Los Angeles has certain advantages in withstanding the rush to move offshore. Writing in the April 1997 issue, he commented that, "for the third consecutive year, apparel employment figures reveal mixed results. For the entire U.S.A., the trend continues downward, thanks in no small part to the devastation that NAFTA and GATT have wrought. On the other hand, for the third year in a row, California has posted a gain! . . . In my opinion southern California will be the last region impacted by NAFTA and GATT because of the nature of the work we are involved with. High-fashion, low-volume, incredibly quick-turn manufacturing does not yet lend itself to worry-free sourcing in Mexico or anywhere else but here. Eventually, NAFTA and GATT are designed to get us too, but not for a long while—at least that is my hope."

The Korean-American Garment Industry Association (KAGIA) was also strongly opposed to NAFTA. According to Chang-Hoon Park, who was president of the association when we interviewed him on 22 October 1992, before NAFTA was implemented, "Korean garment entrepreneurs [have] an underlying sense of anxiety. We are afraid that the *Bong-Je* [garment] industry will be hurt most by NAFTA since it is heavily labor intensive. First, any movement of L.A. manufacturers to Mexico would lead to a decrease in contract orders for Korean firms. It would weaken the dominance of the Korean *Bong-Je* industry in Los Angeles. Second, increased sewing jobs in Mexico would cause a labor shortage here and consequent rise in labor costs. We could not survive the price [competition] with 55 cents-an-hour Mexican labor. Third, most Korean *Bong-Je* firms are small in size and cannot afford to move to Mexico. It is not hard to predict what will happen. They will be forced out of business."

Korean contractors were fiercely opposed, but they viewed the passage of NAFTA as inevitable. To assuage anxiety among its members, the KAGIA formed a committee to explore the effect of NAFTA on the Korean garment industry, and to study what to do about it. Some members insisted that the only way to survive was to move their factories to Mexico and other Latin American countries. The KAGIA even sent a delegation to Mexico to explore opportunities for relocation. In the end, only about a dozen large Korean contractors opened factories in Mexico, Guatemala, and Ecuador in the wake of NAFTA, but they maintained their southern California plants too. The KAGIA has come to believe that NAFTA's impact was not as bad as expected.

LABOR ISSUES

In general, both the GCA and the KAGIA seem to oppose any moves that raise the price of labor, and cheer any actions that lower it. For example, the GCA opposed raising the minimum wage at the national level, and they especially opposed Proposition 210, the California initiative that raised the state minimum wage above the national level. The KAGIA expressed similar opposition. Interviewed by a correspondent for a Korean newspaper on 10 September 1996, the KAGIA president, Sung-Joo Kim, said that, "currently sewing operators with one or two years of experience get paid $4.75 an hour. If the minimum wage of unskilled workers, such as trimmers, rises to $4.75, the experienced workers will surely ask for an even higher wage. A sudden rise in the minimum wage would cause a simultaneous increase in related expenditures such as payroll taxes and insurance premiums. Despite this burden, we cannot ask manufacturers for a higher price to cover the added expense. No matter how we handle the increase, it will eat into our profit margin." Proposition 210 passed in November 1996.

The GCA cheered when the Industrial Wage Commission decided to amend the state overtime provisions by repealing its long-standing provisions requiring employers in California to pay time and a half if their employees work more than eight hours in one day. The federal overtime statute requires the payment of overtime only after a forty-hour work week.[29]

At the local level, the GCA strongly opposed the living wage ordinance, passed by the Los Angeles City Council in April 1997. Writing in the *GCA Newsletter,* columnist Jim Seal considered it as a first step toward a city-wide wage increase extending to the private sector.

The City of L.A. "Living Wage" issue is not the end-game but the beginning of a protracted class warfare campaign to turn public opinion against non-union private contractors and small manufacturers especially garment contractors County wide. . . . L.A. County unions and their allies have a much more ambitious agenda than driving up the labor costs of government contractors. . . . The Living Wage battle was the beginning of an all out assault by a dedicated coalition put together by labor union bosses to expand their influence over companies employing low-wage workers. Labor won because it reached out to the community and painted a picture of greedy owners exploiting immigrant workers. Small businesses were not sufficiently mobilized to present an agenda of economic growth, prosperity, and upward mobility. . . . Labor won the first round but there are many other government mandates yet to be fought.

Here is a clear manifestation of the contractors' ideology. Unionization means domination by "union bosses." When unions fight for the redistribution of some of the wealth to workers, they are seen as engaging in "class warfare." Small business promises prosperity for all, and should be allowed to proceed unimpeded by governmental interference.

Jim Seal also writes a column in the *GCA Newsletter* called "Sacramento Beat," in which he reports on legislative developments. He is fiercely opposed to any proposals by organized labor, all of which he sees as antithetical to the interests of garment contractors. In May 1997 he observed:

Labor unions have an aggressive agenda such as: a contractor Living Wage bill (similar to Los Angeles), a statutorily mandated 8 hour work day, unemployment compensation charges and other related legislation. . . . For many years companies have relied on Republican Governors to veto bills that drive up the costs of doing business or give unions an unfair advantage. However, labor is flexing its muscles because of its role in toppling the Republican majority in the Assembly according to many political pundits. Whether its role is exaggerated or not unions are on the offensive.

For example, every time I am at the capitol there are delegations of labor sympathizers with buttons supporting one union organizing drive or another. Of course, what they want is to force an employer to recognize card-check-off vs. secret ballot elections. The focus of these organizing drives are unskilled minority workers.

What is labor trying to accomplish? According to recent accounts labor wants to create a negative image of Republicans opposing labor backed legislation. Increased membership dues are the "mother's milk" of political action here in L.A. and in Sacramento. The stakes are high for the 1998 Governor's election.

Seal's position is as intensely antiunion as he is pro-Republican. Of course, we cannot be sure how many contractors share his opinions, though the fact that they are published regularly in the newsletter implies support.

JOINT LIABILITY

As we have seen, contractors not only have problems with their workers, but also points of friction with the manufacturers. One of labor's proposals to deal with the persistent violations of labor standards in the apparel industry is to pass joint liability legislation, holding manufacturers responsible for the violations committed by their contractors. Needless to say, manufacturers ardently oppose such legislation, preferring to distance themselves from such violations and deny all responsibility for them. Joint liability attempts to negate this ploy.

Joint liability legislation has been passed by the California legislature a number of times, only to be vetoed by the Republican governors George Deukmejian and Pete Wilson. At the time of writing (early 1999), state assemblyman Darrell S. Steinberg was sponsoring A. B. 633, endorsing joint liability, as part of a larger bill dealing with the underground economy. An interesting question is where contractors stand on such a concept. Writing in the June 1997 *GCA Newsletter,* Robert Reed, a contractor and treasurer of the GCA, expressed the mixed feelings of many contractors. "On the surface it is tempting to gloat over the possibility that the manufacturers who have for so long diverted the work that should have come to us will finally get their comeuppance and be held accountable for their chronic misdeeds. Justice for our tormentors who have exhorted us to work faster, cheaper, and with higher quality while concurrently supporting the massive underground industry, which by breaking all labor laws was able to offer prices which we couldn't begin to compete with legally." This outburst expresses some of the frustration that many garment contractors feel toward the manufacturers. Nevertheless, Reed comes out against joint liability because, in his view, not every manufacturer is guilty of these practices, and it is impossible for manufacturers to police the contractors completely no matter how hard they try. "As much as I feel that there are numerous offending manufacturing entities, it is just not fair for them to be held accountable for behavior over which they have no effective control, and I feel that it would be a catastrophic disaster to our industry as a whole to allow a draconian and all-encompassing measure like this to be imposed upon us. Manufacturers would have no choice but to move all their production out of the state and maybe even the country, leaving us contractors—extinct!!!"

The danger expressed here is that, if public pressure is put on the manufacturers, they will simply leave. The contractors thus feel obliged to support the manufacturers against government regulation, no matter how much they may feel mistreated by them, because ultimately they are dependent upon them for work.

Another example of the contractors' strained relations with manufacturers arose in 1996 in the wake of the passage of the law raising the minimum wage. As reported in the August/September 1996 issue of the *GCA Newsletter*, the association, as did the other contractors' associations, including the KAGIA, addressed an open letter to manufacturers, stating in part:

Dear valued customer:

A mandated increase in the minimum wage is now a reality. We appreciate the efforts many of you made to oppose passage of this costly legislation, but now we must do our best to comply with this new law. . . .

The public (i.e., consumers), when polled about the minimum wage increase favored its passage by wide margins. A corresponding increase in labor prices, offered to contractors to offset this new mandated cost, may result in a slight increase in the retail price of the garments. It is our considered opinion that this increase in retail price is something that the consumer is willing to bear. . . .

Also, by publicizing the voluntary initiative to offset the mandated new labor costs for contractors, the retailers and manufacturers will be in a position to say that they are doing something in a proactive manner to eliminate another excuse for the existence of domestic sweatshops. As you may know, minimum wage violations are a common finding by state and federal labor law enforcement officials. Without immediate relief, these violations may be exacerbated, and our industry's reputation will be further eroded. . . .

The contractors need slightly higher labor prices to offset this new cost. This will be the most equitable way to share the cost of this new burden for all concerned.

Although this letter is extremely polite, it expresses the frustration of contractors that they must bear all the burdens of improved labor standards, which manufacturers are in a position to ignore. This plea undoubtedly fell on deaf ears. The National Retail Federation rejected the argument out of hand, stating that consumers will not accept higher prices.[30]

These quotes from the *GCA Newsletter* and the KAGIA illustrate the complex political stance of contractors. They feel caught between the manufacturers and the workers (or at least the unions). Their political stance seems to be typical of small business: opposition to government regulation, fierce antiunionism, opposition to any measure that would raise the cost of labor (which is *their* direct cost more than it is anyone else's in the industry), and wanting to protect themselves against the flood of imports and the movement offshore. On most issues they seem solidly Republican, yet on the trade question they are closer to segments of the Democratic Party, as well as to the AFL-CIO.

Which Side Are They On?

At first glance, it would seem that there are good reasons for contractors and workers to find common cause. Together contractors and workers would be able to exact higher prices from the manufacturers and each share the benefits. Most of them are immigrants, even if sometimes from different ethnic groups, and most suffer from being racial minorities in this society. Moreover, together they comprise what the industry considers to be its labor costs. Their fates are linked. If a manufacturer moves his production offshore, both contractors and workers lose their livelihood.

The garment workers' union, UNITE, acknowledges that contractors and workers have a common interest, recognizing that contractors, working in concert with a workers' union, could pose a formidable united front to manufacturers. Workers and contractors united could exert considerable control over the flow of production, including the demand for longer-term commitments from manufacturers and higher prices. The contractors could then pay higher wages. There would appear to be a compelling logic for the two lowest tiers of the pyramid to overcome an antagonism that clearly benefits the upper echelons, and to work together to improve their joint position.[31]

Why, then, in Los Angeles today, is a coalition between contractors and organized labor so clearly unthinkable? One reason is ideological: Some contractors come from countries where unions were deemed synonymous with socialism or corruption, and were widely despised, many are evangelical Christians with a deep-seated antipathy toward unions, and all are self-made entrepreneurs who instinctively oppose any challenge to their right to exercise complete control over their businesses without "outside" interference and to make as much money for themselves as possible. Another reason lies in the contracting system itself, which gives overwhelming power to manufacturers. Because any contractor who flirts with the idea of endorsing unionization will wind up an untouchable, shunned by all manufacturers and therefore bereft of all work, contractors *have* to play the game by the manufacturers' rules in order to stay in business. This is an important aspect of the contractors' role as middleman minorities: On behalf of the manufacturers, they help to crush unionization efforts among the workers.

In the union's view, all this would change if unionization were to succeed. If a unionized workforce could force leading manufacturers to agree to use only union shops, contractors would step all over one another in their efforts to get their workers to sign up. Under these circumstances, the union would control the flow of work, and unionized contractors would benefit from the workers' power. Whatever the degree of truth in this theory, in point of fact the garment industry in Los Angeles is almost completely nonunionized, and local contractors remain virulently anti-union. Therein lies the Catch-22 for contractors in Los Angeles: Without already empowered workers to back them up, contractors would commit economic suicide if they called for any empowerment of the workers.

CHAPTER 6
Workers

Copyright, 1997, *Boston Globe*. Distributed by *Los Angeles Times* Syndicate. Reprinted by permission.

On 1 March 1998, as a result of a statewide referendum, the minimum hourly wage in California was raised from $5.15 to $5.75. This was the third increase since September 1996, when the minimum was only $4.25. Soon after, the workers at the Garment Workers Justice Center, a drop-in center run by UNITE (the Union of Needletrades, Industrial and Textile Employees) began to report hearing complaints that garment workers were faced with increased pressure on the job. The weekly wage had increased by 35 percent (some $60 a week) in only eighteen months, yet contractors failed to raise their piece rates accordingly. Some workers were told that they must make the new, higher minimum wage by increasing their hourly rate of production or face the prospect of being fired.[1] Others reportedly were given time to increase their output so that their piece rate reached the newly mandated minimum, but then were docked pay to make up for those weeks in which they did not achieve it.

In other words, rather than following the spirit of the law, the purpose of which was to enhance workers' lives by improving their wages, employers responded by using the new minimum wage as a weapon to force a speedup or to cut earnings. Workers claimed that these pressures were occurring at factories producing nationally known labels, including Ralph Lauren's Polo, JNCO, Calvin Klein, DKNY, J. C. Penney's Arizona, Guess, and Wal-Mart's Kathie Lee line.[2]

The labor squeeze was on, and its impact on workers was not improved by the antiimmigrant sentiment sweeping through California. On 25 March 1998, the Immigration and Naturalization Service (INS) began sweeps, tagged Operation Buttonhole, of garment factories in Los Angeles.[3] In the first three weeks of the program more than seventy-five downtown garment factories, with a combined workforce of over 7,000 workers, were raided, and almost 300 workers were deported. These raids created fear in the large community of immigrant garment workers, many of whom were trying to legalize their immigration status. As the INS expanded its purview to restaurants and other industries employing large numbers of immigrants, workers became increasingly fearful of reporting labor abuses to authorities lest they face reprisal in the form of an INS raid on their factories.

These two developments are but the latest in the saga of the reemergence of sweatshops in Los Angeles. One of the more notorious cases was uncovered on 2 August 1995, when the nation and the world were shocked by the revelation of a garment factory where workers appeared to be held in a condition of near slavery, some reportedly for as long as seven years.[4] The shop was located in El Monte, a community east of downtown Los Angeles. The workers were immigrants from Thailand. They were living and working in an apartment complex surrounded by barbed-wire fences. They worked over eighty hours a week for less than $2 an hour and were detained by the company owners until they had supposedly paid off the debt of their transportation. Some had labored in the factory for years, unsuccessfully pleading for their freedom. They were forced to shop at a store maintained on the premises by the factory owners, and often charging vastly inflated prices, which virtually assured that they would never get out of debt peonage and be able to buy their freedom.

Are these cases, and others like them, aberrations in an otherwise law-abiding industry or are sweatshops a common problem? Who are the garment workers in Los Angeles, and under what conditions do they labor? How do workers feel about these conditions, and how do they respond to them? How are we to understand the return of nineteenth-century conditions at the dawn of the twenty-first?

The term *sweatshop* harks back to the early decades of the twentieth century, when workers slaved for long hours at low pay, in cluttered factories without adequate heating or ventilation. The term does not have a precise definition. We use it here to refer to factories in which at least one serious violation of the labor laws has been found. By that criterion, most garment contracting shops in Los Angeles would qualify as sweatshops.

In January 1998, the United States Department of Labor investigated garment firms in southern California, randomly sampling seventy licensed firms from the five-county area of Los Angeles, Orange, Ventura, Riverside, and San Bernardino, 90 percent of them cases in Los Angeles. These were the cream of the crop as the sampling procedures excluded the unregistered, underground contracting shops that account for between 25 and 33 percent, approximately, of the total. Among the legitimate operators, the department found only 39 percent in full compliance with the wage and hour provisions of the Fair Labor Standards Act. Forty-eight percent violated the minimum-wage law, 54 percent failed to pay overtime, and 51 percent failed to keep proper records. The firms owed an average of $3,631 each in back wages.[5] The prevalence of violations had not declined since a previous survey by the department in 1996, a survey that was based on a sample drawn from a more comprehensive list of firms, obtained from the Employment Development Department, which included some unregistered businesses.

The Department of Labor acknowledges that more violations exist than it is able to uncover. Apart from missing the large number of unregistered factories, the department's investigators find that workers are reluctant to tell government officials about violations in the workplace for fear that their employers will retaliate against them by firing them or calling in the INS.

Leaders in the industry often argue that sweatshops are confined to the underground economy. They feel that the press, the union, and community groups are sensationalizing the issue, giving the whole industry a bad name that it does not deserve and thereby undermining one of the city's most vital economic sectors. But as the 1998 labor department's investigation showed, sweatshops are rampant. High-priced, high-fashion, brand-name, mainstream garments are being produced under illegal conditions. No doubt there are contractors who are completely law abiding (though even they pay wages that are below the poverty level). But manufacturers, under constant pressure from retailers (and sometimes motivated by their own greed), pay the lowest possible prices to their contractors, prices that translate into violations of the labor laws. The manufacturers and retailers may not know, or may choose not to know, that their contractors are operating illegally, but their clothing is nevertheless being made in sweatshops.

In 1990, we joined a state investigation of a factory where it was believed that the workers were living on the premises, their passports having been confiscated.[6] The factory was large, with about 100 workers, and there were signs that workers were indeed living there: a sleeping area with rugs and small stashes of personal belongings, a dark and filthy shower, a washer and dryer, and an eating area filled with groceries. This factory was producing clothing for Monarch Knits and Sportswear, Inc., a well-established firm in Los Angeles, and the garments were being sold in J. C. Penney's stores. Mike O'Connor, a television reporter for KCBS Action News at the time, was also present. He filmed the investigation and presented a series of news stories on the sweatshop problem in Los Angeles. He interviewed Shelly Goldman, the owner of Monarch Knits, who claimed to know nothing of the raided factory, which, it turned out, was subcontracting work from a contractor that Goldman regularly used and that was visited daily by his quality-control inspectors. O'Connor was astounded that Goldman did not notice the much increased productivity that his regular contractor must have attained by employing an additional 100 workers.

O'Connor did some of his own investigating. He went into a downtown building, chosen at random, and spoke to workers there. Some had not been paid for weeks; others were making far less than the minimum wage. He found that they were producing garments for such well-known manufacturers as Rampage Clothing Company, Markham Industries (makers of the Jonathan Martin label), L.A. Glo, Inc. (makers of the Roberta label), and M.C.B. Inc. (makers of the Wild Rose label), clothing that retails in upscale malls, such as the Glendale Galleria. O'Connor also accompanied a health and safety inspection and was shown uncapped gas pipes, blocked exits, and exit doors that opened inward. A fire, as an inspector pointed out, would clearly leave the charred bodies of people frantic to get out piled up behind the door.

The infamous "slave-shop" in El Monte sewed garments that were sold under such labels as Tomato, Clio, B.U.M. International, Anchor Blue, and Airtime. Some of them were the private labels of retailers such as Mervyn's, Miller's Outpost, and Montgomery Ward; others were sold in major department stores or by mass merchandisers such as Robinsons-May, Nordstrom, Sears, and Target.[7] This highly illegal enterprise, for which several licensed factories served as fronts, was producing for the mainstream apparel industry. Larry Jacobs, who works for Stonefield

Josephson, an accounting firm for the apparel industry, has no illusions that El Monte was an abberation or that the sweatshop problem is confined to the underground. "Who among us," he asked, "was all that shocked by the conditions in El Monte? Current industry standards and ways of doing business create situations like the one found in El Monte. . . . Everyone is trying to squeeze contract labor prices! Lower labor prices, higher profits. It's interesting to see how the major retailers have nothing to do with this labor problem. Hah! . . . By leaving the labor pricing system without a floor [i.e., minimum] pricing system, labor abuse will continue to reappear."[8]

For more evidence that brand-name companies are involved in labor violations, one need look no further than the quarterly Garment Enforcement Reports put out by the United States Department of Labor. These reports list not only factories that were found to have violated the labor laws, but also the manufacturers who were using the factories at the time of the violation. The reports began in fall of 1995, and we have reviewed all the reports through spring of 1998. Among the major manufacturers in Los Angeles whose contractors were cited for violations we found some of the industry's most recognizable names: Guess?, Inc. (manufacturers of the Guess and Baby Guess labels), Michael Caruso and Company, Inc. (manufacturers of the Bongo label), Mossimo Inc., Carole Anderson Inc., Rampage Clothing Company, Nina Piccalino Inc., Pepe Jeans USA Inc., Revatex, Inc. (manufacturers of the JNCO label), Lola, Inc. (manufacturers of the XOXO label), Harkham Industries, Inc. (manufactures of the Jonathan Martin label), California Fashion Industries, Inc. (manufacturers of the Carole Little label), Francine Browner, Inc., A.B.S. Clothing Collection Inc. (manufacturers of the ABS USA label), Brasking Inc., L'Koral Inc., Gilda Marx Design Inc., Paris Blues, Inc., Byer California, BeBop Clothing, Inc., Tomato, Inc., Paul Davril, Inc., Topson Downs of California, Inc., Joel and Judy Knapp (manufacturers of the Judy Knapp label), Choon, Inc., Monarch Knits and Sportswear, Inc., Big Bisou Inc. (manufacturers of the Bisou Bisou label), Jalate Ltd., Inc., AZ3 Inc. (manufacturers of the BCBG Max Azria label), and Sirena Apparel Group.

We are not saying that these manufacturers routinely use sweatshops, nor that they are the only manufacturers in Los Angeles who do. They just happened to get caught. The mainstream apparel industry is part and parcel of the sweatshop problem; it is not the victim of unfair smears. Under the current system of production, it is virtually impossible for a manufacturer to avoid using sweatshops. A voluminous academic literature corroborates our conclusion that garment workers in Los Angeles

Table 6. *Occupation in the Los Angeles Apparel Industry, by Ethnicity (percentage), 1990*

Ethnicity	Man-agers	Profes-sionals	Sales-people	Clerks	Craft Workers	Oper-atives	Laborers	Total	Number
European	29.4	42.4	43.5	15.9	10.7	2.1	7.3	8.5	495
African	3.0	3.0	3.2	4.1	2.3	1.1	2.0	1.7	100
Chinese	10.7	9.1	1.1	4.3	5.6	7.7	4.4	7.1	414
Korean	15.5	3.0	3.8	3.8	2.8	2.9	0.8	3.9	223
Other Asian	5.2	6.8	2.7	5.0	3.0	2.5	4.4	3.1	182
Mexican	15.9	15.9	21.1	39.4	49.7	52.4	51.6	46.5	2,691
Central American	4.8	2.3	4.3	10.6	10.9	16.4	15.3	13.7	796
Other Latino	4.8	3.0	3.3	5.4	5.1	6.6	6.5	6.0	350
Other	10.7	14.3	16.8	11.4	9.8	8.4	7.7	9.3	540
Total	7.6	2.3	3.2	8.0	9.8	64.8	1.7	100.0	
Total Number	436	132	184	464	569	3,755	248		5,791

SOURCE: Data only—Bureau of the Census, Public Use Microdata Sample for Los Angeles, 1990. Analysis by authors.

endure considerable hardship and exploitation in an industry structured so as to make sweatshops the norm rather than the exception.[9]

Characteristics of Garment Workers

In April 1998 the Employment Development Department counted 122,500 people working in the apparel industry in Los Angeles County. (This figure is an undercount given the large underground economy.) Obviously not all employees of the industry are sewing machine operators. According to the 1990 census, approximately 65 percent of the people employed in this industry (about 82,000) were classified as "operatives," and 80 percent of those operatives (amounting to slightly more than half of all apparel industry workers) were sewing machine operators (see Table 6).[10] We treat the operatives as the closest equivalent to "garment workers," and if we assume that between a quarter and a third of them are not counted by the EDD, we can estimate that the total number of garment workers in Los Angeles County as of April 1998 was somewhere between 110,000 and 120,000 and the total apparel-related workforce of between 150,000 and 160,000. Ten percent of that workforce consisted of managers and professionals, with approximately the same proportion of clerical and sales workers (11 percent), and craft workers (10 percent). Laborers made up the remainder (two percent).

Women made up roughly two-thirds of the total apparel workforce, but 72 percent of the garment workers. The proportion of male garment workers may sound high at 28 percent and that percentage seems to have been rising over recent years. There is something of a division of labor by gender among garment workers—men are more likely to be cutters and pressers and women more likely to be trimmers—but many men do work at sewing machines alongside women. What used to be a strictly female occupation is no longer. Some workers report that, since 1990, the proportion of men has risen to at least 50 percent, a point corroborated by our study of Korean manufacturers (see Chapter 5). The reasons for this shift, we believe, have to do, in part, with changing United States immigration policy. After the passage of the Immigration Reform and Control Act (IRCA) in 1986, employers were prohibited from employing undocumented workers. Industries in which the plants were larger were more likely to enforce this provision. Undocumented male workers, who at one time had been able to find other, better jobs, are now driven to seek work in the garment industry, which, with its multiple and dispersed small factories and its large underground economy, continues to employ workers without legal papers. The prevalence of illegal practices in the industry on so many other fronts apparently makes disobeying the immigration laws only a minor additional infraction.

It is often argued that employers would prefer "cheaper," more docile female workers. The willingness to hire male workers should, however, come as no surprise, because in the garment industry male workers are no less politically disadvantaged than are their female counterparts. Both male and female workers are likely to be undocumented and therefore vulnerable to deportation if they attract the attention of public officials. Men may even be preferable to women: they are likely to be physically stronger and are less likely to be burdened by family responsibilities that take them away from work. There may also be cultural factors at work. In some Latin American cultures, for example, in Guatemala, men engage in weaving and sewing, so that these are not necessarily seen by men as a form of women's work, beneath their dignity. Possibly contributing to the rising number of male sewing machine operators is the primary method of payment: by the piece, called a piece rate. Workers are paid by the number of operations they have performed rather than by the hour. Because one's productivity, hence pay, is determined by one's own effort, gender may be less relevant. If a woman cannot keep up the same speed as a man, or vice versa, it matters little—both are paid only for the actual work done.

ETHNICITY

The ethnic composition of the workforce in the garment industry has changed. Originally garment workers in New York City and elsewhere on the east coast were mainly Jewish and Italian immigrants. Today, the industry workforce is mainly composed of Asian and Latino immigrants in centers such as New York, San Francisco, Philadelphia, El Paso, and Miami, whereas African-American and white women predominate in the garment factories of the South. In the early years, garment workers in Los Angeles were Jewish, but were principally Mexican by the 1930s. By 1990 the ethnic composition of employees in the Los Angeles apparel industry was staggeringly diverse: There were Europeans, Asians, Latinos, and Middle Easterners from a wide variety of countries, as well as Americans of diverse ethnic backgrounds. Latinos accounted for two-thirds of the industry as a whole. Among Latinos, Mexicans constituted the largest group of apparel industry employees by far, numbering almost half of all workers (47 percent). Central Americans were the second largest group, with 14 percent; other Latinos comprised six percent. Asians (including Chinese, Koreans, and other Asians) accounted for 14 percent of all workers and, among them, the Chinese were numerically most significant (7 percent), followed by Koreans (4 percent). Europeans comprised 8 percent of the industry. African-Americans made up only 2 percent. The remaining nine percent was not identified.

Ethnic diversity in the apparel industry does not mean ethnic equality: Different ethnic groups play different roles. Table 6 shows the ethnic division of labor as of 1990. As can be seen, relative to their overall numbers in the industry, Europeans are overrepresented in managerial and white-collar occupations, Asians, especially Koreans, are overrepresented in management (reflecting their owning and managing contracting shops; about 25 percent are either self-employed or working in a family business), and Latinos, especially Mexicans, are overrepresented among operatives and laborers.

We have observed that most of the Latino workers in the garment industry appear to be dark skinned. In other words, they are usually partly or largely indigenous in origin, a heritage often associated with lower status and discrimination in their native countries. Moreover some Guatemalans are still affiliated with indigenous cultures; Spanish can be their second language and they may not speak it very well. The Indians of the Americas remain among the most exploited of workers in this industry.

Latinos make up 25 percent of the managers, but are fully 75 percent of the garment workers (operatives). Asians constitute about 13 percent of the garment workers, but 31 percent of the managers. Close to 30 percent of the managers, but only 2 percent of the garment workers, are white. One can see in these numbers a fairly severe ethnic division of labor, with whites at the top, Asians in the middle and to some extent, at the bottom, and Latinos mainly at the bottom.

Significantly, African Americans are largely absent from this industry at all levels. As shown in Table 6, only one percent of the garment workers in Los Angeles is African-American. Given the high rate of unemployment among African-American youth, we might expect that garment production would offer opportunity for employment, especially for those who have had limited education. It is not, and various reasons were suggested to us by manufacturers, union officials, and others in the industry: discrimination by employers who believe that immigrants and/or Latinos will work harder for less; the availability of welfare for United States citizens as an alternative to having to work in a low-wage job; and the absence among African Americans of the informal job recruitment networks that are routinely found in both Latino and Asian communities.

Changes in immigration and welfare policies have increased interest in the employment of African Americans as garment workers. Immigration authorities, backed by public antiimmigrant sentiment, are cracking down on the employment of undocumented immigrants. The industry still continues to employ undocumented workers in large numbers, but the INS raids and stepped-up efforts to crack down on the production of fraudulent documents have increased the pressure on garment industry employers to find alternatives. Welfare reform, which is forcing people, especially women, back into the labor market, may provide an important source for the industry. African Americans are obviously not the only welfare recipients, but they may be among those who are pushed to look for garment work.

The Economic Roundtable issued a report about job opportunities for welfare recipients in Los Angeles.[11] Reviewing the report, Alison Neider, a local journalist, mentioned the long-standing justification for low wages in the industry: "To many people involved in the industry, a minimum wage job such as a sewing machine operator is a logical first rung on the ladder of opportunity, a chance to gain needed work experiences and entry into a marketplace with avenues for advancement."[12] Clotee McAfee, an African-American manufacturer, who developed training programs for youth in South Central Los Angeles, in the wake of the 1992 uprising, is one of those who believes in the opportunities afforded by the industry.[13] The authors of the Economic Roundtable report do not. Despite the facts that the local apparel industry is already a regular employer of people now on welfare and that jobs in the industry are growing, Neider commented that "the report warns aid recipients away from entry-level positions such as sewing machine operators, saying such jobs are typified by low wages and sporadic employment. Indeed, the report finds that nearly 40 percent of sewing machine operators with no public assistance are living below the poverty line." Alice Callaghan, the director of the community center Las Familias del Pueblo, concurs. "The pay is low, and there are no health benefits." No "mainstream American worker would take an entry level job as a sewing machine operator. . . . Right now [underground manufacturers] can hire people for $1 or $2 an hour."[14] Nevertheless, McAfee says that the industry is positioning itself to be able to absorb these workers. As a result, we may see more efforts to recruit African-American workers.

Gender and ethnicity interact. For example, among Chinese men, 30 percent were managers and 40 percent were garment workers. Among Chinese women, only 6 percent were managers while almost 80 percent were garment workers. The gender division of labor is less stark for the Latinos, mainly because most men and women alike are found at the bottom of the occupational hierarchy. Thus among Mexican men, 4 percent were managers and 60 percent were garment workers. For Mexican women, 2 percent were managers and almost 80 percent were garment workers. Mexicans remain the most important segment of the garment workforce, with Mexican women predominating, although Mexican men comprise an important (and growing) segment. All told, Latina women make up 55 percent of all garment workers and Asian women make up another 11 percent; two out of three garment workers are thus Latina or Asian women. By way of contrast, Latino men make up 20 percent and Asian men only 2 percent.

CITIZENSHIP

In 1990 about 85 percent of the entire apparel workforce in Los Angeles was made up of immigrants, 15 percent of whom had been naturalized. Even 20 percent of the whites were immigrants, including half who were naturalized. About 33 percent of the Asian immigrants were naturalized citizens compared with between 10 and 15 percent of Latinos. Among Asians, about three-quarters of Koreans were not citizens.

Professionals and sales personnel were much more likely to have been born in the United States than were members of any other occupational group. Garment workers were the least likely: 94 percent of all operatives were immigrants, with less than 15 percent having acquired United States citizenship. In general, there appears to be a strong correlation between the status of a person's occupation and status as a citizen. The higher ranked the occupation, the higher the percentage of United States–born people employed in it; the lower an occupation ranks, the higher the percentage of noncitizens working in it. The one important exception is the occupation of manager, which includes immigrant entrepreneurs who are mainly contractors. Almost 40 percent of the managers had not (yet) become United States citizens.

Regardless of immigration status, ethnicity remains a potent factor in the division of labor in this industry. This may be caused by racial discrimination, but it may also be a product of other characteristics of the groups, such as education, knowledge of English, and especially, availability of capital. The education and backgrounds of immigrants vary widely. Many Latinos are from rural villages, where they received very little formal education. Some are political refugees and may have degrees. They work in the industry because they lack papers or do not know any English. Some Asian workers, especially Koreans and Vietnamese, come from cities and have considerable education. They may work in the industry to gain the experience needed to open up their own contracting shops. Among the Chinese there is more of a dichotomy, with mainland people coming from more rural and educationally disadvantaged areas, while those from Hong Kong and Taiwan are more highly educated (many of the latter either become contractors or enter other fields). On the whole, it is fair to say that most garment workers are handicapped in the labor market because they lack education or a knowledge of English or both.

UNDOCUMENTED IMMIGRANTS

In 1979, Sheldon Maram directed a survey, conducted by the staff of the Concentrated Enforcement Program of the California Department of Industrial Relations, of 499 garment workers.[15] Obviously, these data are old and conditions may have changed considerably since the time they were collected. Nevertheless, they do give us some sense of the employment of undocumented immigrants in this industry. Maram found that 81 percent of the garment workers who responded were un-documented, a ratio that corresponds roughly to the percentage reported by the census as Latino immigrants who are not naturalized. Maram was focusing on "Hispanic" immigrants, (83 percent Mexicans) so does not give us a sense of the numbers of Asian and other garment workers who were not documented.

Maram and his colleagues found that most undocumented garment workers were not migrant workers, but had established permanent resi-dence in the United States.[16] The average wage for Latino garment work-ers was the minimum wage of the time, $2.90 an hour, and a substantial percentage was paid below that. Many did not receive the required over-time pay. Few received the standard fringe benefits of paid sick leave, health insurance, and vacations. Legal Latino immigrants received slightly higher wages than the undocumented did—an average of $3.15 an hour—but they too were unlikely to receive fringe benefits. This study suggests that un-documented workers are common in the apparel industry, and pay a price for their immigration status in the form of lower-than-average wages.

Working Conditions

Our description of conditions in the industry is based on reviews of numerous scholarly studies and government reports, system-atic interviews, and conversations with many garment workers and people who work closely with garment workers. The conclusions we draw are the fruits of ten years spent investigating this industry.[17]

Systematic interviews, of which forty-six were completed, were con-ducted between November 1991 and January 1993 by Gregory Scott. Alba Grande, who had worked in the industry for seventeen years until she was diagnosed with carpal tunnel syndrome, helped translate and tran-scribed taped materials. Workers were recruited by word of mouth, on the sidewalks outside their workplaces, or around lunch trucks, and a "snowball" method of sampling, in which interviewees were asked to iden-tify others who might be interviewed, was used. Participants for longer interviews were paid $10 for their time, although dozens of shorter, more informal conversations contributed to the research as well. About half of the interviews were conducted in the workers' homes, and half occurred at the Garment Workers Justice Center.

All but eight of those interviewed were women, the disproportion a result of our desire to understand the lives of those who experience the harshest conditions. Twenty-three of the workers were undocumented, ten possessed Amnesty Resident Cards, six had green cards, two had alien resident cards, two had migrant workers' permits (*arreglos de los campos*), and one had a temporary protected status (TPS) card. Interviewees ranged in age from twenty-three to forty-six years; the average age was thirty-four. The group was also disproportionately Central American: twenty were from El Salvador, twelve from Guatemala, ten from Mexico, one from Argentina, and one from Ecuador. Respondents had been in the United States from between two to twenty-three years, with an average of nine years. Twenty-seven were currently married; eight (including one man) had children who were still living in their home country. Four were actively involved with the Justice Center, four were somewhat involved, and thirty-six not at all.

As befits the connotations of the word *sweatshop,* working conditions in the garment industry are not pleasant. Wages are low, payment by the piece rate is oppressive, and no benefits are provided. Taxes are sometimes illegally withheld from workers' paychecks, yet are not reported to the IRS. Workers sometimes even report having to provide their own equipment. The industry is cyclical, with no job security. Workers are often harassed by their immediate supervisors. Homework, although illegal, is not uncommon. All in all, the workers on the lowest rungs in this industry have very few resources and no effective defenses.

PHYSICAL CONDITIONS

We have not systematically visited factories throughout Los Angeles County, so our impressions of physical conditions are based on a sampling of those factories to which we have had access, and on interviews and discussions with workers. We suspect that factory conditions vary. For example, garment district factories are mainly located in old, high-rise office buildings, which were not constructed for manufacturing. In contrast, some of the factories in Vernon are located in industrial parks, where cinder block, single-story structures were built for this function. Apart from these more publicly accessible work sites, there are numerous irregular sites, such as small factories tucked away in corners, and even garages serving as sewing factories.

Many garment factories in Los Angeles are found in the lofts of the fashion district. These factories tend to require variances from the city council because they do not conform to the legal standards for manufacturing. Among the hazardous conditions that have been found by inspectors are blocked exits, doors that open inward instead of outward, dangerous wires lying on the floor, and uncapped gas lines. The danger of fire is high.

In 1994 a survey to ascertain the frequency of health and safety violations was conducted by the Targeted Industries Partnership Program, a combined state and federal enforcement effort (see Chapter 8), of a sample of garment shops in California.[18] The survey focused exclusively on sewing contractors, ending up with sixty-nine cases for which they were able to obtain comparable data. Ninety-three percent of the factories, all but five, had health and safety problems. In ten factories a fire would have trapped workers inside because doors were either locked or blocked. In more than 33 percent, safety problems that could result in serious injury or death were found. After a follow-up survey conducted in 1996, it was reported that serious health and safety problems were found in 72 percent of garment factories.

Garment workers also face health and safety problems connected with the work itself. In addition to eye strain, back problems, and repetitive motion injuries, workers suffer from breathing dust and chemicals associated with certain textile treatments. They also sometimes work on sewing machines that have inadequate protection from machinery wheels and electrical wiring. In recent years the Cal-OSHA Standards Board has focused on the dangers surrounding the use of tagging guns. Workers occasionally shoot themselves accidentally, and there is a fear that AIDS can be transmitted this way. (Similar to stapling machines, tagging guns are used to affix tags and shoulder pads to garments.)

PIECEWORK

Garment workers typically work on piece rate, that is, they are paid for each procedure they complete. For example, piece rates for the various parts of a skirt sold by The Limited, Inc. for $54—of which less than $3 went to the workers—were as follows: seventy-two cents for waistband with facing, six cents for hemming the skirt, six cents for hemming the lining, fourteen cents for serging the skirt (overcasting the raw edges of a piece of fabric to prevent raveling), fourteen cents for serging the lining, four cents for cutting threads, ten cents each for making up four belt loops, eight cents each for sewing the belt loops on the skirt, seventeen cents for inserting the zipper, fifteen cents for pressing, and fifteen cents each for ironing the loops.[19] Piecework is similar to the pay system in California agriculture, where farm workers are paid for the number of pounds they pick.

Both California and federal law require that workers be paid minimum wage and overtime even if their output under the piece-rate system is insufficient to meet these standards. The employer is supposed to keep time cards and ensure that the hourly minimum wage is covered and that, when employees work more than eight hours a day (the law in California until 1 January 1998), or forty hours a week (federal, and now state, law), they must be paid 1.5 times their base wage. Contractors are typically very unwilling to pay more than whatever the worker earned by the piece rate, which is pegged to the price that the manufacturer pays the contractor for the garment. If required to pay more than the piece rate, the contractor feels that the money is being taken directly out of his pocket, an unfair extra.

To avoid paying over the piece rate, garment contractors have devised numerous and ingenious schemes. The United States Department of Labor lists the most common. Contractors have been known to:

Have two sets of time cards, one for weekdays and one for weekends, or one for regular hours and one for extra hours.

Alter time cards or not record all hours worked. Contractors may deduct time for meal breaks that workers didn't take. They may deduct time for slow or down periods during the day. They may not record time spent on corrections (rework time). They may not record evening and weekend work. They may change the time cards after the fact to make deductions.

Use fictitious time cards that do not match employees' names.

Require employees to work for different entities owned by the same employer. The hours worked under different firm names or ownership structures are not totaled, so that the actual hours worked are hidden.

"Back into hours," a stratagem by which the contractor pays a promised piece rate, then divides the total earnings for the week by the minimum wage to arrive at a fictitious number of hours worked. He may even make it appear that he is paying overtime, but the rate is not based on real hours worked.

Use the minimum wage rate to calculate overtime, even though regular hourly earnings (made under a piece rate) are higher than the minimum wage.

Pay overtime as a bonus. The contractor pays straight-time rates for overtime hours and then gives workers an extra payment at some arbitrary rate instead of paying proper overtime rates.

Provide cash payments at straight-time rates, with no records kept, for overtime weekend and night work.

List several people on one time card, without a set pay period. For example, home workers are sometimes put on the same card as their regularly employed relatives.

No doubt there are many other scams. Some contractors punch the time clock for their workers at a time of their own choosing, or require workers to work for an hour before clocking in. Inspectors report seeing time cards with exactly the same times punched in and out, suggesting that someone other than the worker is tending to this task. Some factory owners, in filing their quarterly tax documents with the IRS, claim that their workers are independent contractors, and for whom payroll taxes need not be withheld. Nevertheless, they deduct such taxes from the workers' paychecks. Few workers understand the paperwork, and have no idea how to file as independent contractors with the IRS. Contractors sometimes hide the set of books they use for their own accounting, and show inspectors a different set, doctored to appear legitimate, thereby hiding a rat's nest of illegal practices. The variety and creativity of these stratagems demonstrates how motivated the contractors are to avoid paying minimum wage and overtime.

Piece rate has a psychological impact on the workers. In a sense, they themselves control how much money they make by how long and hard they work, but the system encourages self-exploitation. This was an aspect of early twentieth-century sweatshops, where workers would sleep at their machines in order to work every waking hour. Piece rates encourage workers to labor at intense speeds, sometimes to the detriment of their health as they develop back problems, eye strain, and repetitive motion injuries. Nor do workers have any apparent collective interest, because their work has not been socialized, as occurs on an assembly line, where each worker depends on all the others for the pace of the line.[20] Most garment factories in Los Angeles use a modified form of assembly line, known as the progressive bundle system. A worker, seated at a sewing machine, is given a bundle of cut garments. She takes each garment from the bundle and attends to her part of it, sewing on the pockets, for example. When she is done with all the garments in that bundle, she ties it up and passes it on to the next worker for the next procedure, sewing up the seams, for example. Even though the garments are sewn sequentially, there is no pace that would be imposed by a moving belt.[21] Each worker takes as long as the work requires before passing it on. Insofar as this system reduces the dependence of workers on one another, it serves as a disincentive to collective action. The worker feels as though she controls how much she earns. Faster workers feel superior to slower workers, and each one focuses on her own productivity. Even though workers realize that they are being manipulated, it is difficult for them to avoid the effects of the conditions under which they labor. They fear changing the piece-rate system, especially if they are among the quicker workers, believing that if they were paid by the hour, their wages would decline.

Piece rates serve to increase productivity in this industry without the need for capital investment, by intensifying labor, rather than by enhancing its efficiency through improved machinery.[22] It is for this reason that garment factories are described as sweatshops. Labor is sweated from the workers who are made to work incredibly hard, at great speeds, and for long hours. Although piece rates appear to reward productivity, to pay the worker what she really earned, this is a fiction: Contractors are under economic pressure to cut the piece rate when workers become efficient and consequently make "too much." The possibility that workers can make too much is rooted in the employer's basic belief that workers should be paid as low a wage as possible, irrespective of their productivity.

At least one person closely connected with contracting, Joe Rodriguez, the executive director of the Garment Contractors Association, has questions about piece rate. In the June 1997 *GCA Newsletter,* he pointed out that some of the GCA members were experiencing a labor shortage, especially of experienced operators with legal documents. "I feel that in order to attract a work force that is not primarily comprised of recent immigrants, the *method* of compensating operators needs to change. . . . I believe the unattractive aspect of our jobs to most applicants is our total reliance on the piecework method of compensating operators. Some innovations are needed."

Similarly, Paul Ratoff, a consultant to the apparel industry, also criticizes the piece-rate system from a management perspective.[23] He argues that piece rates lead workers to emphasize speed at the expense of quality, and to have no interest in checking the state of the garment as it reaches them. Piece rates discourage cooperation and teamwork, and lead the worker to have no interest in the goals of the firm. Moreover, they breed dissension among the workers. "In a piece-rate environment," he comments, "there often develops a two-tier ranking of workers: the top tier 'higher producers' and the rest of the sewers (lower tier). The higher producers tend to become prima donnas because they receive much of the supervisor's attention. Even with the attention, they are not necessarily loyal employees. If their output drops due to external factors (such as new styles, machine breakdown, etc.), they tend to move on to other plants where they can earn more money. The second-tier employee often resents them, thereby creating friction and an uncooperative atmosphere in the workplace."

We do not for a minute want to suggest that a switch to hourly wages would serve as a panacea for this industry's problems. Workers are right to be suspicious of, and resistant to such a change. Many offshore assembly plants pay workers on an hourly basis, imposing daily work quotas as a means of pressuring workers to labor at maximum speeds, and forcing them to put in overtime hours to complete their quotas. Unrealistic goals are set for young workers, so that they sometimes have to work into the night, as well as take work home with them to finish. But we do believe that replacing the piece-rate system with a *decent* hourly wage would be a significant improvement.

WAGES

The average garment worker in Los Angeles made $7,200 a year in 1990, at a time when the minimum wage for full-time year-round work totaled $8,840, and when the poverty level for a family of three was defined as $10,419, and for a family of four as $13,359. There were some ethnic and gender differences. Mexican men, for example, averaged $8,160 compared with Mexican women, who made $6,500. Chinese women averaged $5,464, whereas other Asian women made $7,500. These differences are not substantial. There can be no doubt that garment workers in Los Angeles earn very low wages indeed.

Another way to gauge this is to calculate the amount of wages that are lost to all garment workers in Los Angeles by the illegal practices of the industry. In 1998, the Department of Labor estimated that, in a typical ninety-day period, the average apparel contracting shop accumulates $3,631 in back wages owed. Stretching this figure out to cover a year, and multiplying it by an estimated 5,000 shops in Los Angeles (a procedure recommended by Jerry Hall of the department), gives us a figure of $72,620,000 in unpaid wages per annum.

Although the average wage is low, some garment workers are able to make more than the minimum wage by working fast and working extra hours. Nevertheless, payment problems abound in this industry. Merced Gonzales [real names are not used], a thirty-five-year-old Salvadoran garment worker who lives with her mother and two children in a housing project near Dodger Stadium, told us that she had worked for fourteen years in the same garment shop, hoping for a raise that never came.

I always take work seriously so that the owner will express satisfaction with my work. Nine years had passed when I asked him for a raise, but what a surprise! He wanted to know, "What's it for?" He shouted his question at me. I left the office and never, never tried for any raise again.

With the Koreans I received $7 for one day of ironing from 7:30 a.m. to 5:00 p.m. Once in a while, they call me to go back to work again. I don't want it since it costs $2.70 for the bus, $3.00 in food, which left me with $1.30.

In some places the wage is the minimum [at the time $4.25 an hour], but others, like the one on Figueroa and Twenty-sixth Street, I worked two weeks and three days for free. The person who hired us said, when we were supposed to be paid for the first week, that the manufacturer did not pay the owner. At the end of the second week, we were sent to the owner, who didn't even know us. Nobody received any money. She [the owner] is Salvadoran and her husband is Mexican. She told the women who were receiving welfare that they better not do anything or she would accuse them of getting welfare while working.

Diego Vasquez, a forty-two-year-old single man from El Salvador, told us that "undocumented workers are preferred because they accept prices like they are. If $5 is missing from the pay, people would rather be silent than go somewhere else. Even though they are paying in cash, when 70 cents out of $41.50 is missing, we don't know why. When you leave the job, the last week is never paid."

Stories of nonpayment abound in the industry. Groups of workers will walk into the Garment Workers Justice Center and report that they have not been paid for three weeks, and now their factory has shut down and the owner has disappeared. Collecting the money owed under such circumstances is very difficult, even for government enforcement agencies.

One successful pursuit was that of the Western Jean Company, an employer of 350 workers. Western Jean was already under investigation by the Department of Labor for wage violations when it failed entirely to make payroll in June 1997, a month before it went out of business. The department was not able to collect from the owners of Western Jean, but did collect $165,000 from a manufacturer, Fashion Resources Inc., that used the contractor. It took seven months for the workers to receive the money, but the department considered this to be an improvement over the usual delay of more than a year.[24]

BENEFITS

Paid only for their direct labor, garment workers rarely receive any benefits. Not only do they typically not receive paid medical insurance, but also they do not usually receive the basic benefits that most United States workers have long taken for granted: paid holidays, vacations, and sick leave. This can be seen as a concomitant of the piece-rate system: They have no guaranteed rights to payment while they are not working.

Nor do they have any job security. If they become sick or give birth, they have no claim to the job. They may arrange with the employer to take time off for necessary emergencies, but there is no system in which their jobs would be held for them. Obviously, a highly skilled and desirable worker may be able to arrange to hold onto her job, but for the majority of workers, who are generally interchangeable in the eyes of the employer, no guarantees are likely to be provided.

Garment workers almost never receive raises. Again this is linked to the piece-rate system. The only way a garment worker can make more money is by working faster or for more hours. Sometimes this intensification and extension of labor leads to reductions in the piece rate, rather than payment for the extra effort. The recent passage of a higher minimum wage by both the federal and state governments has not led to a rise in piece rates for most workers, and has resulted only in speedups and increased job insecurity.

The issue of health coverage is especially troubling because, without it, many garment workers depend on the overloaded county system. The contracting system contributes to this problem. The margins of most contractors are too low to sustain health-insurance payments for garment workers, and the manufacturers, many of whom could afford to pay, deny that they have any responsibility to cover health benefits for the workers who sew their clothes.

In an effort to improve the image of the industry, and counter its sweatshop reputation, the California Fashion Association has instituted a health-insurance program that would lower insurance costs for member companies. The difficulties of implementing such a plan for garment workers were described by Joe Rodriguez of the Garment Contractors Association. "The contractors can't afford any additional costs right now. . . . The prices from the manufacturers don't allow them to offer benefits. . . . For them to pay the premium on behalf of employees is out of the question, really." Rodriguez expects that many firms will not even tell their employees about the plan for fear that it would raise expectations that could not be met.[25]

EQUIPMENT AND TOOLS

Workers are sometimes required to purchase their own production equipment, a practice that is strictly illegal because it essentially means that the cost of the equipment is being deducted from workers' meager wages. Requiring workers to buy their own scissors is not uncommon. A less obvious, but not uncommon, requirement is that they purchase *la pata* (literally, the paw), the foot used to guide the fabric through the stitching channel on the sewing machine, and an expensive item that must be used by even the most experienced garment workers. Workers also sometimes purchase the devices used to fold jeans and other heavy fabrics; without this equipment production would be slow and sloppy in most cases and would consequently go uncompensated. Feet and folders can often be purchased from the factory owners or managers, but, reportedly, at a twofold markup. "Workers using *caballos* [machines used in the production of denim jeans] earn $60 or $80 daily, but the worker must buy the folder, which costs $70 or $100, depending on its brand name. In most factories, workers buy the different feet for the machines. The cheapest might cost $25." The requirement that workers provide some of their own equipment marks the primitive character of this industry. Although it gives the appearance that workers are entrepreneurial part-owners of the means of production, in fact the practice serves as but another means of wresting earnings from the workers.

INDUSTRIAL HOMEWORK

Homework, which is illegal in this industry, is common. For example, when investigating welfare fraud in Orange County in 1989, inspectors found that between 70 and 80 percent of the homes they visited had industrial sewing machines in them.[26] In one instance, according to the Department of Labor, a Latina woman and three of her children, aged seven, ten, and fourteen, averaged $1.45 an hour for sewing they did at home. This example is instructive of the shadowy network of contracting and subcontracting that hides homework and diffuses responsibility throughout the industry. The Valladares family was sewing clothes for En Chante Inc., a dress and sportswear manufacturer in Los Angeles. The garments were sold in J. C. Penney, Wal-Mart, and Sears. En Chante had contracted with a registered contractor, Su Enterprises, which subcontracted to Addison Fashion, a small, unregistered, Viet-namese-owned factory in Garden Grove. Addison farmed out the work to Ms. Valladares's family.[27]

Homework can take a variety of forms. Some home workers spend a full day in the factory and then take work home with them. Others work only at home, receiving work at their homes and having it picked up when it is completed. Some home workers engage in repetitive, partial tasks in the construction of garments; others sew the entire garment. Home workers vary in ethnicity, and include Latinas and Asians. Virtually all of them are women.

Rosa Martha Fregoso studied apparel home workers in Los Angeles.[28] She conducted in-depth interviews and oral histories with eight Latina home workers, seven of whom were Mexican and one Salvadoran. All had legal documentation, and one was a United States citizen. Fregoso found that home workers were among the lowest paid of garment workers. One woman worked in the mid-1980s for a contractor who made women's clothes for swap meets. She was paid 50 cents for sewing complete pairs of pants. Working six days a week, twelve hours a day, she was able to make $200 a week, or about $2.77 an hour, well below the $3.35 minimum wage at that time. Another woman sewed cuffs, collars, and pockets on women's blouses, for a piece rate assigned to each of the tasks. In 1979, when she began working, she made between $80 and $100 a week. Twelve years later, in 1991, she was making between $30 and $150 for the same tasks (pp. 50–52). There is, of course, no record of hours kept for home workers, making it impossible to ensure that they earn the hourly minimum wage. And home workers never receive the overtime premium, nor do they get benefits—no workers' compensation or unemployment insurance, no social security, and no disability protections. They are denied paid holidays, sick pay, medical benefits, and vacation pay. Only one of the twenty employers discussed in Fregoso's study offered any benefits at all: quarterly and end of the year bonuses based on the worker's productivity (pp. 55–56).

Not only do home workers receive low pay; but also they must bear a part of the cost of production. Most must purchase or rent an industrial sewing machine which, according to Fregoso, ranged in price from $250 to $1,600 over the time encompassed by her study (from the early 1970s to 1991), depending on whether they bought a new or used machine. One woman rented an overlock machine for $50 a month. Home workers must also pay for machine maintenance and supplies, as well as covering the cost of utilities. And some must transport the garments back and forth from the contractor, using their own cars. Getting the job can be contingent on being able to provide the transportation (pp. 57–59).

Despite the fact that home workers appear to have some autonomy and to be even more like minientrepreneurs than the piece rate system creates, in fact their autonomy is a myth. Home workers can rarely control the pace of their work. Supervisors use the telephone to pressure them to get the work done and threaten them by making future work contingent on meeting the contractor's schedule. They are working under so much pressure that it is difficult for the women to take care of their children or get the housework done, tasks that are supposedly accommodated by homework (pp. 67–71).

The home workers Fregoso interviewed reported various health problems, among them respiratory problems caused by breathing in cotton dust particles, back pain, allergies, rashes, eye problems, and high blood pressure (pp. 59–61). Feeling the need to be working every spare minute, and rarely having a chance to leave the house, the women also experienced considerable stress, anxiety, and isolation. As one woman put it, she felt like a prisoner in her own home (p. 78).

Home work is often accompanied by child labor. At a minimum, children may be exposed to the danger of playing near moving machinery and breathing cotton dust. Young children may be roped into helping their mother get her work done, trimming threads and folding and packing sewn garments. The labor of these children is unpaid by the contractor.

Despite the exploitation, some home workers choose this option as the best alternative they have. In a patriarchal culture that forces women to be responsible for domestic chores and child care, a mother who sews at home can simultaneously take care of young children and not have to pay for unaffordable child care. Some men may not want their wives to work outside the home, but are willing to permit them to take work into the home. The prevalence of sexual harassment on the job may make working at home preferable. Undocumented status may influence the choice: home workers are less likely to be detected. In addition, because home workers are often paid in cash, they find it easier to avoid taxes; even cash payments made in factories are more easily traced.[29] Fregoso quotes one worker's reasons for getting into homework. "After the birth of my first son, my husband didn't want me to work. But I kept working. Then I got pregnant with my second son and my husband told me again that he didn't want me to continue working. That would mean taking two children to day care. With what I earned, I wouldn't have enough money to pay for child care and transportation to and from work. At that time I was paying $25 for each child which meant $50 total. After paying for child care, transportation, and food for the kids, what would be left of my earnings? So I quit working at the factory and began sewing at home for the same employer."[30]

Most home workers realize that they are being exploited. Most even recognize that, as home workers, they are worse off than any other worker in the entire production system of apparel manufacturing. Nevertheless, given the constraints of their lives, this is the best that they can do and they are likely to defend their right to do it, a position that puts them at odds with the state, which has banned industrial homework, and with unions, which fought hard to ban homework because of the inability to control the exploitation associated with it. Homework raises serious contradictions in that the most victimized of workers find that those who have taken the responsibility for protecting workers—unions and state labor inspectors—prove to be their enemies, ready to throw them out of the work they so desperately need. Meanwhile, contractors, and ultimately manufacturers and retailers, gain from this secondary antagonism, as homeworkers appear to conspire willingly with them in their own exploitation.

SEASONALITY AND LAYOFFS

Apparel manufacturing is a seasonal industry, although in recent years the seasonal fluctuations have been muted by the robust growth of the industry as a whole. The EDD collects monthly employment statistics by which the ebb and flow of employment over the year may be tracked.[31] In 1997, for example, official monthly employment in apparel and textiles in Los Angeles County averaged 114,867 people. The year began with a low of 109,500 workers in January, peaked in May at 116,000, declined to 114,000 in July, then rose steadily throughout the remainder of the year to December, when employment was 117,000. An examination of patterns for the fourteen-year period, 1983 through 1997, shows that employment typically peaks in the spring and bottoms out in the summer, with the peaks and troughs standing at roughly 6 or 7 percent above or below the average. Historically there have been 12,000 more jobs available at the high point of the cycle than there have been at the low point. If we assume that most of this variation is among sewing machine operators, we can assume that as many as 10 percent of the workers are affected by seasonal shifts in employment, which is perhaps why in Los Angeles, apparel sewing is one of the occupations with the highest number of welfare recipients.[32]

Few contractors can rely on a steady stream of work from manufacturers. If a manufacturer has a close relationship to a contractor, he is likely to try to provide that contractor with stable work. Despite the highly competitive nature of the industry, there is value in long-term ties, both between manufacturer and contractor and between contractor and worker. A reliable relationship can pay off in time of need. If a manufacturer needs a rush job done, he can turn to a contractor with whom he has an established relationship in order to be given priority. Likewise the contractor: If he treats them all as disposable, he may find that, when a rush job comes in and he needs workers to put in extra hours, he will not be able to count on them. For these reasons, stabilized networks of relationships do arise in this industry. Typically, for example, a manufacturer may have fairly stable relationships with one or more contractors who constitute his core suppliers. But as a whole, contractors are located in concentric circles of increasing insecurity, where they are struggling to ensure their next job.

Garment workers are *contingent* labor, employed and paid only when their work is needed. If there is no work, they are sent home, or sit around without pay until work arrives. When work is available in abundance, or there is a rush order, they have to work long hours. Both the contractor and the workers work according to the manufacturers' schedules. The availability of work depends on the success or failure of particular fashions, as well as on seasonal variations. The contractor deals with fluctuations in the amount of work by manipulating the number of workers and the hours worked. This arrangement obviously maximizes efficiency and flexibility for the manufacturers and contractors, but the workers have no job security from day to day. Many of the risks associated with fashion and seasons trickle down the system and settle on their shoulders.

WORKERS AS COMMODITIES

A relatively recent innovation in garment contracting is the use of "human resource technology" firms that, like temporary agencies such as Manpower, hire workers who are then subcontracted to employers. For example, Staf-Cor, in Torrance, "buys" the workers in a garment factory and then "leases" them back to the factory owner. Staf-Cor thus assumes responsibility for the wages and benefits of the workers, relieving the contractor of this burden. Such an approach interposes yet another layer between worker and employer, and can contribute to even greater control of the workforce. Abuses of this practice have resulted in court cases involving charges of fraudulent business conduct on the part of such firms.

ABUSES AND HARASSMENT

Compounding the workers' lack of job security is a tolerance of abuse and harassment that pervades the industry. Most garment factories in Los Angeles are small. Many lack bureaucratic rules and a bureaucratic hierarchy to enforce authority. Instead they depend on the personal authority of the owner and his supervisors to maintain control, which lends itself to abuses of all kinds. These include favoritism, the demanding of sexual favors, arbitrary punishments, and arbitrary firings. Workers complain of being yelled at by factory owners or supervisors and sometimes even of being hit. Personal power can be exerted over workers in a multitude of ways, such as not allowing them to go to the restroom or get a drink of water, switching them to an old, slow machine as a way of disciplining them, and cutting their pay. The ability of employers to exert this kind of personal authority encourages workers to curry favor with the supervisor in order to get in his good graces and avoid arbitrary maltreatment. One can easily envision the resulting manipulations engaged in by supervisors and the consequent divisions and resentments that arise among the workers.

Typically, apparel contracting firms have no grievance procedure. Workers can complain to the owner, but as the owner is often the perpetrator, either directly or indirectly through his agent, the supervisor, he is unlikely to provide much satisfaction. There is no independent, neutral system for the arbitration of grievances. Complaining to the employer is likely to bring retaliation. It is hopeless to try to bring about change by complaining, so most workers do not attempt it.

Ana Hernandez, at the time of our interview a forty-five-year-old woman from Mexico, came to Los Angeles with her husband when she was twenty-six. She had a green card, and lived with her husband and four children. Ana began sewing in Mexico when she was twelve years old, making dresses for wealthy women. She told us about her experiences in a previous garment job in Los Angeles.

In that factory we weren't allowed to talk with one another, and we could only use the bathroom less than three times each day because the managers were looking at everyone and asking us: "Why are you going so many times?" They also demanded very high levels of production. It was very severe.

The manager keeps staring at everyone. No one can turn around even to get advice regarding samples. I had an experience where a woman asked me about something that she didn't know about. The manager saw us talking and he came straight to us and said [to the other woman]: "Teresa, go home." We also couldn't make a telephone call even if it was an emergency.

[Piece rates get cut] when you start earning more than they expect you to earn. Then they lower the prices. So if you get a good check, they think it is because the prices are good, not because you are a good worker. If you say no [to reduced prices or increased work loads], the boss will not say anything to you about leaving at that moment. But you will be the next one in line to be fired. They will follow you, keep track of you, and with the first reason or mistake, they will say: "You are fired. Go home."

During a focus-group meeting of garment workers, held by Greg Scott and Alba Grande, one worker commented that, "at work, my boss sometimes shouts at innocent people. I think that he really wishes he could hit us. We can only guess because we don't understand him. A lot of people, women, have complained about the owner's behavior. He throws stuff in the faces of the workers when he gets angry. He treats us like we are animals."

Gloria Arevalo is a twenty-seven-year-old garment worker who is a single mother of one girl and one boy. Before leaving Guatemala in 1988, Gloria studied clothing design. She owned her own clothing shop well before her twenty-first birthday, and she also co-owned a wholesale store that sold beans, sugar, rice and other staples. At the time of this interview, Gloria was working in a Korean-owned factory where she embroidered hats and jackets for college and university bookstores. When we asked Gloria if she had ever witnessed moments when managers or owners would clash with workers either verbally or physically, she said, "I have seen it and it happened to me repeatedly. Four months ago, the manager was a younger man who had worked in my factory for three years. The Korean was abusing him. Can you imagine that happening to the manager? What did workers expect? The manager told the owner one time: 'Please don't shout at me.' The Korean said that he is the owner, so people may be mistreated by him. The manager got fired that day, and the excuse given by the other managers, supervisors, and accountants was that the manager was drunk."

Because apparel firms are small, they typically fall beneath the minimum size necessary to trigger the governmental oversight that would ensure that these kinds of abuses do not occur. A garment worker is always free to file a complaint for discriminatory treatment, but small businesses of this type are much less likely to be investigated, so their practices remain hidden.

FLOOR MANAGERS

More than half of the workers interviewed for this study specifically mentioned abuse from shop-floor managers. Managers are ordinarily employed in shops with more than about twenty people, and they are nearly always Latino. In smaller shops, the wife of the owner is often employed as the manager. The manager's job includes serving as a liaison between workers and the owner, which often translates into preventing workers from confronting the owner directly. Managers oversee production, offer assistance in sewing new or difficult garments, and check the tickets used to determine compensation in the piece-rate system. Managers can treat workers with extreme verbal brutality, behavior that incurs a sense of betrayal in workers of the same ethnicity.

Eva Meraz came to the United States in 1985 at the age of twenty-six and has lived in Los Angeles since her arrival. She did baby-sitting for quite a while and then got a job as a garment worker. Garment work is her favorite occupation, she says, because she knows it the best. Eva is married and has two children, both of whom are living in El Salvador. "Managers do a lot of insulting," she said. "My sister works in a place where the manager is from El Salvador. Recently, the manager almost slapped her in the face. Even though my sister is a Christian, she reacts quickly to those situations. She said: 'Don't ever do that to me.' Usually, managers treat people so badly. However, there are places where owners are also the managers and workers suffer anyway. Our people in this country have already forgotten who they were."

In 1985, Rebeca Martinez completed her high school education in her home country of Guatemala. At age seventeen Rebeca decided to join her older brother in Los Angeles, who was reportedly prospering by selling used automobiles. Rebeca has since worked in the garment industry, in a shoe store, and as a baby-sitter for "wealthy Anglos." While working two or three jobs, she is currently attending school to achieve occupational certification as a secretary.

I didn't like working in this business. I dislike how workers are mistreated, especially by the managers. It didn't only happen with me; it happened to lots of people working in factories. When they had a lot of work, they wanted us to work a lot, otherwise, we just worked two or three hours each day. Then they would send us home. I didn't like the way the manager shouted at everybody, which made people nervous. When it was lunch time, or break time, and if there was a lot of work to do, the manager would let us have only ten minutes for break.

The manager liked to shout and say bad things about the workers, including the girls who were working there. I wasn't working on the machines. I did trimming and the checking of blouses, but many times the manager told girls to hurry up, or similar things that made them nervous since he was the boss and whatever he did was supposedly right, so the girls would start crying. A lot of bad things happened. For example, I got sick one time, and so I arrived about an hour late. I called to tell them the reason I was going to be late. When I got there, everybody was working. The manager told me: "No more work for you." So I went home.

I think the way the workers are treated is not right. People keep this hard feeling inside themselves. They keep everything inside, because they are afraid of losing their job. They take advantage by telling you that if you don't like the job, then just beat it. I left for that reason. They can force people to leave the job because the managers are sure that a lot of people are looking for work.

When a girl was new, the manager stood behind her insinuating sexual things. This really bothered everybody there, but nobody could say anything because he was the manager. He was from El Salvador, but he had an Argentinian accent. The manager was living here for twelve years already.

He did a lot of bad things but it's hard to remember because every day he came up with something new. One day a Mexican girl had to return to Mexico the next day. So as her last day of work, she had a big bunch of work to finish. The manager shouted at her all day long, telling her that she must finish the work before leaving. Finally, the manager shouted very close to her ear and it shocked her. She screamed, and then she started crying, and that made everybody so upset. She stood up, grabbed her purse, and she left. She never came back or said anything, just like everybody does.

They take advantage of people just because they need the money, and because they need the money they are treated like dogs. When you feel you are alone, and all the people are afraid of speaking out, then you prefer to be quiet. I want to say that someone should help them, the workers, so that they don't feel obligated to be there. Please remember, we breathe and feel the same as other people do.

Yolanda Fuentes, a thirty-eight-year-old Ecuadoran woman, lived with her husband while their two children remained in Ecuador. She had twelve years of education in Ecuador, but does not speak much English, and lacks legal documentation. "One day," she told us, "the manager was angry and she started yelling at me. I became very nervous, and then I started crying. I don't know how, but a needle got stuck in my finger, and I started bleeding. I called her over to me and showed her my finger, and she told me, 'I don't want to see that.' And then I said, 'I want to go home,' and she said, 'No, you have to finish.' I said, 'No, I'm sorry, I can't.' And she said, 'Okay, you may go home. But tomorrow you have to be here early, at 7 o'clock.'

Teresa Mendoza was a thirty-year-old woman from Guatemala. She had lived in Los Angeles for nine years. She was single, living with her brother, sister, and sister-in-law. She qualified for amnesty and held a permanent resident card. She described a manager, a Latino who "is always bothering everybody. It's good for me that he is not in my department. A friend of mine told me that he invited her to go on a date. Her answer was no, and that was the reason he fired her. It is unfair that the manager uses this kind of excuse against the women at work."

Marta Garcia, who was born in El Salvador, came to Los Angeles when she was twenty-one, paying a coyote $ 1,500 to bring her across the border. She was pregnant and sick at the time. Now twenty-eight years old, she has been living in Los Angeles with her husband and two children, while two other children remain in El Salvador. She described the behavior of one of her supervisors.

They changed the managers in our shop, and the new one asked me to go out on a date, and I said no. So he said: "If you go out with me then I will accept what you do," instead of forcing me to do his work. When I refused he said: "Well, you have to do this and that." Like he was trading me.

[The Mexican or Latino managers] more often know that we don't have papers and they tell us that. When you try to say something, that you are being treated unfairly, then they say, "Okay, go to the Labor Commissioner with it." Because they know that you won't go because you are afraid. They like people who have recently come to this country because they don't know anything, so it is good for the managers.

MANIPULATION OF IMMIGRATION STATUS

Garment contractors often hire undocumented workers and can threaten to report them to the Immigration and Naturalization Service. Immigration laws, especially the Immigration Reform and Control Act of 1986, have created an enormous hidden economy of falsified legal documents for which immigrants pay between $300 and $500. The owner typically turns a blind eye to false documentation, sometimes even helping employees to obtain it. He agrees to hire the worker as a favor, in return for which the worker promises not to cause any trouble. The worker receives employment and relative security, and the owner is assured a more-or-less docile workforce.

But such an agreement is informal and hardly binding. Changes in ownership, especially in smaller shops, are frequent and rarely announced ahead of time. Suddenly, workers find themselves employed by entirely different people who have different expectations about what they do on the shop floor and off. Often such transitions enable the new owners to fire workers with seniority, a practice that leads workers to file costly claims for workers' compensation. Being on the run in search of work seems endemic to life as an undocumented worker in Los Angeles.

ETHNIC DISCRIMINATION

Discrimination because of ethnicity is common among garment workers. Ethnic differences can also mark favorable treatment. In some factories, employers or supervisors hire people whom they know personally and who receive special favors. Latino workers complain that Asian employers favor their Asian employees, giving them the best jobs and paying them better. Discrimination is also found within subgroups of the same ethnic category. There are, for instance, broad national and cultural differences separating workers from different Latin American countries and even within a given country. In one recent study growing discrimination against Guatemalans and Salvadorans by Mexicans was reported.[33]

The more serious discrimination is that which they cannot see: the institutional discrimination of an industry that is structured to use race, ethnicity, and immigration status to maintain a low-wage labor force. The retailers and manufacturers, who extract the profits, are protected by the screen of Korean and Latino contractors and floor managers who *appear* to be the workers' main oppressors.

PASSIVE RESISTANCE

Garment workers, as Rebeca Martinez put it, have very limited options for fighting back. They "consider themselves incapable of changing jobs or speaking up to stop all of the bad things that happen at work. They would often rather stay at the job, ignoring that something can be done. Some of the reasons why they stay and keep quiet are: They don't have papers, or they don't speak English. For them it is so hard to look outside the factory for work in another place."

In self-defense, many engage in what has been termed "weapons of the weak," that is, they subtly undermine the system while avoiding open confrontations that they are sure to lose.[34] These weapons are often the

only ones available to people who are otherwise vulnerable and powerless. One of the most common forms of resistance is to quit the job in
disgust. Rather than put up with poor conditions and low pay, garment
workers will walk out. This expression of defiance usually leads only to
the acceptance of another, equally poor job. But at least the worker has
had the satisfaction of knowing that she has not allowed a particular employer to abuse her any longer. Workers may respond to their oppression
by resorting to various questionable practices, such as

> Lying in order to receive MediCal, WIC (the special supplemental food
> program for women, infants, and children), or food stamps
>
> Collecting welfare while hiding the fact that one is working
>
> Filing fraudulent workers' compensation claims
>
> Misrepresenting the number of hours worked or pieces sewn
>
> Consenting to sexual relations with the owner in order to enjoy re-
> laxed working restrictions
>
> Helping to transport family members illegally into this country
>
> Working for cash and not filing the proper tax documents with the IRS
>
> Engaging in industrial homework
>
> Purchasing forged documents and representing themselves as legal
> residents

These forms of resistance are fraught with peril and unlikely to produce satisfactory results. Workers can (and do) file formal complaints with
the Labor Commissioner, take contractors to small claims court, and file
workers' compensation claims. However, legal redress is extremely limited, especially for undocumented workers. Even though they have the
right to file a legal claim, many are loath to do so for fear of reprisals. For
all workers, legal or illegal, even such basic evidence of wrongdoing as
pay stubs are seldom available, because wages are so often paid in cash.
Time cards are handled by owners and managers, and therefore can easily be altered. Workers' personal diaries of wages and hours are seldom
admissible in court.

Garment workers also engage in occasional shop-floor actions. The
most galling provocation is to have their piece rate cut, but other grievances may also provoke collective action. Sometimes they present demands to the owner or manager, and sometimes they go to the union
for help.

Opportunities for Upward Mobility

Apparel industry leaders often justify the low wages and poor working conditions of garment workers by describing the jobs as entry level. The implication is that workers will be able to move up and out of apparel work after a while. Moreover, even if the individual garment worker is not able to improve her own position, her children will be in a position to attend United States schools and improve their lot in life. After all, other immigrants have followed this same route, including the apparel manufacturers themselves, who often come from families in which the first generation of immigrants to the United States were garment workers.

Some garment workers are able to move up into contracting. It is our impression that this path to upward mobility is, however, far more available to Asians than it is to Latinos. Some Asians bring capital with them and, although they may start as workers in order to learn the business, they are prepared to acquire a contracting business of their own when they are ready. Presumably some Latino contractors have followed a similar path. But for the vast majority of Latino garment workers, such a move is out of the question. They make barely enough money to survive. Accumulating sufficient capital to open a business is impossible.

Evidence for this comes from our own survey of manufacturers, conducted in 1991. At that time only 4 percent of the manufacturers were Latino, and of the 182 largest firms for which we had data on ethnicity, although 21 were owned by Asians, not one was owned by a Latino. Contracting appears to be a slightly more open pathway to upward mobility for Latinos; three out of ten contractors are Latino, although theirs tend to be the smaller shops. For most Latinos, contracting represents an extremely limited avenue to upward mobility: In 1990, only 2 percent of Mexicans and 3 percent of Central Americans in the industry were self-employed and therefore likely to be contractors, compared with 22 percent of Koreans and 11 percent of Chinese. Other forms of upward mobility within the industry are severely restricted for sewing machine operators. There is no hierarchy of jobs in a typical garment factory, apart from those of a small supervisory staff. Becoming more skilled can improve one's situation slightly, but it does not protect one from seasonal layoffs, arbitrary treatment, or cuts in one's piece rate.

No doubt some garment workers are able to escape from the industry into better jobs, but the prospects are not good. Most garment workers do not speak English, and they would not be learning much at work. They would have to take English classes in their spare time, which is often in short supply. If garment workers are able to leave the industry, chances are they will only get equally dead-end jobs. Some garment workers do, either serially or simultaneously, hold other, low-wage jobs: hotel and restaurant work, domestic service, janitorial service, gardening, and street vending, none of which provides high wages or job security.

The problems of upward mobility for immigrant Latinos in Los Angeles are underscored by Roger Waldinger, who points out that, while Asian immigrants appear to be experiencing some upward mobility, the same cannot be said for newcomers from Mexico and Central America.[35] "A search for immigrant progress will find few glimmers of hope in the record of the past two decades. . . . Already very segregated from other groups in 1970, Mexicans became more and more so, in occupational and industrial terms, over time. . . . Between 1970 and 1990, real earnings in the Mexican immigrant industrial niches declined by over $6,000 a year. . . . There is substantial evidence to indicate that newcomers from Mexico (and Central America as well) find themselves not only at the bottom but at a bottom that is increasingly removed from the top and from which exit is hard to find" (pp. 457–58). Waldinger points out that Mexicans in Los Angeles have a very high proportion of children living in poverty, and that an impoverished background works against their likelihood of success. They are less likely to complete high school than other groups are, and with the decline of good, union jobs in the durable goods industries, there is some question as to how well they will be able to do (pp. 459–60).

Nor is the Los Angeles school system capable of remedying these difficulties. The immigrant parents and grandparents of today's garment manufacturers might have benefited from New York City's excellent public school system during the early years of this century, but the public schools of Los Angeles today are very different: overcrowded, segregated, underfunded, and gang-ridden. Middle-class taxpayers, along with their children and their tax dollars, have moved to the suburbs. It would require a truly heroic effort for the child of a garment worker today to transform this diminished education into a career in business or the professions. Worse, Proposition 187 aimed to deny children of undocumented immigrants access to the public schools altogether. The United States District Court in San Francisco has ruled most of the proposition's provisions illegal. At the time of writing it was not clear whether the newly elected Democratic governor, Gray Davis, would appeal the court's decision. Still, the very idea of closing off public education to the second generation makes a mockery of the optimistic pronouncements of the manufacturers, and must have a chilling effect on the aspirations of garment workers for their children.

The proliferation of sweatshops is likely to be especially acute in those sectors of the industry that resist mechanization, the most fashion-sensitive sectors. The sectors that can use advanced machinery have moved offshore; those oriented towards the production of more fashionable garments, requiring quick turnaround, remain localized in large cities that are fashion centers, such as New York and Los Angeles. Although the workers might be more productive, employers are unlikely to be concerned, because the workers are paid by the piece, a practice that is a throwback to one of the earliest and most primitive forms of wage labor under capitalism.

Nonetheless, the industry today differs in important ways from its counterpart in the early part of the century, when sweatshops were also pervasive. First of all, the roles played by manufacturers in design, grading, patternmaking, cutting, and merchandising have all become much more sophisticated. The division between conception and execution, between mental and manual labor, is virtually complete. The mental aspects of the industry have been heavily computerized and, with the help of such elements as bar-coding and quick-response technologies, the industry has been able to organize and coordinate flexible production systems that range all over the globe. Computerization means that production can be dispersed and shifted around much more easily. Globalization and flexibility have changed the way business is conducted.

Contracting out is also more evolved in Los Angeles today than it was before World War II, or indeed than it is in New York City today. The vastly enhanced ability to shift production to other states, regions, countries, and even continents, makes the current contracting system qualitatively different from its previous form. We believe that the current system of globalized, highly flexible production creates a new kind of labor regime and labor discipline. Workers are kept under control by the mobility and dispersal of the industry. This system, which constantly threatens job loss, and severely inhibits labor struggles, keeps workers toiling at breakneck speed for long hours and low wages. They do not require coercive oversight to achieve the desired effect. In addition, another element of globalization plays into the "new" labor regime in the apparel industry in Los Angeles, and that is the employment of largely undocumented immigrants. Their political vulnerability as noncitizens, and the ability of employers to threaten exposure and deportation, adds to the disciplining effects of global, flexible capitalism.

Another factor that accounts for the reappearance of sweatshops must be mentioned: the weakened position of labor in the United States. Between the New Deal and the 1960s the United States apparel industry saw the near elimination of sweatshops, thanks to a combination of strong union organizing and a federal government committed to protecting workers' rights. Today, both of these conditions are far less significant. The reemergence of sweatshops is a direct product of relaxed government regulation and weakened unionization, a process that began in earnest in the 1980s. The two factors are, of course, not unrelated to each other, because the weakening of government interference in the economy and the attack on strong unions are both part of the same political program.

CHAPTER 7

The Distribution of Wealth

For the oppressors, what is worthwhile is to have more—always more—even at the cost of the oppressed having less or having nothing. For them, to be is to have and to be the class of the "haves." As beneficiaries of a situation of oppression, the oppressors cannot perceive that, if having is a condition of being, it is a necessary condition for all men. . . . To the oppressor consciousness, the humanization of the "others," of the people, appears not as the pursuit of full humanity, but as subversion. The oppressors do not perceive their monopoly on having more *as a privilege which dehumanizes others and themselves. . . . For them,* having more *is an inalienable right, a right they acquired through their own "effort," with their "courage to take risks." If others do not have more, it is because they are incompetent and lazy.*

—Paulo Freire, *Pedagogy of the Oppressed*

According to estimates made by the industry, "the California fashion industry generates more than $63 billion annually. . . . Thirty thousand retailers travel to California each year."[1] This estimate may be a bit exuberant, but there is no question that apparel design, manufacturing, and retailing, along with related occupations, provides many jobs, and generates considerable wealth. Yet this important industry has winners *and* losers. The wealth it generates has many claimants, from the chief executive officers of retailing and manufacturing firms at the top to impoverished immigrant garment workers at the bottom. There is a hierarchy of actors all of whom take a cut from the industry's earnings, with some taking much larger cuts than others can. The multimillionaires at the top may easily earn more in a day than the average worker earns in several years.

In examining the question of who gets rich from the Los Angeles apparel industry and how they do so, we are concerned with a deceptively simple question: How exactly is the money made from the sale of a garment divided up? In an industry in which almost all the firms are privately held and the participants very secretive about their affairs, the answer is not easily found. Our understanding is thus partial at best, based on incomplete and at times fragmentary information. Before we consider who

DRAWINGBOARD / RALL

TED RALL, San Francisco

gets what, we should acknowledge that consumers are among the prime beneficiaries of the apparel industry, even though they are, ultimately, the source of the industry's wealth. They benefit because the apparel industry in Los Angeles provides them efficiently with abundant, stylish, and relatively inexpensive clothing. The industry can rightly be proud of its capacity to produce such abundance, although one could raise questions about the environmental impact — by encouraging the production of far more clothing than most people need through promoting fashion, a form of planned obsolescence involving the massive discarding of useful items — and its manipulation of women by means of suggestive advertising based on impossible images of beauty.

The Actors

Several different types of actors have a stake in this industry. Many are firms rather than individuals, with their own internal ways of dividing up the wealth they generate. A bank or a retailer, for example, may have very highly paid executives, but very poorly paid tellers and sales personnel. The firm may make a great deal of money from the apparel industry, but not all of its employees see that money.

At the industry's top end, there are those who profit significantly from apparel manufacturing and distribution, or at least stand a reasonable chance of doing so. These range from retailers and manufacturers to a handful of contractors with substantial production capacity. This top tier of the industry includes a range of professional and technical service providers, some of whom work directly for retailers and manufacturers, others of whom work independently for a fee. Professionals who service the industry include lawyers, accountants, advertisers, photographers, models, stylists, designers, and consultants who specialize in apparel production and distribution. The buying offices fall into this category, as do the newly developed compliance firms. Indeed, the apparel industry, perhaps like all industries, seems to have an endless capacity to generate new experts and middlemen who provide some essential service that was not thought of before. Less obvious inhabitants of the top end of the industry, but no less important, are the real estate owners and developers of sites where apparel-related functions occur, and the individuals and firms who provide financial backing. The former are the owners of contracting, manufacturing, and retailing property, including mall owners and developers, and mart owners, and the members of the Downtown Property Owners Association; the latter include factors, bankers, stockholders of publicly traded companies, and the investment bankers who engineer the stock offerings.

At the bottom end of the industry one finds the workers, along with a large portion of the contractors. These are the people whose long hours of labor are poorly compensated. Those whose labor most directly contributes to the physical garment are those whose financial share is by far the lowest.

The various levels of government constitute a final, public beneficiary, because they collect taxes generated by the industry. The City of Los Angeles, in particular, has a strong interest in the local apparel industry, both as a source of jobs and of revenue to provide a host of social services. Los Angeles, its people, and its government, would be far worse off were there no apparel industry there.

Salaries and Profits

The wealth generated by the industry is distributed in two ways. The first consists of payment to individuals, for the work they do, in the form of wages and salaries. The other consists of returns to ownership in the form of profit, rent, and interest. Where this money goes is harder to track. Some of it gets reinvested in the companies, but some of it ends up in the pockets of individuals as direct owners or stockholders. The justification for receiving this money comes from having taken the risk to invest in the enterprise. Some of the investors are closely tied to the business and are employed by it; for others it is no more than an investment on which they expect to receive a return. As with all stockholding investments, the expected return can be quite removed from interest in the enterprise itself; the capital gains realized through stock appreciation is a case in point. Some of the people who make high salaries also have an ownership stake in the business. Sometimes the owners, especially of smaller firms, also serve as chief executives of the firms. And sometimes the executives of large companies are granted special stock purchasing options that enable them to become part owners. In either event, these individuals may receive wealth in both forms, as salary and as a share of profit.

How Little Can It Cost?

In the introduction, we illustrated the division of the spoils from a dress that retails for $100. At the top end, the retailer gets $50. At the bottom, the garment maker gets about $6. In Figure 1 we see the gross distribution of the $100, but not the distribution of costs for each level. Nevertheless it is clear that the returns are tilted toward the top. Each level down receives a smaller fraction of the $100. We must recognize that there are costs at every level, not to mention taxes and various other state fees. The $50 that goes to the retailer is not solely profit. It must cover rent, wages and salaries, insurance, legal expenses, advertising, and taxes. Similarly, apart from the textiles, the manufacturer must pay for designers and design technology, engineering, production management, sales personnel, and rent for facilities and a showroom. The contractor, too, must rent his space and rent or purchase his machinery. He has to pay for certain supplies, such as thread, and cover various state charges such as workers' compensation insurance.

To assess how much of the contractor's $15 would be paid to the workers, we asked a number of people in the industry, and received no standard answer. One response was given to us by Randy Youngblood,[2] of Apparel Resources, Inc., a compliance firm in Yorba Linda, who had been invited to give a talk to the Garment Contractors Association. His topic, "Can a contractor charge less than 2.5 times direct labor and still pay the workers' compensation, overtime, and minimum wage required by law?" is important because it reflects the harsh competitive realities of the industry: Contractors are under constant pressure to reduce what they accept from the manufacturer. To charge the manufacturer 2.5 times direct labor costs means that 40 percent of what the contractor gets goes into direct labor. If a contractor lowers his price to the manufacturer, can he still afford to pay his workers the legal minimum?

Robert Walter, the president of the Contractors Association at the time, and teacher of classes on pricing apparel, said there is no standard markup structure.[3] It depends on the continuity of the work, the number of units, and the complexity of the work. The number of units per style drives down the ratio. One very efficient, large contractor, who will only consider a minimum of 10,000 units, is able to charge two times direct labor. Walter's own firm, which accepted much smaller lots, charged 2.75 times labor, and considered 2.5 times to be the lowest ratio it could afford. Charging 2.5 times is difficult, but is probably close to average in Los Angeles, at least for registered contractors who comply with labor laws. Youngblood claimed that higher-end contractors could charge 2.9 times direct cost and still make a profit, but that 2.5 times was frequently used in the industry.

By the standard of 2.5 times direct labor cost, $6 out of the $15 would go to the worker who sewed the $100 dress; the remaining $9 would go to the contractor to cover his costs and profit. In other words, the worker would receive 6 percent of the total retail sales price of the product. This estimate may in fact be a little high; Steve Nutter, former vice president and regional director of the Western States Region of UNITE, estimates the figure to be 5 percent ($5 for a $100 dress), with 10 percent going to the contractor.[4] A detailed analysis of a skirt sold for $54 supports that estimate: For that skirt, only $3 (5.6 percent) went to the worker.

Contractors are under constant competitive pressure to lower their prices to manufacturers, which of course severely reduces what they are willing to pay their workers. Contractors whose markup is more than 2.5 direct labor costs, rather than the industry average do not pay more to their workers; they simply charge more to the manufacturer, pocketing the difference in the process. Low-end contractors who initially charge only twice their direct labor costs in order to get a manufacturer's business will be able to make up the difference by paying their workers less than the standard, especially if they are able to cheat them out of mini-

Table 7. *The Price of a Pair of Shoes: Nike Air Pegasus, 1995*

Retail price	$70.00	
Wholesale price	$21.75	
Retailer's Expenses and Profit		
Sales, distribution, and administration	$5.00	
Promotion and advertising	4.00	
Research and development	.25	
Personnel	9.50	
Rent	9.00	
Other	7.00	
Operating Profit	9.00	
Total	43.75	(62.5%)
Manufacturer's (i.e. Nike) Expenses and Profit		
Materials	$9.00	
Duties	3.00	
Rent and equipment	3.00	
Shipping	.50	
Profit	6.25	
Total	21.75	(31.1%)
Contractor's (Supplier's) Expenses and Profit		
Production labor	$2.75	
Profit	1.75	
Total	4.50	(6.4%)

SOURCE: Steve Pearlstein, "Sizing It Up," *Los Angeles Times,* 13 June 1995, sec. B, p. 3.

mum wage and overtime. We believe that, although the direct labor costs of the larger, more established contractors may amount to 6 percent of the retail price of the garment, the percentage shrinks as one moves down the scale to smaller, more underground firms.

The detailed information necessary for calculating the percentage of the retail price that goes to profits at the various points of the production chain is not available. But footwear is a labor-intensive industry similar in structure to apparel, and just such an analysis was done for the production of a $70 pair of Nike Air Pegasus shoes in 1995.[5] In this case, illustrated in Table 7, we are speaking of offshore production, so that the proportion that goes to labor is even lower than it would be in the United States. As can be seen, $43.75, or 62.5 percent, of a $70 pair of shoes ends up in the hands of the retailers. Most of this money goes to various expenses (including the high salaries of executives), but $9 is retained by the retailer, representing a 12.9 percent profit on sales. Of the $70 retail price, $21.75, or 31.1 percent, goes to Nike, the manufacturer. Again, most of the money goes to expenses, including a proportion to well-paid executives and ad agencies, yet even after those costs, Nike retains $6.25 as profit—a tidy return of 28.7 percent on the wholesale price of $21.75. The contractor's expenses are not clearly specified, because his operating expenses are not listed. Perhaps they are included under Production Labor, which would bring down the figure that the workers receive in wages. In any case, the contractor (supplier) receives $4.50, or only 6.4 percent of the $70. The workers who actually made the shoes receive *at most* $2.75, or 3.9 percent of the retail sales price. The profits realized on the sale of a $70 pair of shoes are substantial: $9.00 to the retailer, $6.25 to the manufacturer, and $1.75 to the contractor, or a total of $17, which is nearly a quarter of the retail sales price (24.3 percent). Meanwhile, the worker receives less than 4 percent. And, of course, profits are calculated *after* the high salaries payable to the chief executive officers and managers of the retailers, manufacturer, and contractors have been deducted.

Clearly the distribution of profits is skewed in favor of the retailer, and as one goes down the hierarchy the proportions decrease, until the worker is left with a tiny percentage. Profits to all the parties concerned add up to at least five times as much as the worker receives. Meanwhile, we have not even begun to calculate how much of the so-called expenses of retailers and manufacturers go to high salaries for executives.

The Accumulation of Wealth

So far we have focused only on the distribution of the selling price of *one* garment. However, as one moves up the hierarchy, not only is more taken out by each level, but each level accumulates more by dealing in greater quantities. This principle is illustrated in Figure 7, for which we use the dollar amounts of the $100 dress presented in Figure 1. (Treating the illustration schematically, we do not allow for markdowns, unsold garments, and so on.)

Let us start at the bottom of the figure, and assume that each contracting shop employs twenty-five workers, each of whom makes one dress. By the previous analysis, each contractor would receive $15 for each dress, out of which $5 would be paid to the worker who made the dress,

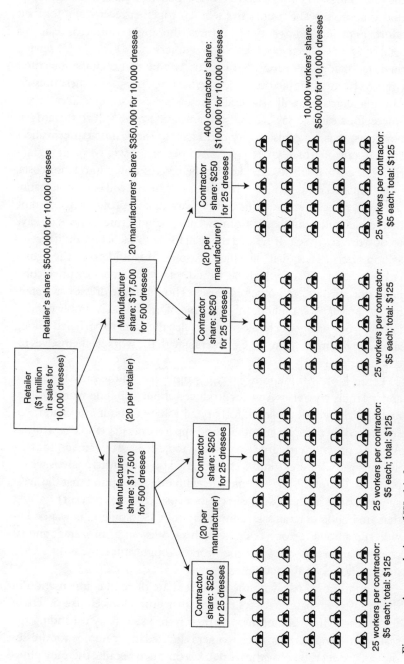

Figure 7. Accumulation of Wealth from 10,000 Dresses Selling for $100 Each

the remaining $10 being used to cover expenses, managerial compensation, and profits. The twenty-five workers together receive $125 for their efforts in producing twenty-five dresses; the single contractor realizes a total of $250. Collectively, the 10,000 workers make $50,000 for sewing the total of 10,000 dresses. Now let us assume that each manufacturer employs twenty contractors who, together, produce 500 of these dresses. The manufacturer will wholesale these dresses to the retailer at $50 apiece, for a total of $25,000. Of this amount, $7,500 will go towards labor costs, that is, to his twenty contractors. The manufacturer realizes $17,500, out of which $11,250 (at $22.50 per dress) will be spent on fabric. (The cost of fabric can, likewise, be broken down into labor costs, other expenses, and profits.) The remaining $6,250 will cover the manufacturer's remaining costs, his compensation, and profit. If we assume that the retailer purchases from twenty manufacturers, he will have 10,000 dresses to sell. If he sold them all for $100 each, he would receive $1,000,000 in sales, half of which ($500,000) would go to the manufacturers, and half of which he would retain to cover executive compensation, profits, and other expenses. Though these dresses are retailing for a total of $1 million, this large pie of $1 million is simply divided into two: one half going to the single retailer, the other to be shared among all those who manufacture the garments, with the workers themselves receiving $5 slivers.

Let us look at this another way. Assume that, in the early 1990s, the apparel industry in Los Angeles produced about $8 billion worth of garments at the wholesale level, for a retail value of about $16 billion. Assume also that there are about 160,000 apparel industry employees in Los Angeles, of whom roughly two-thirds (107,000) are operatives, primarily sewing-machine operators (this is based on the census analysis we reported in Chapter 6). If we continue with our assumption that the average $100 dress includes $5 of direct labor costs (that is, 5 percent), we find that $16 billion in retail sales generates about $800 million in wages. Divided up among 107,000 operatives, this works out to an average annual compensation of about $7,500 per worker, roughly the same as the $7,200 figure reported in the 1990 census.

In addition to receiving the smallest share of total compensation in the industry, apparel workers face another limitation: Unlike others in the industry, they cannot increase their return simply by expanding the scale of their operations. Each worker is limited in the number of dresses she can produce, because the work takes time and because there are physical limits on her productivity. In theory, technological upgrading might slightly increase the workers' productivity, enabling them to earn more under the piece-rate system, assuming, of course, that the technology-induced returns were indeed passed along to workers, rather than used to increase profits along the production chain. But such technological changes do not seem likely in the near future in Los Angeles, and workers remain bound by their physical capacity to sew a certain number of garments in a day. No other level in the hierarchy is so bound. Contractors can make more money by employing more workers, manufacturers can make more money by increasing the size or number of their contractors, and retailers can make more by ordering and selling more garments. At all levels above the factory floor, the ability to make money depends only on the amount of capital that can be raised and the ability to market the product. Manufacturers and contractors can, in other words, accumulate wealth according to the size of their operations. Workers have no such opportunity to accumulate wealth, because the size of their production is determined by their own personal physical limitations. They cannot expand these by employing others, except in the extreme (and illegal) case of taking work home and obtaining the help of their children.

We recognize that dividing the costs at each level into such broad categories as profits, executive compensation, and other expenses obscures the important fact that each of these categories represents concrete people: The factor gets his commission, the landlord his rent, the advertising agency its fee. Ideally, we would be able to break down the expenses in detail, looking at the returns to every actor. Although such an analysis is not possible given the available data, it would certainly reveal that there are enormous disparities in the distribution: in general, the higher on the apparel pyramid the greater the return, a disparity that is reinforced by one's position on the related hierarchy of professional-managerial-technical-occupational status. The workers who make the actual garments are on the very bottom.

Who Get Rich and How Much Do They Make?

In an industry in which the majority of the participants get such meager slices of the pie, it is instructive to review the division of the rest. The data may be sketchy, but it is still possible to move down the line from retailers to contractors and look at some of the professional and managerial occupations associated with the industry.

RETAILERS

Most of the major retailers of apparel are public companies, so that the salaries of their top executives, and their profits, are public information. Indeed, *Women's Wear Daily* publishes summaries of these statistics quarterly and annually, providing the sales and earnings of the company, the chief executive officer's compensation in dollars and as a percentage of earnings, and increases from the previous year.[6] These data are not limited to the apparel industry in Los Angeles; retailers obtain apparel from other production centers, and some of them sell merchandise other than apparel. Although we are unable to assess precisely what proportion of the wealth amassed by the retailers is traceable to the garment industry in Los Angeles, it is obvious from these figures that retailers are an important node of accumulation.

In 1997, the sixty publicly held United States apparel retail firms had sales of $372 billion, up 11 percent from the previous year, when sales were $335 billion. Meanwhile, profits climbed by 25 percent, from $9.2 billion to $11.5 billion. The profit rate in 1997 was 3.1 percent on sales. This figure may seem low, but the absolute amount of money made is huge.

The data about the compensation of chief executive officers are from 1996. In that year, the highest paid retail executive was David Farrell of May Department Stores Co. who received a 123-percent raise from 1995 to 1996, making $5.7 million in the latter year. This was made up of a base salary of $1.2 million, an $818,000 bonus, $3 million in restricted stock awards, and a long-term incentive payout of $684,640.[7] The average compensation of the sixty chief executive officers mentioned was $1,374,000 in 1996, an increase of about 8 percent over the previous year.[8] (This works out to 191 times as much as the average sewing machine operator's yearly compensation of less than $7,200.) Adding up the salaries of these men and women, we find that together they made about $81.8 million in one year. There appears to be only a weak relationship between the chief executive officer's salary and the company's profits. Some companies that lost money, or did worse than they had done the previous year, still gave their chief executive officers substantial increases in compensation. The average increase was about 1 percent, but for several the figure was much higher, up to 15 and 20 percent or more of earnings.

The pay packages of nine chief executive officers of discount chains rose by 45 percent in 1997.[9] Floyd Hall, the chief executive officer of K-Mart for example, received $6.1 million, up from $4.4 million in 1996, a 40 percent leap. His pay represented 2.5 percent of the company's earnings. The chief executive officer of Dayton Hudson Corporation, which owns the mass merchandiser, Target Stores, Inc., received $6.2 million in 1997, up from $5.0 million in 1996. The president of Target itself was paid $2.15 million.

Apart from high compensation, the chief executive officers of retailing companies frequently receive substantial remuneration in other forms. For example, when Myron Ullman, the chairman and chief executive officer of Macy's, left the company in the wake of its merger in 1995 with Federated Department Stores Inc., he received severance pay of about $13 million.[10] Allen Questrom, a former chief executive officer of Federated, who received an incentive bonus of $16 million, was suing the company for $47 million because he believed his bonus should have been $63 million.[11]

We are under the impression that women's apparel is a profit center for many department stores. To give one example, Carter Hawley Hale, the owners of Broadway, a department store chain based in Los Angeles before it was sold to Federated, stated in 1994 that "apparel generates about one-quarter of our revenues, but 60 percent of our profits."[12] In other words, the profitability of women's apparel is much higher for the retailer than are other commodities. Thus the cost of apparel to the retailer is lower relative to its selling price than is the cost of other goods. Some of this lower price must be accounted for by the low price of labor, or, to put it in human terms, the low wages and poor working conditions of garment workers.

The high profits of retailers can be translated into philanthropic activity. For example, in 1993, Dayton Hudson, the parent company of Mervyn's and Target, chains that have a strong presence in California, made grants totaling $3 million to social action and arts programs in California as part of its $24-million nationwide giving program.[13] The company supported United Way, Habitat for Humanity, quality child care, programs that strengthened families, and artistic excellence. Yet, paradoxically, the retailers, represented by the National Retail Federation, and the International Mass Retail Association, also are opposed to raising the federal minimum wage another dollar, from $5.15 an hour to $6.15 by the year 2000.[14]

MANUFACTURERS

Before focusing on apparel manufacturers in Los Angeles, let us consider the national picture. *Women's Wear Daily* publishes the annual earnings and chief executive officers' compensation of publicly owned apparel manufacturers. Because many apparel manufacturers are private companies, the group is small. The listing in 1997 included thirty-five companies.[15] The average earnings for the thirty-five firms declined by eight percent (to $71 million) between 1996 and 1997, having risen by 13 percent the previous year. These figures are somewhat misleading, however, because a single manufacturer, Fruit of the Loom, posted losses of nearly $488 million in 1997, largely the result of a $372 million charge to close plants and write down assets. If we exclude Fruit of the Loom, average earnings for the remaining thirty-four firms increased by 14.7 percent, to $87 million. The combined earnings for all thirty-five companies were $2.5 billion, with considerable variability in profit and loss. (Sara Lee led, with $1 billion in earnings.)

Compensation data reveal that the chief executive officer in these thirty-five firms made, on average, $1,979,341 in 1997, down by 8 percent from 1996. Sixteen of the thirty-five chief executive officers, almost half, received more than $1 million each. The highest-paid chief executive officer, Linda Wachner, the chief executive officer of both the Warnaco Group, Inc. and Authentic Fitness Corporation (the exclusive North American licensee for Speedo swimwear), earned $11.5 million, an increase of 22 percent from the previous year. A few of the listed companies are located in southern California. Maurice Marciano, the chief executive officer of Guess? Inc., was near the middle in terms of executive compensation in 1997, receiving $958,162. Marciano's compensation was down considerably from 1996 ($3.4 million) and 1995 ($3.6 million), years in which he was among the most highly paid chief executive officers of apparel companies in the country. Robert Gray, the chief executive officer of St John Knits, Inc., which is based in Irvine, took home $1.6 million in 1997 and Gerard Guez of Tarrant Apparel Group, private-label specialists, made $950,000.

Reporters for *Women's Wear Daily* commented that "fashion's perks are getting pricier: Private planes, weekend palaces, fleets of cars and art by the modern masters, to name a few. Many a fortune has been made in the fashion business, but the take has gotten larger over the last three years, thanks in part to a rash of public stock offerings. What used to be millions has translated into tens of millions and, for some, tens of millions has translated into hundreds of millions. There's even a handful of billionaires. From licenses to stock sales to huge paychecks supplemented by options and awards—fashion executives are earning big." Ralph Lauren, for instance, was described as owning a 14,000-acre ranch near Telluride, Colorado, where he raised cattle, a mansion on 200 acres in Bedford, New York, a duplex on Fifth Avenue in New York City, a Japanese-inspired house in Montauk, and an Anglo-Indian villa in Jamaica. He also had a valuable collection of antique cars. Apart from a salary of $3.5 million in 1996, he received $135 million from selling a 28.5 percent stake in his business to Goldman Sachs in anticipation of an initial public offering of stock, and $88.4 million in partnership distributions from Goldman Sachs for 1996 and part of 1997.[16]

In 1997 *Apparel Industry Magazine* listed the 100 largest apparel firms (in terms of sales volume) in the United States, attempting to include private as well as publicly held companies.[17] Twenty of these were in California, the second largest concentration behind New York. Those located in southern California are listed in Table 8, together with their rank among the top 100 and, where available, their profits. Unlike the firms headquartered in New York, which reported little production in the New York area, almost all of the California firms reported some production in California. Some of the companies show healthy profits: 13.3 percent for St John Knits, 12.1 percent for Guess, and 11.6 percent for Mossimo. Some of the other companies were not doing as well: 2.1 percent for Chorus Line, and 4.3 percent for Tarrant Apparel. Some of the figures are estimates, and the variability may reflect the particular circumstances of a company at the time. Carole Little, for example, dropped in rank from forty-one to sixty-two because it sold off an apparel division, and reinvested the money in the movie, *Anaconda*. The company had a tie-in between the film and clothing sold under the Reptiles label.

The *Los Angeles Business Journal* collected data in 1997 about the highest paid executives of public companies in Los Angeles.[18] Most of the executives were connected with financial institutions, but six of them were connected with apparel firms. Apart from Linda J. Wachner, the other well-paid apparel executives all came from one company, Guess? Inc. Wachner ranked fifteenth, with a total compensation of $5.5 million from Authentic Fitness Corporation, which is based in Los Angeles. The executives of Guess included: Maurice Marciano, ranked thirty-first, with $3.3 million; Paul Marciano, ranked forty-third, with $2.7 million; Ken Duane, the president of worldwide sales, ranked fifty-third, with $2.3 million; Roger Williams, the executive vice president and chief financial officer, ranked fifty-fourth, with $2.3 million; and Armand Marciano, ranked 58th, with $2.0 million. Together those five executives received $12.6 million in compensation; if we include Linda Wachner's compensation, the six highest-paid apparel executives in Los Angeles took home slightly more than $18 million in 1997. This is sufficient to compensate 2,500 apparel workers for

Table 8. *Apparel Manufacturers in Southern California, by Sales Volume*
1996–1997

Rank[a]		Location	Revenues	Profits
			($ million)	
21	Guess? Inc.	Los Angeles	$551.2	$66.7
24	Bugle Boy Industries	Simi Valley	$487	n.a.
51	Rampage Clothing Co.	Los Angeles	$200[b]	n.a.
52	Tarrant Apparel Group	Los Angeles	$229.9	$10
58	Chorus Line Corp.	Vernon	$206.3	$4.3
59	St John Knits Inc.	Irvine	$203	$27.1
61	Quiksilver Inc.	Costa Mesa	$193.5	$11.7
62	Carole Little (California Fashion Industries, Inc.)	Los Angeles	$185.5	n.a.
80	Laundry by Shelli Segal (Podell Industries Inc.)	Los Angeles	$156	n.a.
87	BCBG Max Azria (AZ3 Inc.)	Vernon	$132	n.a.
96	Mossimo, Inc.	Irvine	$108.7	$12.6

SOURCE: Andree Conrad, "The Year Profit Became Fashionable," *Apparel Industry Magazine,* June 1997, pp. 20–30.

a In listing of 100 apparel firms in the United States, ranked by size of sales volume.
b Estimate.

a year, at the industry average of $7,200 per worker. If we assume that Wachner's Authentic Fitness Corporation and the Marcianos' Guess? Inc. together employ the equivalent of 10,000 full-time garment workers, those six executives, by simply sharing half of their $18 million in earnings could contribute $900 to each of their workers' annual incomes, giving them a 13 percent pay raise. (Guess is, however, rapidly moving its production to Tehuacán, Mexico, where labor costs are a tenth of those in the United States; the Marcianos' annual compensation would stretch considerably further in Tehuacán than it does in Los Angeles.)

The high and growing rates of compensation for executives in the United States have received serious criticism from a number of sources.[19] In 1997, the best-paid executives at America's 365 largest companies earned 35 percent more than they had the year before, and in 1996, they earned 54 percent more than they had in 1995. By way of comparison, the average factory worker's paycheck grew by only 2.6 percent in 1997, and the average white-collar worker's pay increased by only 3.8 percent. This discrepancy has contributed to a growing inequality that is much more marked in the United States than it is in other industrial countries.

THE PROFESSIONALS AND MANAGERS

Professionals and managers hold a broad range of jobs, and include managers below the rank of chief executive officer, lawyers and accountants, designers, advertisers and models, people who run buying offices, merchandising experts, and so on. They are all considered to have special knowledge or skills, and are paid high salaries for their services. We take two examples, advertising, and managerial and professional services, to illustrate the level of earnings accruing to those who serve the top end of the apparel industry.

Retailers and manufacturers spend enormous amounts on advertising, as a glance at the *Los Angeles Times* confirms. In mid-1997 a full-page advertisement cost approximately $30,000. Major retailers, such as Robinsons-May and Macy's buy several pages every day, week after week.[20] Nike, to take a well-known example, spent $211 million on advertising in 1997; Levi Strauss & Co. spent $100 million. More than $30 million a year is spent on advertising such major apparel brands as Polo Ralph Lauren, Calvin Klein, Wrangler (jeans), Tommy Hilfiger, and Dockers.[21] Experts maintain that manufacturers need to spend at least $5 or $10 million to stand out from the crowd.[22] According to the president and creative director of an advertising agency in Massachusetts, a successful men's wear company must spend between $5 and $7 million in advertising, and a women's wear company, between $10 and $15 million. To launch a new business, it is necessary to spend up to 15 percent of expected sales.

Although most of the big spenders on advertising are not based in Los Angeles (Guess? Inc., which spent $19 million on advertising in 1997, is an exception), manufacturers there do spend considerable amounts on billboards, bus benches, and newspaper and magazine advertisements.[23] In 1993, advertising agencies on the West Coast averaged a 16-percent commission on accounts ranging up to $200 million a year.[24] Guess's highly creative advertising campaigns once set an industry standard with their provocative mixture of supermodels, sexual suggestiveness, and denim; Paul Marciano is still the creative genius behind these campaigns.

The multimillion dollar advertising budgets are divided among several people, including the owners of the manufacturing companies, executives and professionals connected with such media as magazines and television, advertising agencies, models, photographers, and others. Models, for example, begin at $250 an hour for New York runway shows, average $750 an hour, and earn as much as $10,000 a day.[25] The stylists

Table 9. *Executives' Salaries, Manufacturers of Women's Wear in California, by Title, 1996*

President	$325,000
Division president	$200,000
Executive vice president, sales	$265,000
Executive vice president	$260,000
Executive vice president, marketing	$250,000
Vice president, sales and merchandising	$220,000
Vice president, sales	$180,000–$225,000
Regional sales manager	$120,000
Showroom manager, Los Angeles	$135,000
Showroom manager, New York	$150,000
Assistant/Seller	$50,000–$80,000
Sales manager/account executive	$66,000–$180,000
Sales	$30,000–$126,000
Sales executive	$100,000–$650,000
Account executive	$23,000–$157,500

SOURCE: J. Blade Corwin, "California Sales Pay Packages Varied and Lucrative," *Apparel Industry Magazine*, April 1997, p. 33. Among the firms that responded to the survey were Carole Little (a label of California Fashion Industries, Inc.), Chorus Line Corporation, David Dart, Inc., Francine Browner, Inc., Guess? Inc., Jalate Ltd., Inc., Harkham Industries, Inc. (under the label Jonathan Martin Fashion Group), Joel and Judy Knapp Corp. (under the label Judy Knapp), Karen Kane Co., Inc., Podelle Industries, Inc. (under the label Laundry by Shelli Segal), Platinum Clothing Company, Inc. (under the label Platinum), Rampage Clothing, Inc., Topson Downs of California, Inc., and Lola, Inc. (under the label XOXO).

NOTE: The names used for various positions are those adopted by the various firms in their responses; they do not necessarily have the same meaning in each firm.

who select their clothes earn between $1,500 and $2,500 a day; the best stylists make considerably more.

In 1996, *Apparel Industry Magazine* surveyed thirty-one of California's leading women's wear firms, and obtained detailed information about compensation for the executives from twelve of the companies.[26] In Table 9 we present the results. Most executives earn over $100,000 a year, and many earn two to three times that amount. Even assistant sellers, who start at $50,000, do reasonably well, and can expect to move up if they are successful. There are also independent sales representatives who operate showrooms in places such as the CaliforniaMart, who typically receive a commission of between 10 and 15 percent as well as a showroom fee.[27]

In 1992, in a study of fifty chief operating officers of privately held apparel firms throughout the country, it was found that the average officer took home $206,000 in base salary, $70,000 in year-end bonus, and received an annual pension contribution of $15,000, for a total compensation of $291,000. Additionally, the officers received comprehensive family health-insurance coverage, life insurance equal to three times their base salary, a paid vacation for four weeks, and an employment agreement covering thirty-six months with a six-month severance package.[28]

Apparel firms obtain specialized services from law and accounting firms. According to one study, in 1994 senior partners in major Los Angeles law firms made between $300,000 and $650,000 or more, and received such perks as expense accounts of between $5,000 and $10,000 for meals and entertainment, theater and sports tickets, and company-paid cellular phone costs. Local attorneys' incomes had risen by 26 percent in the previous five years.[29]

CONTRACTORS

Contractors run privately owned companies, and it is difficult to assess how much wealth they amass. Garment contracting is a risky business, with considerable turnover. Many contractors fail and go out of business. Others collect enough capital to open more factories or invest in other enterprises, including real estate. In investigating Korean contractors (described in detail in Chapter 5), Ku-Sup Chin found that their median annual income was about $50,000, with 40 percent reporting incomes over $70,000, and ten individuals reporting incomes over $200,000. Seventy percent owned their own homes. Koreans are among the more successful of the contractors, so that the figures may be higher than average. The range of earnings among garment contractors is probably quite large. Nevertheless it seems safe to say that, on the whole, they are able to provide a comfortable living for their families, including college education for their children. Many own suburban homes and cars. Indeed, as one industry analyst remarked, "Go to the parking lot of any contractor and you will see Lexuses and BMWs."[30] They are middle class in a way that most garment workers can only dream about.

Fashion as a Lifestyle

Writing for the *New York Times,* Stephanie Strom described some of the immense wealth of the Marciano brothers, the owners of

Guess? Inc.; her information derived from the prospectus for a private placement to buy out one of the brothers, Georges, in 1993.

In recent years, [the four Marcianos] have drawn millions of dollars in salaries, perquisites, rent, licenses, and side deals. That was in addition to the $204 million they received before taxes as their share of profits in the last three years. Georges also was paid $8.7 million in salary, bonuses, and other compensation last year; each of his brothers was paid more than $5 million. Their $25 million in compensation accounted for about 18 percent of the company's administrative expenses. All four brothers have cars and drivers at their disposal, and Paul and Georges have bodyguards. The company carries about $25 million worth of art and $18 million in aircraft on its books, presumably for the benefit of the brothers. The company is active in real estate—family-owned real estate. Guess? leases two buildings for more than $2 million a year from a limited partnership [that] lists the brothers as its sole partners. . . . The company also sold the brothers its corporate offices and distribution operations in Los Angeles for $24 million and then leases the buildings back for about $2 million a year. . . .
    In 1989, the company began its retail operations by buying twenty-one stores from none other than the Marciano brothers. . . . And earlier this year, Guess? bought a 51 percent stake in a TV and record company, G & C Entertainment, Inc., owned by Paul and Georges. It then lent G & C $487,000, which the entertainment company used to repay loans the two brothers made to it.[31]

The Marciano brothers are very wealthy individuals. And they have much more wealth than is disclosed in that document. A glimpse of the wealth can be obtained from the court records of the divorce of Armand Marciano, the least wealthy of the brothers. Armand divorced his wife Patricia in 1993, and in the course of wrangling over the division of property, at least some of his wealth was revealed.[32] As of December 1991, Armand had $4.3 million worth of marketable securities. He owned a house in Beverly Hills worth $4.2 million, a house in Pt. Lechuza worth $2.9 million, and a number of other properties. The couple had jewelry and furs worth $626,139, fine art worth $249,699, antiques and furnishings worth $310,752, a Rolls Royce, two Mercedeses, a Ferrari, a Range Rover, and what appears to be a yacht named *Wild Guess II*. Armand's assets reportedly totaled $19.149 million. His investments in Guess and related properties alone were worth $13.7 million. At the time of his divorce, Armand's gross income from Guess was $17,539,842, or $1,461,662 a month, which translated into a disposable monthly income of $773,123. On 8 August 1996, Guess sold 7,000,000 shares of stock at $18 per share in an initial public offering, raising $126 million for Maurice, Paul, and Armand.

Most of this money was not reinvested in the company, but instead was taken by the brothers as compensation.[33]

Many of the wealthy apparel industry owners, managers, and professionals are very generous with their money. Prolific donors to charities and to political causes, they do not hoard their wealth; on the contrary, they use it, in part, to "give back" to their community. Nevertheless, there is an enormous gulf between top and bottom in this industry. The lifestyles of top retailers and manufacturers, along with the professionals who serve them, stand in stark contrast to those of the persons who make the clothing.

We believe that this system is wrong. There is a broad social injustice at work. We are not contending that the beneficiaries of the system plotted for this to happen. They simply do what everyone else is doing, and get what the system allots to them. This is the way the market seems to work. But the market does not have a conscience. It does not take care of the social welfare. The beneficiaries of the system, even if they are not personally greedy, nevertheless support with all the considerable power at their command a system that ends up benefiting them and hurting others. Herein lies their culpability.

PART III
Fighting Back

CHAPTER 8
Government Enforcement and Retention Efforts

Two interrelated problems face the apparel industry in Los Angeles. One is the return of sweatshops, and the other is the flight of the industry, especially to Mexico. These two issues have been joined in a shotgun marriage with a knot that is very difficult to unravel. If we succeed in raising labor standards, which is an inevitable concomitant of eliminating sweatshops, the industry will, it is widely believed, then leave Los Angeles, because labor costs will be too high to sustain a local apparel industry. In curing the disease, we may kill the patient.

In speaking of the flight of the industry, we are not referring to the manufacturers themselves. That Los Angeles will continue to be a design center and a center for managing the production of apparel is not in question. The issue is whether the contracting and production base will remain. Most employees in the industry work in the contracting shops. The threat of offshore production is that the manufacturers will cease to use local contractors who employ local workers, and instead, will contract out the production in Mexico (and elsewhere), using the labor force there, at a fraction of the cost.

Enforcing the Law

Sweatshops are associated with the contracting system. When manufacturers (and retailers) contract out the actual production to small shops, they are essentially using these shops as labor contractors. This system in the apparel industry is very similar to the labor contracting system used in agriculture. In both cases, employees typically are paid by the piece and suffer the worst working conditions. The economics of the contracting system encourages the development of thousands of small

3/27/97

shops. These shops are spread out over the Los Angeles basin (as well as Orange County and other counties in southern California). Their large numbers and small size make them very difficult to police. Many avoid any contact with law enforcement agencies by operating completely underground, that is, by remaining unregistered and not paying taxes. Even if caught, they are able to close down and reopen in a new location under a new name and the authorities are unable to trace them. Meanwhile, the workers lose their jobs and may never be compensated for the work that was stolen from them.

The issue of responsibility is muddied because manufacturers shift their production around among contractors, and some contractors work for several manufacturers. But the fact is that the manufacturer never relinquishes title to the goods that are sent out for assembly and processing. The manufacturer always owns the garment parts as well as the final, assembled product. Law enforcement agencies need to find a way to hold

GOVERNMENT ENFORCEMENT   223

manufacturers (and retailers) responsible for the conditions under which their garments are produced. If the incentive to contract out work to illegal operators is removed, it is assumed that the illegal operators will be driven out of business.

THE PURVIEW OF THE STATE

The Division of Labor Standards Enforcement (DLSE), part of the California Department of Industrial Relations, was created in 1975 as a consolidation of two earlier agencies, the Division of Industrial Work and the Division of Labor Law Enforcement. The consolidation promised improved enforcement and efficiency, but only the latter was implemented: The number of field enforcement positions increased only marginally, to fifty-eight from fifty-three a year earlier. Subsequent increases were more than outweighed by the transfer of staff into other functions, not to mention the substantial growth in the number of low-wage workers to be monitored.

Briefly, from 1978 to 1983, the DLSE ran a Concentrated Enforcement Program (CEP), which was to become the largest and most coordinated effort to curb labor abuses in state history. The CEP did not take the typical approach of responding to complaints from workers but actively pursued enforcement in the field by developing a program of identifying abuses even without complaints. The CEP focused, in order of priority, on four industries, apparel, restaurants, nursing homes, and agriculture. One-third of all the program's inspections were of garment firms in Los Angeles. The program was relatively well staffed, with about sixty field and support workers. Its twelve person "strike force" conducted systematic and well-publicized neighborhood sweeps in which garments would be seized and criminal charges filed when violations were countered. Recruiting many of its agents from ethnic communities in Los Angeles, the program acquired insider's knowledge and linguistic access to the industries it monitored. The activities were closely coordinated with those of other agencies concerned with labor law enforcement, including the Employment Development Department, the IRS and the state Franchise Tax Board, state and county health departments, and county and city business license departments.

During its five-year existence, the CEP conducted more than 5,000 inspections in the Los Angeles apparel industry alone. It found that 56 percent of all garment factories violated minimum wage and/or overtime laws, and 75 percent kept faulty records. Some $3.8 million in fines was collected for wage and overtime violations. But the CEP's very success led to its undoing, and the program fell victim to budget cutting and probusiness lobbying under the incoming Deukmejian administration. Its functions were folded into a new agency, the Bureau of Field Enforcement, the total staff of which consisted of ninety-nine inspectors for all the government's enforcement programs. After that, the vigorousness of field enforcement declined, dissipated further by exploding numbers of low-wage workers and factories. The Division of Labor Standards Enforcement shifted its efforts into other areas, including public works and medium- and high-wage industries. The number of garment industry sweeps declined, and the number of inspections and amounts of fines levied fluctuated at around one-half to two-thirds of the levels attained by the Concentrated Enforcement Program, even as employment in the industry grew by one-third between 1983 and 1991. In 1990, for example, only 2,900 apparel workers received back wages owed them by employers, at a time when 137,000 workers were officially known to be employed in the state. In 1991, the bureau's backlog of cases reached 4,000. Between three and six months might elapse before it could act on a specific complaint. A single inspector was responsible for all the industries in downtown Los Angeles, including those in the garment district.[1]

In 1992, the Department of Labor Standards Enforcement once again turned its attention to the apparel industry, creating the Targeted Industries Partnership Program (TIPP) in collaboration with the federal Department of Labor and other state agencies. Apparel and agriculture were the two industries targeted for special attention (see p. 238 below). From this time on, all state enforcement efforts connected with the apparel industry were covered by TIPP.

Registration. Part of the California Labor Code deals solely with garment manufacturing. Known as the Montoya Act because of its promotion by State Senator Joseph Montoya, the garment manufacturing section of the Labor Code (sections 2670–2692) became law on 1 July 1982. It requires all garment manufacturers to register with the state, sets forth bonding requirements, defines misdemeanors, and establishes civil and criminal penalties (including confiscation). Garment manufacturer is broadly defined to include "any person, whether an individual, partnership, corporation, or association, including but not limited to, an employer, a manufacturer, a jobber, a wholesaler, a contractor, or a subcontractor, who sews, cuts, makes, processes, repairs, finishes, assembles, or otherwise prepares any garment or any article of wearing apparel, designed or intended to be worn by any individual, for sale or resale."[2] When registering, the applicant must have documented that he or she has a current workers' compensation insurance policy. One must take tests showing knowledge of state laws on labor standards and occupational safety and health. Employers are required to post proof of registration. Employers who have been cited or penalized in the previous three years are required to deposit a bond of up to $5,000 with the state, the money to be used to pay employees who have not been paid minimum wage or overtime. One of the strongest provisions of the law is that apparel manufacturers who contract with unregistered garment firms are held to be the employers of the workers in those firms, and are jointly liable for violations of labor standards. The Labor Commissioner (who is the head of the Department of Labor Standards Enforcement) may confiscate garments made in unregistered shops, and may revoke the registration of contractors for three or more violations of labor standards in a two-year period.

Joint Liability Legislation. Several efforts have been made to pass more stringent legislation at the state level. These efforts have been strongly championed by the garment workers' union (initially the ILGWU, subsequently UNITE). One major goal has been to pass joint liability legislation, holding the manufacturer (and possibly the retailer as well) financially liable for any violations of labor law that occur in the contracting shops used, regardless of whether the firm is registered or not.

Joint liability legislation was first introduced by Assemblyman Tom Hayden, the Democratic Party representative for Santa Monica, in March 1990, following a well-publicized series of raids on sweatshops in Los Angeles and Orange County that revealed widespread abuses of the labor laws, including below-minimum wage pay, the use of child labor, and reliance on illegal homework. The specific case prompting the effort to pass a joint liability law concerned Juana Valladeres and her three young children. The Valladeres family was owed $23,000 in back wages, but their contractor, Addison Fashion, who was producing garments for the manufacturer En Chante, went out of business. Under existing law, the Valladereses had no recourse for obtaining the money they were owed. The proposed joint liability legislation would hold En Chante accountable.[3]

Needless to say, industry leaders strongly opposed the legislation. Bernard Brown, the executive director of the Coalition of Apparel Industries of California (CAIC) at the time, warned that overregulation would destroy the industry. "We are trying," he said, "very desperately trying to clean up the act in our industry, [but] if indeed there's a liability act we can't live with, we'll just move out of California."[4] Bernard Lax, who succeeded Brown as executive director, also strongly opposed joint liability. As he put it, "There have been sweatshops since day one; it is, after all, the second oldest profession."[5]

Clothing manufacturers lobbied strongly against the measure, which quickly became a partisan issue. Although joint liability legislation several times made it successfully through state legislatures by the Democratic Party, it was vetoed by the Republican governors, first George Deukmejian, then Pete Wilson. The Conservative Caucus of the Assembly argued that the passage of joint liability legislation would drive the industry out of the state entirely, and asserted that sweatshops were a necessary evil. "People do not work in sweatshops to enjoy a break from six-figure incomes and expense-account lunches. They work long hours for low wages in lousy conditions because they have no better alternative. . . . If public policy denies them that alternative, they can increase the supply of workers already competing for low-wage jobs and further depress wages, they can turn to crime, or they can try welfare, homelessness and starvation. . . . [Contractors] will not raise wages, reduce hours, and install air conditioning, because if they do, some other wicked s.o.b. who does not do those things will undercut their prices."[6]

The discovery of the slave shop in El Monte unleashed new efforts to pass joint liability legislation, this time led by State Senator Hilda Soliz, the Democratic Party representative for El Monte. In August 1998, faced with growing pressure to clean up the sweatshop problem, and following the passage of a strong antisweatshop law that was supported by New York's Republican governor, Governor Wilson signed a new law that redefined garment manufacturers to include those that have no direct employees and who contract out all operations.[7] Retailers who produce private-label garments are also covered. Joint liability is still, however, limited to unregistered contractors.

Assembly Bill 633, signed into law by Governor Davis in October 1999, takes a step in the direction of joint liability by imposing a "wage guarantee" on manufacturers and retailers (in their private-label production), who must now assure, along with their contractors, that workers are paid minimum wage and overtime. The Labor Commission is authorized to enforce the measure and revoke the registration of any manufacturer who fails to pay an award.

Corruption in the DLSE. The fortunes of the Division of Labor Standards Enforcement took a turn for the worst on 16 September 1997, when state authorities announced that Howard Hernandez, who had been a labor standards investigator and veteran inspector for seventeen years, was arrested for extorting money from a garment contractor by threatening to shut down the firm or confiscate goods for a minor violation.[8] As a result, the newly appointed state Labor Commissioner, Jose Millan, reported that he would pair up his inspectors when they were conducting raids, rather than have them go out alone.[9] In the whole of 1996 the agency had inspected about 800 shops; now that they had to work in pairs the thirty-five inspectors would be able to inspect only about 400 shops. Millan also announced that inspectors would be rotated out of garment duty after a maximum of two years. Given the difficulty of ferreting out violations at the best of times, this policy, too, would weaken the effectiveness of an already weakened program.

Immigrants and State Law.   Immigration policy is a federal responsibility. But, despite the large number of undocumented workers in California, state labor law was not clear about their rights. In July 1998, a state appeals court ruled that undocumented workers have the same workplace rights as other employees have.[10] Undocumented immigrants can now sue for being paid less than the minimum wage or for being subjected to unsafe working conditions. These rights were already protected under federal law; the new ruling allows workers to file cases in California, where they can recover more in damages.

THE PURVIEW OF THE FEDERAL GOVERNMENT

Under the Fair Labor Standards Act, the Wage and Hour division of the federal Department of Labor (DOL) enforces labor standards in the apparel industry. The act, which was originally established in 1938, requires the payment of minimum wage, specifies wages and conditions for overtime work, and prohibits both homework and child labor (the minimum working age is sixteen). It also requires that employers keep records for each worker, including social security number, forms that establish legal United States residency,[11] and a breakdown of hours and compensation (total hours worked each week, the basis of pay computations, regular pay, overtime pay, total gross pay, specified deductions, and net pay).

For many years enforcement efforts relied on traditional means of investigation: responding to workers' complaints or conducting occasional sweeps that would reveal violations. But it became evident that this approach was not leading to any change in the industry. Indeed, conditions appeared to be worsening in the Los Angeles area. Rather than continue with business as usual, department officials in Los Angeles, led by Rolene Otero, the head of the Wage and Hour division, decided to take seriously the challenge posed by sweatshops in the apparel industry. Under the contracting system, it was argued, factory sweeps were doomed to failure, because sweatshop conditions were in large part a response to price squeezes by retailers and manufacturers. The imposition of stiff penalties on a particular factory merely hastened its demise. The only way to assure compliance among contractors, the department felt, was a backdoor approach to asserting the liability of the manufacturer. The staff came up with two related ideas: the concept of hot goods and the introduction of compliance agreements.

Hot Goods. Turning back to the Fair Labor Standards Act, the staff rediscovered the principle (a part of the original legislation) that, if goods are made in violation of the law, they may not be shipped across state borders. This principle became a weapon that could be used against manufacturers, regardless of their denial of responsibility for what went on in their contracting shops. If the goods were made under illegal conditions, no matter where, they became "hot goods" and manufacturers could not ship them. Most manufacturers in Los Angeles produce for a national market, so the threat of not allowing them to ship was potent.[12] In order to "cool off" such hot goods, the department required that restitution be made by, for example, paying the wages owed to the workers.[13]

By insisting that a manufacturer was responsible for the conditions under which its garments were made, at least for those that cross state lines, the department was able to introduce the principle of joint liability. Because the shipping of the goods was the province of the manufacturer, the protection provided by a legal separation between manufacturer and contractor was stripped. "The hot goods provision," according to the department, "does not apply to a 'good faith' purchaser that acquires the goods in reliance on written assurances that the goods were not 'hot,' unless the purchaser had notice that the goods actually were 'hot.' However, manufacturers or retailers that own the goods at the time the violations of the minimum wage and overtime provisions take place do not qualify for this 'good faith' exception. Retailers generally will qualify for the exception unless they know, or have reason to know, that the goods were made unlawfully. If a retailer knows that its supplier has sold 'hot goods' in the past and does nothing to assure that the goods it receives are not 'hot,' it may lose its 'good faith' exception."[14]

One of the weaknesses of the hot goods provision of the act is that there are no clear punishments for violation. If the department takes a manufacturer to court for shipping hot goods, the judge is likely to say, "Don't do it again," and ask the department what it wants done. The department will then ask the judge to insist that the company sign a compliance agreement with the agency.

Compliance Agreements. Recognizing that it would never have enough personnel to police this mobile, far-flung, often outlaw industry, the Department of Labor had to find a way to make the industry police itself. The mechanism was an agreement between the manufacturers and the department that manufacturers would work only with contractors who complied with the Fair Labor Standards Act. The manufacturers would also agree to set up a compliance program that would provide education and investigations, and would send regular reports back to the department about the conditions in their shops. Should the department find an irregularity in one of their shops, the manufacturers were to correct it immediately.

Once the manufacturers' responsibility for the contractors' conduct was established, the department could use other threats, such as large fines for egregious violations in the contractors' shops or the possibility of public exposure and embarrassment.[15] The department pursued four levels of enforcement of this provision. For a first violation, the manufacturer was notified and asked for a letter of assurance that no further violations would be found. A second violation required that the manufacturer sign an assurance of compliance (the Short Form). A third violation led to a request that the manufacturer sign a compliance agreement (the Long Form) in which the department specified the remedy. A fourth violation would lead to a lawsuit.[16] The compliance program agreement (the Long Form) requires the manufacturer to have his contractors sign an agreement instituting an Employer Contractor Compliance Program (ECCP). The manufacturer will then review the ECCP with the contractor, monitor and keep records on the contractor's compliance, and make the records available to the Department of Labor. The agreement specifies that manufacturers should pay unpaid back wages in their contracting shops, but, because these payments are to be treated as fines payable to the department, the manufacturer could avoid any implication of being a joint employer of the contractor's workers.

The first company that the Los Angeles office of the department went after was Guess? Inc. Finding at least five Guess contractors with major violations, including five instances of child labor, the department threatened Guess with a suit that could have led to a court injunction, followed by millions of dollars in fines and possibly a jail sentence, but also offered Guess the opportunity to sign a compliance agreement and be the first company to do so. After difficult negotiations, Guess signed its own particular version of the Long Form in 1992, and did, indeed, become the first apparel manufacturer in Los Angeles and in the United States to implement a compliance program, which affected its approximately 100 local sewing contractors.[17] Guess hired Connie Meza to be its first compliance director and instituted a nine-point program of compliance:

On-site education for workers in their native languages

Informing workers of their rights

A toll-free hot line for contractors' employees

Training and technical assistance programs to teach contractors how to comply with the law

Encouragement and assistance for contractors in using recommended payroll services

Audits of contractors' payrolls; time and motion studies to ensure that Guess? pays its contractors adequately

Monitoring by quality-control personnel

On behalf of the contractor, payment of back wages directly to the workers

Refusal to do business with any contractor who will not participate in the program.[18]

Guess also agreed to pay $573,000 to compensate for unpaid back wages for workers who were illegally denied overtime pay or minimum wage. The company donated $10,000 to Rebuild L.A., an organization for youth employment that was developed in the wake of the 1992 riots, and gave $25,000 worth of clothing to charities serving needy families with children.[19]

The Department of Labor was hoping to get other manufacturers to sign the Long Form, following Guess's example.[20] Much, of course, depended on the willingness of Guess to comply with the agreement. "[Guess] can do one of two things," said Bernard Lax of the CAIC. "They can make it a circus or they can set a progressive example for the entire industry."[21] In June 1993, the department published a list of 157 garment manufacturers that had been contacted during the previous two years.[22] At the time, about twenty manufacturers on the list had reportedly signed the Long Form. In fact, getting companies to sign the Long Form was harder to accomplish than officials had expected. The apparel manufacturers were extremely resistant and signed only under duress, when they were caught in flagrant violation of the law and with no other way out. By mid-1998 the department had signed Long Form agreements with sixty of the largest companies, including: Z Cavaricci Inc., Nina Piccalino, Inc., Francine Browner, Inc., Swat/Fame, Inc., Chorus Line Corp., and Rampage Clothing Co.

In early 1995, the department won a precedent-setting case against Sungdo, a sportswear manufacturer in Los Angeles and division of a South Korean retailer. One of Sungdo's fashion T-shirt contractors owed $15,000 in back wages. The company had already had to pay $223,000 in back wages for another of its contractors. The judge for the case declared that manufacturers may not invoke a good-faith defense, claiming they were unaware that their contractors were not paying their workers properly. Manufacturers sometimes tried to argue that the language on the back of the Adams Form absolved them of all responsibility. But Judge Manuel Real ruled that this defense did not apply because the manufacturer owned the materials throughout the sewing process and thus had a proprietary interest in the sewing shop.[23] This was a principle that the Department of Labor had been trying to establish, so the officials in Los Angeles were delighted to get such a clear court ruling.

In February 1998, the department won another precedent-setting case, this time against Fashion Headquarters, Inc., a garment manufacturer in New York City. Fashion Headquarters, which made clothing for Lerner's, a subsidiary of The Limited, Inc., employed the contractors MSL Sportswear and Laura and Sarah Sportswear, which, the department claimed, owed $214,000 in back wages to seventy-three workers. The court issued an injunction against the shipping of hot goods, and ordered the manufacturer to assess whether its pricing was adequate to cover minimum wage and overtime before contracting with garment sewing shops. Moreover, because Fashion Headquarters was a private-label manufacturer for a retailer, retailers were put on alert that the department was serious about going after their private-label production. "As a result of the department's uncovering of violations by MSL Sportswear, Inc., and Laura and Sarah Sportswear, Inc., in December [1997], four national retailers, Wal-Mart, K-mart, Nordstrom, and The Limited, agreed to step up their efforts to ensure that their private-label fashion lines are not made in sweatshop conditions and to increase unannounced monitoring of their contractors."[24]

Reactions in the Industry. The Department of Labor's efforts have produced considerable reaction in the Los Angeles apparel industry. Manufacturers have done everything they could to get out of signing compliance agreements. In a typical reaction David Plummer, the president of Sungdo's operation in Los Angeles, said, "We are moving out; we are going to Mexico. . . . I am in the garment business. I am not in the labor-enforcement business." The report continued: "Plummer said he is frustrated by Labor's targeting apparel manufacturers for violations he views as solely the responsibility of contractors. And while he said the company plans to follow the agency's latest demands for a monitoring program, he said regardless of the oversight, many sewing shops will still circumvent the law. 'The contractors "yes" us to death. Then they go behind our backs and do it again. What are we going to do? I know we are going to be busted again,' Plummer said, labeling the agency's threat of delaying shipment of apparel until contractor back wages are paid a form of extortion."[25]

Manufacturers' and contractors' organizations held meetings at which staff from the Department of Labor explained their program and intentions. The Garment Contractors Association recognized that its membership, which tends to consist of the older, larger, more law-abiding contractors, stood to benefit on the whole by having illegal contractors either pushed out of business or made to comply with the law. The department's efforts would help to eliminate unfair competition. However, the association also felt that contractors were being blamed for all the problems in the industry, when manufacturers surely played a role in constructing the sweatshop system by squeezing contractors to the point where they could no longer afford to pay even minimum wage. Joe Rodriguez of the association told us that his members don't want the manufacturers to do the enforcing.[26]

A reporter for *California Apparel News* described the reactions of one contractor to the compliance program. "Rejecting the new agreement, Spencer Miller, owner of My Joy of California, a contracting shop, said he has operated legally for fifteen years. 'I've been operating long enough to know that a manufacturer controls the prices and a 25-cent difference in price can make the difference in a shop operating legally or illegally.' Outraged, Miller asked why a contractor can't review a manufacturer's books to see if prices are fairly distributed. 'Why am I perceived as the bad guy and the manufacturer is the good guy?' "[27]

The manufacturers, at least those represented by the Coalition of Apparel Industries of California, responded with even more ambivalence.

On the one hand they did not want to appear to condone illegality. On the other hand, they wanted to insist that they were not legally responsible for what contractors did. They wanted to avoid even a hint of joint liability, claiming that they could then be open to financial liability for actions over which they had no control. Nevertheless, the executive director of the coalition, Bernard Lax, exhorted manufacturers to acknowledge that the department was serious and that the manufacturers themselves had to play a role in cleaning up the industry. He believed that this would be good for the industry in the long run. Yet at the same time Lax was somewhat critical of the aggressive posture of the Department of Labor, which he characterized as implying, "I'm the new sheriff in town." This, he claimed, had angered many powerful people in the industry, whose attitude was simply, "We're powerful. This, as other things, will pass."[28]

Consequences. In theory, manufacturers who participate in the compliance program are subject to considerable embarrassment if the department finds violations in their shops, because the names of the contractors, and of the manufacturers who use them, are published in the department's quarterly reports, which are available to the general public, posted on the department's website, and distributed to retailers, in the hope that the retailers will put pressure on the manufacturers to bring their shops into full compliance. In practice, however, manufacturers do not routinely inform the department of the violations they uncover in their self-monitoring efforts; such information is provided only when the department uncovers a violation and requests a report. As the departments' district offices conduct only about 300 investigations a year, it seems unlikely that most violations will be uncovered. Moreover, because manufacturers who sign the Long Form are presumably making a good-faith effort to monitor their contractors, they are exempted from lawsuits or the seizure of hot goods when violations do occur. This provides a strong incentive for manufacturers to participate in the program, even if they suspect that some of their contractors are in violation, because it affords some degree of protection against sanctions and bad publicity.[29] The district office has only one legal representative with a staff of three, and is hardly in a position to sue. The district director Gerald Hall candidly admitted, "We're a paper tiger."[30]

The compliance agreements have had a number of unintended effects. Partly in order to use contractors that were in a better position to comply with the law, and partly to reduce their oversight bills by limiting the number of shops requiring investigation, manufacturers have tended to place their orders with fewer but larger contractors. The contractors believe that the agreements have put more power into the hands of the manufacturers, who could withhold work or deny pay for the contractor's slightest infraction. And when the Department of Labor charges the manufacturer for a violation, he can turn around and pass the fines on to the contractor, who already has his own fines to pay.

Another unintended effect has been the creation of an industry, the business of compliance consultancy, firms that monitor contractors for manufacturers—for a hefty fee. This new compliance industry is not without its detractors. Joe Rodriguez of the Garment Contractors Association holds that monitoring "has spawned an industry which doesn't add value—the new millionaires in the compliance industry [are] making us less competitive."[31] The largest compliance firm, California Safety Compliance Corporation, offers seminars to contractors for $450, on-site inspections for $300 per contractor, contractor monitoring for $100 per contractor, and so on.

Another spin-off from the compliance program is the Compliance Alliance, organized in June 1995 by Richard Reinis, an apparel attorney. The group consists of apparel manufacturers in Los Angeles who decided to take the initiative to create their own monitoring program modeled on the Department of Labor's standards. The original members were L'Koral Inc., Jalate Ltd., Inc., Little Laura of California, Podell Industries, Paris Blues, Maxine of Hollywood, Inc., BeBop Clothing, Inc., and Joni Blair of California, Inc. As of July 1998, the Alliance claimed a membership of sixteen large manufacturers who, reportedly, accounted for about a fifth of southern California's total production.[32] In exchange for the self-monitoring, the department agreed to refrain from initiating litigation against member companies if the firm agreed not to ship "hot goods." The department also agreed to inform retailers of remediation steps that the manufacturer was taking if the manufacturer had already notified the retailer of hot goods violations.[33]

The Compliance Alliance's "trust me" approach has been criticized. Even Bernard Lax, of the Coalition of Apparel Industries of America, has characterized the actions of the Alliance as a Band-Aid approach, because it did not establish professional standards for the compliance officers who are hired to monitor the contracting shops.[34] The Alliance's founder and head, Richard Reinis, responded to his critics by claiming that "it may be a fox in the chicken coop, but at least the fox has to pay attention."[35]

Is Monitoring Effective? How well is the fox paying attention? This is a controversial issue, but some unexpected difficulties have surfaced with self-monitoring programs. Workers are afraid to reveal problems to monitors for fear that the contractors will fire them. Even if monitors do uncover problems, their only recourse is to ask the contractor to fix the problem or have the manufacturer threaten to stop giving work. Because both contractor and workers have an interest in not losing the work, they are motivated to collude in covering up the problems. A reporter for the *New York Times* described some of these difficulties as they were revealed in Guess's internal monitoring.

The reports show that over a four-year period Guess monitors found repeated violations at three factories with the same owner: Pride Jeans, Price Jeans, and Price Fashions. In May 1993, an inspector reported, "This shop needs to be watched very carefully because it has the tendency of cheating employees very easily." The next month, an inspector found that many workers did not punch time cards or receive overtime when they worked more than eight hours. In March 1994, an inspector found 160 employees working, but just 113 clocked in. In June 1994, like the previous June, monitors found that the company did not pay overtime after eight hours of work. In February 1996, an inspector reported that "something is 'fishy' " with Pride's payroll methods. Despite this monitoring, last November federal inspectors found that Pride had failed to pay $135,067.03 in overtime to 146 workers.[36]

A similar situation was found at Jeans Plus, another contractor to Guess. There federal inspectors reported that workers were owed $80,000 in back wages, even though Guess inspectors had given it a clean bill of health.

There is some systematic evidence about the effectiveness of monitoring that suggests that the Department of Labor's program is not working very well. The combined state and federal Targeted Industries Partnership Program conducted random surveys of contractors in southern California in 1994, 1996, and 1998 to ascertain compliance with federal and state labor laws. Roughly seventy contractors were selected in each year. Although the overall compliance rate increased from 22 percent in 1994 to 39 percent in 1996, it then remained unchanged in 1998. In other words, despite four years of self-monitoring, 61 percent of the factories in Los Angeles were still violating the labor laws. Minimum wage violations had actually increased slightly between 1996 and 1998 (from 43 percent to 48 percent), and overtime violations remained unchanged at about 54 percent. Gerald Hall, the department's district director, was clearly disappointed that the agency's efforts had borne little fruit.[37]

What about those firms that engaged in self-monitoring? In 1996 and 1998 the Targeted Industries Partnership Program distinguished monitored from unmonitored shops. Much to the dismay of labor officials, the overall rates of compliance among monitored shops dropped from 58 percent in 1996 to only 40 percent in 1998; compliance with minimum wage laws dropped from 73 percent to 56 percent; and compliance with overtime laws dropped from 61 percent to 48 percent. In an understandable effort to put a good face on disappointing results, a distinction was made between "effectively monitored" shops and shops that were simply "monitored."[38] The results were then only slightly more promising: "effectively monitored" shops (about a quarter of the total) had an overall compliance rate of 56 percent, including overtime compliance of 56 percent and minimum wage compliance of 72 percent. The average amount of back wages owed at "effectively monitored" shops was reportedly only $1,413, about half that of all monitored shops ($2,955) and about a quarter of that at unmonitored shops ($5,324).[39] "The results," said Hall, "indicate that a well-monitored shop, one that a manufacturer is really looking at, is much more likely to be in compliance. But still, the overall levels aren't good."[40]

Hall's conclusion must surely rank as an understatement: Even the contractors that were being "effectively monitored" were revealed to be violating wage and hour requirements flagrantly. Because the survey included only *registered* contractors, those in the substantial underground economy, where abuses are known to be almost universal, were not even counted. Whatever its impact on violations of laws on wages and hours, monitoring appears to have little effect on violations of health and safety laws, which Cal-OSHA has found in a high percentage of shops.

In sum, despite its courageous, path-breaking efforts, the Department of Labor has achieved limited results. Even though it recovered nearly $1.3 million in back wages for more than 3,130 apparel workers throughout California,[41] this is a small fraction of the $73 million in back wages that we estimate was owed in southern California alone. The ingenuity and dedication of the department's leaders in pushing their program of forcing manufacturers and retailers to take responsibility must be acknowledged. The monitoring program's shortcomings are mainly a product of the realities of the apparel production system as a whole. In a production system in which each layer squeezes the one below it, in which relationships are hidden behind a thick curtain of secrecy, in which legal lines of authority and accountability are all but nonexistent, and in which the budgets for enforcement are minimal, it is not surprising that self-monitoring is ineffective. We do not mean to suggest, however, that monitoring should be abandoned. It may be an important part of a comprehensive campaign against sweatshops, especially if monitors are not confined to the company and its own agents.[42]

Immigration Raids. United States immigration law makes it illegal to hire workers without legal immigration papers. That law is routinely violated in the apparel industry in Los Angeles, but the provisions of the Fair Labor Standards Act (FLSA) apply to all workers, irrespective of their immigration status. Indeed, if they did not, the incentive to hire undocumented workers would rise dramatically in all low-wage industries. A below-standard sector would emerge in the workforce, clearly marked off by immigration status, and the Department of Labor would not be able to do anything about it. Moreover, the existence of such a sector would push down the wages of all workers, who would be forced to compete with the undocumented.

The Immigration and Naturalization Service and the Department of Labor have somewhat conflicting missions. The former wants to ferret out all undocumented workers for possible deportation; the latter needs to enforce the provisions of the Fair Labor Standards Act for all workers, including the undocumented. If the Department of Labor cooperates too closely with the Immigration and Naturalization Service, its own mission is weakened, because undocumented workers will not reveal violations of the labor laws to the department if they know that they will be turned over to the immigration authorities. In their efforts to avoid any detection by either agency, sweatshops would retreat further underground.

Neverthless, in July 1992, the Department of Labor signed a Memorandum of Understanding with the Immigration and Naturalization Service that it would cooperate with the immigration authorities if it found violations. The memorandum was signed for strictly pragmatic reasons. The Department of Labor is faced with a very constricted budget, but the immigration service has been given billions of dollars to spend on enforcement. To gain more money for its own enforcement mission, the labor department agreed to help the immigration service.

Describing the memorandum as "a pact with the devil,"[43] Gerald Hall reported that most of the garment workers the department sees are undocumented, but it has never turned anyone over to the immigration service, and whenever it inspects a factory, the workers are told that the department is not connected with the immigration service. Before raiding garment shops in early 1998, the immigration service did not inform the

Department of Labor, which was, according to Gerald Hall, "angry about it and let them know."[44] Moreover, when the immigration service does deport people, the Department of Labor steps in to ensure that workers are paid the back wages they are owed before being deported. Nevertheless, the existence of the memorandum lurks in the background as a possible impediment to the department's effectiveness, and rumors circulate among workers that reports of violations to the Department of Labor will be followed up with a raid by the immigration authorities.

Targeted Industries Partnership Program (TIPP). In November 1992, following up on an idea presented by the state Labor Commissioner, Victoria Bradshaw, the governor of California, Pete Wilson, created the Targeted Industries Partnership Program (TIPP), a program in which the work of federal, state, and local agencies is coordinated to enforce labor laws and educate employers and employees about the laws.[45] The target industries are garment manufacturing and agriculture because of their long histories of violation of labor, employment tax, and health and safety laws. The program has four lead agencies: the Division of Labor Standards Enforcement (DLSE), the Division of Occupational Safety and Health (Cal-OSHA), the Employment Development Department (EDD)—three Californian agencies, and the Wage and Hour division of the United States Department of Labor (DOL). Making no attempt to address the structural conditions of the industry that lead to widespread labor law violations, the program works on the assumption that violations are in large part the result of ignorance, and that education is a key component of any solution. "From the beginning, TIPP's philosophy stressed that an essential ingredient of effective enforcement is effective education. TIPP's goal is to ensure that minimum labor standards for employees are met, not to ensnare unwary employers in a web of regulations and fines. TIPP has found that many employers are often poorly informed about those standards and about the consequences of their violation."[46] Among the methods used for "reaching and teaching employers about labor and health and safety laws" are printed materials, meetings, focus groups, and employer-initiated seminars, although it was noted in TIPP's 1994 Annual Report that "progress has been slower in the garment industry where employer groups are not as well organized. Nevertheless, TIPP believes that employer groups in the garment industry are gradually becoming more sophisticated and, with persistent encouragement from TIPP, may develop their own educational seminars." TIPP also seeks to reach employees, through local outreach meetings, focus groups, and "pocket-sized employee rights cards that inform farm and garment workers about their basic labor rights." Since 1996, it has offered a garment hot-line (800/803-6650) for reporting suspected violations.

TIPP was initiated as a pilot project in 1992, and was extended indef-initely in 1994. The Employment Development Department was added to the three founding agencies (Division of Labor Standards Enforce-ment, Division of Occupational Safety and Health, and Department of Labor) in 1996, as a means of reaching the underground economy more effectively. The basic idea behind TIPP is to increase the efficiency and ef-fectiveness of law enforcement by combining the resources of the vari-ous government agencies and sharing information. For example, a gar-ment firm must be registered with the Division of Labor Standards to operate legally, but if the firm owes back wages under an assessment made by the Department of Labor, it will not be allowed to operate until the back wages are paid. TIPP also avoids the duplication of effort by as-signing one agency to perform an investigation and share the results with the others. TIPP has begun to develop partnerships with other agencies, including the IRS and the Franchise Tax Board in California, and with la-bor agencies in other states.

TIPP conducts unannounced "sweeps" in which various agencies are coordinated in a concentrated enforcement effort in a particular region. It also conducts inspections in response to complaints by individual work-ers. Both types of investigation cover wage and hour issues, occupational health and safety, child labor, employment tax, and workers' compensa-tion insurance coverage. In 1996, TIPP decided to narrow its focus to the repeat offender.

Organizers of the program readily acknowledge that the garment in-dustry is one of the worst offenders. "The garment industry has a dis-proportionate number of employers who pay less than the minimum wage, do not pay required overtime rates, and who violate employment tax and safety laws. Such employers frequently employ undocumented workers who often do not file complaints with state or federal agencies. Legitimate garment manufacturers operate at a distinct disadvantage."[47]

In early 1994 TIPP conducted a baseline survey of a random sample of California garment shops and found widespread violations of health and safety and labor laws. As might be expected, industry leaders were very unhappy with the results of this survey. Bernard Lax, the executive director of the Coalition of Apparel Industries, believed that the sample could not have been random, and that the government was "painting the whole industry with the same brush." He continued to believe that many people are obeying the law.[48]

One of the problems faced by TIPP was the uneasy marriage between state and federal government officials. Not only were state officials part of a Republican administration and federal officials part of a Democratic one, but also they disagreed about approaches. The Division of Labor Standards Enforcement did not favor self-monitoring programs, which were the crown jewel of the Labor Department's effort, and favored instead, increasing direct enforcement by government inspectors. Thus representatives of the Division of Labor Standards Enforcement failed to appear at the press conference announcing results of the 1996 TIPP survey because so much emphasis was on the supposed benefits of self-monitoring.[49] The Department of Labor felt sandbagged over the raid on the Thai-run garment factory in El Monte, when the staff of the Division of Labor Standards Enforcement criticized the department for not discovering it earlier.[50] The presidential and gubernatorial elections in 1996 exacerbated the problems.

Other Initiatives

THE SECRETARY OF LABOR STEPS IN

Robert Reich, the former United States Labor Secretary, took up the sweatshop issue with considerable energy, thereby making many enemies in the industry. He engaged in a number of unpopular initiatives, among them an attempt to put pressure on retailers to ensure that the garments they sold were not made in sweatshops.[51] Needless to say, leading retailers were not pleased and the result was a closed-door meeting with officials from Federated Department Stores, Dayton-Hudson Corp., Montgomery Ward, Sears, J. C. Penney, and Wal-Mart.[52] Reich, with the help of Maria Echaveste, an administrator in the Wage and Hour division tried to set a more conciliatory tone at this meeting and to enlist the retailers' help rather than engage in an adversarial relationship with them.

In December 1995, the Department of Labor began publishing a Trendsetter List of retailers and manufacturers who were supposed to have made outstanding efforts to combat sweatshops, and who therefore should be patronized for the holiday season.[53] It favored companies that had signed monitoring agreements with the department and produced cries of outrage from industry leaders, many of whom claimed they had never been found to use sweatshops so had not been tapped for the monitoring program.[54] "The list is a real disservice to hundreds of thousands of other retailers who are doing business every day in a highly ethical manner," said Tracy Mullin, the president of the National Retail Federation. "This is a

PR stunt."[55] Apparel manufacturers in Los Angeles also criticized the list.[56] Richard Reinis, of the Compliance Alliance, complained that retailers would use the list to cancel orders or sue manufacturers, heightening the already existing tension between retailers and manufacturers. Maria Echaveste, who was representing the Department of Labor, claimed that the list was a work-in-progress that would be revised and extended over time.

Starting in May 1996, the Department of Labor began to issue reports of violations by sewing shops, revealing the names of the manufacturers for whom violators were sewing.[57] Most of the violators were in southern California and New York.[58] The list, which was issued quarterly after the first one, came to be entitled the No Sweat Garment Enforcement Report. It was intended to induce manufacturers to keep better control over their contractors. However, as usual, industry leaders did not take the pressure lying down. According to a reporter writing in *Women's Wear Daily,* "the report has only stoked bad feelings among apparel makers and retailers concerning the Labor Department's push to get them to assist federal and state officials in weeding out sweatshops from among the nation's 22,000 contractors. 'It's a black eye. If they want to publish a list, make it one with just the people who have been cited, fined or punished,' said Larry Martin, president of the American Apparel Manufacturers Association, pointing out that almost all of the violations are by contractors and not the vendors who gave them the work."[59] Once again the manufacturers sought to distance themselves from their contractors' illegal actions. Reich justified the list, claiming that retailers had asked for it, saying that they did not have adequate information about offenders to make sure that the clothing they purchased was made in compliance with the law. The National Retail Federation denied that this was what the retailers were looking for.

In July 1996, Reich called an "antisweatshop rap session," attended by about 300 representatives from leading apparel manufacturers and retailers.[60] The Fashion Industry Forum, as it came to be called, was held at Marymount University in Virginia. Reich's efforts to put the sweatshop issue on the map had not gone without effect, as the meeting's relatively high attendance indicates. Both domestic and offshore labor standards in the industry were addressed by the Department of Labor. What Reich was looking for, according to newspaper accounts, was a renewed commitment by industry leaders to address the sweatshop problem seriously.

Alexis Herman, Reich's successor as Secretary of Labor, did not immediately take up his cause, and industry leaders breathed a collective sigh of relief after she had been in office for a few months.[61] Their relief was short-lived. In October 1997, having been in office about six months, Herman developed some new antisweatshop initiatives, including a program, called "Getta Clue," to enlist youth in the fight against sweatshops.[62] Upon request, the Department of Labor would send packets of information to schools, scout troops, and other youth groups. To announce the new program, the department held a joint news conference with Theodore Mc-Carrick, the Catholic archbishop of Newark, who revealed plans to add sweatshop issues to the curriculum of the archdiocese's schools. The agency also created a poster entitled *Life Cycle of a Blue Jean, Sweatshop Style* and, after detailing the various actors in the production process, carried the caption, "Bottom Line—How much did you pay for your last pair of jeans? And how much of that went to the workers who made those jeans? Think about it!"

The California Fashion Association (CFA) did not look favorably on this effort, and sent a delegation, led by Lonnie Kane, to meet with administrators in the Department of Labor, and ask to be allowed to comment on the materials. According to a report in *Apparel Industry Magazine,* "A committee of CFA members reviewed the materials and formulated a detailed letter to [Department of Labor] officials, citing the team's analysis of the materials as 'inaccurate and harmful.' 'We are taking issue with the content of the brochure and have requested that it be revised substantially. We are continuing to pursue this matter and will seek a remedy that does not tarnish the reputation of legitimate manufacturers,' says Kane."[63]

Also instigated by Alexis Herman is a program to involve banks and factors in bringing the apparel industry into compliance with the law.[64] Rather than threatening these financial entities with legal action, the department is urging lenders and factors (buyers of receivables) to require their manufacturers to monitor their contractors, arguing that they have a financial interest in the sweatshop issue because, if hot goods are seized, the banks and factors will lose money. In May 1998, officials from the department met with the CFA and some representatives of financial institutions, who appeared open to considering greater involvement. However, a couple of manufacturers, including Guess, Inc. and Karen Kane Co., expressed concern about such a move, fearing that it might lead financial agents to raise interest rates if minor violations were found, or that it would discourage the emergence of new, small manufacturers.

THE APPAREL INDUSTRY PARTNERSHIP

In August 1996, President Clinton created a task force to look into the sweatshop issue and come up with some recommendations within six months.[65] One of the initial ideas for this group, promoted by Reich, was to develop a "no sweat" label. Karen Kane Co., whose chief executive officer was the president of the California Fashion Association, was one of the initial participants. The American Apparel Manufacturers Association, as usual, thought this was a bad idea, stating that the federal government should use a different approach to the sweatshop issue: step up immigration law enforcement, and use the United States Customs to bar sweatshop-made imports.

The task force came to be called the Apparel Industry Partnership (AIP); its twenty-three members included representatives from UNITE and human rights groups. A major controversy arose over the issue of how factories should be monitored to assure that they were not violating labor standards.[66] The union and human rights groups called for more stringent monitoring than industry leaders were willing to allow. The former wanted to have community and religious leaders who live near the factories be an integral part of the monitoring process, which industry leaders did not like. Belatedly, in April 1997, the panel came up with its recommendation:[67] a nine-point code of conduct, aimed especially at offshore production, that included bans on forced labor, harassment or abuse, and child labor, requirements that companies pay the prevailing local minimum wage and overtime, and that they acknowledge the rights of freedom of association and collective bargaining.[68]

The group planned to continue meeting to hammer out more details, and hoped to get other apparel firms to join the association, which would be charged with overseeing the monitoring of the industry. One manufacturer, Warnaco Group Inc., quit the group at this point over the issue of external monitoring. The director of Global Exchange, a human rights group in San Francisco, argued that the agreement was not strong enough to protect workers. "Recognition of the rights [of freedom of association and collective bargaining] is certainly a positive step. Unfortunately, many U.S. companies choose to work in countries or free-trade zones where independent organizing is illegal and where workers who stand up for their rights are severely repressed. To give this recognition of workers' rights meaning, U.S. companies must pressure local governments to allow workers the freedom to organize, call for the release of all those jailed for their organizing efforts, and require companies to rehire in their own factories workers who have been fired for organizing."[69] In June, 1997, Karen Kane Co. followed Warnaco's lead and resigned from the task force, objecting to the proposal for external monitors. Kane had been represented on the panel by Stan Levy, who had formerly been general counsel for Guess? Inc. "Levy said even requiring the involvement of these grass-roots leaders [local religious, labor and community groups] is like dictating to contractors, companies, and workers who should represent the workers. . . . Another issue of concern to Kane about the task force plans is whether companies that belong to the monitoring association would assume liability for their contractors since they are mandating worker conditions, Levy said."[70] Again, the manufacturers wanted to avoid being seen as joint employers, and being held accountable thereby for conditions of "their" workers.

On 2 November 1998, the AIP published an agreement to form a nonprofit Fair Labor Association (FLA) to implement the AIP's provisions. Companies would join, adopt the FLA's Code of Conduct, and comply with a limited monitoring program. Companies that followed the fair labor practices would become certified as abiding by the FLA's standards and could sew a label into their products stating that they were made under fair conditions. The two unions that had participated in the AIP and the ecumenical Interfaith Center for Corporate Responsibility withdrew from the AIP at this point, believing that the FLA standards were far too weak and that the association would serve as a public relations tool for firms that were still paying less than a living wage, coercing workers to work sixty- or seventy-hour weeks, and denying workers the right to organize and bargain collectively.

The Clinton administration also participated in a first-ever "sweatshop summit" with the European Union in Brussels on 20 February 1998.[71] The event indicated that conditions in garment factories around the world have become a major concern in a number of countries. The British government has developed an Ethical Trade Initiative, and a Clean Clothes Campaign has been developed in Amsterdam. The United States touted the efforts of the Apparel Industry Partnership, and an important international conversation has begun.

PENDING LEGISLATION

At the end of 1998, legislation against sweatshops, proposed by Representative William Clay and Senator Edward Kennedy, was working its way through Congress. The Stop Sweatshops Act would amend the Fair Labor Standards Act of 1938 to make manufacturers and some retailers jointly liable for any wage, hour, and homework violations perpetrated by their contractors. The bill hoped to establish joint liability for both manufacturers and retailers at the federal level.[72]

In August 1998, New York State passed the Unpaid Wages Prohibition Act, the first full joint-liability act passed in the United States. It holds apparel manufacturers fully accountable for sweatshop conditions in their contracted factories.[73] The one weakness in the law, that it does not cover retailers who engage in private-label production, is a result of successful lobbying by the New York Retail Council. UNITE played a key role in the passage of this legislation. Among its provisions, the law shifts the burden of proof from workers (who rarely have strong documentation that they were not properly paid) to employers (who have to demonstrate that they did pay workers legally). It sets a civil penalty for repeated or willful nonpayment of wages at 200 percent of the wages owed. The repeated nonpayment of wages, previously a misdemeanor, became a felony, with a maximum criminal penalty of $20,000. The law prohibits the state Department of Labor from settling for less than the full amount the employer is proven to owe. These and similar provisions make it more difficult to evade law enforcement and to be able to treat the consequences of infraction as a mere cost of doing business.

The enforcement effort could be greatly enhanced by a number of state and federal legislative reforms.[74] One vital provision would be to compel manufacturers and contractors to disclose their connections. The veil of secrecy that surrounds these relationships protects manufacturers from being exposed as sweatshop users. The Department of Labor has taken steps to reveal the connections where they have found violations, but those cover only a small minority of cases and the information is often revealed too late. Manufacturers and contractors could be compelled to post lists of who works for them, or for whom they work, either outside their buildings or on the Internet. Disclosure should cover not only local contracting relations, but also international ones.

Another potentially important piece of legislation would cover pricing by retailers and manufacturers. Prices are often set without regard to the legal costs of actually making a garment, so such standards would compel retailers and manufacturers to prove that they had costed their garments at a legal level, and not just accepted whatever the market would bear even if it is illegal. This idea is already written into the Department of Labor's Long Form agreements, but has yet to be actively implemented. Legislation would set industrywide standards.

Keeping Production at Home

Attempts to eliminate sweatshops encounter the threat of the industry's being driven offshore or to Mexico. Industry leaders frequently raise this threat and some have already acted on it. Is there a way to clean up the apparel industry and still keep it in Los Angeles, or are the two goals inevitably contradictory?

INCENTIVES FOR BUSINESS

Because the apparel industry is so mobile, various governmental agencies, both here and in other countries, have to compete with one another over the location of firms. Jurisdictions, such as the City of Los Angeles and the State of California, want to maintain the industry and lure more garment companies because of the jobs and tax base that they provide. Apparel firms are, therefore, given various financial incentives to make the location more alluring.

The Riordan administration has taken some specific steps in creating an economic climate in Los Angeles that is friendly to business. When he was elected mayor in late 1994, he created the Los Angeles Business Team to keep companies from leaving the city, and to persuade companies from out of the city and state to move here.[75] As expressed in its mission statement, the goals of the Business Team are to "communicate powerful messages in support of the business retention, expansion, and attraction program through marketing, public relations, and advertising; promote Los Angeles as a business-friendly city; counteract perceptions that the City is antibusiness; and help blunt the effectiveness of other cities' and states' attempts to lure business away from Los Angeles." The city is somewhat limited in what it can do. In general, it cannot make deals with individual companies and acts mainly as a broker and marketing arm for state and federal programs. "The city is mainly concerned with a company's bottom line as a means of getting [companies] to come here or stay here," according to a member of the Business Team.[76] The twenty-five-person team answers questions about using the various state and federal economic zones, helps firms to obtain permits quickly, enables them to gain long-term discounts on utilities, helps them to find the best site on which to build or relocate, and can provide them with financing programs at below-market rates. The team also proposed cutting local business taxes for five years when a company moves to the city from outside Los Angeles and freezing taxes for five years for those already here.

The various zones function to provide businesses with tax breaks in order to encourage them to employ low-income workers and revitalize inner-city neighborhoods. California adopted an enterprise zone program in 1986 and some 1,800 enterprise zones were created throughout the state, largely in anticipation of a similar program of federal zones that would reinforce local efforts. Los Angeles currently contains three such major zones, one of which, the Central City Enterprise Zone, encompassing roughly 68,000 residents in four square miles, covers the garment district area.[77]

The federal enterprise zone program received a major boost in 1994, with the Clinton administration's national competition for empowerment zones that would bring $100 million each to six cities. The program was created partly in response to the riots in Los Angeles in 1992, and the city was widely regarded (in Washington as well as Los Angeles) as certain to receive funding. The city's proposal, encompassing neighborhoods ranging from Pacoima to South Central, was optimistically entitled "Building Together from the Ground Up." Through a combination of federal grants and tax breaks, it would have provided $100 million in funding directly for job training, child care, and similar programs; payroll tax breaks as high as 20 percent of wages; and highly accelerated business depreciation on the purchase of new equipment. The overall benefit was predicted to reach as much as $500 million.[78]

The city's proposal was not accepted. It was judged to be excessively vague, long on platitudes but short on specifics, relying instead on California's importance for Clinton's prospects of being reelected president. Part of the difficulty was that, given federal restrictions (empowerment zones could contain no more than 200,000 residents in twenty square miles), more time was spent on negotiating the political boundaries of the zone than on preparing the proposal itself, which was left to a private consulting firm, Hamilton, Rabinovitz and Alschuler, that had only three months to complete its work (at a cost of $220,000).[79]

This setback for city officials, although embarrassing, proved not to be fatal; Los Angeles was simply too politically important to be cut out of federal programs entirely. The empowerment zone proposal was turned down in late December 1994; by the following May, the Clinton administration, in a high-profile announcement made by Vice President Gore, announced the award of $450 million to capitalize a nonprofit community development bank in Los Angeles, the fulfillment of a long-time dream of administration officials.[80] The award, consisting of grants and loan guarantees from the United States Department of Housing and Urban Development, would be used by the community development bank for loans to private banks and nonprofit development organizations, which would leverage loans estimated at as much as $2 billion to community organizations, private developers, and small and medium-sized businesses.[81] The apparel industry was its first target.[82] The area encompassed by the program includes low-income areas in downtown Los Angeles, including sections of the city where the garment industry is concentrated.[83]

One problem with these kinds of programs is their lack of accountability. We spent many fruitless hours trying to ascertain whether any apparel company had received tax breaks under any of the various zone programs, how much, and whether any effort had been made to assess whether the programs had, indeed, increased jobs for the targeted populations. We discovered that the information about tax rebates is kept secret, and it appears that no oversight is done to ensure that the promises are fulfilled.

FOCUS ON THE APPAREL INDUSTRY

Mayor Riordan recognizes the importance of the apparel industry to Los Angeles.[84] He speaks with pride about the fact that the industry in Los Angeles has zoomed past New York, and that it provides a mixture of high-quality and entry-level jobs. He has made efforts to bring major fashion shows to Los Angeles. He amended parts of the city tax code in 1997 by eliminating manufacturing as a basis for imposing business taxes on wholesalers and retailers. And he calls on industry leaders to pressure him to do more. Early in his administration the mayor appointed an apparel specialist in his Office of Economic Development. He convened the New Fashion Industry Roundtable, which brought together most of the major power-players in the industry (page 110). The California Fashion Association was created as a result of the roundtable meeting and it has become a visible and vocal advocate for the industry. The city has also endorsed the development of a Business Improvement District in the Fashion District, so that buyers would be more comfortable in the area. The mayor agreed to participate in the CaliforniaMart's Designer of the Year Award ceremony at the Beverly Hilton in October 1998. According to a member of the Los Angeles Business Team, "We really want to make clear that we're supportive of the [apparel] industry."[85]

Apart from general efforts to encourage the apparel industry to remain in Los Angeles, approaches have been made to specific firms, urging them to remain by offering them a package of favors and incentives. Three companies that took up the city's offer were California Fashion Industries, Inc., Guess? Inc., and Superba, Inc.

California Fashion Industries, Inc., the company producing the Carole Little label and one of the flagship apparel companies in Los Angeles, suffered $11 million in damages during the riots in 1992. After fortifying its complex at Martin Luther King Boulevard and Main Street, the company began to seek a new location that would not only prove safer, but also would house its rapidly growing staff (projected to double from 800). The coowners, Leonard Rabinowitz and Carole Little, had been thinking about moving the company to Nevada when a former distribution center for the May Company became available. Although California Fashion Industries was willing to spend $10 million on purchasing, renovating, and expanding the facility, the company was concerned about becoming entangled in the red tape of the permit process. A meeting with Riordan, who personally reassured Rabinowitz that the permit application would be expedited, convinced the company to remain in Los Angeles.[86]

In the early 1990s the Marciano brothers, the owners of Guess? Inc., talked of moving their headquarters and production system out of Los Angeles. When word got around that they were talking of leaving, the governor's office called the California Trade and Commerce Agency, which pulled together a Red Team, including someone from the mayor's office. The team met with the Marcianos, and told them, among other things, of all the tax abatements they were entitled to because their headquarters are located in an enterprise zone and a revitalization zone.

The Los Angeles Business Team met with Superba, a tie producer whose clients include Tommy Hilfiger, when it was planning to expand and began to look for a new location. The company was being approached by such governmental entities as the City of Industry, Vernon, and even a city in Kansas. The team leader, Rocky Delgadillo, described the meeting. "So we get in there, and say 'Think about how we can keep you where you're at.' We reminded them that moving costs are not an insignificant consideration. We also remind them that the Department of Water and Power is owned by the city. Why not seek a long-term discounted contract?"[87] Delgadillo also pointed out that empowerment zones are a marketing tool used by the Business Team. By taking advantage of a federal tax credit of $3,000 for each employee, a company such as Superba could save $210,000. The company remained, and added 100 new employees to its existing staff of 700.

TAX CONCESSIONS AND A LIVING WAGE

The fact that various governmental jurisdictions must compete with one another to attract or keep apparel firms leads to a situation in which very wealthy entities and individuals are offered ways of saving themselves money—typically out of the public coffers. Meanwhile, the pressing needs of low-wage workers are set aside as less important. The assumption is made that, if the job-producers remain in Los Angeles, the problems of the workers will automatically be solved. In fact, the wealthy take advantage of all the breaks they are offered, and get richer; the incomes of low-wage workers stagnate.

This conflict lies at the heart of the debate over the living wage. Workers and their advocates object to the fact that public moneys (including tax concessions) are given to already wealthy companies, even when those companies pay their workers rock-bottom wages and fail to cover such basic necessities as health insurance. Advocates of a living wage argue that, if companies receive subsidies from the government, they should have an obligation to pass on some of their gains to their employees. To the extent that one of the unstated advantages of settling or remaining in Los Angeles is the availability of low-wage, immigrant workers, the conflict between the retention of the industry and the elimination of sweatshops cannot be resolved.

The issue of accountability for receiving subsidies is being reviewed by the Los Angeles Alliance for a New Economy (LAANE), an outgrowth of the Living Wage Coalition. The alliance, led by Madeline Janis-Aparicio, is exploring the ways in which the city sudsidizes businesses, including the activities of the Community Redevelopment Agency, the use of industrial development bonds, the uses of the city's Economic Development Budget, and so forth. The purpose of this project is to see whether the benefits of these public expenditures extend to workers and communities, rather than merely ending up in the hands of wealthy developers. The Alliance wants businesses that receive subsidies to be held accountable for providing benefits to the rest of the city's population.

The City of Los Angeles is clearly important in maintaining the apparel industry here, but we believe that its role cannot be limited to offering breaks to businesses while ignoring the problem of sweatshop production. City officials need to develop a *comprehensive* plan, not only for maintaining the industry, but also for upgrading its labor standards. Workers and their advocates and representatives must be included in the development of the plan. It is not enough simply to offer breaks to businesses and assume that, in providing jobs, they will benefit the community, regardless of the quality of those jobs. More wealth put into the hands of the wealthiest residents will not dissuade them to stop exploiting immigrant workers unless they are vigorously prohibited from doing so.

TECHNOLOGY AND TRAINING

The technology of most apparel manufacturing processes has changed little during the past century.[88] Work on soft, three-dimensional fabric is still highly labor intensive.[89] The principal technological changes have been in automated fabric cutting, embroidering and buttonholing, and electronic point-of-sale inventory systems. Some limited changes have been made in sewing technology, particularly in the development of computerized and specialized sewing machines. Nonetheless, apparel production in Los Angeles still depends on low labor costs and minimal investment in plant and equipment.

The argument for improved technology is simple: The apparel industry in southern California cannot remain competitive in today's global production system if it relies only on the low cost of its labor. Too many other countries can offer still lower labor costs. In a race to the bottom, Los Angeles will clearly be the loser. The industry in Los Angeles needs to develop other sources of competitive advantage.

Southern California Edison Company. Barry Sedlik, the manager of the Business Retention Group of Southern California Edison Company, was one of the first to consider the need for change. In March 1993, he invited a group of industry leaders to try to develop a coordinated strategy for retaining the apparel production base in southern California. The group, which became known as the Apparel Industry Roundtable, held regular meetings, hired a consulting firm to conduct research, and published a report in 1995.[90] In the report two possible futures were envisaged for the apparel industry: It could continue the current course or take what was described as the "value path"—illustrated in Figure 8. "By taking no concerted action to date, the industry has focused on solely maintaining its low-cost labor force. In effect, southern California's apparel firms have tried to compete head-to-head with the low-cost apparel centers of the world. . . . If the industry continues down its current course, expected (given industry trends) losses in employment will accelerate and future wages and profitability will be constrained" (p. 20). In the report, it is pointed out that productivity gains have been made in Los Angeles through slow growth in wages. "The fact is, southern California has fallen behind both domestic and international competitors, *even some of its lowest labor cost competitors,* in applying the array of production and communication technologies available to the industry" (p. 22). If the industry continues on its current course, Edison predicted that, in ten years (2005), industry output will have shrunk from $8 billion to $7.7 billion, and in twenty-five years (2020), it will have declined to $6.4 billion, and that employment will have fallen from 141,000 in 1995 to 112,000 in 2005, and to 65,500 by 2020.

The alternative, the "value path," involves taking action to revitalize the industry. The report recommends a two-stage approach: Stage one, called Competing through Value, entails significant new investment in increased productivity through the adoption of new technologies and production methods, along with investments in training workers. Stage two, called Competing through Trade, involves a long-term vision of capturing a larger share of the world market. If this strategy were to be followed, an output growth to $10.3 billion in ten years and $16.6 billion in twenty-five years is predicted. Employment is expected to decline to 136,000 in ten years and to grow again to 140,000 by 2020.

The value path is accompanied by higher wages. Edison estimated the average apparel industry wage in 1995 as $17,559. Note that this figure includes all employees of the industry, including designers, computer operators, and so on, and not just sewing machine operators whose wages are much lower. Edison predicts that, by following the current course, the average apparel wage will rise to $20,800 in 2005 and to $32,700 by 2020, but by pursuing the value path, it should rise to $34,400 in 2005 and to $40,700 in 2020. Of course the accuracy of all these predictions can be questioned, but at least the intent is clear: To increase technology and training, improve productivity, and raise wages.

Edison argued that competitive advantage is found in four areas: cost, speed, quality, and distinctiveness. The group asserted that technological upgrading could raise the quality of goods, diminishing flaws in cutting and sewing, leading to a more consistent product, hence higher volume. Enhanced technology could also improve service by providing faster turnaround and adaptability. "The industry is also behind in employing improved production techniques, such as modular production, proven to increase production and worker satisfaction" (p. 22). The group suggested that the industry develop a relationship with Mexico "not unlike the mutual competitiveness achieved by Hong Kong and South China" (p. 29), in which Los Angeles provides high-value services (design support, sales, merchandising, logistics, and finances) while Mexico provides low-cost labor.

For Competing on Value, Edison recommended three courses of action: to improve the production chain, to increase market opportunities, and to improve government relations. Many of the ideas were predicated on the hope that leaders of the apparel industry in Los Angeles would act in concert. "Collaboration will be the industry's first challenge. There

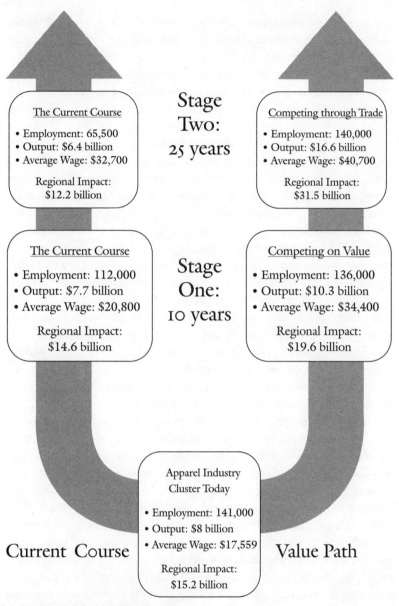

Stage Two: 25 years

The Current Course
- Employment: 65,500
- Output: $6.4 billion
- Average Wage: $32,700

Regional Impact: $12.2 billion

Competing through Trade
- Employment: 140,000
- Output: $16.6 billion
- Average Wage: $40,700

Regional Impact: $31.5 billion

Stage One: 10 years

The Current Course
- Employment: 112,000
- Output: $7.7 billion
- Average Wage: $20,800

Regional Impact: $14.6 billion

Competing on Value
- Employment: 136,000
- Output: $10.3 billion
- Average Wage: $34,400

Regional Impact: $19.6 billion

Current Course

Apparel Industry Cluster Today
- Employment: 141,000
- Output: $8 billion
- Average Wage: $17,559

Regional Impact: $15.2 billion

Value Path

SOURCES: Modeling by DRI/McGraw-Hill.
DATA: U.S. Bureau of Labor Statistics.
NOTE: Employment and Average Wage are computed (in constant 1992 $) for the entire Apparel Cluster, including sewing/contracting jobs, higher-paying designer/manufacturing jobs, and the jobs in the financial and other services that are supported by the industry. Average wages rise due to higher wages in apparel sewing/manufacturing, which increase in line with productivity increases and the increased demand by the industry for services—particularly business, financial, and export services.
Copyright © 1995 by Southern California Edison Company.

Figure 8. A Two-Path Scenario for the Southern California Apparel Industry

is a long list of obstacles which have historically prevented the diverse and fragmented southern California apparel industry from working together" (p. 36), among them the facts that the industry is made up of fiercely independent entrepreneurs, that the various sectors of the industry are often unaware of one another's problems, that short-term cost-based relationships hinder frank and open communication, and that the industry has many small enterprises fighting for survival.

In order to foster communication, Edison created an Apparel Industry Roundtable, which held meetings between March 1993 and March 1994. A number of other initiatives grew out of this pioneering effort, including the mayor's Fashion Industry Roundtable, which led to the creation of the California Fashion Association (see page 110) and the Apparel Roundtable Educational Consortia, chaired by Sharon Tate of Los Angeles Trade Technical College (see page 108). One of the accomplishments of the roundtable was the passage in Sacramento of the California Apparel Industry Revitalization Act of 1994, which requires the secretary of trade and commerce "to direct all relevant components of the Trade and Commerce Agency to coordinate state resources for specified purposes relating to supporting the apparel industry in the state."[91] The act, like the recommendations of the roundtable itself, was short on specifics. In the time since the Edison report was issued and the act signed into law (some five years as of this writing), there has been no significant upgrading of the apparel industry in southern California.

One avenue to improving the performance of the local industry would be to increase funding for the apparel industry office within the Department of Trade and Commerce to establish a district office in Los Angeles. That office would be responsible for providing technical, managerial, and financial support and training to contractors, establishing links between the garment industry and other economic development agencies, and coordinating public agencies that share an interest in advancing the industry. In a similar vein, additional funding could be provided to support incubator projects that demonstrate upgraded technologies and production techniques, as well as provide contractors with necessary technical support and management training (including training in fair labor practices). Incubator projects could also enable employees to improve their skills and foster the use of computers in production as well as design.[92]

Possible Models. Los Angeles is not the only apparel center in the United States that faces the twin threats of industry flight and the return of sweatshops. Both New York and San Francisco face the same dilemma, and both have experimented with what might be termed "corporatist" solutions, that is, efforts to bring together capital, labor, and government in a joint effort to upgrade the industry, to the benefit of both business and workers. In both cities, the union (UNITE), pushing for training for workers and improved factory standards, has been an important partner.

In San Francisco the project, called Garment 2000, brings together manufacturers, contractors, organized labor, San Francisco City College, the City of San Francisco, and the United States Department of Labor. The goal is to revitalize the apparel sector in the Bay Area by encouraging higher-value and higher-quality, rather than high-volume, production. The project organizers want to deploy new technologies, develop just-in-time production capabilities, and link production sites to retail outlets. The tools they emphasize are workforce development (training), technological improvements, demonstrations, simulations, and access to capital. They offer an array of programs, from workshops in business management to on-site technical assistance to a teaching factory.

Apparently the program has met with some success. According to a newspaper report, workers who went through the training program (in mid-1996, before the rise in the minimum wage) were able to increase their wages from $5 to $6 an hour.[93] Moreover, in a recent survey, the Department of Labor found an encouraging rate of compliance with federal law: 37 percent in New York, 39 percent in Los Angeles, and 79 percent in San Francisco.[94] Certain characteristics of the apparel industry in San Francisco make programs such as Garment 2000 likely to succeed. The industry is much smaller, the manufacturers are well organized, the union has made greater inroads in the industry, and the climate in San Francisco is more favorable towards unions than it is in Los Angeles.

In New York, the Garment Industry Development Corporation (GIDC) is a nonprofit consortium of business, government, and labor that was originally instigated by the ILGWU, and became incorporated in 1984. The corporation helps apparel firms with real estate, marketing and technology, and training to upgrade the skills of both managers and workers. Supported by the city and state of New York, the industry trade associations, and a number of UNITE (originally ILGWU) locals,[95] it offers a variety of programs, too numerous to mention here.[96] The main point is that the consortium is able to raise public money to support its various efforts to upgrade the industry. In 1997, it received a $200,000 grant from the United States Department of Labor to expand programs and services. With the support of a state grant, it also developed a Fashion Industry Modernization Center in Chinatown that opened in the spring of 1998.[97]

The consortium is recommending that the New York apparel industry take advantage of the desire by many retailers to shorten the time between ordering and receipt, for both new orders and reorders. It urges that New York get out of low-end production, where competition is based on price, and focus more on the high end, and urges the industry to pursue exports, taking advantage of the popularity abroad of Made in the USA or Made in New York labels. In practical terms, however, "the highly fragmented structure of the industry, with its secretive and competitive history makes the role of change catalyst difficult. [The corporation] is trying to counteract this by operating demonstration projects that *show* manufacturers and contractors that change is possible. Then, it hopes, it will be able to make a significant impact on the industry."[98] The situation in New York is considerably more complex than it is in San Francisco. Still, compared with Los Angeles, New York has several advantages, namely, better-organized manufacturers and a stronger (though weakened) union. Both of these components contribute to the corporatist approach of cooperation among business, labor, and government. In none of the efforts in Los Angeles is organized labor invited to the table, and some people in the industry there say they would *never* sit at the same table as the union.

UPGRADING THE CONTRACTORS

The single biggest problem facing technological upgrading is the current contracting system. Because contractors generally do not have a reliable flow of work, they are reluctant to invest extensively in modernized equipment even if favorable financing were available. The situation is exacerbated by the conditions of employment, under which workers are paid a piece rate and are employed only when they are needed. This system discourages loyalty among employees and makes it unreasonable for contractors to invest in training their workers. Turnover at such firms can be high, as workers keep on searching for a new job or a better situation. The piece-work system also encourages speed, rather than quality, as workers seek to maximize the number of pieces completed. Because more skilled workers are able to build up speed, hence earnings, they may be reluctant to undertake changes that may lead, initially, to cuts in their pay.

Almost all contracting shops in Los Angeles use the progressive bundle system, which requires only the narrowest of skills (see page 179). Also, it is a highly inefficient method of producing garments, because bundles of cloth sit on the floor for days as they inch their way through the assembly process. Large quantities of product are warehoused at the production site, awaiting the next step. This halting through-put means that inventory accumulates in the contractors' factories and not on the sales floor. The goal of any reorganization of production is to decrease the time that a particular garment remains on the shop floor, so that the turnover time is diminished. There are at least two readily available alternatives to the standard progressive bundle system, namely, the unit production system (UPS), and modular production. The unit production system depends on a central computer, which is used to dispatch garment parts on hangers over a system of rails to workers. Not only does this increase the speed with which garments can be completed, but also the fact that the garment is hanging rather than being bundled up reduces the need for pressing. In modular production workers form teams that work together to finish a whole garment. This system requires greater skill on the part of workers, who must be able to change tasks readily, but it also enables them to put together a garment very quickly, while making the work more interesting. These innovations are more common in the South, where garment firms are much larger, and where there is a potential labor shortage. *Bobbin* and *Apparel Industry Magazine,* trade magazines that have a southern base, are filled with examples of firms using the new systems, and are continually urging contractors to try them out.

Yet few contractors in Los Angeles have adopted the new systems, both because of the capital investment required and because they require investment in training workers. Neither manufacturers nor retailers are demanding these or other production practices or equipment from their contractors. From the contractors' point of view, the foremost consideration of manufacturers and retailers is *price.* The retailers and manufacturers have tremendous bargaining power to set contract sewing prices. Retail buyers are concerned with quality, especially in terms of product styling, fabric, and timely shipping, but not to the extent that they care about the production system itself. Contractors believe that, if manufacturers or retailers do not care about the mechanics of production, investment in technological upgrades is wasted. Joe Rodriguez, the executive director of the Garment Contractors Association, summarizes the situation succinctly: "If in fact the manufacturers and retailers can always say 'squeeze every last penny out or we'll go elsewhere,' what can contractors do? The high-tech plants in the South are simply out of the reach of Los Angeles. Who here can afford a $75,000 machine?"[99] The demand for skilled production workers is low. Familiarity with a specific sewing machine operation is all that most contractors require. Facility on several types of machines is desirable but not required. Industrywide there is little formal training of machine operators, and what little training is done happens on the job.

Local contractors could benefit from long product runs, repeat orders, and a more predictable work load. Large sewing orders that would help local contractors to stabilize their production sufficiently to make it worth investing in upgrading are, unfortunately, unlikely to be placed in Los Angeles. They tend to be sourced offshore. If those kinds of production runs could be secured by the adoption of more efficient technologies in the region, it might be possible to entice local contractors to consider upgrading. But this is a chicken and egg problem: Without predictability they dare not invest, and without investment, the more stable production will not be done here. Local sewing contractors are more likely to be relied upon for shorter runs, rush orders, or one-time batches for the spot market, ordered in such limited quantities that offshore production is not cost effective. More complicated garments requiring quality oversight are also more likely to be sewn locally.

Owners and managers of contracting shops frequently bemoan the fact that they suffer from a shortage of skilled workers who could work on a variety of machines. But, because of the price pressures and instability, they are unwilling to pay for skilled workers or institute training programs. The problems are compounded by the fact that apparel contractors are, correctly, seen as risky ventures by the financial community. Because of the contractors' vulnerability and instability, financial agencies do not consider lending them money to upgrade their equipment and technology. Even if a contractor decides to try to pursue the high road, he will be hard-pressed to raise the necessary capital.

In sum, the contracting and piece-rate systems, which provide flexibility for the manufacturer and retailer, lead to unpredictability and instability for contractors and workers. Because this flexible system allows manufacturers and retailers to set very low prices, they are satisfied with the results and have little incentive to change. Meanwhile, contractors have little to gain from improving either their production systems or working conditions. There appears to be no internal dynamic that leads away from the low-wage (sweatshop) low road.[100]

A STRATEGIC ALLIANCE

Because of pressure from offshore competition, stepped-up governmental enforcement efforts, and a renewed effort on the part of UNITE to organize garment workers in Los Angeles, some industry leaders are attempting to retain a strong apparel manufacturing base in the region. These leaders include members of the Apparel Industry Roundtable, the California Fashion Association, the Garment Contractors Association, and the North American Integration and Development Center at the University of California, at Los Angeles.

To address the fragmentation of the industry, and the unequal relationship between contractors and manufacturers, a strategic alliance has been proposed that would both seek to create alliances between contractors and manufacturers, and to prepare contractors to borrow from commercial banks so that they could afford to upgrade their technology. The theory holds that, if the contractor were to agree to purchase equipment, the manufacturer, who would then benefit from lower costs and more efficient production, would guarantee to provide the contractor with work for a specified period of time. Both would benefit, and the industry would be stabilized. Because of this alliance, the contractor would be more creditworthy, and would therefore be in a more favorable position to obtain loans from commercial banks. Moreover, the pump would be primed with seed loans from the Small Business Administration, the North American Development Bank, or the Los Angeles Community Development Bank. This model has existed in a much more direct form: A few manufacturers already provide low-interest or interest-free loans to their regular contractors so that they might upgrade equipment or expand their factories.

Closely related to technology upgrading and business development for contractors is an effort to link training to the alliance between manufacturer and contractor. A few modest courses are being offered for management and workers. However, public support for training is limited. Most state and local economic development and employment training policy is based on the assumption that some sectors, such as apparel, are inherently poorly paid and that policymakers should support the growth of inherently well-paid sectors rather than help transform the low-wage ones. The largest federal training program, the Job Training Partnership Act, has been aimed at people without jobs, rather than at upgrading the incumbent workforce. The main source of funding for training of incumbent workers in California is the Employment Training Panel, but most of the money is spent on durable goods manufacturers. The apparel industry has received only one or two grants over the past several years.

There has been some upgrading and training in recent years. Following the riots in 1992, Rebuild L.A. (now the Community Development Technology Center) was created to address the needs of neglected, lower-income communities. The organization's Apparel Network has developed a close collaboration with Edison, the Los Angeles Trade Technical College, the Garment Contractors Association, the Fashion Industry Alliance, and the Textile and Clothing Technology Corporation (TC2), which is based in North Carolina. This collaboration has had several successes, having obtained a technology grant from IBM Corporation to help set up an apparel technology resource center at Trade-Tech, software donations from equipment companies, opportunities for numerous TC2 workshops, and collaboration with the Los Angeles Community Development Bank and the North American Development Bank for making capital more accessible to contractors and manufacturers.

Another of the results of the Roundtable convened by Southern California Edison was the notion that alliances between manufacturers and contractors could provide access to financial resources. Provided they were guaranteed work by the manufacturers, contractors, with the aid of the California Fashion Association's Technology-Education Council and the North American Integration and Development Center, would find it possible to obtain loans from the Small Business Administration and the North American Development Bank. In July 1996, Southern California Edison awarded a $50,000 grant to the Technology-Education Council to support the organization of strategic alliances in order to upgrade technology, equipment and workers' skills. Qualifying alliances would be eligible for loan guarantees from the North American Development Bank, so that commercial banks would be willing to lend to the risky apparel industry. The goal was to get commercial banks involved in the process of upgrading the industry. However, the domination of the California Fashion Association by manufacturers made it difficult for that organization to support an agenda for the benefit of contractors. Recognizing this problem, Edison has asked that its grant include a diverse base of contractors. Some manufacturers have even expressed the concern that any sharpening of the business skills of the contractors would make them less likely to accept contracts that force them to pay lower and ever-lower wages. (Except briefly, at the initial Apparel Industry Roundtable meetings, organized labor has not been involved in any of these initiatives. Once the unions ceased to participate, hostility toward them became very evident. Competitive pressure for lower costs made unions and higher wages anathema.)

So far the efforts to develop strategic alliances and to gain financing for them have not met with much success. The Community Development Technology Center and Los Angeles Trade-Technical College continue in their efforts to upgrade the industry, focusing on training both for contractors and workers. The problem may lie in the unwillingness of manufacturers to develop stable bonds with contractors, because that would reduce flexibility and distance from the harsh labor conditions of the industry. The manufacturers may not see what they have to gain, and the option of moving to ever cheaper sources of labor promises clear benefits. Without the aid of strong external pressures, from workers, unions, and community groups, it is hard to see how any but a tiny minority will voluntarily pursue the high road. However, if pressure is effectively applied from a number of sources, the various high-road initiatives that have been opened may come into fuller play.

Government efforts to clean up the apparel industry are riddled with contradictions. On the one hand, agencies are eager to bring the industry into compliance with the law of the land. On the other hand, they are afraid of driving factories out of business or out of their jurisdiction. Moreover, in the battle between labor and capital, government agencies are much more likely to hear from and be pressured by business interests than by workers—especially in this industry, where the workforce is overwhelmingly immigrants, many without legal documents. The result is that governmental entities tend to favor business, even though some of the individuals who work for the government are zealously eager to bring an end to sweatshops. Thus, no matter how well intentioned government might be, it is very difficult to bring about fundamental change in the industry without external pressure. Legislative reform, for example, will require an aroused public to ensure that it is passed.

CHAPTER 9
Worker Empowerment

I came to Washington thinking the answer was simply to provide people in the bottom half with access to the education and skills they need to qualify for better jobs. But it's more than that. Without power, they can't get the resources for good schools and affordable higher education or training. Powerless, they can't even guarantee safe workplaces, maintain a livable minimum wage, or prevent sweatshops from reemerging. Without power, they can't force highly profitable companies to share the profits with them. Powerless, they're as expendable as old pieces of machinery.

—Robert B. Reich, *Locked in the Cabinet*

The return of sweatshops to the United States apparel industry has been attributed to a number of causes. Among the factors often cited is the decline of the welfare state and the weakening of the once-powerful garment worker unions.[1] These two factors are closely intertwined in that a strong labor movement helped to build the welfare state, and the welfare state in turn provided support for labor organizing and the formation of a strong labor movement. The weakening of these twin supports for workers' rights and a decent standard of living for United States working-class families has contributed to the erosion of labor standards in the apparel industry in Los Angeles, and to the appearance of widespread violations of labor law in the thousands of garment factories located there.

The apparel industry of today is not what it was in the first half of the twentieth century. The new, flexible, global system of production does not lend itself readily to the solutions of the past. Employers of workers in the United States face a realistic threat from their competitors who are producing offshore using labor that costs considerably less. Similarly, firms that take advantage of all the benefits associated with contracting put pressure on those that do not, driving all to move toward this cost-cutting approach. Market forces are pushing developments with hurricane force, and the efforts by government agencies to ameliorate the worst effects

FEIFFER®

FEIFFER © 1997, Jules Feiffer. Reprinted with permission of Universal Press Syndicate.
All rights reserved.

for working people, both here and abroad, seem pitifully weak in the face
of the gale.

What is to be done? Typically the issue gets addressed in terms of public policy, that is, what can those with power do to bring about change?
In this chapter we focus on the victims of the system, the workers themselves, to determine if there is anything *they* can do. We see the problem
of sweatshops as a problem of powerlessness. Left unchecked, market
forces will run roughshod over workers who have no ability to fight back.
The maldistribution of wealth and power will only get worse unless workers are able to build resistance to these forces. Otherwise, the polarization between rich and poor will grow, and wages and working conditions
for garment workers will worsen.

Workers need power. They can only counter the power of business by
pushing against it. There are many routes to power, but the most important approach historically has been through organization, that is,
through unionization. Corporations are organized into disciplined entities that face workers with the ability to exercise considerable power.
Workers are fragmented into isolated individuals with almost no power.
Only when they form organizations that can act as an equally disciplined
force against the domination of the employer, do they have a chance of
effective resistance. This idea was enunciated clearly by Chief Justice
Charles Evans Hughes of the United States Supreme Court in support
of the passage of the National Labor Relations Act in 1935. "Long ago

we stated the reason for labor organizations. We said that they were or-ganized out of the necessities of the situation; that a single employee was helpless in dealing with an employer; that he was dependent ordinarily on his daily wage for the maintenance of himself and family; that if the employer refused to pay him the wages that he thought fair, he was nev-ertheless unable to leave the employer and resist arbitrary and unfair treat-ment; that union was essential to give laborers opportunity to deal on equality with their employer."[2]

How can garment workers empower themselves? Are the trade unions of the AFL-CIO able to rise to the task? Are the strategies of the 1940s and 1950s still applicable, or do we need new approaches? It is our belief that the challenge of organizing garment workers portends the challenges that will face the workers of many other industries in the expanding global, flexible political economy. If workers and unions can figure out how to develop the power of workers in *this* industry, they should be able to suc-ceed in many others.

Garment Workers' Unions

Garment workers' unions were among the most powerful trade unions in the first half of the twentieth century, and they played an important role in shaping the legislation that aims to protect workers today. The Fair Labor Standards Act and the National Labor Relations Act both provided important support for garment workers, the former by setting basic labor standards, and the latter by protecting the right to form independent trade unions and engage in collective bargaining. To-day, the United States labor movement is in deep trouble. The disman-tling of the welfare state, the rise of antilabor conservative thinking (es-pecially in the Republican Party, but also among centrist Democrats), the restructuring of the global economy, the hegemony of neoliberalism, and a right-wing assault on the labor movement have taken their toll. True, some of the difficulties faced by the labor movement can be attributed to its own, internal problems. These include old bureaucratic structures that are unresponsive to a changing workforce composed more of women and immigrants, the tendency to put more energy and resources into servic-ing members than into organizing new members, and a failure to develop new and creative techniques for dealing with the flexible, global work en-vironment.[3] Nevertheless, the major problem lies in the fact that corpo-rations have abandoned the old social contract under which they worked with the unions to arrive at a mutually beneficial agreement: industrial peace in exchange for job security and a middle-class standard of living, at least for white male workers.

The National Labor Relations Board (NLRB) has been weakened, resulting in a decline in successful organizing drives, and an even worse decline in successfully negotiated union contracts, as was shown by the Dunlop Commission.[4] The threat to close plants and the ability to shift production offshore has also had a chilling effect on union organizing efforts.[5] Employers' efforts to thwart union organizing in the private sector have grown more aggressive. Many companies now hire professional consultants to keep their firms free of unions.[6] Between 1992 and 1995, more than 33 percent of the firms in the United States that were faced with NLRB representation elections illegally fired workers for union activity, more than 50 percent threatened to shut down all or part of the company if the union succeeded in organizing the facility, and between 15 and 40 percent made illegal changes in wages and working conditions, gave bribes and favors to union opponents, or used electronic surveillance against union activists.[7] The situation is much worse in the United States than it is in any of the other industrialized countries of the world.[8] By 1998, only 14 percent of the United States labor force was unionized, and only 11 percent of the workers in the private sector, down from a high of 37 percent in 1946.[9]

The organizing of garment workers has proven more difficult than most organizing, and the garment workers' unions have suffered a severe decline in membership. Part of the decline can be attributed to the loss of apparel jobs as the industry has shifted offshore. But the unions have even lost ground among the workers who remain in this country. In 1995 the two major remaining unions, the International Ladies Garment Workers' Union (ILGWU) and the Amalgamated Clothing and Textile Workers' Union (ACTWU) merged to form UNITE (Union of Needletrades, Industrial and Textile Employees). By the end of 1997, UNITE represented about 300,000 workers, down from the 800,000 workers represented by the two component unions in the late 1960s. As the I in UNITE suggests, the union is no longer focusing exclusively on garment workers, but is moving into other industries where organizing is not as difficult.

Difficulties in Organizing Garment Workers

The apparel industry poses special problems for union organizing because of its flexible and global production. The problems plague the union across the country, but are especially prominent in Los Angeles, where garment workers are virtually unorganized. This has not always been the case. Mexican immigrant women, who made up the majority of the workforce, were once able to organize successfully, engaging in a strike of 7,000 dressmakers in 1933.[10] Union membership reached its height in 1948, when 12,000 workers, over 50 percent of the workers at that time, belonged.[11] Yet by 1998 UNITE represented only a few hundred garment workers in Los Angeles.[12] Why has it been so difficult to organize the garment workers there?

THE STRUCTURE OF THE INDUSTRY

The garment industry in Los Angeles specializes in women's wear, the most seasonal, fashion-sensitive, and, therefore, riskiest sector of the industry. Manufacturers try to externalize the risk by having their production done by contractors on a contingency basis. The contracting system is more advanced in Los Angeles than it is anywhere else in the country, and may be described as the epitome of flexible production. The manufacturer is able not only to minimize risk by employing contractors only when he needs them, but also he can shift work around to obtain the best deal. Most manufacturers have few commitments to their contractors; should a significantly better deal be offered, they can move to accept it.

The mobility of the industry, both locally and globally, makes union organizing very difficult. It is impossible for workers in any one contracting shop to organize because, once the manufacturer finds out about it, he will switch the work to another contractor and the workers will lose their jobs. Even if a contractor were sympathetic to unions—highly unlikely, in the Los Angeles context—he could honestly tell his workers: "If I support your efforts, I will lose all my business, and you will all lose your jobs." That is because a unionized contractor will almost certainly be boycotted by the manufacturers, who have ample alternative (non-union) places to take their business within Los Angeles, elsewhere in the United States, and offshore. Moreover, even if workers could successfully organize a contracting shop without the contractor's going out of business, they would win very little, because profit margins at the contracting level are so narrow.

The impossibility of organizing a single contractor raises the obvious issue of attempting to organize a manufacturer and all of his contractors, the approach that, historically, characterized the highly successful efforts of the ILGWU in New York City. This approach makes a great deal of sense because the manufacturer is the profit center, from whom tangible gains can be won. However, treating all of a manufacturer's contractors as a single production system poses a number of difficulties. For one thing, manufacturers are very secretive about their contractors. There is no public information about which contractors work for which manufacturers. Thus workers have no idea where their fellow workers who are sewing for the same manufacturer are employed. Moreover, the list of contractors keeps changing from month to month. Even if workers or the union could obtain a good list at one point in time, they have no way of knowing how long it will remain in effect. Most contractors work for more than one manufacturer and the mix of manufacturers that they work for, and the proportions of work from each, keep changing.

Consider, for a moment, what this means for organizing. The union can develop an organizing committee in a contracting shop, at great effort and personal risk to the workers, only to find that the targeted manufacturer is no longer sending work to that factory. The workers involved suddenly find themselves irrelevant to the organizing drive. Moreover, if the manufacturer wishes to avoid unionization, as do almost all the apparel manufacturers in Los Angeles, he will move work away from that particular contractor if he receives the slightest hint that the workers are organizing in that plant. When workers find that they lose their jobs as a result of an organizing effort, even when the loss is clearly the result of the manufacturer's efforts to thwart unionization, they understandably become wary of union organizing, and sometimes downright antagonistic toward the union itself. Industry leaders, of course, make much of any factory closing that can be connected with union organizing efforts, emphasizing that the union is to blame for jobs that may be lost.

We do not want to suggest that garment manufacturing is infinitely mobile, nor that all the cards are in the hands of the manufacturers. Some manufacturers do develop longer-term relationships with some of their contractors, and a few sometimes even invest in their contractors' enterprises. It can be difficult to find a new contractor who produces goods that are up to your standards of quality. And it takes time to finish up the jobs you already have in any one contracting shop so that you do not lose that work. UNITE has sought, with mixed success, to exploit these cracks in the system, by attempting, before the manufacturer can respond by moving production elsewhere or offshore, to get specific manufacturers to agree to work only with union shops.

THE NATIONAL LABOR RELATIONS ACT

The National Labor Relations Act (NLRA) governs the rights of workers to join and form unions of their own choosing. The presumption of this aspect of labor law, first passed in 1935, is that unions are good for the United States economy because they regulate and limit labor conflict. Moreover, they help to correct a power imbalance that favors the employer over the employees.

The peculiar structure of the apparel industry and its impediments against organizing receive a moment's recognition in the form of the Garment Industry Proviso, found in section 8(e) of the NLRA: Although it is an unfair labor practice to engage in secondary boycotts against any other employer or any other person engaged in commerce, an exception is made in that a labor action against an apparel manufacturer can be extended to its contractors and vice versa. In the words of section 8(e), " 'any other person' shall not include persons in the relation of a jobber, manufacturer, contractor, or subcontractor working on the goods or premises of the jobber or manufacturer or performing parts of an integrated process of production in the apparel and clothing industry."[13] This provision opens the way to organizing a manufacturer and his contractors as a single unit.

As we have pointed out, the spirit and letter of the NLRA have been flouted by employers in recent decades. Low-wage, immigrant-employing industries are especially likely to engage in illegal antiunion actions, and the garment industry is a prime example. NLRB elections have proven to be a notorious failure in the low-wage, immigrant industries. All three of the major immigrant-organizing unions in Los Angeles, HERE (Hotel Employees and Restaurant Employees), SEIU (Service Employees International Union, especially in its Justice for Janitors campaign), and UNITE, have come to realize this. The difficulty is that employers in these industries do everything in their power to threaten and intimidate workers. They fire union leaders, demonstrating to other workers the dangers of union activity. They give raises and promotions to antiunion activists to show workers the rewards of sticking with the company against the union. They blame the union for job loss. They fight to define bargaining units so that antiunion elements are included. They delay and appeal every ruling so that workers' energy and enthusiasm are drained, along with the union's resources. Many of these actions are illegal, but the penalties for them are so weak that they can be disregarded by the employer as just another cost of doing business. For example, if an employer illegally fires union leaders, the only restitution is that they be "made whole." They are to be reinstated and paid back wages, minus the amount they have earned at other jobs in the interim. No fine is levied for violation of the law. After all these antiunion activities and having cleared the path to almost certain victory for themselves, they call for a free election.

The ILGWU's experiences in Los Angeles in organizing through NLRB elections are telling. Two examples, a decade apart, clearly show the many roadblocks and pitfalls that accompany efforts to unionize workers under the provisions of the NLRA. In October 1988, the ILGWU started a campaign at a shirt manufacturer named Heng's.[14] The company employed 300 workers, and 253 of them (84 percent) signed authorization cards in support of union recognition. In December the union filed for recognition. On 14 December, the company fired fourteen members of the twenty-two-member workers' leadership committee. On 15 December, the union filed (under section 8(a)3 of the NLRA) an Unfair Labor Practice complaint, claiming that the workers had been fired for union activity. On 15 January 1989, the union filed a petition for an election. The NLRB held a first hearing about the election on 2 February 1989. The company raised questions about the eligibility of between thirty and forty workers, requiring that each be interviewed individually. This process took until 24 February. Another fifteen days were taken up in writing briefs. On 20 March 1989, the written arguments were presented. On 30 April the NLRB made its decision and ordered that the election be held. Workers, especially those who lacked immigration papers, were then fired, harassed, and intimidated, and the NLRB did nothing about the firings. The election, which was held 30 May, resulted in the defeat of unionization, with only 57 votes in favor of the union (24 percent) out of 237 votes cast. This enormous change in the workers' support of the union was the result of the union-busting activities of the employer. Heng's denial of raises to prounion workers, its firing of union activists, and its bringing in the Immigration and Naturalization Service to intimidate workers contributed to a climate of fear that turned the tide against the union. It is worth pointing out that, even if the union had won the election, the company would have contested the results, causing another three-month delay until the NLRB could issue a decision, a decision that the firm would likely have appealed further. (One year after the elections, in June 1991, the NLRB determined that three workers had been fired for their union activities, and ordered Heng's to pay each of them the minuscule sum of $3,000.)

The other example of union-busting activities comes from the UNITE campaign against Guess? Inc. In addition to relying on the labor of thousands of contracted workers for whom it claims no direct responsibility, Guess does its cutting and warehousing in-house, and so directly employs several hundred blue-collar workers for those tasks. When Guess workers started organizing with UNITE, the company engaged in an all-out antiunion attack. In 1998, the NLRB charged Guess with a series of violations. The company decided to settle the matter out of court, perhaps to minimize the unfavorable publicity and to maintain the position that it had not actually been found guilty. In addition, Guess was required to post a notification and to read to all employees a long list stipulating the company's conduct in response to the illegal practices that the NLRB had identified. This list shows the kinds of activities that Guess was alleged to have perpetrated—activities that are typical of antiunion efforts:

> We will not discharge, lay off, or otherwise discriminate against our employees because of their activities on behalf of UNITE or any other labor organization.

> We will not threaten our employees with discharge, or with any unspecified reprisals, because of their union or other protected concerted activities.

> We will not coercively interrogate our employees regarding their union activities or support, or the union activities or support of our other employees.

> We will not solicit grievances from our employees and/or promise to remedy grievances as a means of dissuading our employees from supporting UNITE or any other labor organization.

> We will not threaten that we will close and/or move our facility to another country if employees select UNITE or any other labor organization as their representative.

> We will not make statements or engage in other conduct that unlawfully creates the impression that our employees' union activities are under surveillance, and we will not engage in unlawful surveillance of our employees' union activities.

> We will not unlawfully sponsor, organize, direct and/or participate in antiunion events or activities.

> We will not make statements to our employees that it is futile to select UNITE as their representative.

> We will not tell our employees that they were denied higher raises because of their union activities.

We will not coerce, interrogate, and poll our employees regarding their union sentiments by unlawfully offering or distributing antiunion paraphernalia to our employees, or by unlawfully asking our employees to engage in antiunion events or activities, or by unlawfully recording the names of our employees who indicate their willingness to participate in antiunion events or activities.

We will discontinue the TRAC II and TRAC committees [organizations of workers that were created by the company to foster antiunionism].

In addition, Guess agreed to pay nineteen workers the wages they had lost as a result of being fired in August 1996, and the same for two workers fired in 1997. They also agreed, presumably because the NLRB had determined that the layoffs were the result of the workers' union activities, to recall eleven workers who had been laid off.

It is easy to see how these kinds of activities would undermine the efforts of workers to organize themselves. When union leaders are fired (illegally), other workers are less willing to step forward. Threats of closing or moving offshore underscore the dangers of attempting to organize. The power of companies to threaten and intimidate union sympathizers, and to encourage and reward antiunion personnel, can overwhelm even those workers who strongly want to be unionized.

UNDOCUMENTED WORKERS

Ever since the passage of the Immigration Reform and Control Act (IRCA) in 1986, United States immigration law and policy have made it increasingly difficult for undocumented immigrants to find work. It is illegal for employers to hire them, and sanctions are supposed to be enforced against employers who do. Nevertheless, the apparel industry continues to be a major employer. Do these workers have the right to organize under the NLRA?

There is an obvious conflict between the IRCA and the NLRA. Under the NLRA, all workers have the right to organize, regardless of immigration status. If they did not, and if a group of workers existed in the United States labor market who were not free to organize, those workers would become preferred employees and they would drive out of work those who have legally protected rights to organize.

The passage of the IRCA complicates this principle because, if it is illegal to hire undocumented workers, what happens if they are found to be undocumented during a labor dispute? If they are illegally fired during the course of union organizing, can they be reinstated, as can legal residents? Or will they face deportation? If the latter, their right to organize becomes hollow; they have a right without a remedy. Moreover, if such workers can be deported, even if their rights have been violated under the NLRA, the employer has an added incentive to hire them, because, should any union organizing occur among them, the drive can quickly be squelched by exposing their immigration status and demanding that they be deported. Of course, this can be a little tricky because the employer should not have employed undocumented workers in the first place. However, he can ostensibly discover the undocumented status of workers during the course of the organizing drive, thereby legitimately getting rid of them then. Moreover, he can claim that he does not owe these workers any back wages because they should never have been employed by him in the first place.

Note that, even from the standpoint of a law that hopes to eliminate undocumented immigration, this dynamic does not serve its purposes. If undocumented immigrants are attractive to employers, the flow of immigration is likely to be stimulated. Only when there is no advantage to employing undocumented immigrants will potential employment cease to serve as a magnet.

The problem is illustrated by the case of UniHosiery, a sock manufacturer, where about eighty workers went on strike 14 March 1994. The workers asked the ILGWU for help in dealing with some grievances they had against the company. Three weeks later, the company suspended about fifty workers, claiming that their Social Security numbers were questionable. The company claimed that it reviewed the Social Security numbers because of burglaries in the factory. The union thought this was a trumped-up excuse to break the strike and filed unfair labor practices charges with the NLRB. In this case the NLRB accepted the company's argument that the fortuitous discovery of the workers' undocumented status had nothing to do with the labor dispute. The strike was broken.

Nevertheless, there are signs that the NLRB is taking steps to address the Catch-22 faced by undocumented workers caught between immigration and labor laws. The NLRB issued a decision in 1995 stating that its traditional remedies are available to undocumented immigrants who have been subjected to unfair labor practices.[15] The case involved two mechanics who, in 1991, were illegally discharged for their union activities with the Teamsters. The NLRB found flagrant and pervasive unfair labor practices by the company, including unlawful discharges, threats to fire workers, coercive interrogations, promises of benefits if employees voted against the union, and coercion in obtaining affidavits revoking union authorization cards. The NLRB initially ordered the company to offer the customary benefits of immediate reinstatement and back pay, but in July 1993, decided to address the case of the two undocumented workers separately. Reaching a decision two and a half years later, in December 1995, which shows how slow the process can be, the NLRB declared that "IRCA and the NLRA can and must be read in harmony as complementary elements of a legislative scheme explicitly intended, in both cases, to protect the rights of employees in the American workplace. . . . We conclude that the most effective way for the Board to accommodate—and indeed to further—the immigration policies IRCA embodies is, to the extent possible, to provide the protections and remedies of the NLRA to undocumented workers in the same manner as other employees. To do otherwise would increase the incentives for some unscrupulous employers to play the provisions of the NLRA and IRCA against each other to defeat the fundamental objectives of each, while profiting from their own wrongdoing with relative impunity."[16] The NLRB ordered the company to offer back pay to the two workers, along with reinstatement, conditional on their being able to supply the necessary work eligibility documentation under IRCA. Needless to say, the latter is the rub. If workers cannot obtain a work permit, can they still be reinstated? And if not, will the employer not have succeeded in effectively curtailing organizing among undocumented workers because they expose themselves to possible deportation?

One potential loophole in this case is the fact that the employer knew that the two workers were undocumented at the time they were hired. The NLRB holds that, "in the ordinary case, when the IRCA requirements have been met, there may be no need for this additional condition," namely, that the illegally fired workers rectify their status before being reinstated. In other words, if workers were treated by the employer as having proper papers when they were hired, then their immigration status cannot be used to block their reinstatement.[17]

THE POLITICAL ENVIRONMENT

The political climate facing garment workers in Los Angeles is harsh. Antiimmigrant sentiment is running at record levels in California, accentuating the already enormous power imbalance between a largely undocumented workforce and the elites of one of the city's leading manufacturing sectors. Moreover, the local elites have teamed up with national political leaders in an effort to further curb the union's efforts. All of this has contributed to a climate of intimidation that has been felt even by the authors of this book.

The political climate confronted by immigrant workers in all industries is always difficult. The political environment may, however, be worse for garment workers than it is for most other immigrants, some of whom have been more successful at organizing.[18] Although we do not have proof, we believe that the percentage of undocumented workers is higher in this industry than it is in most others. Thus the attack on the undocumented has more serious ramifications for organizing in the apparel industry. Garment workers suffer from severe political disabilities as rightless workers. The owners in this industry may not have extra political clout, but the gap between what clout they have and that of the garment workers is substantially larger than it is in other industries. When leaders of the garment industry threaten to move to Mexico, for example, government officials at all levels stand up and take notice, offering numerous concessions in an effort to induce the industry to stay. A classic example of the situation was the mayor's creation of the California Fashion Association, described in Chapter 4. Although the CFA is now independently funded, it received a kick-start from the mayor's office and continues to maintain close ties with him. The CFA includes a Labor Committee, the chair of which is Stan Levy, previous counsel for Guess and continued active supporter of the company in its efforts to prevent unionization. This Labor Committee does not have a single representative from labor on it—neither a union official nor a rank-and-file worker. Thus a public entity, the city, has helped to create an organization that is manifestly probusiness and antilabor, reflecting the relative power and access of each.

Local elites have found support for their antiunion efforts in Washington as well. In 1998, Congressman Pete Hoekstra, a Republican from Michigan and a member of the Subcommittee on Oversight and Investigations of the House Committee on Education and the Workforce, launched an investigation entitled Failures and Promises of the Garment Industry, as part of the project called American Workers at a Crossroads. Expressing horror at conditions in many garment factories, especially in New York's Chinatown, the subcommittee (popularly known as the Hoekstra Committee) sought to blame the Department of Labor and UNITE for the return of sweatshops. Both organizations decided to boycott the subcommittee's hearings on the grounds that they were biased.

The hearing in Los Angeles, which we attended, was held on 18 May 1998. It appeared to be a concerted effort to discredit UNITE, in the larger service of further weakening the legal power of organized labor. Behind the committee's attacks on UNITE were two legislative goals. First, the subcommittee was pushing to eliminate the Garment Industry Proviso of the NLRA that allows garment unions to treat apparel manufacturers and their contractors as a single, integrated system of production. Second, the subcommittee appeared to be aiming at eliminating the union's right to collect "liquidated damages," a fine paid by manufacturers who break their contract with the union by using nonunion shops. This right was granted under the bipartisan 1959 Landrum-Griffin Act, which sought to discourage manufacturers from breaking their union contracts by levying penalties for doing so.[19] In recent years, UNITE has invoked this measure to discourage companies from moving offshore by making manufacturers pay for the practice. Given the enormous cost differentials between domestic and offshore production, and the sizable profits in the industry, many companies have simply chosen to pay UNITE the damages as a cost of doing business, and then relocate their factories. Between 1987 and 1996, UNITE collected nearly $100 million in liquidated damages from companies that have moved their production offshore, money that has been used in support of the union's organizing efforts. The Hoekstra hearings were aimed at discrediting these collections, by arguing that the money was simply being used to feather the union's nest, rather than in support of workers.[20]

Although the rhetoric of the subcommittee is proworker, its real sentiments are antiunion. The committee (or at least its Republican leadership and majority) supports the global, flexible strategy of apparel manufacturers that would allow them to shift production wherever and whenever they want. Having observed the hearings, we surmise that Hoekstra himself believes that union interference in the free market ultimately hurts workers, that their employers are the workers' best friends and that empowerment of workers is unnecessary. The Hoekstra Committee's investigation, which was being watched very closely by the industry, received sympathetic coverage in the trade press, which strongly suggests to us that an influential segment of the apparel industry is determined to eliminate the remaining vestiges of union power. Apparel manufacturers in Los Angeles are among the leaders in this endeavor. Among the people who testified before the Hoekstra Committee was Lonnie Kane, the president of the California Fashion Association. He blamed loss of jobs in the industry on UNITE, expressed his disapproval of the ability of the union to pressure the manufacturer when attempting to organize a contractor, and argued in favor of permitting manufacturers to monitor their contractors themselves as the best solution to the sweat-shop problem. Kane probably speaks for most of the apparel manufac-turers in Los Angeles, articulating their fierce opposition to the union.

We ourselves have encountered the industry's ability to reach state of-ficials to protect their interests against those of workers and to intimidate those whom they see as challenging their interests. In August, 1997, the *Los Angeles Times* asked one of the authors (Edna Bonacich) for an opin-ion piece responding to an article entitled "Sweatshop Raids Cast Doubt on Ability of Garment Makers to Police Factories" that was published in the *New York Times*.[21] In her response, entitled "Garment Sweatshops Won't End till Workers Have Power," Edna commented that, "a couple of weeks ago, state investigators announced they had uncovered five cases of illegal industrial homework, some connected with contractors who sew for Guess? Inc. Guess has an agreement with the United States Depart-ment of Labor to monitor its contractors for violations and should have found these problems. What went wrong?"[22] Three days later, an expen-sive ad (occupying a third of a page) appeared in the *Los Angeles Times* and the *New York Times* contradicting this statement, and claiming that state inspectors had "found no violations regarding Guess? garments." (The advertisement identified Edna as someone "who describes herself as a professor of Sociology at U.C. Riverside.") Edna asked the two news-papers for an opportunity to respond to the advertisement, but her re-quest was denied. Sociology professors can ill afford to buy significant advertising space in two major newspapers, so Edna instead wrote a let-ter to Lonnie Kane, the president of the California Fashion Association, asking him to distribute her response to his membership, stating

Guess claims that the recent homework raids by the California State Division of Labor Standards Enforcement have nothing to do with Guess because no Guess clothes were identified among the confiscated garments. Since writ-ing my op-ed piece, I have learned that California Labor Commissioner Jose Millan has reported that Guess clothing was, indeed, found among the con-fiscated items in this raid. But my argument did not depend on this. The point was that contractors that Guess admitted using, and therefore regularly in-spected, were engaged in illegal homework. If Guess's compliance program were truly effective, its monitors should have uncovered and ended the con-tractors' illegal practices, regardless of whether the clothing being sewn at home at the particular time of the raids happened to be Guess clothing. Their inability to uncover the homework supports my arguments.

In early September both authors attended a meeting of the Jewish Coalition on Sweatshops.[23] The coalition had just received a fax from Stan

Levy, at the time external counsel for Guess and an active member of the California Fashion Association, quoting three paragraphs from a letter written by the State Labor Commissioner, Jose Millan, to Edna. Edna had not yet received Millan's letter, so Levy's fax came as something of a surprise. How was Levy in a position to quote a letter written to Edna, that she had not yet seen, and that she did not receive until the following day? How, too, did he come to possess the letter when there was no indication on it that he had been sent a copy?

In writing to Edna, Millan denied that he had ever claimed that Guess clothing was found during the homework raids. He attached, however, another letter, written by Thomas Grogan, the assistant chief of the Division of Labor Standards Enforcement, to Stan Levy, written in response to a request for information about the recent homework raids. Grogan said that "the results of those investigations did not reveal any apparel that belonged to Guess. DLSE personnel did find Guess labels in two locations." This raised an interesting question: If garments from contractors that usually sew clothing for Guess were being illegally sewn in peoples' homes, and Guess labels were also found in some of those homes, is it not reasonable to conclude that the two might be connected?

The legal answer to this question arrived on 12 September 1997, when Edna received a letter from Mitchell, Silberberg and Knupp, the law firm retained by Guess. The law firm claimed that Edna had defamed Guess, citing once again Jose Millan's letter to her, which apparently Guess and its law firm had now seen. Mitchell, Silberberg and Knupp demanded that Edna retract her accusation that Guess was involved in illegal industrial homework and implied that they would sue if she refused. Edna's reply, citing the letter from Grogan about finding the two labels and citing an article published in the *Los Angeles Times* in which it was reported that Guess admitted to employing two of the contractors who employed two of the home workers, provoked a second threatening letter. Mitchell, Silberberg and Knupp demanded an immediate written retraction and an apology to Guess or, they said, they would have no choice but to sue her.

At this point Edna called Jose Millan to try to find out whether someone had pressured him to write the letter to her, to inform him of how Guess was using it, to see if he approved of this usage and, if he did not, to ask him to intercede. Millan reported that he had been told to write the letter by his boss, the head of the Department of Industrial Relations, and the only person who, according to the notation on the letter, had been sent a copy. He did not know how Stan Levy and Guess obtained it, and he disapproved of its being used to threaten a lawsuit. He said he would try to intervene. Meanwhile, Edna obtained help from Ben Bycel, a member of the Jewish coalition, a lawyer and law school dean, and previous head of the Ethics Commission of the City of Los Angeles. Bycel intervened because, he said, he hates "to see the abuse of power by large corporations like Guess." Part of the response Bycel drafted and Edna sent stated:

I have reviewed your letters of September 12 and 18, 1997. Needless to say, I would like to avoid litigation with a giant corporation such as Guess and a prestigious law firm such as yours, so I will attempt to clear up what appears to be a minor misstatement on my part.

When I heard from two different sources, around August 15, 1997, that State Labor Commissioner Jose Millan had reported that investigators had found Guess labels among the confiscated items in the homework raids of July 16 and 17, 1997, I assumed that the labels were attached to clothing. This was a mistake any of us would have made because very few people, especially garment workers, merely collect or take labels home in order to bring them back to work the next day. This assumption was incorrect on my part. . . . .

You can be assured that I will never again make the assumption that just because Guess labels were found in the homes of two illegal homework operations, that in fact the sewing of Guess clothing was being done in those homes on the day of the raid or any other day.

The beauty of this reply is that it did not afford Guess any opportunity to use quotes from the letter in its defense. Edna never heard another word from Mitchell, Silberberg and Knupp on this matter, perhaps because the letter silenced them, or perhaps because Jose Millan contacted them.

What is most interesting to us in this brief foray into the world of litigation is the fact that such effective pressure was put on the State Labor Commissioner. He had no reason to have seen the letter that was written to Lonnie Kane of the California Fashion Association and he admitted to Edna that he was told by a political appointee in the Wilson administration to write the letter to her. The fact that Stan Levy received a copy of the letter before she did strongly suggests to us that he played a role in getting the letter written. Needless to say, no garment worker in Los Angeles has this kind of political access.

THE WORKERS' ATTITUDES

Successful union organizing among garment workers in Los Angeles obviously depends to a considerable degree on the workers themselves. How do the garment workers feel about unionization? Are they ready to form or join unions? Do they feel the need for change, or are they content with where they are in the social hierarchy? How likely are garment workers, overwhelmingly immigrants from Mexico, Central America, and to a lesser extent, Asia, to join a unionization effort? There is considerable variation in the apparel workforce in both ethnicity and immigrant status. We have not conducted a systematic survey of workers' attitudes, but have gained some impressions from research done by our students and others and from our own extensive discussions with workers' advocates and a fair number of garment workers. The biggest divide exists between Latino and Asian workers, so let us start there.

Asian garment workers are very diverse, coming from a number of countries, including China, Vietnam, Thailand, and Cambodia.[24] Within each group there is also diversity. Some are first generation wage-earners from peasant backgrounds, others are from cities and towns with experience of city living. In general, they probably come to the United States with more education than do the majority of Latino garment workers. Most Asian garment workers in Los Angeles are women, more so than among Latinos. They also tend to be older than the Latino workers. Some Asians see their work in a garment factory as a stepping stone. They use their work time to learn the business and save money so that, with the help of family and friends, they can become contractors. Not all Asian workers see such an opportunity for themselves. They may be working to help supplement the family income, and do not see themselves as the primary wage earner. They feel reluctant to complain about their wages and working conditions, believing that they are engaged in a justified sacrifice for their children. Some also collect welfare to supplement their meager earnings and are afraid of being caught for welfare fraud.

Asian workers are also more likely than Latinos are to be working under paternalistic conditions. This may be especially true in Chinatown. Employed by someone they know, who is struggling to establish a successful factory, they feel an obligation to the owner for giving them the work. The owner may allow the worker to have a flexible work schedule, to pick up children from school, for example, and the worker, in turn, will not complain if her pay check is late. In factories where the workforce is both Asian and Latino, the Asians tend to have connections with the owners and supervisors, and are more likely to hold better positions. This tends to drive a wedge between the two groups of workers. However, the concept of better in a garment factory is relative; these jobs would hardly be coveted by anyone who had other opportunities.

The issue of political consciousness and potential activism among Asian workers is complex. Those who are ambitious to move up into entrepreneurship may shun unionism as antithetical to their ideology. Or, eager to accumulate capital more quickly, they may welcome the increased pay that a union can bring them. Women who see garment work as a sacrifice that they are making for their families may find it difficult to stand up for themselves in a union struggle, but may also value the health insurance that they can win through unionization. In sum, among Asian workers there are both sources of resistance to unionization and perceptions of its advantages.

The Latinos, too, are diverse, coming from different countries with different historical experiences though, unlike the Asians, they share a common language in Spanish. (For some Latino garment workers, notably those from indigenous cultures, Spanish is, however, a second language.) Most Latino garment workers are Mexican and many have come to the United States because of economic dislocations in their homeland. In contrast, more of the Central Americans are likely to have come to the United States as political refugees, from the civil war in El Salvador and years of repression in Guatemala.

Latino garment workers, like Asians, include both displaced peasants who are first-generation wage-workers, and urban dwellers, but we suspect that a higher proportion of Latinos than Asians come from the countryside. They have lower levels of formal education, on average, than the Asians have, and many fewer of them come with any resources—in terms of capital or experience—that might enable them to become entrepreneurs or contractors.

The Latino men and women are probably somewhat younger, on average, than the Asian workers are, and they are more likely to be the sole or major supporter of their families. We suspect that their belief in the necessity of sacrificing oneself for the next generation is strong, but not as strong on average as that found among the Asian workers. Rather, they are likely to have a keener sense that they are being exploited, but many also consider it futile to try to bring about change.

Latino workers are more likely to be employed in shops where the owner is of a different ethnicity. Certainly there are exceptions to this rule; Mexican and Central American contractors do employ workers from their own country of origin. Still, the predominant pattern for Latino garment workers is to be employed by an Asian, often Korean, contractor. This arrangement precludes the development of paternalistic ties between the contractor and the employees. Instead, the relationship is strictly businesslike, without favors being granted in either direction. The more alienated relationship in these factories, where the lines between owners and workers are sharper than they are in many of the factories where Asian workers are employed, tends to foster more of a consciousness among Latinos of seeing themselves as exploited workers.

A larger proportion of Latino than Asian workers lack immigration papers, so they live in fear of exposure and possible deportation. The passage of the Immigration Reform and Control Act in 1986, and of Proposition 187 in California in 1995, aimed specifically at the undocumented, has caused a deterioration in the political climate for these workers, making organizing increasingly difficult. Nevertheless, successful union organizing drives have been conducted with undocumented immigrants, so that fear of deportation is not a complete impediment.[25]

Immigrant garment workers vary in their previous political experiences. Some of the Central Americans have had a great deal of experience with political struggles in their homelands, as have some of the Mexicans, especially those who come from Mexico City. But many have been exposed to corrupt unions or to regimes that assassinate union activists. These experiences, or the lack of experience with political struggle, may serve as a handicap for union organizing. Similarly, Asian workers have experienced both communist and anticommunist regimes, and their politics have been affected accordingly.

In our view, the main problem in organizing garment workers in Los Angeles does not lie in the various characteristics of the workforce, important though they are in finding the best ways for workers to develop an organization. Most garment workers know that they are being exploited and dearly want to improve their situation. The main problem lies in their extreme vulnerability. If they speak up, they are likely to be fired; if they organize, their factory will almost certainly close. If the undocumented complain, they may provoke an immigration raid. The possibilities of losing their jobs and being deported inspire fear in the workers, who, quite reasonably, are reluctant to provoke such consequences. This fear is exacerbated by their poverty, which gives them little room for maneuver. The ever-present threat that the industry will move to Mexico serves as an additional barrier. Even if the workers can win a union contract, how long would they be able to maintain it? Won't the manufacturer immediately start scouting around for other locations? Won't there be a quiet but inevitable loss of apparel manufacturing jobs in Los Angeles. In sum, the problem from the workers' point of view has less to do with a lack of awareness of being exploited and much more to do with the seeming impossibility of their winning any long-lasting gains as a result of union organizing. Faced with job loss and deportation, how many workers will take the risk? Only if there is hope of a reasonably clear victory will workers join in a unionizing effort.

Some UNITE leaders argue that, in the face of industry flight, it is better to be organized than to be unorganized. If the apparel industry is moving to Mexico in any case, unionized workers could protest against its flight. More substantively, a union contract could impose costly terms on the manufacturer for moving or negotiate a percentage of the work that must remain in the country. It has yet to be shown that the promise of such long-term protections is likely to be persuasive to workers who face immediate risks from organizing.

THE UNION OF NEEDLETRADES, INDUSTRIAL AND TEXTILE EMPLOYEES

A number of criticisms have been leveled at UNITE as an organization by those who are sympathetic to the empowerment of workers (as distinguished from the barrage of attacks from industry leaders and their supporters). These criticisms have an element of truth to them. UNITE is mainly run from the East Coast. Its top leadership does not reflect the ethnicity of the majority of garment workers. The union lacks a long-term commitment to organizing garment workers. It has suffered from internal conflicts that have been exacerbated by the merger of the ILGWU and ACTWU, and there has been far too much turnover in personnel and organizing leadership.

The union does, however, have many strengths. Virtually all of the UNITE organizers in Los Angeles are Latino, and most of them were garment workers before they became organizers. The organizing department's affairs are conducted almost exclusively in Spanish, and organizing efforts are rooted directly in the experience and lives of the workers, with little distance between the organizers and the workers. UNITE organizers are highly dedicated, working very long hours for low pay. They drive workers to and from meetings, visit workers in their homes, spend endless hours planning strategy, and frequently work late into the night. They are smart, militant, and deeply committed to bringing about greater social justice.

When UNITE organizes workers, it may appear as though it is an outside agent that is foisting its agenda on them. Opponents of unionization argue that UNITE is manipulating the workers for its own ends, irrespective of what is in the interests of the workers. We do not believe that this is the case. The union sees its role as drawing upon its experience to teach workers how they can collaborate to win gains for themselves. Union organizers see themselves as catalysts for change, bringing about a transformation in the workers' understanding of their circumstances. Only a union comes close to having the resources and political power to challenge rich and powerful manufacturers and retailers, affording workers even the minimal protections against being fired or underpaid. Moreover, UNITE continues to be an advocate of garment workers' rights in many arenas, including legislation. Thus, while the existing union may not always be the perfect instrument for empowering the garment workers, it is the only institution that comes close to playing this role.

Approaches to Unionization

At the time of writing, UNITE was in the midst of the Guess campaign, an effort to organize the largest apparel manufacturer in Los Angeles. The campaign began under the leadership of David Young, the organizing director of the ILGWU, but with the merger into UNITE, leadership (and approaches to the project) changed. Mauricio Vázquez eventually became the organizing director. The outcome of this campaign, which was still undetermined, will undoubtedly have an effect on UNITE's ability to organize garment workers in Los Angeles in the future. Others are studying the history of the Guess campaign, and we refer the reader to their forthcoming work.[26] Meanwhile, many of the ideas discussed below have been used at some point during the effort to organize Guess.

We discuss eight basic approaches to organizing garment workers in Los Angeles, assessing their strengths and weaknesses. In practice, they are not mutually exclusive and, in fact, often overlap and are implemented together. The eight approaches are NLRB elections, jobbers' agreements, corporate campaigns, cross-border organizing, uniting with contractors, sectoral and geographical organizing, community organizing, and workers' centers.

ELECTIONS UNDER THE NATIONAL LABOR RELATIONS BOARD

Elections under the aegis of the National Labor Relations Board would appear to be the ideal way to organize garment workers.

The union would meet with workers at a particular factory or group of factories, discuss with them the pros and cons of unionization, and they would decide democratically whether or not they want to be represented by the union. The NLRB would then hold the election, ensuring that democratic rules are followed, and the garment workers would either become unionized or not.

In the apparel industry in Los Angeles this approach has pitfalls. Even if workers were able to negotiate a contract with their immediate employers, the contractors, they would win very little because the real profit centers of the industry are the manufacturers and retailers. More importantly, the contractor would almost certainly be boycotted by the manufacturers who would not be willing to employ a contractor whose price was higher than the others, let alone one known to have labor problems, which might threaten work schedules. The unionized contractor would receive no work and would go out of business; the workers would have won the election, but lost their jobs. In addition, knowing that he would be driven out of business if a union election were won in his shop, the contractor is highly motivated to do everything he can, legal and illegal, to break the union.

Garment industry employers will sometimes call for elections, claiming that this is the only fair and American thing to do, that workers should have a free choice, and that they support a secret ballot. But these calls are completely cynical, arising only after the company has engaged in various union-busting practices and feels confident that the workers will vote against the union. We feel safe in saying that almost no apparel manufacturer or contractor in Los Angeles would simply allow a union election to occur without interference in his plant.

Clearly legal and procedural reforms are needed in the NLRB process. Such reforms would still not, however, address the difficulties posed by the contracting system, which enables manufacturers, the real employers, to shift work away from unionized factories and thereby destroy any organizing effort in the long run, if not at the time of the election.

JOBBERS' AGREEMENTS

The idea of a jobber's (or Hazantown) agreement comes out of the ILGWU's long experience of organizing in the women's apparel industry back east. The term *jobber,* which means a manufacturer who contracts out all the labor, is still used in New York even though it does not apply to the industry in Los Angeles. A jobber's agreement holds the manufacturer responsible for conditions in his contracting shops by getting him to sign a contract that ensures that he will use only unionized contractors, and will pay them the union scale and benefits. It is the union's version of joint liability, a version that is far more powerful than any government efforts to make manufacturers take responsibility for their contractors, because it is backed by a union contract. Under such an agreement, the manufacturer cannot boycott union contractors, but on the contrary, is bound to use them.

The challenge in obtaining a jobber's agreement is to organize the entire production system of a manufacturer at one time, both the workers who are employed in his headquarters (maybe sample-makers, cutters, or warehouse workers), and the workers in the dispersed contracting shops. If the workers in these various locations can be brought together to unite around the issue of gaining a union contract across the entire system, they may be able to succeed in getting the manufacturer and the contractors to sign.

The basic strategic approach that has been used to organize such a dispersed production system is to turn the manufacturer's advantages in contracting out into weaknesses. The fact that the manufacturer does not have strong and stable ties with his contractors means that the links between the manufacturer and his contractors can be severed. The physical dispersal of production also opens up the possibility that the flow of garments between various plants may be disrupted. Moreover, because of the time-sensitivity of the fashion business, even temporary interruptions in the flow of production can be very costly, especially if they happen at the peak of the season.

The ties between the manufacturer and his contractors can be broken by various means. The workers in key contracting shops may go out on strike. Workers may picket certain shops or the company's warehouse, and may be able to persuade truckers not to cross their picket lines. Contractors who have other clients may decide not to work for the one manufacturer that the union is trying to organize for the period of the labor dispute so as to avoid all the disruption. The manufacturer has probably not been loyal to him, so the contractor has little reason to see him through these tough times. The union may also be able to get some contractors to sign "me too" agreements under which they agree tentatively to settle with the union in the event that a jobber's agreement is signed and, meanwhile, avoid labor strife.

Although the manufacturer may be able to move production to other shops in order to avoid those contractors where workers are organized and engaged in various forms of protest, the fact is that, in the height of a publicized labor dispute, it is difficult for the manufacturer to find others who will work with him and risk having a picket line thrown at them. As soon as the union is able to trace the work to a new contractor, it can meet with the contractor and warn him of the consequences of working for a manufacturer that is fighting with the union. Thus the advantage to the manufacturer of being able to shift production can be minimized during an organizing campaign.

The strength of this approach lies in tying the manufacturer to the contractors, so that workers can win significant gains. Moreover, such an organizing drive is usually combined with a corporate campaign and community organizing, so that other aspects of the company's functioning, apart from its production, are also under attack. The purpose of such a multifaceted attack is to drive a firm, which otherwise would fight unionization to the bitter end, to negotiate with the union. Some may feel that such a "coercive" approach should not be necessary in a democratic society but, from the union's perspective, given the antiunion animus of the employers, nothing short of forcing them to the bargaining table will succeed.

We perceive a few problems with the jobber's agreement approach. First, it is extremely difficult to coordinate all the parts of the dispersed production system so that they are ready to take action at the same time. The organizer who is coordinating such a struggle has to deal with numerous fronts at one time. Second, for the union the problem of secrecy is intense because the employer is likely to deploy his many resources to preempt such an effort before it gets off the ground. The need for secrecy obviously impedes organizing and it weakens the development of democratic structures among workers as the union is building support. Third, such an organizing drive is most likely to succeed right away or not at all. The longer the struggle is drawn out, the more the employer is able to engage in evasive action, including devising methods for moving work away from contractors with strong union support. The ability to shift production is deadly to the morale of the workers, who find their factory losing work or closing down, at least in the short run, and begin to fear whether they will ever be able to win back their jobs.

A fourth problem with organizing for a jobber's agreement is that it lends itself to top-down organizing. In other words, it is possible to put sufficient pressure on the manufacturer so that he agrees to sign with union contractors. The contractor may sign with the union, not because of pressure from his workers, but because he knows that a union contract will guarantee him stable work. The workers thus become irrelevant to the signing of the union contract. The contractor is motivated to sign whether the workers want a union or not. Now there is nothing inherent in a jobber's agreement that precludes workers' participation in the struggle to win it. Indeed, driving the manufacturer to the bargaining table may depend on strong activism of various sorts among the workers. Nevertheless, workers may find themselves as members of a union without having much say in it. Moreover, the fact that their bosses, the contractors, are now eager union members, leads to an unsettling dynamic between workers and contractors; the antagonistic relationship between the workers and their immediate employers is muted by the union contract, and the union may end up dealing directly with the contractor rather than with the workers.

These problems acknowledged, there still has not yet been devised a more effective method of organizing the kind of dispersed production system characteristic of the apparel industry. Achieving such agreements may be exceedingly difficult, in practice. But, once signed, they provide the strongest protection for garment workers and contractors against the movement of the work away from organized shops.

CORPORATE CAMPAIGNS

Because the corporate campaign is not unique to the apparel industry, we touch on it only lightly. The labor movement as a whole has become much more sophisticated at researching the companies it is trying to organize and finding other points of vulnerability apart from their production systems. Such vulnerabilities lie in the various plans and relationships of the company. For example, its stockholders may be dismayed to learn about certain company practices and may be willing to put pressure on the company to settle quickly with the union. When unions themselves are among the stockholders, their part ownership can be used to influence the company.

The fashion industry would appear to be especially vulnerable to one form of this kind of pressure, namely, challenges to a company's image. Fashion depends on the selling of an image, rather than simply the selling of a product. The image-selling aspect of apparel has accelerated in recent years, as certain key brand names have, by spending millions of dollars on advertising, managed to create identities with which their consumers identify. The strength of image in fashion is also its weakness. If an image is tarnished, it can quickly drop out of public favor, leading to plummeting sales. Unions (and other organizations concerned with labor abuses) can try to take advantage of the vulnerability of a brand's public image by developing unfavorable associations with that name as a means of pressuring the company to negotiate with its workers. Corporate campaigns often put pressure on retailers to drop the brand by getting consumers to question salespeople about production conditions, by calling for a consumer boycott, and so forth. In consequence, the company's sales decline. The value of a company's stock may also be affected. Falling sales and stock prices, or the perception that such drops are likely to occur if the campaign continues, may lead owners to decide that it is imperative to settle the labor dispute.

A major weakness of this approach arises if it is not linked to a strong worker-organizing component. Corporate campaign pressure on a company may, indeed, hurt its sales or stock prices, which in turn may lead the company to cut prices and wages and to lay off workers. In other words, workers may suffer from the consequences of a boycott (for example) and, if they are not actively involved in the campaign, will feel that these efforts by others to help them are unwelcome. Unless the workers participate fully in the decision to boycott, unless they understand that they may suffer some immediate repercussions, and without their informed consent, the approach can backfire, leading to the alienation of the very workers the union is trying to organize.

CROSS-BORDER ORGANIZING

If capital can freely shift its production from one country to the next in an effort to find the lowest living standards and most politically oppressed workers, the efforts of workers anywhere to improve their conditions will be undone. Workers worldwide need to join together to set standards and protect the political rights of all, so that capital cannot pit one group against another. This proposition applies as much to the apparel industry as to any other, and perhaps more to apparel, which is the most globalized of industries. For example, the constant threat of apparel manufacturers in Los Angeles to move to Mexico clearly needs to be thwarted by unionization among Mexican workers, who will not allow themselves to be exploited any more than United States workers will. The same principle applies wherever the industry moves.

This necessity is so obvious that it barely needs stating. Yet the pitfalls in achieving it are legion. We mention only a few. First, poor countries need industrial development. Encouraging globalizing capitalism is often the only apparent option available to achieve this goal. No other feasible models exist today (even if we might want to experiment with alternatives). What poor countries have to offer capital is their workforce at bargain prices. Both governments and workers can see that, if demands for improved conditions come too quickly, all will be lost. Capital and industry will flee.

Second, efforts by workers and unions in the richer countries to reach out to workers in poorer countries can be interpreted by the latter as a form of protectionism. Workers in the richer countries, wanting to protect their own jobs against flight, do not want those jobs to move to the poorer countries. To workers in the poorer countries, this seems as if they are selfishly holding on to an advantage and are not willing to share it. Why should an impoverished worker who cannot feed her family fight to stop a factory from moving to her country and providing her with a job?

Third, the history of the AFL-CIO in Latin America and other areas of the world often raises concerns among workers' movements in those countries. The United States labor movement, at least as represented by some of its political alliances, has too frequently given the appearance of aligning itself with the exploitative practices of United States capitalists in the poorer countries. Why should workers in poor countries support the fights of such so-called allies now that they are suddenly waking up to the fact that global capitalism hurts them too? Where was the AFL-CIO when the marines were invading their country and destroying its democratic movements?

Fourth, we often lack a clear model for implementing international labor organizing. Do we mean that union organizers from the richer countries send their representatives to help the offshore workers on the assumption that they cannot help themselves? Too often, unfortunately, that is the way it looks. From the perspective of workers in poor countries, the response is likely to be: "Who are *you* to help *us?* You are part of the problem, not part of the solution. Get out of here and let us figure out our own problems." (Needless to say, both the parallels to racism within this country, and the reality of racism in relation to workers in poorer countries, is evident.)

Despite these problems, UNITE has made some attempts and has had some success in helping garment workers to organize both in the Dominican Republic and in Guatemala. Ralph Armbruster-Sandoval reviewed the case of a factory owned by Phillips-Van Heusen in Guatemala, in which the workers were successful in winning a union contract with the help of UNITE and other solidarity organizations.[27] So far, however,

little progress has made in the very important Mexican garment industry. Mexico has unions of its own, of course, though most of them are
under the tight control of the government-dominated Confederación de
Trabajadores de México. Some independent unions have emerged, such
as the Nineteenth of September National Garment Workers' Union,
formed in the wake of the earthquake in Mexico City on 19 September
1985, which killed 800 garment workers.[28] Unfortunately, this particular
union has lost much of its former strength, making it difficult for UNITE
to find the needed allies.[29] Nevertheless, to the extent that the United
States workforce and labor movement come to consist of and be led by
people of color, immigrants, and women, the chances of forming alliances
across borders improve.

AN ALLIANCE WITH THE CONTRACTORS

At first glance, it would seem that there are good reasons
for contractors and workers to find common cause. If contractors joined
together with workers, they would be able to insist on higher prices from
the manufacturers and be able to pay the workers adequately. They have
in common the fact that they are mainly immigrants, even if sometimes
from different ethnic groups, and most suffer from being racial minorities in this society. Moreover, together comprising what the industry considers to be its labor costs, their fates are linked. If a manufacturer moves
his production offshore, both the contractor and the workers lose their
jobs.

Of course, there are many factors that make such an alliance difficult.
One is the ethnic difference that characterizes many contracting shops in
Los Angeles. Another is the anger that many workers feel toward the contractors, their direct employers. Because they feel cheated and disrespected,
the idea of working in coalition with their bosses is almost unthinkable.

The contractors themselves have divided interests. Because the manufacturer provides them with work, they have to keep on his good side.
Without the work, they are out of business. Nevertheless, if contractors
were to organize themselves, as a kind of union, they could exert considerable control over the flow of production, and, for example, demand
longer-term commitments as well as higher prices.

The advantage of aligning themselves with workers is that such a contractors' union becomes much more plausible if the workers support it.
Because workers make up the majority of the people in this industry, their
combined power would be considerable. If workers and contractors decided together to strike against the manufacturers, they would bring pro-

duction to a halt. Workers can do this on their own, but having the contractors stand with them would certainly strengthen their hand. (Of course any such effort raises the possibility that the industry would respond by moving to Mexico more quickly.)

According to David Young, who was the organizing director for the ILGWU in Los Angeles for a number of years, the key to the leanings of contractors depends on the location of power. Young's opinion was based on the experience of trying to work with contractors while attempting to win union representation for workers. When manufacturers have the power, Young believes, the contractors side with them. When workers have the power, the contractors are more likely to side with them. For example, if the union is able to win a jobber's agreement from a manufacturer under which the manufacturer agrees to work with union contractors, contractors will flock to the union. Under these circumstances, the union controls the flow of work, and union contractors are the beneficiaries of the workers' power.

At the time of writing the contractors in Los Angeles were generally fiercely antiunion. In part this antipathy is cultural. Some Korean contractors, for example, are conservative Christians with deep-seated antiunion sentiments. No doubt the entrepreneurial values that lead a person into self-employment clash with the notion of sharing power and control with anyone else, least of all one's employees. But mainly contractors *have* to be antiunion in order to stay in business. Thus the role of the contractors as a middleman minority has another important aspect: They help to crush unionization efforts among the workers for the manufacturers. They are the front line of antiunionism in this industry. Nevertheless, all of this could change. Contractors may feel so embattled by manufacturers, especially in the face of constant threats to move production to Mexico, that they may become more open to finding common cause with the workers and the union.

SECTORAL AND GEOGRAPHICAL ORGANIZING

One of the difficulties in going after a single manufacturer and his production system is that he fears that, if he acknowledges the union, he will be put at a price disadvantage with respect to his competitors. Thus the ideal approach might be to organize an entire sector, as a competitive unit, at the same time. If the contractors in that sector have some degree of distinctiveness in terms of skills and machinery, so much the better. One can, for example, attempt to organize all the swimwear manufacturers and contractors at the same time, binding them to a single contract. As an extension of the jobber's agreement approach, sectoral organizing would also take advantage of corporate campaigning.

The biggest problem with this idea is the amount of resources it requires. Identifying the relevant manufacturers and contractors is a major research undertaking made more difficult by the secrecy of the industry. And organizing in so many locations at once is certainly costly. Nevertheless, this approach has considerable potential. Its success depends on the selection of a sector that is unlikely to move production to Mexico or elsewhere.

Another, similar approach would be to organize the workers in a geographical area of the Los Angeles basin where the garment industry is especially concentrated, such as the downtown garment district, Vernon, or El Monte. Organizing might be attempted on a door-to-door basis. This approach requires a completely different system for signing contracts, because the manufacturers in the area who employ contractors out of it, and the contractors who work for manufacturers outside the area would all have to be tied into larger arrangements. Still, this approach could create a worker-centered movement that is linked with the concepts of community organizing and building a workers' center.

COMMUNITY ORGANIZING

The phrase, community organizing, as used by unions, can have at least two distinct meanings. First, it can refer to outreach to middle-class supporters and other allies, who can help put pressure on the industry in general or on a particular campaign target. These community supporters can become participants in the corporate campaign, helping to demonstrate against the company, publicize its labor abuses, and spread the word about a boycott. The community that is mobilized helps to provide the troops that exert community pressure on the company. The troops may include various liberal organizations, other trade unions, religious groups, women's groups, students, artists, politicians, and so forth. The second type of community organizing involves organizing within the workers' community. In the garment industry context, it involves organizing around the broader issues facing the Latino and Asian immigrant communities, including the political assaults on both legal and illegal immigrants. The idea is to link the hardships faced by garment workers to the broader agenda of the immigrant communities.

The fact that garment workers are so poorly paid contributes to the general impoverishment of the immigrant community—remember the

$73 million a year in unpaid wages—and the political underrepresentation of Latinos, in particular, makes it much harder for garment workers to protect themselves against economic exploitation. Their positions as workers, as women, and as immigrants under attack, reinforce one another in the overall oppression of the group. The struggle to improve their situation thus extends beyond winning a union contract to winning political power for the community in general and to supporting the rights of women within the community and in the society at large. The various types of struggle are all connected. The union can attempt to align itself with the political aspirations of the Latino community, even as Latino leaders come to recognize that the labor struggle is an important part of winning rights and respect for the Latino community. (Similar statements can be made for segments of the Asian communities, though they are more heterogeneous both in class and ethnic terms.[30])

WORKERS' CENTERS

The idea behind workers' centers is that the organizing of garment workers needs to proceed, irrespective of a particular organizing drive. A workers' center can accomplish a number of purposes. It can provide services to garment workers (who are generally in great need of help in dealing with wage claims or with immigration problems). It can help to educate workers, not only about their rights, but also about the political economy in which they find themselves. It can provide workers with the tools they need to understand their world and begin to fight back. It can provide an environment where workers can engage in lower-risk political struggles rather than a full-fledged organizing drive. The importance of political action cannot be overemphasized because it is in the course of political struggle that workers are able to learn that victories can be won. The very act of participation is radicalizing because it undermines the oppressive belief that the employers are all-powerful and that change is impossible.[31] In sum, a workers' center can provide the basis for building a general movement of garment workers. It is a form of worker-centered organizing, regardless of where people are employed.

UNITE has developed a few workers' centers, called Justice Centers, in New York and Los Angeles.[32] The Los Angeles Garment Workers' Justice Center has experienced ups and downs over the years. The center has helped many workers win back wages owed to them, as well as aiding workers in dealing with problems arising from their immigration status. Too often the center has been overwhelmed by trying to provide basic services to a very needy population. At the time of writing, the center, led by Isaura Lucero, was in the process of evaluating its past experience and attempting to pursue the more fundamental goals of developing an educational and political program.

We believe that this kind of worker-centered organizing is essential for building a *long-term* garment workers' movement in Los Angeles. The Justice Center can work in tandem with particular organizing drives, by helping to prepare workers for participation in such drives, by providing workers to support those drives, and by giving the workers who are engaged in a particular drive a place to go and a support structure even if their factory has been boycotted by the manufacturer. The Justice Center can also serve as a community center for garment workers who, too often, as the newest immigrants, live under conditions of social fragmentation and who need to build social support networks.

Any organizing effort by the garment workers in Los Angeles may simply speed up the the flight of the industry to Mexico. Indeed, although they are unlikely to admit it, we suspect that many apparel manufacturers in Los Angeles regard shifting their production as a form of insurance against local organizing. But small lots in the most fashion-sensitive sectors will probably always be produced in Los Angeles. So will replenishment stock. The number of garment factory jobs may decline in the future, but the industry will not completely disappear. Meanwhile, any attempt to eliminate sweatshops in Los Angeles (and around the world) must include worker empowerment as an essential component.

CHAPTER 10
The Antisweatshop Movement

Jeff Danziger, © *The Christian Science Monitor*

As we have seen, neither governmental enforcement nor efforts to unionize workers are likely, by themselves, to bring an end to sweatshops. The reality is that the system of global, flexible production has created a reign of terror for garment workers in Los Angeles. Most immigrant garment workers are too afraid to report illegal practices in their factories to government authorities and they are even more afraid to join a union organizing drive. Workers typically file claims with the government or come to the union for help only after they have lost their jobs or their factory has closed (often without paying the workers).

This does not suggest that government enforcement efforts should not be strengthened and that worker empowerment through unionization is not a critical component to bringing an end to sweatshops. Rather, these forces *by themselves* are unlikely to succeed. They have not succeeded yet and, if anything, things appear to be getting worse for Los Angeles's garment workers, despite their best efforts.

The current system of employment for garment workers shares some features with the old system of slavery in the United States South. In both cases, workers suffer from a racialized social order that disenfranchises them and makes it very difficult for them to rise up in protest. Under slavery, individuals would occasionally revolt, but the revolts were always crushed. Southern slaves had no chance of winning their freedom by revolting. The planters were not only entrenched locally, but also held considerable sway in the federal government.

Sweatshops may not constitute the same level of atrocity as slavery did, but they come close to it and occasionally actually cross the line, as did the factory in El Monte. In the garment industry in Los Angeles, workers are not only marked off by their race, but also by a combination of their immigration status and race. Some might argue that race has nothing to do with it, but we contend that antiimmigrant policies and sentiments are laden with racial overtones, especially in regard to Mexicans. In any case, immigration status marks off an especially deprived group of workers in a manner that is quite similar to that of the slave system. In addition, apparel industry leaders are, like the plantation aristocracy, able to put pressure on government agencies in an effort to limit their so-called interference with the operations of the industry. The logic of capitalism, and especially of the global, flexible, new world order, under which corporations are likely to flee to new locations or new countries if their demands are not met, compels government agencies to temper their pressures on the industry. Like revolts by slaves, revolts by sweatshop workers are easily crushed. They may not be crushed by the direct and brutal methods of slave-owner's regimes, but they are crushed nonetheless, leaving workers without the means of survival.

The parallel to slavery is important because it suggests the need for an abolitionist-type movement as a significant adjunct to the efforts by workers and government agencies to eliminate sweatshops. The abolitionist movement, which included former slaves, played a critical role in arousing the moral disgust of the nation towards slavery. Similarly, in the case of the return of sweatshops, the public at large needs to become aware of what is happening and to exert moral pressure to bring about change. We need a modern-day abolitionist movement that joins with workers and unions and puts pressure on the government and the industry to bring about needed change. Such a movement is forming and gaining momentum. Indeed, the antisweatshop movement has already played a major role in a number of reforms.

The significance of the antisweatshop movement extends far beyond the apparel industry. It represents nothing less than an attack on the entire system of global, flexible production and the social inequality and suffering that it is creating. The movement asserts that this way of doing business, including contracting out and denying responsibility, moving production to areas of the world where workers are most oppressed and least able to defend themselves, pitting workers around the world against one another in an effort to lower labor costs, and in general, the attack on the power of labor while businesses and their managers and professionals enrich themselves, is unacceptable. The antisweatshop movement is a challenge to the new capitalist world order as a whole. Needless to say, the movement cannot prevail without the support of garment workers and unions. What we are describing is the emergence of a coalition between workers and community groups. Both are essential for bringing an end to sweatshops. Neither group can end them alone but, working together, the coalition can move mountains.

Community Groups

Community groups of all kinds are getting involved in the sweatshop issue in a variety of ways and for a variety of motives. Part of their force lies in the fact that they claim to speak for the consuming public. The entire flexible, global production system is ostensibly geared toward providing consumers with what they want, so, if consumers object to the conditions under which their clothes are being made, the industry will be forced to change its practices. Unlike traditional labor organizing, which is aimed at the point of production, these efforts are aimed at the point of consumption. This shift of focus has at least one potential advantage: Globalization enables manufacturers to shift their production sites to avoid militant workers, but they cannot so easily avoid militant consumers. If there is one thing to which United States retailers and manufacturers will respond quickly and decisively, it is pressure from consumers. Even the *threat* of consumer pressure can be sufficient to turn the most hard-nosed retailer or manufacturer into a crusader for labor reform and the elimination of sweatshops, at least in their public pronouncements.

The essence of consumer objections lies in moral considerations. Some consumers believe it is wrong to wear garments that have been made by people working in sweatshops, either here or abroad. They want to be able to buy clothes without feeling guilty about the conditions under which they were made. Consumers who understand something about the dynamics of the industry may question the enormous discrepancy between the low wages of garment workers and the high salaries and profits realized by leading retailers and manufacturers.

In 1995 and 1996, researchers at Marymount University in Arlington, Virginia, conducted a national survey of 1,000 adults to find out how strongly consumers felt about sweatshops. The results should send a clear message to all retailers and manufacturers. In both years the results of the survey showed that 80 percent of the consumers polled would avoid retailers that sold clothing made in sweatshops, and that over 60 percent would be more inclined to shop in stores that cooperated with law enforcement officials to prevent sweatshops. More than 80 percent would be willing to pay an additional dollar for a $20 garment if it were guaranteed to be made in a legitimate shop, a percentage that held up even for low-income respondents (those earning less than $15,000 a year). The large majority (70 percent) held manufacturers, rather than retailers, responsible for preventing sweatshops.[1]

Industry leaders assume that most consumers are indifferent to the conditions under which the products they buy are made, and are much more concerned with the quality, fit, style, and image of a garment. The millions of dollars spent on advertising by the industry encourages a focus on those characteristics, diverting attention away from the working conditions of garment workers. Industry leaders also claim that the price of labor directly determines the retail price of the garment, and that any increase in that price will be felt by the consumer as a rise in the cost of apparel. They count on the belief that consumers will not be willing to pay more to salve their consciences.

Many social movements, including the abolitionist movement, have resulted in significant social change without having the active support of the majority. A dedicated minority of activists, surrounded by a majority that is mildly sympathetic, can achieve significant results. If a growing social movement demands that sweatshop practices be ended, the apparel industry will have to take notice: An industry that lives by image is very vulnerable to an unfavorable image.

The kinds of community organizations involved in antisweatshop work have been growing. It is impossible for us to present a comprehensive list of all the antisweatshop organizations here, but they include religious groups, student groups, human rights groups, ethnic organizations, women's groups, workers' advocates, immigrants' advocates, lawyers, and political organizations. Interested people may contact San Francisco–based Sweatshop Watch, a coalition of many of the California organizations, which maintains an excellent website.[2] Some of the organizations are national in scope, including the National Labor Committee, the Guatemala Labor Education Project, Global Exchange, the National Interfaith Committee for Worker Justice, and the Stop Sweatshops Campaign. Others are statewide and include California's Sweatshop Watch and the Jessica McClintock campaign, organized by Asian Immigrant Women's Advocates. Others based in Los Angeles include Common Threads, the Los Angeles Jewish Commission on Sweatshops, and the new Coalition for Garment Workers.

Special note should be taken of the role of religious organizations in the growing antisweatshop movement. Apart from the groups already mentioned above, established religious organizations such as Witness for Peace and the People of Faith Network are becoming involved in antisweatshop work. In southern California, Mobilization for the Human Family, a coalition of mainstream Protestant churches, has formed an antisweatshop committee. The Jewish Commission is reaching out to other religious communities to form an ecumenical effort to eradicate sweatshops in Los Angeles. The religious community played a vital role in the abolitionist movement and may come to play a similar role in the antisweatshop movement.[3]

Some community organizations focus on offshore production. The Coalition for Justice in the Maquiladoras (led by Mary Tong) is an example of such an organization. Most of the efforts of the National Labor Committee (led by Charles Kernaghan) have been aimed at improving conditions in Central America, Haiti, and China, though the committee is also engaged in more general projects, including the establishment of a Season of Conscience, an appeal to consumers during the holiday season. The committee targeted particular companies, including The Gap, Disney, and Wal-Mart, for their offshore production practices.[4] Global Exchange (led by Medea Benjamin) has been joined by other organizations in targeting Nike, another offshore producer.

At the same time, organizations and individuals in growing numbers are becoming aware that the sweatshop problem is not confined to the less-developed world, but is firmly entrenched in our own cities. The National Labor Committee, which was responsible for bringing attention to the fact that clothing endorsed by the celebrity Kathie Lee Gifford and sold by Wal-Mart was being made in sweatshops overseas, was also able to link her line to a sweatshop in New York City.

The garment workers' union, UNITE, has sometimes played a role in stimulating the development of community organizations or working as a partner with independent groups. Robert Reich, the Labor Secretary in the first Clinton administration, has also been influential in raising public awareness about sweatshops, thereby stimulating organizations to form or to step up their activities. It cannot, however, be assumed that most of the groups mentioned were created by the government or the union. On the contrary, they have typically formed apart from these two institutions, sometimes even from a stance that is critical of them.

Although the community groups do not have the vast amounts of money available for advertising that the industry commands, they are nevertheless able to spread their concerns by less costly means: presentations, workshops, teach-ins, reports, investigations, demonstrations, picketing, news releases, and conferences. Their principal power lies in the fact that they speak for, and have access to, consumer interests. They reach out to draw in other consumers, hoping to arouse ever-extending waves of concern about sweatshops and overcoming the false dichotomy between workers and consumers. Some of these groups also question the system of global capitalism, with its increased reliance on flexible production systems, that is resulting in the enrichment of the few and the growth of mass poverty. The fundamental values of the system are placed into question by these groups, as they seek to pressure corporations to take account of human (and environmental) values and not just profits. Put another way, they seek to make it unprofitable for companies to disregard social concerns.

Apart from their importance as consumers, community groups may sometimes exert influence as investors and stockholders. If financial agents begin to face a public outcry about investment practices, they can be made to act in ways that put serious pressure on the industry. An example was the movement that, in discouraging investment in companies that operated in South Africa, contributed to the overthrow of Apartheid there.

The methods used by community groups are numerous and various. The most obvious is a boycott against companies that pursue undesirable practices. But boycotts are only one of an array of actions available to community groups and are not necessarily the most effective. Diffuse lists of labels that are categorized as good guys and bad guys have limited effectiveness because they result in highly idiosyncratic buying practices that carry no clear message to a company. It is far more effective either to join an organized boycott aimed at changing the practices of a particular company or to engage in other forms of activism aimed at the structure of the industry itself. Let us review some of the types of activities.

EDUCATING THE PUBLIC

One of the first challenges that community groups take on is that of educating the public about what is going on in the industry. They collect information, conduct investigations, and disseminate their findings as broadly as possible through lectures, workshops, newsletters, reports, videos and, increasingly, the Internet and the World Wide Web. Universities are playing an important role in holding educational conferences, workshops, and teach-ins. Such forums have been held at a number of places, including Clark University in Massachusetts, the University of California at Santa Cruz and Santa Barbara, New York University, and Marymount University in Virginia. At the conference at Marymount, for example, the Labor Secretary, Alexis Herman, was the keynote speaker, and she was followed by academics and industry representatives who discussed research, education, and the industry. The proceedings of the conference have been published.[5] The book *No Sweat* was the product of a conference organized by the American Studies Program at New York University, UNITE, and *The Nation* magazine.[6] This conference included testimony from workers and union and community representatives, as well as academics.

ORGANIZED BOYCOTTS

A nationwide boycott against a particular company is a focused effort that can satisfy the desire of consumers to engage in ethical shopping practices. It is more likely to be successful in changing a company's practices than are individual efforts to adhere to good-guy shopping lists. One of the more successful organized boycotts was the campaign against Jessica McClintock by the Asian Immigrant Women's Advocates (AIWA). The organization, located in Oakland, a city in the San Francisco Bay Area, is concerned with all Asian immigrant women in the region, not solely with garment workers. However, because so many Asian women do work in the garment industry, they became a focus of AIWA's organizing efforts. AIWA adopted a worker-centered approach to organizing, developing the workers' consciousness gradually, through various social and educational programs, while building community support for the women's plight as garment workers.[7]

The Jessica McClintock campaign arose when one of McClintock's sewing contractors, Lucky Sewing Company, declared bankruptcy, owing its workers several months' pay. AIWA demanded that McClintock take responsibility for paying those workers. McClintock refused, arguing that, having paid Lucky for sewing her clothing, she had no legal responsibility for covering the contractors' obligations to its workers. AIWA, arguing that McClintock had a moral (if not legal) responsibility to the workers, promptly launched a nationwide publicity campaign and boycott against the manufacturer. For three years AIWA held demonstrations at stores where her clothing was sold, built support for a boycott on campuses, and especially encouraged the involvement of Asian-American students in an effort to create a new generation of activists around social issues. A high point of the campaign was a segment on the widely viewed television program, *Sixty Minutes,* which proved especially embarrassing to McClintock. Eventually, under pressure from the Secretary of Labor, McClintock arrived at a settlement that included not only paying the back wages of the laid-off Lucky workers, but also supporting a garment workers' education fund, an outreach campaign to inform garment workers of their rights, and a toll-free hotline in English and Cantonese. To the end, McClintock denied legal responsibility, but AIWA had successfully established that she had a moral duty to pay the workers.[8]

PRESSURING PURCHASING AGENTS

Community groups can also put pressure on institutions that purchase clothing, another approach that is more likely to be effective than are individual purchasing strategies. Among the institutions confronted have been churches whose private schools require uniforms, school sports teams, and cities, counties, and universities that sell garments with their logos. For example, the city of Bangor, Maine has developed a Clean Clothes Campaign, the purpose of which is to ensure that all clothes sold in local stores are made according to "established international standards of ethical production." The city is requiring that retailers develop an inventory of so-called clean clothes and support national antisweatshop campaigns, and is asking consumers to provide moral support and economic incentive for the retailers to participate. They encourage community members to participate in a number of ways, such as holding slide presentations, joining a Clean Clothes Action Group, working on a newsletter, doing office work, joining a team that works with store managers, helping with fundraising projects, doing art work, writing letters to newspapers, providing theater or music for special events, and helping to maintain a website. Bangor sees its campaign as "reclaiming community values" and hopes to become a model for the nation.[9]

PRESSURING RETAILERS

Retailers, one of the most important categories of purchasing agents, have come under increased pressure from the Department of Labor to take responsibility for the clothes they sell. The legal situation is somewhat murky, because retailers cannot be held legally responsible for selling hot goods if they were purchased in good faith, that is without the retailers' knowing that the goods were produced under illegal conditions. Their legal responsibility is clearer in the production of their own private-label items, especially when they employ contractors directly. Such production is a rapidly growing part of total retail sales. The Department of Labor publishes lists of violating contractors and the manufacturers for whom they sew, and sends them to the retailers. Thus the retailers know which labels are suspect, and should find it harder to claim a good faith exemption. Meanwhile, the manufacturers who are so exposed feel the threat that they might be dropped by the retailer if they do not clean up their act. (Of course, retailers are probably very reluctant to drop established resources, no matter how the clothes are made.) Apart from government pressure, community groups can and have put pressure on retailers to cease ordering garments known to have been produced in sweatshops. The Korean Immigrant Workers' Advocates, for example, developed a Retailer Accountability Campaign in an effort to move retailers to change their practices. They engaged in regular demonstrations at targeted retailers, such as Robinsons-May, which refused to take any responsibility for the Thai workers in El Monte even though some of the clothes they sewed were sold by the retailer.

CODES OF CONDUCT

One of the popular forms the apparel industry has developed for dealing with external pressure from community groups is to adopt codes of conduct that seek to guarantee that a company's products are made under acceptable standards. Several major retailers have adopted such codes, claiming that they ask their suppliers to sign them and expect them to provide garments that are made only under legal conditions. Because the retailers generally do not have programs for ensuring that the codes are enforced, they serve mainly as a mechanism for deflecting responsibility to the manufacturers and to ward off public criticism and pressure by community groups.

A battle over codes of conduct has developed on universities across the United States. The target is the $2.5-billion collegiate licensing industry, by which universities receive a royalty from manufacturers who sell T-shirts, sweatshirts, jerseys, baseball caps, and other items bearing the school emblem. As of the end of the 1998–99 academic year, student groups on some thirty campuses were demanding that apparel bearing their university's logo be made only in factories that pay their workers a living wage, rather than the much lower minimum or prevailing wage in various countries. Students were also calling for full disclosure of the location of factories where the garments are actually sewn, factory monitoring by independent human rights or religious groups, and the right of workers to organize unions and engage in collective bargaining. Needless to say, these demands are revolutionary for an industry that insists on secrecy, wants to cut labor costs to the bare bones, and seeks to avoid the unionization of its work force.

Students on some campuses have engaged in militant protests, including the occupation of university administrative offices. Among those who were compelled by student activism to strengthen their codes of conduct are Duke, Georgetown, Brown, Princeton, Yale, the University of Wisconsin-Madison, and the University of Michigan. Students at those universities have won commitments from their administrations to abide by at least some of their demands. The nine-campus University of California is also facing a tide of student activism around this issue. The university enacted a code of conduct over the summer of 1998, but students (and some faculty) believe that the code is weak and does not address the major reforms that are being demanded. Meetings with administrators and teach-ins are being held to insist that the university set a decent standard for its licensees. In April 1999 students held a well-publicized rally at the Oakland offices of the UC President. The coalition of students, representing different campuses, opposed the university's participation in the Fair Labor Association (FLA), calling instead for a student and faculty voice in determining licensing policies.

A nationwide coalition of student groups, the United Students Against Sweatshops (USAS), was formed in the summer of 1998 to help coordinate these efforts. By means of websites, an Internet subscribers' group, and occasional face-to-face workshops, this coalition provides an extraordinary degree of coordination among geographically dispersed campus groups. Students discuss and develop common demands for codes of conduct and share strategies for achieving their goals. They also seek to foster cooperation between universities in enforcing codes of conduct.

Universities and their suppliers are both trying to find ways to circumvent this pressure. The Collegiate Licensing Company (CLC), which handles the licensing for approximately 200 universities and 2,000 retailers, is working with the Association of Collegiate Licensing Administrators to adopt codes of conduct that will blunt the students' demands. One alternative that universities are pursuing is affiliation with the FLA, a nonprofit organization that was created by the Apparel Industry Partnership to oversee monitoring. The FLA is governed by representatives from manufacturers, a handful of nongovernmental organizations engaged in monitoring, and participating universities. USAS strongly opposes the affiliation of universities with the FLA, which advocates standards that are considerably weaker than those that already exist at a number of universities. Among the students' concerns are the FLA's failure to require a living wage and its relatively weak monitoring provisions, which fail to require public disclosure of violations or even publication of the names and addresses of factories. The FLA also allows companies to select and pay their own monitors, a practice that, students fear, will enable firms to be certified "sweatshop free" while covering up violations.

Apart from the actual standards set by codes of conduct, the biggest problem is their enforcement. Who will ensure that they are actually being followed? And how can consumers and community groups be convinced that the codes are not just public relations gimmicks, aimed to lull critics and avoid further pressure without being accompanied by any serious efforts to make real changes? Despite these concerns, the fact that more and more companies and organizations feel the need to adopt such codes shows that the antisweatshop movement is having an effect.

MONITORING

One way to ensure that the standards that companies claim to follow are actually being implemented is by monitoring them. The Department of Labor has played a major role in attempting to compel manufacturers to take responsibility for monitoring their own contractors. Of course, the department has no jurisdiction outside the boundaries of the United States, but the president's Apparel Industry Partnership attempts to apply the principle of monitoring to offshore production as well.

Monitoring is a source of controversy. Some industry leaders have reluctantly acceded to self-monitoring and even to monitoring by compliance firms that they themselves employ, but they draw the line at having their factories and contractors inspected by outsiders. Community groups pressure for more involvement in the oversight of garment production.

They want to be able to inspect factories themselves, or arrange for inspections by groups they trust, such as local human rights advocates or religious representatives. They tend to be critical of self-monitoring, believing that apparel firms will not make any real effort to clean up their contracting shops unless outsiders watch over them closely. They believe that the companies are too motivated by competitive pressures and the need to earn profits to take the moral issues seriously, and that only those who are directly concerned with the well-being of the workers can be trusted to ensure that strong codes of conduct are being implemented in practice.

One of the problems with codes of conduct and with monitoring is that they can induce a manufacturer to take work away from a violating contractor. This possibility virtually invalidates efforts to improve conditions for the workers, who end up losing their jobs. Knowing that they are likely to lose their jobs, workers are unwilling to speak out about illegal and abusive practices, which only makes monitoring more difficult. Effective monitoring depends on the cooperation of the workers, who alone can reveal the well-hidden malfeasance of their employers. Codes of conduct and monitoring systems need, therefore, to require that the manufacturer will stay and clean up the illegalities, and not run to the next (possibly equally illegal) contractor, or the next country, where workers have even less protection. Community groups have usually educated themselves about the global economy and are aware of the mobility of the apparel industry. Thus, when they expose conditions in a particular factory or country, their purpose is explicitly *not* to drive the manufacturer to an even lower-wage country or region, but rather to force it to take responsibility for labor conditions, to stay and clean up the conditions it helped to create.

This was an important feature of the campaign against the Gap, led by the National Labor Committee (NLC) in 1995. Teenagers at Mandarin International, in the San Marcos free-enterprise zone of El Salvador, were working for 56 cents an hour, sometimes for eighteen hours a day. They were trying to organize a union; predictably, Mandarin's management fired union activists. Two young workers toured the United States, arousing public outrage. The Gap, Inc., stating that it was disturbed by the allegations even though it claimed to find no evidence in support of them, removed its work from Mandarin. This was not, however, the outcome that the NLC sought, because it left Mandarin free to engage in similar abuses while producing for other manufacturers and retailers. The NLC continued to push for the reinstatement of the fired workers, insisting that the Gap maintain its work there and install an independent, third-party monitoring system to oversee conditions. Eventually the Gap agreed to negotiate with the NLC, leading to the creation of a monitoring system under the aegis of Salvadoran organizations, including the human rights departments of Jesuit University and the Catholic archdiocese.[10]

PRESSURING CELEBRITY ENDORSERS

The NLC achieved a resounding success by embarrassing the television talk-show host Kathie Lee Gifford. Wal-Mart was paying her $9 million a year in royalties for using her name on a private-label line. Some of these clothes were being made at Global Fashion in Honduras, where workers, whose ages ranged as low as thirteen and fourteen, earned about $900 a year. Gifford, a supporter of family values, was exposed before a huge television audience. After initially denying the abuses, she conducted her own investigation and came to the conclusion that they were true. This led her to support efforts to clean up the apparel industry, giving the issue of sweatshops considerable public exposure.[11]

PRESSURING MANUFACTURERS

A growing element in the antisweatshop movement is the insistence that apparel manufacturers disclose the names of the contractors they use, both here and abroad. Very secretive about whom they work with, manufacturers claim this secrecy is a precaution against their competitors who might steal their contractors away. In practice, the absence of information about contracting relations protects the use of sweatshops. Companies can move to the far corners of the earth, and it is very difficult for anyone to ascertain the location of their contract factories, let alone uncover the labor conditions there. If consumers are to have a choice about how their garments are produced, and if community groups are to monitor factories, this veil of secrecy must be lifted.

Charles Kernaghan of the NLC is raising the issue of disclosure in connection with the committee's campaign against Wal-Mart. Charging that Wal-Mart produces 85 percent of its private-label garments offshore, despite its advertising that the goods are "made right here," the NLC is insisting that Wal-Mart divulge the locations of its factories, which number in the thousands.[12] This requirement can certainly be extended to other manufacturers and retailers and is being fought for by students in their efforts to strengthen universities' codes of conduct.

LEGAL ACTION

Lawsuits are often important mechanisms for establishing precedents and compelling change in practice, particularly in countries such as the United States, where the enforcement of existing laws would go at least part way toward eradicating the problem of sweatshops (although not toward providing an adequate income for most garment workers). Some community groups are staffed with lawyers that are able to pursue legal action. This was one of the main weapons used by the Asian Pacific American Legal Center in its efforts to achieve redress for the Thai workers in El Monte. Julie Su, an attorney and activist, led the effort, naming not only the contractors who directly employed the workers, but also the manufacturers and retailers who profited from their enslavement.[13] The case was extended to include seventy Latino workers who worked in a sister company that was linked to the Thai factory. Four major companies, including the retailers Mervyn's (owned by Dayton Hudson Corporation) and Montgomery Ward, and the manufacturers B.U.M. International and LF Sportswear, agreed to pay 150 workers $2 million. A separate settlement was reached with Hub Distributing, the parent company of the retailer Miller's Outpost, for an undisclosed amount. As usual, the companies made no admission of wrongdoing because they settled the case out of court.[14] However, as Su pointed out, "If they weren't guilty, they wouldn't be paying. This case has established a precedent that workers can sue and win."[15]

In January 1999, the largest legal action taken so far against sweatshops based in the United States was filed in three state and federal courts in California and Saipan. The suits were filed by New York law firm Milberg Weiss Bershad Hynes and Lerach, joined by UNITE, Global Exchange, Sweatshop Watch, and the Asian Law Caucus on behalf of more than fifty thousand garment workers in Saipan in the United States commonwealth of the Northern Mariana Islands. The suits charge a group of major apparel retailers and manufacturers, including the Gap Inc., Tommy Hilfiger Corp., Wal-Mart Stores Inc., Dayton Hudson Corp., J. C. Penney Co., J. Crew Group Inc., Limited Inc., May Department Stores Co., Nordstrom Inc., Sears, Roebuck and Co., and Warnaco Group Inc., among others, with employing garment contractors who recruited workers from China and the Philippines to work under prisonlike conditions. The suits, which seek more than $1 billion in damages, claim that garment workers work up to twelve hours per day, seven days a week, often without overtime pay. They are kept inside by barbed wire fences and armed guards. They signed contracts of indenture, paying up to $7,000 for the privilege of obtaining the jobs supposedly in the United States.[16]

LEGISLATIVE REFORM

Community groups have also played a role in pushing for legislative change, often in tandem with UNITE and its predecessors. The passage in New York of the Joint Liability Act in 1998, and the passage in California of a law that holds retailers jointly liable for private-label production if they use unregistered contractors, are products of a growing public concern about sweatshops. Moreover, the president's Apparel Industry Partnership was, without doubt, created in response to concerns about the scandalous labor conditions in this industry, both here and abroad.

Antisweatshop groups are pushing a host of legislative proposals at both the state and federal levels. These proposals include the appending of stronger provisions for the protection of labor to new trade agreements. The potential for this kind for pressure has not gone unnoticed by the Clinton administration. In a keynote address to the World Trade Organization in May 1998, President Clinton stated the need for institutions such as the WTO to address labor standards in the global economy, including the right to collective bargaining, freedom of association, and the abolition of bonded and child labor.[17]

Community Groups in Los Angeles

At least three distinctive community groups have formed in Los Angeles around the sweatshop issue. All three of the groups focus upon conditions in Los Angeles, although they are not unmindful of the larger global context that is shaping local conditions. These groups are Common Threads, the Los Angeles Jewish Commission on Sweatshops, and the Coalition for Garment Workers.[18]

COMMON THREADS

Common Threads was a women's group that developed around the idea that the apparel industry affects women at a number of levels.[19] Not only are most of the garment workers in Los Angeles women, but also the primary product of the industry there is women's

wear. Common Threads believed that women, as consumers, were manipulated by advertising that uses sexual objectification and ultrathin
models. The group, which drew inspiration from early twentieth-century
middle-class women's support of striking garment workers in New York,
saw its primary mission as supporting garment workers' efforts to organize themselves.

Common Threads prided itself on its lack of bureaucracy. It did not
develop any formal leadership or committee structure; it was independent, free-wheeling, and creative, engaging in activities that were unusual
for the labor movement. The group developed a slide show, making numerous presentations for schools and community groups, along with a
satirical fashion show as a form of street theater. It also created an artists'
collective that developed a couple of posters that were used for late-night
postings around the city. The artists' crowning achievement was an exhibition in the large display windows of an abandoned Robinsons-May
department store downtown. The exhibition, entitled *Hidden Labor: Un-
covering Los Angeles's Garment Industry,* was funded by a grant from the
Community Redevelopment Agency and opened 4 May 1997. It covered
the history of union struggles in the garment industry (including the
Guess campaign) with photos, interviews with workers, and artifacts. As
might be expected, industry leaders objected to the public funding of such
an exhibit. Ilse Metchek of the California Fashion Association complained
that the redevelopment agency did not consult industry groups before
supporting the project. "We would have loved to have had some input
into it. People never hear the entrepreneur's side of the story."[20] (The
Community Redevelopment Agency requires developers to contribute 1
percent of their development costs to a public art fund.) Mickey Gustin
of the CRA responded to Metchek's objections, stating that the exhibit
was about "a piece of history that should be told. It's important for the
workers to be heard from as well." (With this reaction, similar to that provoked by the Smithsonian's exhibit, *Between a Rock and a Hard Place: A
History of American Sweatshops, 1820–Present,* it would seem that the power
elite of the apparel industry in Los Angeles wants to control all messages
about the industry and does not want the other side to be heard.)

Members of Common Threads actively supported UNITE's efforts to
unionize Guess? Inc.'s contractors. They met with Guess's workers in an
effort to understand their problems better and to show solidarity and participated in a number of demonstrations in the Guess campaign, proudly
displaying a large banner that read "The Community is Watching." Common Threads even organized a literary reading at the Midnight Special

bookstore in support of the Guess workers. This activity caught the eye of the company, which filed a lawsuit against Common Threads, accusing the organization of defamation. Common Threads responded by publicly decrying the attack on the free speech of a small, unfunded community group. Guess? Inc. eventually dropped the suit, because it made the company appear to be a big bully picking on a small group of women. When the news arrived that the lawsuit was dropped, Common Threads promptly held another literary reading at the Midnight Special, "The Literary Reading that Guess? Could Not Shut Down," which was far better attended than the first had been.

At the time of writing, Common Threads has more or less dissolved, though some of the artists' activities continue. Many of the members who were students have graduated and moved on, a number of them to jobs in the labor movement. Those who participated believe they learned something of value in terms of active involvement in a struggle for change and do not regret that the organization reached an end.

THE LOS ANGELES JEWISH COMMISSION ON SWEATSHOPS

The Los Angeles Jewish Commission on Sweatshops[21] was formed in June 1997 by several Jewish organizations that were concerned about reports of substandard labor conditions in the garment industry in Los Angeles. It consists of Jewish organizational leaders, rabbis, and other community leaders representing a substantial range of the organized Jewish community. Its original cochairs were Carol Levy (at the time executive director of the American Jewish Congress, Pacific Southwest Region), Evely Laser Shlensky (the immediate past national chair of the Commission on Social Action of Reform Judaism), and Rabbi Leonard Beerman (the founding rabbi of the Leo Baeck Temple in Los Angeles).[22]

The commission drew on Jewish history and religious tradition for its inspiration, because both are richly intertwined with all aspects of apparel manufacturing and an abiding concern for justice for workers. Since the early twentieth century, Jews have been involved with nearly every aspect of the garment industry, from providing an immigrant workforce at the beginning of the century to playing the role of leading manufacturers today. Many of the early immigrants were active participants in the nascent labor movement, particularly the ILGWU.

Jewish religious tradition strongly respects the dignity of labor, an important theme in Jewish religious writings for centuries. There is a range of labor protections in the Bible and Talmud, including calls for the prompt payment of wages, the workers' right to strike, and limitations on the number of hours and conditions under which people can be expected to work. Employers are liable for work-related injuries caused by negligence, and workers are prohibited from accepting unsafe working conditions.

The purpose of the commission has been to gather information about the operation of the industry through a series of public and private hearings and eventually to come up with proposals for improving conditions that would be consistent with Jewish traditions of social justice. Over a period of approximately nine months, the commission met with representatives from all segments of the industry, including workers, the union, manufacturers, retailers, contractors, and federal and state labor and health and safety officials. Its report, issued in January 1999, calls on religious and community groups to educate themselves on conditions in the Los Angeles apparel industry and pressure retailers, manufacturers, and lawmakers to end sweatshop abuse. Among its recommendations, the commission advocates the passage of federal and state joint-liability legislation, strong codes governing apparel licensing or purchases by universities, schools, and local government, independent monitoring, and the protection of the right of apparel workers to unionize. As of this writing, the commission was laying plans to engage in outreach to synagogues and Jewish student organizations, as well as to work with other segments of the religious community in Los Angeles to implement its proposals.

Shortly after the commission issued its report, one of the cosponsoring organizations, the Southwest Region of the American Jewish Congress (AJC), was shut down by the national office in New York City. Initially the staff in Los Angeles were given only a few days to clear out their offices, and the regional board was disbanded. This seemingly precipitous decision was recommended by the AJC's finance committee, on the grounds that the Southwest Region had for years failed to raise sufficient money to cover its expenses. Skeptics wondered about the sudden timing of the closure, especially as the problems were allegedly of long-standing duration. Skeptics also noted that the head of the national finance committee—the person who spearheaded the closure—also was president of Republic Business Credit Corporation, the fifth-largest factoring company in the United States. An outgrowth of Republic Factors, Republic Business Credit Corporation boasted a factoring volume of nearly $6 billion in 1999 and offices in New York City, Charlotte, North Carolina, and Los Angeles. The company is an active member of the Los Angeles apparel power elite and a player in the California Fashion Association, an organization that is strongly and publicly critical of the Jewish Commission's report.

THE COALITION FOR GARMENT WORKERS

Toward the end of 1997, a group of organizations met in Los Angeles to promote the goals of providing services, developing an educational program, and engaging in lower-risk political actions with garment workers. The group, tentatively called the Coalition for Garment Workers, brings together the union and a number of community groups, including the Asian Pacific American Legal Center, the Coalition for Humane Immigrant Rights of Los Angeles, the Korean Immigrant Worker Advocates, the Mexican American Legal Defense and Education Fund, the Legal Aid Foundation of Los Angeles, Beit Tzedek (a Jewish group that offers free legal services to the poor), and UNITE's Garment Workers Justice Center. Each of the community groups has engaged in organizing and providing services and has had plenty of experience in working with garment workers.

The group is attempting to reach out to garment workers by providing them with legal services (with the help of student interns), and encourages them to participate in UNITE's Justice Center and to develop a political movement. The coalition hopes it can establish a division of labor so that the Justice Center will be relieved of some of its responsibility for services, and all the organizations can help with the development of an educational and political program. So far, the group has conducted a number of workshops for Latino and Chinese workers to teach them about their rights and to provide them with legal assistance, if needed. The coalition has made contact with a few Catholic churches and is in the process of helping a small group of garment workers at St. Vincent's church in downtown Los Angeles to set up workshops for church members.

The coalition has also held meetings with staff from the state Department of Labor Standards Enforcement and the federal Department of Labor, in an effort to get them to be more responsive to workers' claims and grievances. The group is attempting to get the agencies to implement the law they are charged to uphold more effectively, as well as to develop worker-friendly policies and procedures. By showing the agencies that several community groups are watching them closely and demanding accountability, the coalition hopes to get the agencies to become more ac-

tive in the antisweatshop struggle. For example, coalition members chal-
lenged the Department of Labor to sue for breach of contract manufacturers who have signed the Long-Form agreement promising to monitor
their contractors, but whose contractors are still breaking the law. The coalition argued that, without penalties, the agreement can end up shielding
manufacturers from the confiscation of their hot goods. The coalition
also urged the department to implement a provision in the Long-Form
agreement that the manufacturer be held accountable for establishing pricing policies that allow for legal production. In late September 1998, the
coalition organized a hearing before the two agencies at which garment
workers testified and presented their grievances and demands. The hearing aimed to demonstrate to the government, and indirectly to the industry, that garment workers will no longer remain silent about their oppression and exploitation, but intend to band together and insist on
change.

Given the attention that the sweatshop issue is attracting, it is indeed con-
ceivable that sufficient pressure will be mounted to minimize or eliminate them in this country. Part of the key, at least in southern California,
will be the rise in Latino political power. Already, the influence of Latino
voters and politicians is being felt, and as their numbers swell, the political climate in the region is bound to change. Obviously not every Latino
holds egalitarian social values, but the majority appear to support such
values, and their elected representatives are often outspoken critics of the
prevailing system of race and class inequality.

The Latino community has yet to adopt the garment workers' issues
with the same fervor that it embraced the farm workers. Yet there are many
important parallels between the two groups of immigrant workers. Garment workers in Los Angeles can be seen as the urban equivalent of the
farm workers. Both groups produce a basic commodity (food and clothing) under highly exploitative conditions. If the Latino community were
to take on sweatshop conditions as a major issue, it could build upon,
and invigorate, the multifaceted efforts that are already being made.

The key question is whether, if the antisweatshop movement is successful, the industry will inevitably leave Los Angeles. Does the industry
depend on low-wage labor? Will all the forces that are concerned with
keeping the industry here be able to overcome this imperative? In part,
the answer lies in developments abroad. If workers and their supporters
in the developing world are able to resist the levels of exploitation they
currently face and are able to establish decent standards for garment pro-

duction, the industry will have fewer places to run to. Meanwhile, pressures by community groups that are closely watching offshore conditions could make this a less attractive option. Los Angeles is not an island. What happens here inevitably depends upon what happens in the rest of the world.

The struggle over sweatshops extends far beyond the question of how our clothes are made. It is a struggle over the future of the new world order of neoliberal economics. The global, flexible system of production, touted for its greater business efficiency, is also exhibiting a darker underside, the mushrooming of sweatshops, here and abroad. When people stand up and fight against sweatshops, they are expressing their opposition to the entire system that produces them. A line of resistance is being drawn. We are witnessing a challenge to the United States corporate juggernaut that appears to rolling over the entire world. Will the resistance build up sufficient momentum to cause a change in direction? We believe that it can and will. Like the abolitionist movement, the antisweatshop movement, working in tandem with workers and their organizations, is creating such moral outrage that the system will be forced to make significant changes. This volume, we hope, will contribute to that process.

Afterword
The Larger Questions

In this book we have focused on the costs, to the *workers* who sew the clothing, of the way that apparel is currently produced. But there are other problems with the system and other groups that are hurt by it. We mention them only fleetingly here, because a full discussion of the issues would require another book.

An issue that concerns us deeply is the fact that women spend much more money on apparel than do men. In 1997, of the $180 billion spent on apparel in the United States, almost 50 percent ($89 billion) was spent on women's wear. Only 29 percent ($51 billion) was spent on men's wear and the remaining 22 percent ($40 billion) on children's and infants' wear and uniforms.[1] The implications of this fact are enormous. Women are expected to be consumers, to the point where the mere act of shopping can become a pathology. Women learn to seek meaning in their lives by shopping; they are urged to "shop 'till they drop," buying clothing they do not need and often can ill afford. Women are encouraged to focus on their appearance much more than men are, an unhealthy preoccupation that is fostered by the fashion industry in order to sell products. Indeed, the fashion industry promotes impossible images of female beauty, unhealthy thinness, standardized perfection of face and figure, and an obsession with youth. Much like the entertainment industry, the fashion industry exploits female bodies, often using sexually charged photographs to sell garments. There is a kind of seduction of young women, urging them to buy clothes in order to find romance as the solution to all of their problems.

The pace of change in women's fashions has escalated in recent years, another consequence of the industry's need to create ever-new markets for its products. Instead of four seasons a year, apparel companies now have a continually changing stream of new designs. Retail stores must keep changing the clothes that are hanging on their racks in order to draw women in to buy the latest fashions. The pressure to get women to keep buying new clothes feeds back on the way these garments are produced. It is the craziness of constantly changing fashion that produces the need for flexibility on the part of the manufacturers, hence the small contracting shops and sweated labor. These two realities are parts of a single whole. It is significant that, for the most part, men's wear is not part of the same wild fashion cycle and, as a consequence, men's wear tends not to be produced under the same fragmented system.

We are not suggesting that fashion does not have its delights, nor are we advocating a world where women dress in drab uniforms. Nevertheless, aspects of the fashion scene seem to us to be escalating beyond what is reasonable and healthy for a society. We do not advocate fashion censorship, but nor do we think it unreasonable to raise questions for public discussion about the meaning and desirability of these trends. The fashion industry encourages consumerism, an obsession with spending money and accumulating material objects. In our opinion, the values represented by consumerism can be detrimental to human beings. They bolster concern with superficial matters, steering young people away from organizing their lives around what could become more meaningful pursuits. Moreover, consumerism fosters the growing exploitation of our planet and the rapid exhaustion of its precious resources. The explosion of apparel consumption is indicative of this erosion.

Of course, we must also recognize the maldistribution of the clothing that is made. Some countries, notably the United States, and particularly its middle class, buy a hugely disproportionate share of the total garment production of the world. Profit-driven consumerism helps to create a situation where the Third World poor, both here and abroad, cannot afford to buy the clothes they make, even as the more privileged classes in the United States are drowning in an abundance of clothing. The distribution of clothing consumption across the world is irrationally skewed, so that those who already have an abundance are pressed to buy more and more, while those who have too little must send still more to those who have an abundance.

The global distribution of clothing production also has irrational elements. Capital flight to the poorest countries might, in the long run, enable some of those countries to develop, raise their living standards, and jump on the consumer bandwagon, but we doubt that this will happen in most countries, at least not in the near future. So long as countries and places compete with one another to underbid production costs, and so long as the industry is mobile enough to move to the lowest bidder, globalization contributes to poverty and exploitation in already poor countries such as Haiti or Guatemala, and to growing poverty in the United States.

We do not support protectionism on the part of the United States. We also do not think that the United States should hold onto good jobs and export menial, low-wage, polluting industries. We believe that our economic and political system should strive to provide a decent standard of living, meaningful work and a rich life for *all* the world's inhabitants. Perhaps a system could be devised to distribute apparel production among the various countries of the world so that they are not pitted against one another. Perhaps such a system would loosen the controls on fashion and design exercised by the West and would allow new types of cultural variation to find expression.

An alternative approach concerns the possibility of regional development strategies coupled with regional social standards. NAFTA is inevitably creating an integrated North American production zone that crosses national boundaries. Yet national borders are sharply maintained when it comes to the mobility of labor. Clearly we need to think about North America not simply as a zone of free capital investment, but also as an area where the rights of workers (and human rights, in general) need to be specified on a regional basis. Like the European Union, we need to be establishing a floor for decent standards (such as a living wage) and labor rights for all workers in the region, regardless of where they live or work. In particular, the rights of immigrant workers need to be protected. Perhaps we should be working toward a notion of regional citizenship for all workers employed in the NAFTA countries, eventually to cover all the countries to which a free-trade agreement is extended.

Our system seems to be rushing forward without controls, careening down the track toward various types of disaster, both social and ecological. But changing the system at a fundamental level seems impractical, at the moment. In this book, we have tried, for the most part, to suggest reforms that are not completely unfeasible, as a way to move away from sweatshops and still keep a flourishing apparel industry in Los Angeles. But, while we urge that space be made for these reforms, including space for a strong workers' movement, ultimately we believe that these larger questions must be addressed. Perhaps a movement of workers and the community together, should it gain some political power, will be the means of doing so.

Notes

Notes for Introduction: The Return of the Sweatshop

1. Gerald Hall, the District Director of the Department of Labor (DOL) in Los Angeles, made this statement at a meeting of DOL officials with the Coalition for Garment Workers, a coalition of advocate groups for garment workers (to be discussed in Chapter 9), in Los Angeles, 9 July 1998.

2. For a brief review of the history of sweatshops and the struggles against them, see Alan Howard, "Labor, History, and Sweatshops in the New Global Economy," pp. 151–72 in *No Sweat: Fashion, Free Trade, and the Rights of Garment Workers,* ed. Andrew Ross (New York: Verso, 1997). For more details, see Nancy Schrom Dye, *As Equals and as Sisters: Feminism, the Labor Movement, and the Women's Trade Union League of New York* (Columbia: University of Missouri Press, 1980); Philip S. Foner, *Women and the American Labor Movement: From Colonial Times to the Eve of World War I* (New York: Free Press, 1979); Jack Hardy, *The Clothing Workers: A Study of the Conditions and Struggles in the Needle Trades* (New York: International Publishiers, 1935); Joan M. Jensen and Sue Davidson, eds., *A Needle, a Bobbin, a Strike: Women Needleworkers in America* (Philadelphia: Temple University Press, 1984); Annelise Orleck, *Common Sense and a Little Fire: Women and Working-Class Politics in the United States, 1900–1965* (Chapel Hill: University of North Carolina Press, 1995); Joel Seidman, *The Needle Trades* (New York: Farrar and Rinehart, 1942); Leon Stein, ed., *Out of the Sweatshop: The Struggle for Industrial Democracy* (New York: Quadrangle, 1977); Gus Tyler, *Look for the Union Label: A History of the International Ladies' Garment Workers' Union* (Armonk, N.Y.: M. E. Sharpe, 1995).

3. Leon Stein, *The Triangle Fire* (New York: Carroll and Graf, 1962).

4. This figure is arrived at by taking the average back wages owed per factory for ninety days, $3,631, multiplying it by four to get the back wages owed per year, and then by the estimated 5,000 contractors in Los Angeles. This method of calculating was suggested by Gerald Hall of the DOL, who at a meeting between the DOL and the Coalition for Garment Workers held on July 9, 1998, also reported the amount collected in back wages, per annum.

5. The Los Angeles City Council passed a living wage ordinance in early 1997: Holders of municipal contracts and firms receiving substantial financial aid from the city must pay their employees at least $7.25 an hour, plus health insurance, or $8.50 an hour without specified benefits. At the time, the state and federal minimum wage was $4.25 an hour. See Jean Merl, "Defiant Mayor Vetoes 'Living Wage' Ordinance," *Los Angeles Times,* 28 March 1997, sec. B, p. 3. The concept of a living wage has emerged in Los Angeles and other cities, where it has become clear that a minimum-wage job without benefits puts a family well below the official poverty level. Those who must labor under such conditions are the working poor.

6. Throughout this book references to Los Angeles indicate the County of Los Angeles, which is the equivalent of the metropolitan area. The City of Los Angeles is only one, though the largest, of a number of cities in the county, which also includes unincorporated areas. References to the city will clearly differentiate it from the county.

7. A large and growing literature treats these developments, for example, David Harvey, *The Condition of Postmodernity* (Cambridge: Blackwell, 1989); Ankie Hoogvelt, *Globalization and the Postcolonial World: The New Political Economy of Development* (Baltimore: Johns Hopkins University Press, 1997); Kim Moody, *Workers in a Lean World* (New York: Verso, 1997); and Beth A. Rubin, *Shifts in the Social Contract: Understanding Change in American Society* (Thousand Oaks, Calif.: Pine Forge Press, 1996).

8. See Michael J. Piore and Charles F. Sabel, *The Second Industrial Divide: Possibilities for Prosperity* (New York: Basic Books, 1984) and Joseph B. Pine, *Mass Customization: The New Frontier in Business Competition* (Boston, Mass.: Harvard Business School Press, 1993). For critiques of the "new flexibility," see Harvey, *Condition of Postmodernity;* Alain Lipietz, *Mirages and Miracles: The Crisis of Global Fordism* (London: Verso, 1987); and Richard P. Appelbaum, "Multiculturalism and Flexibility: Some New Directions in Global Capitalism," pp. 297–316 in *Mapping Multi-Culturalism,* ed. by Avery Gordon and Christopher Newfield (Minneapolis: University of Minnesota Press, 1996).

9. Kate Bronfenbrenner, Sheldon Friedman, Richard W. Hurd, Rudolph A. Oswald, and Ronald L. Seeber, eds., *Organizing to Win: New Research on Union Strategies* (Ithaca, N.Y.: ILR Press, 1997), 2–3.

10. Another large literature deals with this topic. See, for example, Saskia Sassen, *The Mobility of Labor and Capital: A Study in International Investment and Labor Flow* (Cambridge: Cambridge University Press, 1988); Paul Ong, Edna Bonacich, and Lucie Cheng, eds., *The New Asian Immigration in Los Angeles and Global Restructuring* (Philadelphia: Temple University Press, 1994).

11. Bennett Harrison and Barry Bluestone, *The Great U-Turn: Corporate Restructuring and the Polarizing of America* (New York: Basic Books, 1990).

12. Kurt Hoffman and Howard Rush, *Micro-Electronics and Clothing: The Impact of Technical Change on a Global Industry* (New York: Praeger, 1988).

13. American Apparel Manufacturers Association, *Focus: An Economic Profile of the Apparel Industry* (Arlington, Va.: AAMA, 1998), 4. The apparel retail market in the United States reached $180 billion in 1997.

14. Imports have also affected the apparel industries of other advanced industrial countries. See Ian M. Taplin and Jonathan Winterton, eds., *Rethinking*

Global Production: A Comparative Analysis of Restructuring in the Clothing Industry (Aldershot, England: Ashgate, 1997).

15. Kitty Dickerson, *Textiles and Apparel in the Global Economy,* 2d ed. (New York: Macmillan, 1995), 202–206, 225–26.

16. See Ian M. Taplin, "Flexible Production, Rigid Jobs: Lessons from the Clothing Industry," *Work and Occupations* 22 (November 1995): 412–38; and "Rethinking Flexibility: The Case of the Apparel Industry," *Review of Social Economy* 54 (Summer 1996): 191–220.

17. Pine, *Mass Customization.*

18. American Apparel Manufacturers Association, *Focus 1998* (Arlington, Va.), p. 10. In New York City there has recently been a slight rise in apparel employment. The city's apparel and textile manufacturing employment peaked in the mid-1970s at 250,000, but had dropped to 82,500 by 1996. In 1997 it rose to 84,000. "Rebirth of New York's Apparel Industry," *Apparel Industry Magazine,* March 1998, p. 12.

19. Daniel Taub, "L.A. Beats Out Chicago as No. 1 Manufacturing Center," *Los Angeles Business Journal,* 9 March 1998, p. 5. See also Louis Uchitelle, "The New Faces of U.S. Manufacturing: California's Vision of the Future: Thriving, But with Fewer High-Wage Jobs," *New York Times,* 3 July 1994, sec. 3, p. 1; Jack Kyser, *Manufacturing in Los Angeles* (Los Angeles, Calif.: Economic Development Corp., 1997).

20. Taub, "L.A. Beats Out Chicago," p. 5.

21. Goetz Wolff, "The Apparel Cluster: A Regional Growth Industry," pamphlet prepared for the California Community College Fashion Symposium, CaliforniaMart, Los Angeles, April 1997.

22. Paul M. Ong, *The Widening Divide: Income Inequality and Poverty in Los Angeles* (Los Angeles, Calif.: Graduate School of Architecture and Urban Planning, University of California, Los Angeles, 1989).

23. California Legislature, Assembly Select Committee on the California Middle Class, *The Distribution of Income in California and Los Angeles: A Look at Recent Current Population Survey and State Taxpayer Data* (Sacramento, 1998). The chairman of the committee is Assemblyman Wally Knox.

24. Examples of the growing literature on the restructuring of Los Angeles include: Mike Davis, *City of Quartz: Excavating the Future of Los Angeles* (London: Verso, 1990); Michael J. Dear, H. Eric Schockman, and Greg Hise, eds., *Rethinking Los Angeles* (Thousand Oaks, Calif.: Sage, 1996); Cynthia Hamilton, *Apartheid in an American City: The Case of the Black Community in Los Angeles* (Los Angeles, Calif.: Labor/Community Strategy Center, 1987); Labor/Community Strategy Center, *Reconstructing Los Angeles from the Bottom Up* (Los Angeles, Calif.: Labor/Community Strategy Center, 1993); David Reid, ed., *Sex, Death and God in L.A.* (Berkeley, Calif.: University of California Press, 1994); David Rieff, *Los Angeles: Capital of the Third World* (New York: Simon and Schuster, 1991); Gerry Riposa and Carolyn G. Dersch, eds., *City of Angels* (Dubuque, Iowa: Kendall/ Hunt, 1992); Allen J. Scott, *Technopolis: High-Technology Industry and Regional Development in Southern California* (Berkeley, Calif.: University of California Press, 1993); Allen J. Scott and Edward W. Soja, eds., *The City: Los Angeles and Urban Theory at the End of the Twentieth Century* (Berkeley, Calif.: University of Cali-

fornia Press, 1996); Edward W. Soja, *Postmodern Geographics: The Reassertion of Space in Critical Social Theory* (London: Verso, 1989); Edward W. Soja, Rebecca Morales, and Goetz Wolff, "Urban Restructuring: An Analysis of Social and Spatial Change in Los Angeles," *Economic Geography* 59 (1983): 195–230; Roger Waldinger and Mehdi Bozorgmehr, eds., *Ethnic Los Angeles* (New York: Russell Sage, 1996).

25. Kristin Young, "The Living Wage Debate," *California Apparel News,* 31 January–6 February 1997, 6–7. Both the California Fashion Association, an organization of the major manufacturers, and the Downtown Property Owners Association, the major garment district real estate owners, opposed the ordinance.

Notes for Chapter 1. Manufacturers

1. According to Gerald Hall, the district director of the Los Angeles office of the Department of Labor, the number of apparel manufacturers in Los Angeles has been growing in recent years and is approaching 2,000. This number has not been verified.

2. Tom Adler, independent designer, PCH/Style-land Company, interview with authors, 24 June 1992.

3. Ibid.

4. Matt Kingman, production manager, PCH/Style-land Company, interview with authors, 26 August 1992.

5. Julie McElwain, "Dual Identity: Many of Today's Successful Manufacturers are Becoming Tomorrow's Top Merchants," *California Apparel News,* 17 June–23 June 1994, p. 8.

6. Characteristically, the actual sewing of the clothing is done in more than a thousand independent contracting factories throughout the world. Like most apparel manufacturers, the Gap, a retailer, does no direct manufacturing of its own.

7. The distinction between department and specialty stores will be discussed in Chapter 3. Briefly, department stores sell apparel and other goods, such as furniture, appliances, and housewares. Specialty stores concentrate on apparel.

8. Neal Breton, of Breton Industries, a prominent manufacturer, told us in an interview on 3 August 1992, that, although only a decade earlier, one could start a garment business for $50,000, by 1992 the price of entry was more than triple that amount.

9. Barbie Ludovose, "The Start of Something Big: The Next Cool Label Just May Be behind a Garage Door." *Los Angeles Times,* 30 May 1996, sec. E, p. 1, E4.

10. Cohn also founded Kaspare Cohn Hospital, which initially served persons associated with the garment industry. Kaspare Cohn Hospital became Cedars of Lebanon Hospital, eventually merging with Mount Sinai Hospital to become Cedars-Sinai Medical Center. Many prominent figures in the apparel industry today sit on the hospital board.

11. Bruce Corbin, regional vice president for administration, Union Bank, interview with the authors, 2 September 1992.

12. Thomas J. Ryan, "IPOs: Door Still Open, but not Wide." *Women's Wear Daily*, 1 December 1997, pp. 27–28; and "Selective Welcome Awaits Fashion IPOs." *Women's Wear Daily*, 13 April 1998, pp. 14–15.

13. *California Apparel News*, 1–7 January 1999, p. 4.

14. Larry Jacobs, "Sex, Lies and Factoring," *California Apparel News*, 26 December 1997–1 January 1998, p. 2.

15. Peg Brickley, "Apparel Manufacturers Turn to Factors for Everything from Fast Cash to In-Depth Forecasting," *Apparel Industry Magazine: Factoring Supplement*, February 1997, FS1.

16. Larry Jacobs, "Credit or Not," *California Apparel News*, 22–28 November, 1996, p. 7.

17. Sidney Rutberg, "Factors Log Solid Growth but not from Apparel and Textiles," *Women's Wear Daily*, 23 February 1998, pp. 16–17.

18. We wish to thank Farinaz Farshad for the excellent research she conducted on factoring.

19. States of California, Department of Finance, Demographic Research Unit, "Historical Census Populations of Places, Towns, and Cities in California, 1850–1990," (1998) available: http://www.dof.ca. gov/html/Demograp/histtext.htm.

20. Charles S. Goodman, *The Location of Fashion Industries, with Special Reference to the California Apparel Market* (Ann Arbor: University of Michigan Press, 1948), pp. 50–57.

21. Goodman, *Location of Fashion Industries*, p. 51.

22. Begun in 1964, the mart today spreads over three thirteen-story buildings that contain over 3 million square feet of retail space, house more than 1,500 showrooms representing over 10,000 collections. More than fifty fashion shows are produced there annually, including twenty specialty markets. CaliforniaMart, "CM Profile"; http://www.californiamart.com/About/cm_profile.html [2 February 1999].

23. The Standard Industrial Classification (SIC) 23: Apparel and Other Textile Products, includes both contractors and manufacturers. As a result, the Bureau of the Census, in its *County Business Patterns* and its *United States Census of Manufacturers*, which provide information about the the apparel industry in Los Angeles, combines the two categories, making the published data almost useless for understanding the industry.

24. To come up with our own estimates, we combined various sources. These included all manufacturers who registered with the state of California in order to obtain a license in 1989 and 1991; Dun & Bradstreet reports for 1990 and 1991; listings obtained from Fabric Marketing Resources, a private consulting firm, for 1991; and the Textile Association of Los Angeles directory for 1991. Once these sources were combined and duplicates eliminated, we came up with a total of 1,452 apparel manufacturers in Los Angeles, half of which had annual sales volumes of less than $1.2 million.

We wish to thank Patricia Hanneman for her indispensable help in creating, correcting, and analyzing this complex computer file. Chris Arnold and Brad Christerson also provided invaluable assistance with the analysis.

25. We have information on year of opening for 1,122 of the firms.

26. Don Lee, "Fashion Forward," *Los Angeles Times*, 26 April 1998, sec. D, p. 1.

27. Only three firms reported designing high-fashion couture apparel.

28. Our combined data bank had sales volume information on 1,269 firms. Because almost all of the apparel manufacturing firms in Los Angeles are privately owned, we used estimates of sales volume figures provided by Dun & Bradstreet and Fabric Marketing Resources.

29. We have data on direct employment for 909 firms (62.6 percent of the total). These 909 employed a total of 33,078 people, or an average of 36.4 per firm. If we assume that the 909 firms employ roughly twice as many people as the 543 firms for which we lack data, the total employment would be about 43,000 people.

30. We have the zip codes of all 1,452 of our manufacturing firms, which are spread out across 207 different zip codes. While three-quarters of these zip code areas have five firms or fewer in them, a mere eight have twenty or more firms, and three that lie in the downtown garment industry, 90014, 90015 and 90021, have more than 100 firms each.

31. See Fashion District of Los Angeles; available: http://www.dpoa.com/. A rough approximation would include five zip code areas: 90015 (with 243 manufacturers), 90014 (with 119), 90021 (with 105), 90007 (with 74), and 90079 (with 50). The last is the special zip code allocated to the CaliforniaMart. Some of the fifty manufacturers who gave this address may simply be listing their showrooms rather than their headquarters, although at least one garment firm we interviewed did use the mart as its office for contracting out production.

32. Zip code 90058, comprising much of Vernon, has fifty-seven apparel manufacturers. The "growth region" also includes zip code 90011, with eighteen firms.

33. California Employment Development Department, *Annual Planning Information: Los Angeles–Long Beach Metropolitan Statistical Area* (Sacramento, Calif.: Employment Development Department), 1993, 6.

34. Mimi Avins, "Rags and Riches." *Los Angeles Times,* 19 January, 1996, sec. E, p. 1; Kim-Van Dang, "Vendors of Vernon: NAFTA or No, the City of Vernon Is Home Sweet Home for Now to Some of the Biggest Players in L.A.'s Garment Industry," *Women's Wear Daily,* January 1994, p. 14. See also George White, "Rag Trade Flees to Suburbs: High Cost of L.A. Plant Space Is Driving Many Garment Manufacturers to Cities Such as Vernon," *Los Angeles Times,* 27 November 1989, sec. D, p. 5.

35. As a whole, apparel manufacturers in the city of Los Angeles average only $6.3 million in annual sales and 34.9 employees per firm.

36. Michell Glass, vice president of production, Cherokee Inc., interview with authors, 14 August 1991.

37. "Two Pair Pants Come with This Coat—A Perfect Fit: History of Jews in the Southern California Apparel Business." *Legacy: Journal of the Southern California Jewish Historical Society* 1 (spring 1988).

38. We have data on ethnicity for the owners of 1,362 firms. These data must be regarded as approximate because, with the exception of 184 of the largest firms, whose owners or managers we interviewed directly, ethnicity was inferred from the surname of the owner. Although ambiguous surnames were categorized as "other," our identification likely contains some errors.

39. Shelly Branch, "How Hip-Hop Fashion Won over Mainstream America," *Black Enterprise,* June 1993, p. 110; William Kissel, "Hot Urban Cool," *Los Angeles Times,* 24 July 1992, sec. E, p. 1.

40. Elizabeth Hayes, "Designer Denim," *Los Angeles Business Journal,* 27 April 1998, 38; "Biggest Black-Owned Business," *Los Angeles Times,* 5 July, 1996, sec. D, p. 2.

41. A. J. Nett, "Vision Quest." *Bobbin,* July 1995, pp. 86–88; James Flanigan, "Primed for Profit," *Los Angeles Times,* 13 September 1995, sec. D, p. 1; Karen E. Klein, "For Uniform Firm, a Sales Approach That Wears Well," *Los Angeles Times,* 29 October 1997, sec. D, p. 6.

42. Larry Jacobs, "Where Have All the Flowers Gone?" *California Apparel News,* 24–30 April 1998, p. 12.

43. The survey was conducted by Jean Gilbert, who did an excellent job of contacting the subjects and following up with the interviews. The data were then input by Patricia Hanneman, who helped analyze them. Using such sources as Dun & Bradstreet and Fabric Marketing Resources, we identified 255 apparel manufacturers in Los Angeles County with sales over $10 million a year (although once we completed the interviews, sixteen of those firms reported sales of less than $10 million). We were able to complete 195 interviews, producing 184 that were usable; some firms turned out to be located outside of Los Angeles County.

44. Cherokee licenses the right to manufacturer women's casual denim and sportswear, shoes, girls' apparel, sunglasses, and watches under its name; 70 percent of its revenues is derived from its licensing arrangements with Target. See Hoover's On-Line, http://www.hoovers.com/capsules/45345.html); see also, Cherokee, Inc., Securities and Exchange Commission Form 10-K for fiscal year ending 31 May 1997; EDGAR ON-LINE, available: http://www.edgar-online.com/bin/gethist/ ?doc-A-844161-0000898430-97-003053 [2 February 1999].

45. Kristin Young, "Cheers, California: Midyear Financial Report." *California Apparel News,* 18–24 July 1997, p. 6.

46. John Calvert of Stonefield Josephson Consulting speaking at an Apparel Industry Roundtable meeting, 1/10/96. See Chapter 8 for a description of the roundtable.

47. Don Lee, "Brazilian Koreans: A Force in Fashion." *Los Angeles Times,* 30 April 1998, sec. A, p. 1.

48. Quoted in Rose-Marie Turk, "An Eye for Style," *Los Angeles Times,* 2 June 1994, sec. E, p. 4. See also Kristi Ellis, "Rampage CEO Banks on Restructuring Judy's Inc.," *California Apparel News,* 5–11 February 1993, p. 2; Kim-Van Dang, "Rampage on a Retail Roll," *Women's Wear Daily,* 9 March 1994, p. 24.

49. "Clothier Declares Bankruptcy," *Los Angeles Business Journal,* 14 July 1997, p. 22; Kristi Ellis, "Russe Bid Wins Rampage," *Women's Wear Daily,* 24 September 1997, p. 36; "Charlotte Russe Outbids Wet Seal for Rampage Sites," *California Apparel News;* 19–25 September 1997, p. 6.

50. "BUM Files Chapter 11 to Drop Its Stores," *Women's Wear Daily,* 12 April 1996, p. 2; Kristin Young, "BUM International Files Chapter 11," *California Apparel News,* 12 April 1996, p. 3.

51. Yes Clothing Company, Securities and Exchange Commission Form 10-K

for fiscal year ending 31 March 1995, EDGAR ON-LINE, available: http://www.edgar-online.com/bin/gethist/?choice=2-180259&nad=0.

52. George Randall, chief executive officer of Yes Clothing Company, interview with authors, 3 March 1992.

53. Yes Clothing Company, Securities and Exchange Commission Form 10-K405 for fiscal year ending 31 March 1997; EDGAR ON-LINE, available: http://www. edgar-online.com/bin/gethist/?choice=2-733731&nad-0 [2 February 1999].

54. Donna K. H. Walters, "A Blossom Rises from the Ruins," *Los Angeles Times,* 3 May 1993, sec. D, p. 2.

55. Donna K. H. Walters, "Carole Little Sews Up Deal with Mayor Riordan," *Los Angeles Times,* 16 July 1993, sec. D, p. 2; A. J. Nett, "Big Expansion for Carole Little," *Bobbin,* October 1994, pp. 76–79.

56. Hoover's On-Line; available: http.//www.hoovers.com/capsules/42561. html.

57. Scott Collins, "A Hollywood Segue: Fashion to Screen," *Los Angeles Times,* 14 April 1997, sec. F, p. 1; Louise Farr, "Snake Charmers," *Women's Wear Daily,* 17 April 1997, p. 20.

58. George White and Vicki Torres, "L.A. Apparel Maker Rocked by Three Slayings," *Los Angeles Times,* 18 May 1995, sec. D, p. 1; Paul Lieberman, "Gunman Convicted in Clothing Firm Slaying," *Los Angeles Times,* 14 February 1996, sec. B, p. 1.

59. Kristin Young, "Outrageous Fortune," *California Apparel News,* 22–28 August 1997, pp. 8–9; Larry Kanter, "Move Over Calvin Klein," *Los Angeles Business Journal,* 13 October 1997, p. 28. Anne D'Innocenzio, "BCBG Acquires Browner," *Women's Wear Daily,* 23 July 1996, p. 2; idem, "Contemporary's New Personality," *Women's Wear Daily,* 27 March 1996, pp. 8–9; "California Designers Recognized," *Bobbin,* February 1996, p. 63; Geraldine Baum, "Storming the Tents," *Los Angeles Times,* 5 April 1996, sec. E, p. 1.

60. Jalate Ltd., Securities and Exchange Commission Form 10-K405 for fiscal year ending 31 December 1997; EDGAR ON-LINE, available: http://www. edgar-online.com/bin/gethist/?choice=2-988504&nad=0.

61. Ibid.

62. *Business Wire,* available: http://www.businesswire.com [7 April 1998].

63. Tarrant Apparel Group, Securities and Exchange Commission Form 10-K405 for fiscal year ending 31 December 1997; EDGAR ON-LINE, available: http://www.edgar-online.com/bin/gethist/?doc=A-944948-0000898430-98-000690 [2 February 1999].

64. *Business Wire;* accessed 23 February 1998.

65. Ibid.; accessed 27 April 1998.

66. Guess? Inc., Securities and Exchange Commission Form 10-K405 for fiscal year ending 31 December 1997; EDGAR ON-LINE, available: http://www. edgar-online.com/bin/gethist/?choice=2-98511&nad=0.

67. Richard Behar and Shaifali Puri, "Guess What's Behind This IPO?" *Fortune Magazine,* 14 October 1996, p. 133.

68. Ibid., p. 135.

69. Christopher Byron, *Skin Tight: The Bizarre Story of Guess v. Jordache—Glamour, Greed and Dirty Tricks in the Fashion Industry* (New York: Simon and Schuster, 1993).

70. Jim Schachter, "Lawyer Awarded $23.1 million in Guess Suit," *Los Angeles Times,* 26 April 1994, sec. D, p. 1.

71. George White, "Ex-Guess Chairman Sues over Trademark Use," *Los Angeles Times,* 29 December 1993, sec. D, p. 4.

72. Guess? Inc., Form 10-K405.

Notes for Chapter 2. Offshore Production

1. Rhonda L. Rundle, "Guess Transfers Manufacturing to Mexico amid Labor Charges," *Wall Street Journal,* 14 January 1997. Stuart Silverstein, George White, and Mary Beth Sheridan, "Guess Inc. to Move Much of L.A. Work South of Border," *Los Angeles Times,* 15 January 1997, sec. A p. 1; Elena de la Cruz, "Firma Guess traslada operaciones a Mexicó," *La Opinión,* 15 January 1997.

2. Roger Waldinger, *Through the Eye of the Needle: Immigrants and Enterprise in New York's Garment Trades* (New York: New York University Press, 1986), 54–56.

3. Sally Kurtzman, interview by authors, 3 March 1992.

4. See, for example, Chung-In Moon, "Trade Frictions and Industrial Adjustment: The Textiles and Apparel Industry in the Pacific Basin," *Pacific Focus* 2, no. 1 (1987): 105–33.

5. United States Department of Commerce data presented in Gary Gereffi, "Global Sourcing and Regional Divisions of Labor in the Pacific Rim," pp. 51–68 in Arif Dirlik, ed., *What Is in a Rim? Critical Perspectives on the Pacific Region Idea* (Boulder, Colo.: Westview Press, 1993).

6. GATT data, cited by Kitty G. Dickerson, *Textiles and Apparel in the International Economy* (New York: Macmillan, 1991), tables 6–12 through 6–14.

7. Data from *Demand, Production and Trade in Textiles and Clothing: Statistical Report to the Secretariat.* Textiles Committee, General Agreement on Tariffs and Trade (GATT), United Nations Statistical Division, 1993.

8. United States Bureau of the Census, *United States General Imports.* (Washington, D.C., 1992).

9. General Agreement on Tariffs and Trade (GATT), Textiles Committee, *Demand, Production and Trade in Textiles and Clothing: Statistical Report to the Secretariat* (New York: United Nations Statistical Division, 1993).

10. United States Department of Commerce, International Trade Commission, Office of Textiles and Apparel, "Major Shippers Report: Section One: Textiles and Apparel Imports by Category"; available: http://otexa.ita.doc.gov/ msr/catv0.htm [30 May 1998]. Imports of apparel only from Mexico in 1997 reached $5.1 billion, from China were $4.5 billion and from Hong Kong were $3.9 billion; ibid., available: http://otexa.ita.doc.gov/msr/catv1.htm [30 May 1998].

11. In 1996, the value of imports of apparel and related textiles totaled $48 billion; the value of exports was $8.1 billion. United States Department of Commerce, Office of Trade and Economic Analysis, "Trends Tables: Apparel and Other Textile Products (SIC 23)" in United States Industry Sector Data; available: http://www.ita.doc.gov/industry/otea/usito98/tables/23.txt [30 May 1998].

12. American Apparel Manufacturers Association, *1997 Focus. An Economic Profile of the Apparel Industry* (Arlington Vt.: AAMA, 1997), chart A, p. 4.

13. Subsequently, paragraph 9802, but still commonly referred to as 807.

14. The MFA followed several earlier multilateral restrictive agreements among the major trading nations, the most important of which was the so-called Long-Term Arrangement, which was in force from 1962 until it was superseded by the MFA. For a detailed history of the regulation of textiles and apparel, see Vinod Aggarwal, *Liberal Protectionism: The International Politics of Organized Textile Trade* (Berkeley, Calif.: University of California Press, 1985); also, see chapter 10 (on which much of the present discussion is based) of Kitty G. Dickerson, *Textiles and Apparel in the International Economy,* 2d ed. (New York: Macmillan, 1995).

15. Currently United States quota restrictions are triggered when exports to the United States exceed one percent of a country's total trade.

16. Another effect of quotas has been to encourage the illegal transshipment of goods from low-wage countries with limited quotas (such as China) through higher-wage countries with large quota allocations (such as Hong Kong and Taiwan). Such "submarined" goods constitute a large volume of global apparel trade, providing much work for United States customs officials, authors' interview with Thomas Gray, Special Agent, United States Customs Office, Hong Kong, 29 November 1991.

17. United States Department of Commerce, International Trade Administration Office (NAFTA), "NAFTA Key Provisions"; available: http://iepnt1.itaiep.doc.gov/nafta/3002.htm [May 30 1998].

18. Both authors have written on this topic in the past, so we refer our readers to these works for more extensive treatment. See Richard P. Appelbaum, David Smith, and Brad Christerson, "Commodity Chains and Industrial Restructuring in the Pacific Rim: Garment Trade and Manufacturing," pp. 197–204 in *Commodity Chains and Global Capitalism,* ed. Gary Gereffi and Miguel Korzeniewicz (Westport, Conn.: Greenwood, 1994); Edna Bonacich, Lucie Cheng, Norma Chinchilla, Nora Hamilton, and Paul Ong, eds., *Global Production: The Garment Industry in the Pacific Rim* (Philadelphia: Temple University Press, 1994); Richard P. Appelbaum and Brad Christerson, "Cheap Labor Strategies and Export-Oriented Industrialization: Some Lessons from the East Asia/Los Angeles Apparel Connection," *The International Journal of Urban and Regional Research* 21, no. 2 (June 1997): 202–17; Brad Christerson and Richard P. Appelbaum, "Global and Local Subcontracting: Space, Ethnicity, and the Organization of Apparel Production," *World Development* 23, no. 8 (1995): 1363–74.

19. Brent Klopp, senior vice president for production planning, Bugle Boy Industries, interview by authors, 11 October 1991. All information concerning Bugle Boy is from this interview.

20. Don Lee, "Fashion Forward," *Los Angeles Times,* 26 April 1998, sec. D, p. 1.

21. "B.U.M. moves to Rhode Island," *California Apparel News,* 2 October 1997, p. 7.

22. Jeff Richards, production manager, B.U.M. Equipment, interview by authors with the assistance of Edward Tchakalian, 19 August 1994.

23. Gene Light, senior vice president for manufacturing, Chorus Line Corp., interview by authors with the assistance of Edward Tchakalian, 25 August 1994.

24. Silverstein, White, and Sheridan, "Guess Inc. to Move."

25. Interview with Kenneth Martin, senior vice president for manufacturing and sourcing, Carole Little, interview by authors with the assistance of Edward Tchakalian, 1 September 1994. Martin was murdered in December 1994, in a string of killings and attempted murders of Carole Little personnel that occurred between 1993 and 1995 (see Chapter 1).

26. Mitch Glass, vice president for production, sourcing and scheduling, Cherokee, Inc., interview by authors, 14 August 1991.

27. Judi Kessler, "Southern California: Transition takes Hold," *Bobbin,* October 1998, pp. 30–38.

28. Larry Kaner, "Levi's Move Overseas Paralleled in L.A. Apparel Trade," *Los Angeles Business Journal,* 8 March 1999, p. 5.

29. Cited in Larry Kanter, "Guess Defection Unlikely to Spark Garment Exodus." *Los Angeles Business Journal,* 20 January 1997, p. 1.

30. Cited in Kristi Ellis, "The Southern Draw," *Women's Wear Daily,* Los Angeles Fall I, March 1997, pp. 26–29. See also Kristin Young, "Guess Move Begs Question: Is California Business Friendly?" *California Apparel News,* 17–23 January 1997, p. 3.

31. Young, "Guess Move."

32. "Union Files New Charges against Guess," *Los Angeles Times,* 18 January 1997, sec. D p. 2.

33. This issue is complicated by the contracting system, under which Guess can shift its contracting offshore without moving its headquarters out of Los Angeles. Because the contractors, both here and in Mexico, are ostensibly independent, Guess can claim that *it* has not moved offshore, even though its production has.

34. Rundle, "Guess Transfers Manufacturing."

35. This is the number of licensed factories; there are reportedly at least as many "underground" factories.

36. The delegation included representatives of the National Interfaith Committee for Worker Justice, the National Association of Working Women, the Women of Color Resource Center, the Commission on Social Action of Reform Judaism, the Los Angeles Jewish Commission on Sweatshops, the Rural Organizing Project of Oregon, UNITE, and the Highlander Research and Education Center.

37. National Interfaith Committee for Worker Justice, "Cross-Border Blues: A Call for Justice for Denim Workers in Tehuacán Maquiladoras (pamphlet), National Interfaith Committee for Worker Justice, Chicago, Ill., June 1998, 5.

38. Silverstein, White, and Sheridan, "Guess Inc. to Move."

39. Rick Wartzman, "Apparel Data Look Great (But Don't Count on It)," *Wall Street Journal,* 15 January 1997.

40. Ellis, "The Southern Draw." In fact, the number of jobs between September 1996 (112,700) and February 1997 (112,800) was virtually unchanged; in 1997 some 7,300 jobs were added (from 109,700 in December 1996 to 117,000 in December 1997); State of California, EDD.

41. Silverstein, White, and Sheridan, "Guess Inc. to Move."

42. Quoted in Wartzman, "Apparel Data Look Great."

43. Jeff Mowdy, production manager, Francine Browner, Inc., interview by Edward Tchakalian, 22 August 1994.

44. Kanter, "Guess Defection."

45. Ibid.

46. Mowdy, interview. In mid-1996 Francine Browner, Inc. was bought by BCBG Max Azria, a growing fashion powerhouse, leaving unclear what the future sourcing policies of the company will be; Kristin Young, "BCBG Acquires Francine Browner," *California Apparel News,* 28 July to 1 August 1996, 4.

47. Gus Leonard, interview by authors, May 1995.

48. Kanter, "Guess Defection."

49. Ibid.

50. Ellis, "The Southern Draw."

51. Ibid.

52. Joel Kotkin, "Is Having a Garment Industry Worth All the Trouble?" *Los Angeles Times,* 19 January 1997, sec. M p. 6.

53. Don Lee, "Fashion Forward."

54. Allen J. Scott, "The Craft, Fashion, and Cultural Products Industries of Los Angeles: Competitive Dynamics and Policy Dilemmas in a Multisectoral Image-Producing Complex," *Annals of the Association of American Geographers* 86 (1996): 306–23; Allen J. Scott and David L. Rigby, "The Craft Industries of Los Angeles: Prospects for Economic Growth and Development," *CPS Brief,* California Policy Seminar 8 July 1996 Berkeley; David L. Rigby, "The Apparel Industry in Southern California," Geography Department, University of California at Los Angeles, 1995.

55. Allen Scott, "Craft, Fashion, and Cultural Products," 307.

56. For an interesting discussion, see Harvey L. Molotch, "Art in Economy: How Aesthetics and Design Build Los Angeles," *Competition and Change: The Journal of Global Business and Political Economy* 1 no. 2 (1995): 145–85; and "L.A. as Product: How Design Works in a Regional Economy," pp. 225–75 in *The City: Los Angeles and Urban Theory at the End of the Twentieth Century,* ed. Allen J. Scott and Edward W. Soja (Berkeley, Calif.: University of California Press, 1996).

57. See Chapter 1 for a brief discussion of the history of the apparel industry in relation to Hollywood.

58. See, for example, Michael E. Porter, *The Competitive Advantage of Nations* (New York: The Free Press, 1990); Allen J. Scott, "Flexible Production Systems and Regional Development," *International Journal of Urban and Regional Research* 12 (1988): 171–86; Michael J. Piore and Charles F. Sabel, *The Second Industrial Divide: Possibilities for Prosperity* (New York: Basic Books, 1984); Michael Storper and Richard Walker, *The Capitalist Imperative: Territory, Technology and Industrial Growth* (New York: Blackwell, 1989). For a case study of the importance of agglomeration in the electronics industry of southern California, see Allen J. Scott, *Technopolis: High-Technology Industry and Regional Development in Southern California* (Berkeley, Calif.: University of California Press, 1993).

59. H. Hakansson, ed. *International Marketing and Purchasing of Industrial*

Goods, 2d ed. (Chichester, England: John Wiley, 1982); T. H. Willis and C. R. Hutson. "Vendor Requirements and Evaluation in a Just-in-Time Environment," *International Journal of Purchasing Management* 10 no. 4 (1990): 41–50; Mark Granovetter, "Economic Action and Social Structure: The Problem of Embeddedness," *American Journal of Sociology* 9 no. 3 (1985): 481–510; Richard Walker, "The Geographical Organization of Production-Systems," *Environment and Planning* 6 no. 4 (1988): 377–408.

60. Sidney Morse, interview by authors, 28 October 1992.

61. David Morse, at the time managing partner of CaliforniaMart, interview by authors, 7 January 1992.

62. Sidney Morse, interview.

63. CaliforniaMart; available: http://www.californiamart.com/About/cm_profile.html [11 June 1998].

64. Susan Morse-Lebow, at the time responsible for financial operations, interview by authors, 27 August 1992. This projected building was never undertaken, although millions of dollars were invested in it. "Thank God we didn't do it," said Susan. "We cut our losses."

65. This description of CaliforniaMart comes from its promotional materials, including a Press Fact Sheet, a History, and the regularly released Directories.

66. Susan had just had a child at the time of our interview, and was pregnant again, which limited her involvement in the family business. David decided to devote his full energy to Mart Management International, becoming the sole partner of what had initially been another family venture to develop an Asian version of the CaliforniaMart. The Trade Mart Singapore billed itself as the region's first integrated resource center for the wholesale fashion trade by linking Hong Kong, Indonesia, Malaysia, the Philippines, South Korea, Taiwan, Thailand, and Singapore in an effort to become "the centre of Asia's fashion business." The $140-million project was a joint venture between Mart Management International and Parkway Holdings of Singapore. In 1998, Trade Mart Singapore offered some 300 wholesale fashion showrooms and offices; Trade Mart Singapore; available: http://www.tmsinfo.com [11 June 1998].

67. Sidney Morse, interview. This assertion was contested by Bruce Corbin, the regional vice president for administration of Union Bank, who claimed that the high interest rates of the early 1980s had long since declined, and that money was available, but that the difficulties in the industry (which he characterized as "treacherous") made most manufacturers bad credit risks (Bruce Corbin, interview by authors, 2 September 1992).

68. Cash-and-carry refers to the production of goods that are already manufactured and are available for immediate sale to retailers; conventionally, garments are manufactured only on specific orders from retailers.

69. Corbin, interview; Ronald Jones, CPA and managing partner, Moss Adams LLP, interview by authors, 9 November 1992.

70. Marty Josephson, interview by authors, 4 November 1992.

71. Jones, interview; Josephson, interview.

72. For example, in May 1997 representatives of the Economic Development Corporation in Los Angeles met with leaders in art and design education, including representatives of Otis College of Art and Design and the Fashion Institute of

Design and Merchandising to investigate the feasibility of hosting an annual international *L.A. by Design* show that would feature the apparel, entertainment, furniture, toy, and food industries; *California Apparel News,* 16 May 1997, 4.

73. "Education: How Do You Keep the Apparel Industry Stocked with Talent?" *California Apparel News,* 3 to 9 July 1998, sec. A, p. 1.

74. S. J. Diamond, "Designing the Future," *Los Angeles Times,* 15 November 1992, sec. E, p. 1.

75. These include El Camino College in Torrance, Fullerton College, Glendale College, Long Beach City College, Los Angeles Valley College in Van Nuys, Orange Coast College in Costa Mesa, Palomar College in San Marcos, Pasadena City College, Rancho Santiago College in Santa Ana, Saddleback College in Mission Viejo, and San Diego Mesa College; *California Apparel News,* 18 to 24 June 1993, 10.

76. For a more detailed discussion, see Bonacich et al., *Global Production.*

Notes for Chapter 3. Retailers

1. Kurt Salmon Associates, Retail Services Group. "Retailing: The Changing game." *Bobbin,* January 1989, p. 56.

2. Matt Kingman, production manager, PCH Style-Land Company, interview by authors, 26 August 1992.

3. Barry Bluestone, Patricia Hanna, Sarah Kuhn, and Laura Moore. *The Retail Revolution: Market Transformation, Investment, and Labor in the Modern Department Store* (Boston: Auburn House, 1981). See also Thierry J. Noyelle, *Beyond Industrial Dualism: Market and Job Segmentation in the New Economy* (Boulder, Colo.: Westview, 1987), 19–49.

4. Noyelle, *Beyond Industrial Dualism,* 20–21.

5. Bluestone, et al., *Retail Revolution,* 15–29. Noyelle, *Beyond Industrial Dualism,* p. 21, adds a sixth type, distinguishing mass merchandisers, such as Sears and J. C. Penney, from department-store chains such as Macy's and Marshall Field.

6. Gary Gereffi, "The Role of Big Buyers in Global Commodity Chains: How U.S. Retail Networks Affect Overseas Production Patterns" (paper presented at the sixteenth annual Political Economy of the World System Conference, Durham, N.C. April 1992).

7. Nordstrom, Inc. "How We Got Our Start"; available: http://www.nordstrom-pta.com/aboutus/ _aboutus.html [26 June 1998].

8. Michael Steinberg, chairman of Macy's West, cited in Kristin Young, "Federated Says It Will Boost California Economy," *California Apparel News,* 5 to 11 April 1996, p. 3.

9. Isadore Barmash. *Macy's for Sale* (New York: Weidenfeld and Nicolson, 1989).

10. For a full account of the early years of the Campeau story, see John Rothchild, *Going for Broke: How Robert Campeau Bankrupted the Retail Industry, Jolted the Junk Bond Market, and Brought the Booming Eighties to a Crashing Halt* (New York: Simon and Schuster, 1991).

11. Cathleen Ferraro, "R. H. Macy Finally Runs Out of Miracles," *Business Investor's Daily,* 28 January 1992, pp. 1–2.

12. Federated Department Stores, "History," 1998; available: http://www.federated-fds.com/ index.shtml [27 June 1998].

13. Sidney Rutberg, "Federated's Broadway Buy: Wall Street's Paper Chase," *Women's Wear Daily*, 28 August 1995, p. 23.

14. "Financial Advisors to Make $4M on Broadway Deal," *Women's Wear Daily*, 28 August 1995, p. 23.

15. "Broadway's Dworkin Could Reap $5M due to Federated Merger," *Women's Wear Daily*, 25 August 1995, p. 2. This was a lot less than was made by Roger Farah when he left R. H. Macy after serving just two months as president. He was given a severance pay of $14 million.

16. Federated Department Stores, Inc., "FDS at a Glance"; available: http://www.federated-fds.com/index.html) [27 June 1998].

17. Hoover's On-Line, "Federated Department Stores, Inc.: Capsule"; available: http://www.hoovers.com/cgi-bin/brand_EDGAR_mlist.cgi?mode=full&symbol=FD [26 June 1998].

18. Cathleen Ferraro, "Dayton to Pay $1.04 bil for Marshall Field," *Business Investor's Daily*, 20 April 1990, p. 1; Nancy Garman, ed., *Directory of Foreign Investment in the U.S.: Real Estate and Businesses* (Detroit, Mich.: Gale Research, 1991), 428; Cathleen Ferraro, "BAT to Sell Saks Fifth Avenue to Arab Group for $1.5 Billion," *Business Investor's Daily*, 26 April 1990, p. 34.

19. In 1972, there were only eight square feet of retail space per capita, with average sales of about $235 per square foot (in 1992 dollars). Dick Silverman, "Has Expansion Boom Finally Brought Retail to Saturation Point?" *Women's Wear Daily*, 30 October 1997, p. 10.

20. Vicki M. Young, "Bankruptcies Ebbing," *Women's Wear Daily*, 15 July 1998, p. 30.

21. James Flanigan, "Can the Department Store Survive?" *Los Angeles Times*, 16 August 1995, sec. A p. 1.

22. Jackie Jones, "Forces Behind Restructuring in U.S. Apparel Retailing and Its Effect on the U.S. Apparel Industry" (1993), United States International Trade Commission; available: http://www.usitc. gov/332s/ITTREXMP.HTM [24 March 1999]. See also, Gary Gereffi, "The Organization of Buyer-Driven Commodity Chains: How U.S. Retailers Shape Overseas Production," in *Commodity Chains and Global Capitalism,* Gary Gereffi and Miguel Korzeniewicz, eds. (Westport, Conn.: Greenwood Press, 1994); Richard P. Appelbaum and Gary Gereffi, "Power and Profits in the Apparel Commodity Chain," pp. 95–122 in *Global Production: The Apparel Industry in the Pacific Rim,* eds. Edna Bonacich, Lucie Cheng, Norma Chinchilla, Norma Hamilton, and Paul Ong (Philadelphia, Pa: Temple University Press, 1994).

23. Kristin Young, "Cheers, California: Midyear Financial Report," *California Apparel News,* 18 to 24 July 1997.

24. Kurt Salmon Associates, "A Survival Course for the Nineties," *KSA Perspective,* 1990.

25. Hoover's On-Line, "The May Department Store Company: Capsule"; http://www.hoovers.com/cgi-bin/brand_EDGAR_mlist.cgi?mode=full&symbol=MAY [27 June 1998].

26. David Morse, interview by authors, 7 January 1992.

27. Stanley Hirsh, interview by authors, 6 February 1992.

28. Mona Danford, interview by authors, 27 August 1992.

29. John Metzger, the founder and chief executive officer of Creditek, a financial services outsourcing company based in New Jersey, quoted in Jane Applegate, "Apparel Makers Seeking to Reduce Shipping Charge-Back Penalties," *Los Angeles Times*, 12 August 1997, sec. D, p. 10.

30. Sammy Lee, vice president of Contempo Casuals, interview by authors, 14 May 1993.

31. Standard and Poor's, *Industry Surveys: Textiles, Apparel and Home Furnishings: Basic Analysis*, no. 163, 9/28/95, p. T99.

32. Standard and Poor's, *Industry Surveys: Textiles*.

33. KSA, "Retailing."

34. William Kapler, Kapler and Associates, interview by authors, 1992.

35. Karen J. Sack, "Retail Current Analysis: Productivity and Value Pricing Lure Customers," pp. R62–64, in Standard and Poor's, *Industry Surveys*, 9 January 1992.

36. Joan Berk, interview by authors, 29 June 1992.

37. Jim Cunningham, vice president for offshore sourcing, The Gap (Far East) Ltd., Hong Kong, interview by authors, 28 November 1991.

38. Sack, "Retail Current Analysis," pp. R62–63.

39. Andy Reinhardt, "Business at Net Speed," *Business Week*, 21 June 1998, p. 134.

40. American Apparel Manufacturers Association, *Flexible Apparel Manufacturing* (Arlington, Va.: AAMA, 1988).

41. Reinhardt, "Business at Net Speed," 138.

42. Robert D. Hoff, "The 'Click Here' Economy: On-Line Sales Are Soaring," *Business Week*, 22 June 1998, p. 124.

43. The publishers of *Business Week*, envisioning $327 billion in "e-commerce" by 2002 (it is only $20 billion today), are positively giddy in proclaiming, in their annual report on information technology, that the new age "is nothing less than the collapse of time and space between partners," "Doing Business in the Internet Age," *Business Week*, 22 July 1998, p. 124. See also Joe Pine, *Mass Customization: The New Frontier in Business Competition* (Cambridge, Mass.: Harvard Business School Press, 1992).

44. Neil Gross, "The Supply Chain: Leapfrogging a Few Links," *Business Week*, 22 June 1998, p. 140.

45. Bob Greenburg, an accountant with Moss Adams, one of the largest apparel accounting firms in Los Angeles, quoted in Kristin Young, "Cheers, California," 11.

46. Bureau of Wholesale Sales Representatives, *The Retailer: The Basics of Apparel Retailing* (Atlanta, Ga.: Bureau of Wholesale Sales Representatives, 1990), 17.

47. Standard and Poor's, *Industry Surveys: Textiles*, T93.

48. Bureau of Wholesale Sales Representatives, *The Retailer*, 19.

49. Bill Chapman, accounting manager for Seattle Pacific Industries, quoted in Applegate, "Apparel Makers," sec. D p. 10.

50. Ellen Bradley, a principal with Frederick Atkins buying office, interview by authors, 3 March 1992.

51. Laura Bird and Wendy Bounds, "Stores' Demands Squeeze Apparel Companies," *Wall Street Journal,* 15 July 1997, sec. B, p. 1.

52. Sammy Lee, interview.

53. Danford, interview; Barbara Fields, president, Barbara Fields Buying Office, interview by authors, 14 August 1992.

54. Bradley, interview.

55. Fields, interview.

56. Danford, interview.

57. Bradley, interview.

58. Fields, interview.

59. Bradley, interview.

60. Ruth Bregman, partner in Arkin/California, interview by authors, 23 September 1992.

61. Hoover's On-Line, "Company Capsule: The Gap"; available: http://www.hoovers.com/capsules/ 11469.html [28 June 1998].

62. Cunningham, interview.

63. Sharon Edelson, "Fueled by Designers, Private Label Moves to a Higher Plateau," *Women's Wear Daily,* 1 March 1999, p. 8.

64. Matt Kingman, managing director, Impact Textiles Company Ltd., Hong Kong, interview by authors, 30 September 1996.

65. Danford and Bradley, interviews.

66. Kingman, interview, 26 August 1992.

67. Ellen Newborne and Stephanie Anderson, "Look Who's Picking Levi's Pocket," *Business Week,* 8 September 1997, pp. 68–72.

68. Greg Johnson, "Levi Struggles to Reclaim Share As Tastes Shift," *The Detroit News,* 9 November 1997; available: http://www.detnews.com/1997/biz/9711/10/11090030.htm [28 June 1998].

69. Compound annual growth rate, 1987–1997. Gap sales grew by 23.2 percent in 1997 alone. Hoover's On-Line, "Company Capsule: The Gap."

70. Newborne and Anderson, "Look," 68.

71. Neil Breton, head of Breton Industries, interview by authors, 3 August 1992.

72. Hoover's On-Line, "Company Capsule: Bugle Boy Industries"; available: http://www.hoovers.com/capsules/40690.html [28 June 1998].

73. Hoover's On-Line, "Company Capsule: Guess"; available: http://www.hoovers.com/cgi-bin/brand_EDGAR_mlist.cgi?mode=full&symbol=GES [28 June 1998].

74. Standard and Poor's, *Industry Surveys: Textiles,* T75–T81.

Notes for Chapter 4. The Power Elite

1. See Chapter 7 for an examination of the distribution of wealth in the industry and the results of the power relations described in this chapter.

2. Our information comes from annual listings by *California Apparel News* of leaders in the industry, members and boards of directors of various influential organizations, the attendance at charitable events, and coverage in the apparel press.

3. Bruce Corbin, interview by the authors, 2 September 1992.

4. Our analysis relied on data provided by Dataquick, a commercial real estate information broker that sells access to an electronic database of all parcels in the state of California. The records we studied were obtained by Dataquick from the Los Angeles County Assessor's office, and are updated quarterly. The data were collected by David Waller, then a graduate student at the University of California at Riverside, between August 1992 and February 1993.

5. Julie McElwain, "CFA and CAIC Merge: Fashion Association Surviving Entity." *California Apparel News,* 3 to 9 April 1998, p. 3.

6. Kristi Ellis, "Industry Moves to Enhance Image: Apparel Businesses Unite to Clean Up the Area, Insure Buyers' Safety and Keep Fragmentation at Bay," *Women's Wear Daily,* October 1995, pp. 18–21.

7. "$300,000 HUD Grant Awarded." *Downtown Property Owners Association News,* Fall 1995, p. 2.

8. "With New Look, It's Now 'Fashion District.' " *Los Angeles Times,* November 1995, sec. B p. 2.

9. Kristi Ellis, "Mayor Riordan Convenes Industry Roundtable," *California Apparel News,* 24 February to 2 March 1995, p. 8.

10. "Los Angeles," *Women's Wear Daily,* March 1999, p. 6.

11. Idem, "Apparel Leaders Form Association," *California Apparel News,* 18 to 24 August 1995, p. 5.

12. Ibid.

13. California Fashion Association, advertisement; *California Apparel News,* 13 to 19 November 1995, p. 5.

14. We thank Nir Oliver for putting us on to this rich vein of research by casually mentioning the United Jewish Fund's Fashion Division at a dinner party. It was through the Fund that we learned of other charities supported by people in the apparel industry.

15. Jewish Federation Council of Greater Los Angeles, United Jewish Fund, 1998; available: http://www.jewishla.org/html/united_jewish_fund.html [14 June 1998].

16. Tracy Baum, Judy Fischer, and Karen Schetina, interview by authors, 30 June 1992.

17. Barbara Markell, development associate, community relations, Cedars-Sinai Medical Center, interview by authors, 11 August 1992; advertisement book from 1992 Fashion Industries Guild dinner dance. According to the ad book, some of the money raised was used to endow the Seventh Floor South Patient Tower Barry Morse Rehabilitation Center, the Harvey S. Morse Conference Center, the Arrhythmia Electrophysiology Research Program, and to purchase two two-dimensional echocardiograph machines. In 1991 the *Fashion Industries Guild* made its last payment on the Florence and Duke Becker Building; Sidney "Duke" Becker, a partner of the Morses, had been one of the principals of the CaliforniaMart.

18. Sharon Canady, director, Merchants Group, City of Hope Hospital, interview by authors, October 1992. See also, *Legacy of Hope: Celebrating City of Hope's 80th Anniversary,* (Los Angeles: City of Hope, 1993), p. 6; and "Two Pair Pants Come with This Coat—A Perfect Fit: History of Jews in the Southern Cal-

ifornia Apparel Business," *Legacy: Journal of the Southern California Jewish Historical Society* 1 (spring 1988): 9.

19. Karen Paull, director, Professionals and Finance Association, City of Hope, interview by authors, 8 February 1994.

20. Canady, interview; a colloquialism (*schmatte* means "rag" as in "rag trade").

21. Lee Graff, chairman and chief executive officer of Graff Californiawear, and Cece Robman, interview by authors, 30 November 1992. We are grateful to Sharon Canady for setting up this interview for us.

22. Paull, interview.

23. The California Fashion Creators was an organization that became obsolete with the opening of CaliforniaMart. It was looked at with nostalgia by some prominent members of the industry, including Norma Persky of the Coalition of Apparel Industries of California, who said, "That was a different era, when manufacturers worked together. Competition wasn't so vicious. They were a different breed" (interview by authors, 8 November 1996).

24. Sidney Morse, interview by authors, 9 November 1992.

25. George White, "Sweatshop Exhibit Gives Voice to Abuse," *Los Angeles Times,* 19 April 1998, sec. D, p. 1.

26. Quoted in "Industry Says No to Museum Exhibit," *California Apparel News,* 19 to 25 September 1997, p. 16.

27. Quoted in Joanna Ramey, "Trade Groups Snub Smithsonian Exhibit," *Women's Wear Daily,* 12 September 1997, p. 15.

28. Quoted in George White, "Plan for Sweatshop Exhibition Draws Fire," *Los Angeles Times,* 11 September 1997, sec. A, p. 1.

29. George White, "Trade Group Now Supports Sweatshop Exhibit," *Los Angeles Times,* 27 March 1998, sec. D, p. 3; "NRF Reverses Position, Backs Smithsonian Sweatshop Show," *Women's Wear Daily,* 30 March 1998, p. 14.

30. Kristin Young, "Smithsonian Exhibit Splits Trade Groups," *California Apparel News,* 10 to 16 April 1998, p. 1.

31. Idem, "The Living Wage Debate," *California Apparel News,* 31 January to 6 February 1997, pp. 6–7.

32. Morse, interview.

33. Stanley Hirsh, interview by authors, 6 February 1992.

34. Jonathan Bernstein, interview by authors, 23 September 1992.

35. George Randall, interview by authors, 3 March 1992.

36. "Wage Survey of Manufacturers, Contractors Under Way: Network Wants to Give Clear Picture of Industry to Pols, Others," *California Apparel News,* 10 to 16 April 1998, p. A-6. The survey has since been published: Linda J. Wong, "The Los Angeles Apparel Industry Wage and Occupational Survey: 1998 Report" (Los Angeles: Community Development Technologies Center, 1999).

37. Jack Kyser, "Advice to Industry: Dress Yourself for Success," *California Apparel News,* 10 to 16 April 1998, p. A-2.

38. Quoted in Alison A. Nieder, "Welfare to Work Inspires Opposing View of Industry," *California Apparel News,* 5 to 11 June 1998, p. 9.

39. Kristin Young. "Debate over Smithsonian Exhibit Heats Up," *California Apparel News,* 29 August to 4 September 1997, p. 4.

40. Joel Kotkin, "A Union's War on Workers," *Wall Street Journal,* 9 December 1997, p. A22.

41. "Just Deserts? Joel Kotkin Believes California's Apparel Industry Must Work Quickly to Shed its Unseemly Image," *California Apparel News,* 11 to 17 April 1997, pp. 12–13.

42. February 1998, pp. 3–4.

43. Richard Reinis, quoted in "Fashion Leaders Go to Washington," *California Apparel News,* 18 to 24 July 1997, p. 5.

44. Alan C. Miller and Dwight Morris, "Political Gold Rush in L.A.," *Los Angeles Times,* 26 January 1992, sec. A, p. 1.

45. Glenn F. Bunting and Dwight Morris, "109 Donors Top Federal Limits in Campaign Contributions," *Los Angeles Times,* 15 November 1993, sec. A, p. 1.

46. *California Apparel News,* 6 to 11 November 1993, p. 17.

47. Bunting and Morris, "109 Donors."

48. Dan Morain, "Garamendi's Campaign Running on Lean Funding," *Los Angeles Times,* 10 April 1994, sec. A, p. 1.

49. Greg Goldin, "Trials and Errors: Gil Garcetti's Troubled Tenure as D.A.," *L.A. Weekly* 22 to 26 March 1996, 29–34; Alan Abrahamson, "Garcetti Rivals Hammer at Propriety Issue," *Los Angeles Times,* 14 March 1996, sec. B, p. 1.

50. Goldin, "Trials and Errors," 33–34.

51. Abrahamson, "Garcetti Rivals," sec. B, p. 6.

52. Ruth Galanter, member of Los Angeles City Council, interview by authors, 15 March 1993.

53. Idem.

54. Kristi Ellis-Krapf, "Council Sustains May Co. Veto," *California Apparel News,* 29 November to 5 December 1991, p. 8.

55. Louis Sahagun, "Wide Expansion of Garment District Proposed," *Los Angeles Times,* 6 August 1992, sec. B, p. 1.

56. Idem.

57. Joshua Leonard, CPA, Langdon Reider Strategic Real Estate Services, interview by authors, 4 November 1992.

58. William Kissel, "Splitting at the Seams," *Los Angeles Times,* 29 January 1993, sec. E, p. 3.

59. Karl Schoenberg, "Bringing Life Back to City's Heart," *Los Angeles Times,* 14 December 1993, sec. A, p. 18.

60. Quoted in Kissel, "Splitting at the Seams."

61. Sidney Morse, interview by authors, 28 October 1992.

62. Idem.

63. Kissel, "Splitting"; and Dean E. Murphy, "Officials Try to Keep Apparel Firms from Bolting Downtown," *Los Angeles Times,* 14 November 1992, sec. B, p. 3.

64. Murphy, "Officials."

65. Kristi Ellis, "Water Garden Site Wins Tenant Vote," *California Apparel News,* 18 to 24 December 1992, p. 2.

66. Kim-Van Dang, "California Mart Tenants Wooed Again," *Women's Wear Daily,* 28 July 1993, p. 12.

67. Benjamin Mark Cole, "Edison, Snyder Woo Tenants from Major Downtown L.A. Site," *Los Angeles Business Journal,* 5 July 1993, p. 1.

68. Dang, "California Mart Tenants."

69. An anonymous real estate expert quoted in *California Apparel News,* 19 to 25 November 1993, p. 2.

70. Cole, "Edison, Snyder," 34.

Notes for Chapter 5. Contractors

1. The literature on ethnic and immigrant entrepreneurship is vast, extending far beyond the garment industry. Works in this genre that focus on apparel include Nancy L. Green, *Ready-to-Wear, Ready-to-Work: A Century of Industry and Immigrants in Paris and New York* (Durham, N.C.: Duke University Press, 1997); and Roger D. Waldinger, *Through the Eye of the Needle: Immigrants and Enterprise in New York's Garment Trades* (New York: New York University Press, 1986). A conference was organized by the Institute for Migration and Ethnic Studies at the University of Amersterdam in 1997, the focus of which was a comparative analysis of immigrant entrepreneurship in the apparel industry in Europe and the United States. For critiques of this perspective, see Edna Bonacich, " 'Making It' in America: A Social Evaluation of Immigrant Entrepreneurship," *Sociological Perspectives* 30 (1987): 446–66; "The Social Costs of Immigrant Entrepreneurship," *Amerasia Journal* 14 (1988): 119–28; "The Role of the Petite Bourgeoisie with Capitalism: A Response to Pyong Gap Min," *Amerasia Journal* 15 (1989): 195–203; and "The Other Side of Ethnic Entrepreneurship: A Dialogue with Waldinger, Aldrich, Ward, and Associates," *International Migration Review* 27 (1993): 685–92.

2. As Paul Tsang, the general manager of Unimix, a company in Hong Kong that sources Asian apparel production for American and European manufacturers unabashedly expressed it, "I don't mind if it's a military government in Burma, I just hope the government doesn't change. If a bunch of school kids come into the streets, I worry." Interview by authors, 28 November 1991.

3. Other, possibly more important, profit centers are the real estate owners and bankers, but their role is beyond the scope of this volume, for the most part. We may, in the future, explore it in more depth.

4. It has been estimated that, at most, 30 percent of all workers in Los Angeles found their jobs in a traditional ethnic economy, in which employer and worker were from the same ethnic group (Ivan Light, Richard Bernard, and Rebecca Kim, "Immigrant Incorporation in the Garment Industry of Los Angeles," working paper no. 4.9, Center for German and European Studies, University of California at Berkeley, Berkeley, Calif. 1997). This figure holds only if the unlikely assumption is made that employers from a particular ethnicity hire *only* workers from the same ethnicity. In fact, such a percentage is very likely much smaller.

5. For a general description of middleman minority theory, see Edna Bonacich and John Modell, *The Economic Basis of Ethnic Solidarity: Small Business in the Japanese American Community* (Berkeley, Calif.: University of California Press, 1980), chapter 2.

6. A large and growing literature treats tensions between Koreans and Blacks, sometimes from a middleman minority perspective. See Pyong Gap Min, *Caught in the Middle: Korean Communities in New York and Los Angeles* (Berkeley, Calif.:

University of California Press, 1996); Kyeyoung Park, *The Korean American Dream: Immigrants and Small Business in New York City* (Ithaca, N.Y.: Cornell University Press, 1997); In-Jin Yoon, *On My Own: Korean Businesses and Race Relations in America* (Chicago, Ill.: University of Chicago Press, 1997). For a report of the special targeting of Korean stores during the uprising in Los Angeles, see Paul Ong and Suzanne Hee, "Losses in the Los Angeles Civil Unrest, April 29–May 1, 1992," Center for Pacific Rim Studies, University of California at Los Angeles, 1993.

7. Manufacturers are not the only ones who point the finger at contractors whose ethnicity is viewed as the source of the problem. John Y. Cho, head of the Korean-American Garment Industry Association (KAGIA) when we interviewed him, 2/21/93, claimed that Vietnamese contractors were responsible for running illegal shops that pay subminimum wages. Cho's position was reaffirmed by a subsequent director of the KAGIA, J. H. Lee, in testimony before the Jewish Commission on 23 April 1998. In a similar vein, Rito Gutierrez, the owner of Cal-Arts Contracting Company, whom we interviewed on 18 September 1991, faulted what he called Orientals as responsible for the many abuses that are found in the industry.

8. Standard Industrial Classification (SIC) 23, apparel and other related textile products.

9. United States Department of Labor, Stakeholders' Meeting, 5/27/98.

10. Don Lee, "Fashion Forward," *Los Angeles Times,* 26 April 1998, sec. D, p. 1.

11. Under the 1981 Montoya Act, all firms engaged in garment manufacturing are required to register with the State of California.

12. Don Lee, "Fashion Forward."

13. Bureau of the Census, *County Business Patterns,* United States Department of Commerce, Washington, D.C., 1996.

14. See chapter 1, note 23, for an explanation of SIC 23-a Standard Industrial Classification category; number 23 pertains to the textile industry.

15. This data set was compiled for us by Patricia Hanneman, to whom we owe a debt of gratitude.

16. Those that could not be matched by computer were then done by hand, using informants from the principal ethnic groups; 497 could not be matched at all, usually because only a business name, not an owner's name, appeared in the data.

17. Cho, interview.

18. This calculation was done by Ku-Sup Chin, then a graduate student at the University of California at Irvine and working under the direction of David Smith. Chin's survey of Korean contractors is discussed at length, later in this chapter. In 1993, *County Business Patterns* enumerated 94,423 garment workers in Los Angeles County. Combining the number of Korean firms registered with the state with the membership list of the Korean-American Garment Industry Association, and eliminating overlaps, Chin identified 942 Korean-owned firms in 1993. From his survey he determined that the average number of employees in Korean factories was fifty-four. Multiplying this average by 942 firms yields a total of 50,868 garment workers employed by Korean contractors, over half of the total of 94,423.

19. Since the late 1980s numerous factories have opened in Garden Grove,

Westminster, Santa Ana, and other cities in Orange County, which is home to the more than 100,000 Vietnamese immigrants who have settled there since 1975. As recently as 1983 there were reportedly only a handful of garment factories there. Many of the current factory owners were boat people from Vietnam, as were the large number of Vietnamese people who worked alongside Latino immigrants in their factories. Although located in newly constructed, light-industry complexes, these factories reportedly are among the most exploitative in the region, with higher rates of violation of minimum wage, industrial homework, and child labor laws. A detailed analysis of Orange County sweatshops is beyond the scope of this book. Journalistic accounts can, however, be found in the series of articles by Sonni Efron that appeared in the *Los Angeles Times* in 1989 and 1990. See also Ralph Frammolino, "Sweatshop Sweep Finds Labor Violations," *Los Angeles Times,* 25 February 1992, sec. B, p. 3.

20. This and the subsequent section are co-authored by Ku-Sup Chin, who served as our research assistant for this part of the project.

21. Hyung-Ki Jin, "A Survey on the Economic and Managerial Status of Sewing Factories Owned and Operated by Korean Contractors in the Los Angeles Area" (Industrial Research Institute for Pacific Nations, California State Polytechnic University, Pomona, Calif., 1981).

22. Darrel Eugene Hess, "Korean Immigrant Entrepreneurs in the Los Angeles Garment Industry," (masters thesis, University of California, Los Angeles, 1990).

23. Subsequently Ku-Sup Chin worked with Socorro Sarmiento to conduct sixty-five interviews with Latino workers employed by Korean garment contractors in the summer of 1993. For a more detailed discussion of the results of this survey, see Ku-Sup Chin, Socorro T. Sarmiento, and David A. Smith, "Exploiting Migrants: The Los Angeles Garment Industry and Global Restructuring" (Program in Social Relations, University of California at Irvine, 1997).

24. For an early analysis of Korean immigrant entrepreneurship in Los Angeles, see Ivan H. Light and Edna Bonacich, *Immigrant Entrepreneurs: The Koreans in Los Angeles, 1965–1982* (Berkeley, Calif.: University of California Press, 1988).

25. Piece rate is the standard way of paying garment workers in the apparel industry in Los Angeles. We discuss it in more detail in Chapter 6.

26. Our survey figures correspond roughly to the estimates of John Cho, of the Korean-American Garment Industry Association. In 1993 Cho guessed that about 10 percent of Korean contractors earned more than $250,000, and that between 20 and 30 percent made between $20,000 and $50,000.

27. Chin, Sarmiento, and Smith, "Exploiting Migrants."

28. As part of this project, Edward J. W. Park interviewed several Korean jobbers and manufacturers. See his "From Entry to Entrenchment: Korean Americans and the Los Angeles Garment Industry, 1970–1995" (paper presented at the meetings of the Pacific Sociological Association, Seattle, 1996).

29. *GCA Newsletter,* July–August 1997.

30. George White, "Garment Contractors Urged to Seek Higher Pay from Retailers," *Los Angeles Times,* 1 October 1996, sec. D, p. 2.

31. Successful alliances between workers and contractors are rare indeed, although they have occasionally surfaced in other industries, such as agriculture.

For example, nearly a century ago, in 1903, the Japanese-Mexican Labor Alliance in the sugar beet industry in Oxnard, California, was organized by contractors and their employees, and was able to hold a successful strike. See Tomas Almaguer, *Racial Fault Lines: The Historical Origins of White Supremacy in California* (Berkeley, Calif.: University of California Press, 1994), chapter 7.

Notes for Chapter 6. Workers

1. Workers testifying before the Los Angeles Jewish Commission on Sweatshops, 25 March 1998, corroborated this point.

2. Perhaps manufacturers were not entirely to blame for this. In October 1996, when the first of several minimum wage increases went into effect, the National Association of Retailers and the United States Department of Labor jointly held a meeting for manufacturers and contractors at the CaliforniaMart. The retailers made it clear they were unwilling to pay much more for apparel to accommodate the minimum wage increase. The department made it equally clear it would not tolerate sweatshops. According to one manufacturer who attended the meeting, Jim Garibay, the production manager for MGT Industries, which makes lingerie, "The message was, 'find a way to manufacture your goods without passing on the costs to retailers.' They were also concerned that the only way we could do it was to set up illegal shops." A number of manufacturers who were present concluded that the not-so-hidden message was that they should move their production offshore. (Quoted in Sam Quiñones, "Garment Industry Thrives on Continental Drift," *United States/Mexico Business Observer* [October 1997]: 46.)

3. Kristi Ellis, "INS 'Operation Buttonhole' Sweep Collars 75 Undocumented Workers," *Women's Wear Daily,* 29 April 1998, p. 13; "The Hire Wire," *Women's Wear Daily,* Special on Los Angeles (June 1998): 14–16; Kristin Young, "INS in Downtown Sweep," *California Apparel News,* 17 to 23 April 1998, 4; Sandra Hernandez, "Immigrants Rounded Up: INS Deports Hundreds in Garment Factory Raids," *L.A. Weekly,* 24 to 30 April 1998, 17.

4. George White, "Workers Held in Near Slavery, Officials Say," *Los Angeles Times,* 3 August 1995, p. 1. For a full account, see Julie Su, "El Monte Thai Garment Workers: Slave Sweatshops," pp. 143–49 in *No Sweat: Fashion, Free Trade, and the Rights of Garment Workers,* ed. Andrew Ross (New York: Verso, 1997).

5. "Labor Department Survey: No Change Since '96 on Compliance," *California Apparel News,* 29 May to 4 June 1998, 1.

6. This raid was reported by Bob Baker, "Alleged Sweatshop with 100 Thai Workers Closed by State," *Los Angeles Times,* 19 July 1990, sec. B p. 3.

7. Su, "El Monte Thai Garment Workers."

8. Larry Jacobs, "Wisdom for Hire," *California Apparel News,* 22 to 28 September 1995, 14.

9. Maria Angelina Soldatenko, "The Everyday Lives of Latina Garment Workers in Los Angeles: The Convergence of Gender, Race, Class and Immigration" (Ph. D. diss., University of California at Los Angeles, 1992); Rosa Martha Fregoso, "The Invisible Workforce: Immigrant Home Workers in the Garment Industry of Los Angeles" (master's thesis, University of California, Berkeley,

1992); Gregory Scott, "The Everyday Politics of Domination and Resistance: An Ethnographic Inquiry into the Local Production of Garments for the Global Market" (master's thesis, University of California, Santa Barbara, 1992); M. Patricia Fernandez-Kelly and Anna M. Garcia, "Hispanic Women and Homework: Women in the Informal Economy of Miami and Los Angeles," pp. 165–79 in *Homework: Historical and Contemporary Perspectives on Paid Labor at Home,* ed. Eileen Boris and Cynthia R. Daniels (Urbana, Ill.: University of Illinois Press, 1989); idem, "Informalization at the Core: Hispanic Women, Homework, and the Advanced Capitalist State," pp. 247–64 in *The Informal Economy: Studies in Advanced and Less Developed Countries,* ed. Alejandro Portes, Manuel Castells, and Lauren A. Benton (Baltimore, Md.: Johns Hopkins University Press, 1989); M. Patricia Fernandez-Kelly and Saskia Sassen, "A Collaborative Study of Hispanic Women in Garment and Electronics Industry" (final report to the Ford, Revson, and Tinker Foundations, May 1991); and M. Patricia Fernandez-Kelly and Anna M. Garcia, "Power Surrendered, Power Restored: The Politics of Work and Family among Hispanic Garment Workers in California and Florida," pp. 215–28 in *Challenging Fronteras: Structuring Latina and Latino Lives in the United States,* ed. Mary Romero, Pierrette Hondagneu-Sotelo, and Vilma Ortiz (New York: Routledge, 1997).

10. This section is based on an analysis of the 1990 census, using the 5 percent Public Use Micro Sample (PUMS) data. We began by selecting Los Angeles County, and within that, people employed in the apparel industry. This yielded a PUMS sample of 5,791, suggesting a total apparel industry "population" of 115,820. Although nearly a decade old, the PUMS data are the only reliable, detailed demographic information on the apparel workforce.

11. Peter Force, Daniel Flaming, Julia R. Henly, and Mark Drayse, *By the Sweat of Their Brow: Welfare to Work in Los Angeles* (Los Angeles, Calif.: Economic Roundtable, 1988).

12. Alison A. Neider, "Welfare-to-Work Inspires Opposing Views of Industry," *California Apparel News,* 5 to 11 June 1998, p. 1.

13. Ibid.; Nicole Simon, "Dream a Little Dream," *California Apparel News,* 15 to 21 July 1994, p. 20.

14. Neider, "Welfare-to-Work," p. 8.

15. Sheldon L. Maram, "Hispanic Workers in the Garment and Restaurant Industries in Los Angeles County: A Social and Economic Profile," working papers in United States-Mexican Studies, no. 12 (University of California at San Diego, 1980); Sheldon Maram and Stewart Long, *The Labor Market Impact of Hispanic Undocumented Workers: An Exploratory Case Study of the Garment Industry in Los Angeles County* (Employment and Training Administration, United States Department of Labor, Washington, D.C., 1981).

16. Maram, "Hispanic Workers," p. xiv. Having permanent residence meant that many undocumented workers were eligible for amnesty under the Immigration Reform and Control Act, which was passed in 1986.

17. This section is co-authored with Gregory Shawn Scott, who received his doctorate from the University of California at Santa Barbara under the chairmanship of Richard Appelbaum. For a fuller report of parts of this research, see Gregory Shawn Scott, "The Everyday Politics of Domination and Resistance:

An Ethnographic Inquiry into the Local Production of Garments for the Global Market" (master's thesis, University of California at Santa Barbara, 1992); and "Sewing with Dignity: Class Struggle and Ethnic Conflict in the Los Angeles Garment Industry" (Ph.D. diss., University of California at Santa Barbara, 1997). For an interview study of garment workers, see Soldatenko, "The Everyday Lives." Traci C. Lew, an undergraduate student at the University of California at Riverside, also helped with this section by reviewing a number of governmental hearings on conditions in the apparel industry.

18. Stuart Silverstein, "Survey of Garment Industry Finds Rampant Labor Abuse," *Los Angeles Times,* 15 April 1994, sec. D, p. 1.

19. Susan Headden, "Made in the U.S.A.," *United States News and World Report,* 22 November 1992, p. 48.

20. Some efforts are being made to socialize apparel assembly with modular production: A group of workers standing around a table and helping one another construct a garment together. Modular production has gained virtually no foothold in Los Angeles and is mainly practiced in the South, where labor shortages have required an upgrading of the work.

21. A few contractors in Los Angeles have introduced the unit production system, known as UPS. Each garment is treated as a unit, and computers are used to send the garments from one worker to the next on an overhead rail. The pace of work is still, however, determined by the workers.

22. This is not to say that no technological innovations have been introduced in sewing. There have been improvements in sewing machines and other aspects of garment assembly. Nonetheless, the basic labor involved in sewing—a woman joining pieces of material at a sewing machine—has not changed much since the invention of the sewing machine. Most of the improved technology has been introduced either in the earlier phases of design and cutting or in the system of distribution. See Kurt Hoffman and Howard Rush, *Micro-Electronics and Clothing: The Impact of Technical Change on a Global Industry* (New York: Praeger, 1988).

23. Paul Ratoff, "The Piece-Rate Dilemma for Manufacturers," *California Apparel News,* 22 to 28 October 1993, p. 8.

24. Queena Sook Kim, "Wages Won," *L.A. Weekly,* 30 January to 5 February 1998, p. 18.

25. Daniel Taub, "Apparel Trade Association Offering Health Insurance," *Los Angeles Business Journal,* 1 June 1998, p. 10.

26. Sonni Efron, "Sweatshops Expanding into Orange County: Thousands of Immigrants Find Themselves Sewing for Low Wages in Third World Conditions," *Los Angeles Times,* 26 November 1989, sec. A, p. 1.

27. Idem, "Mother's Plight Turns a Home into a Sweatshop," *Los Angeles Times,* 27 November 1989, sec. A, p. 1.

28. Fregoso, "Invisible Workforce."

29. See Fernandez-Kelly and Sassen, "A Collaborative Study," pp. 108–11, for interviews with apparel home workers in Los Angeles who made similar statements.

30. Fregoso, pp. 64–65.

31. State of California, Employment Development Department, "Los Angeles County Historical Monthly Labor Force Data, 1983–Current"; available: http://www.calmis.cahwnet.gov/htmlfile/msa/lalb.htm [29 March 1999].

32. Force, et al., *By the Sweat.*

33. Tomas Rivera Policy Institute, "Diversifying Southern California's Latino Mosaic," Claremont, Calif., 26 March 1997. See also, Julio Laboy, "Mix of Hispanic Culture Is Source of Workplace Tensions, Study Finds," *Wall Street Journal,* 26 March 1997.

34. James C. Scott, *Weapons of the Weak: Everyday Forms of Peasant Resistance* (New Haven, Conn.: Yale University Press, 1985).

35. Roger Waldinger, "Ethnicity and Opportunity in the Plural City," pp. 445–70 in *Ethnic Los Angeles,* ed. Roger Waldinger and Mehdi Bozogmehr (New York: Russell Sage Foundation, 1996).

Notes for Chapter 7. The Distribution of Wealth

1. California Fashion Association, advertisement, *California Apparel News,* 27 September to 3 October 1996, p. 15. Eighty percent of the industry in California is located in southern California.

2. Randy Youngblood, Apparel Resources, Inc., interview by authors, 30 July 1993.

3. Robert Walter, interview by authors, 26 June 1996.

4. Steve Nutter, "The Structure and Growth of the Los Angeles Garment Industry," in *No Sweat: Fashion, Free Trade and the Rights of Garment Workers,* ed. Andrew Ross (New York: Verso, 1997), 200.

5. Steve Pearlstein, "Sizing It Up," *Los Angeles Times,* 13 June 1995, sec. E, p. 3.

6. "1996 Retail Compensation," *Women's Wear Daily,* 30 June 1997, p. 11; "Retail Results for the Fourth Quarter and Full Year," *Women's Wear Daily,* 20 April 1998, p. 18. Unfortunately, for 1996 the newspaper gives profits and the compensation for chief executive officers, and for 1997 it gives sales and profits. In our discussion we combine these data.

7. Jennifer L. Brady, "Retail Execs' Paychecks Bloom." *Women's Wear Daily,* 30 June 1997, p. 10.

8. The average increase was skewed downward by the fact that Allen Questrom had received a payout of $11 million from Federated Department Stores Inc. the previous year.

9. Thomas J. Ryan, "Pay Packages Surged Ahead 45 Percent for Heads of Discount Chains," *Women's Wear Daily,* 3 June 1998, p. 1.

10. David Moin, "Myron Ullman to exit R. H. Macy on Jan 31 with $13M Severance," *Women's Wear Daily,* 20 September 1994, p. 1.

11. Thomas J. Ryan, "Allen Questrom Sues Federated for $47 Million," *Women's Wear Daily,* 2 February 1998, p. 1.

12. Dianne M. Pogoda, "CHH Will Boost Private Label to 25% of Women's Inventory," *Women's Wear Daily,* 18 November 1994, p. 16.

13. "Dayton Hudson Donates Millions," *California Apparel News,* 17 to 23 December 1993, p. 2.

14. Joyce Barrett, "Stores Grapple with Proposed Minimum Wage Hike," *Women's Wear Daily,* 15 June 1998, p. 12.

15. Thomas J. Ryan, "Biggest Bucks Go to Power-Brand Execs," *Women's Wear Daily,* 20 July 1998, p. 24.

16. Thomas J. Ryan and Lisa Lockwood, "The Age of the IPO: Fashion Execs Wear Crowns of Royalty," *Women's Wear Daily,* 17 April 1997, p. 1.

17. Andree Conrad, "The Year Profit Became Fashionable," *Apparel Industry Magazine,* June 1997, p. 20.

18. Ben Sullivan, "Bankers, Financiers Dominate Ranks of L.A.'s Highest Paid," *Los Angeles Business Journal,* 23 to 29 June 1997, p. 1.

19. See, for example, Graef S. Crystal, *In Search of Excess: The Overcompensation of American Executives* (New York: Norton, 1991).

20. See, for example, Dianne M. Pogoda, Sophy Fearnley-Whittingstall, and Rusty Williamson, "Ad Plans: Big Stores, Big Bucks," *Women's Wear Daily,* 5 October 1994, p. 8.

21. "The Big Spenders: Top 100 Fashion and Beauty Advertisers," *Women's Wear Daily,* 15 May 1998, sec. 2, p. 8.

22. Lisa Lockwood, "The High Price of Fashion Fame," *Women's Wear Daily,* 27 September 1996, p. 10.

23. Idem, "Fashion's Deep Pockets," *Women's Wear Daily,* 15 May 1998, sec. 2, p. 4.

24. Pamela Sellers, "The Reel World: The Top West Coast-Based Apparel Ad Agencies," *California Apparel News,* 11 to 17 June 1993, p. 10.

25. Lisa Lockwood, "7th on Sixth, Agencies Reach Accord on Models' Show Fees," *Women's Wear Daily,* 14 October 1993, p. 2.

26. J. Blade Corwin, "California Sales Pay Packages Varied and Lucrative," *Apparel Industry Magazine,* April 1997, pp. 30–33.

27. Avis Cardella and Lisa Bruno, "The Rap on Reps," *California Apparel News,* 24 to 30 December 1993, p. 7.

28. Bill Seitchick, "Hired Hands: The Big Payoff," *Bobbin,* June 1992, pp. 86–90.

29. Samuel Greengard, "What They Earn," *Los Angeles Magazine,* March 1994, pp. 66–73.

30. Youngblood, interview.

31. Stephanie Strom, "A Debt Offering Reveals a Fashion Family's Feud," *New York Times,* 6 August 1993, sec. D, p. 1.

32. Los Angeles Superior Court, Case BD082355.

33. "Guess Stumbles Down Wall Street Runway," *Los Angeles Times,* 6 August 1996, sec. D, p. 3.

Notes for Chapter 8. Government Enforcement and Retention Efforts

1. This section draws on the excellent work of Beverly A. Pitman, "California Garment Industry: The Role of Field Enforcement in the State of California's Policing of Minimum Wage and Overtime Pay Violations" (paper prepared for the ILGWU, Los Angeles, 1992).

2. Division of Labor Standards Enforcement, Garment Manufacturers, La-

bor Code. (ii) Reference: Sections 2671(a) and (b), Labor Code, State of California, Division of Labor Standards Enforcement; available: http://www.dir.ca .gov/dir/t8/13630.html.

3. Sonni Efron, "Hayden Launches Campaign to Crack Down on Sweatshops," *Los Angeles Times,* 3 March 1990, sec. B, p. 1.

4. Quoted in Efron, "Sweatshop Bill Puts Heat on Manufacturers," *Los Angeles Times,* 28 February 1990, sec. A, p. 1.

5. Bernard Lax, interview by authors, 1 November 1993.

6. Ralph Frammolino, "Two Sweatshop Bills Clear First Hurdle," *Los Angeles Times,* 5 April 1990, sec. A, p. 3.

7. Arthur Friedman, "Vendors, Contractors Both Liable under New California Labor Law," *Women's Wear Daily,* 13 August 1998, p. 11; "Labor Liability Extended to One-Person Shops," *California Apparel News,* 21–27 August 1998, p. 36.

8. Don Lee and Stuart Silverstein, "Labor Official Is Suspected of Extortion: State Inspector Is Accused of Squeezing Thousands of Dollars from a Los Angeles Garment Shop Owner," *Los Angeles Times,* 16 September 1997, sec. D, p. 1; "Calif. Nabs Inspector on Extortion Charge," *Women's Wear Daily,* 22 September 1997, p. 20.

9. Don Lee, "State Will Pair Labor Inspectors after Agent's Arrest: Commissioner Is Enacting Changes. Fewer Garment Shop Inspections Are Likely," *Los Angeles Times,* 17 September 1997, sec. D, p. 1; Kristin Young, "Investigators Reined in after Agent's Arrest," *California Apparel News,* 19 to 25 September 1997, p. 4.

10. Davan Maharaj, "Court Upholds Immigrants' Rights in the Workplace," *Los Angeles Times,* 30 July 1998, sec. A, p. 1.

11. I-9 forms, required since the Immigration Reform and Control Act went into effect in 1986.

12. Sonni Efron, " 'Hot Goods' Law Revived As Anti-Sweatshop Tool," *Los Angeles Times,* 28 September 1989, sec. A, p. 3. " 'Hot Goods' Statute Bans Interstate Shipment of Merchandise Made in Violation of Labor Laws," *Los Angeles Times,* 28 November 1989, sec. A, p. 1.

13. Rolene Otero, Los Angeles District Director, United States Department of Labor, interview by authors, 30 November 1992.

14. United States Department of Labor, *Protecting America's Garment Workers: Wage and Hour Enforcement Approach* (Washington, D.C.: 1996).

15. Stuart Silverstein, "Fashion Firms Told to Police Contractors," *Los Angeles Times,* 11 June 1993, sec. D, p. 1.

16. Otero, interview.

17. Kim-Van Dang, "Guess to Inspect, Report to U.S. on Contractors," *Women's Wear Daily,* 6 August 1992, p. 15; Otero, interview.

18. Stanley W. Levy, "Guess? Fights Sweatshops by Monitoring Contractors," *Apparel Industry Magazine,* November 1992, p. 106.

19. Dang, "Guess to Inspect."

20. Joanna Ramey, "Guess-Labor Dept. Contractor Pact Only the First," *Women's Wear Daily,* 6 August 1992, p. 15.

21. Quoted in Stuart Silverstein, "Guess? Pact to Curb Sweatshop Abuses Praised: But Some Manufacturers Question Whether the Apparel Maker Will Diligently Police Its Contractors," *Los Angeles Times,* 6 August 1992, sec. D, p. 3.

22. Kristi Ellis, "Labor Department Targets Garment Manufacturers," *California Apparel News,* 11 to 17 June, 1993, p. 2.

23. Joanna Ramey, "L.A. Sportswear Firm Cited by Labor Dept.," *Women's Wear Daily,* 23 December, 1994, p. 10; Kristi Ellis, "District Court Ruling Sets Precedent for Labor Department," *California Apparel News,* 6 to 12 January 1995, p. 3.

24. United States Department of Labor, news release, 10 February 1998.

25. Ramey, "Los Angeles Sportswear Firm."

26. Joe Rodriguez, interview by authors, 16 November 1992.

27. Kristi Ellis, "Garment Contractors Voice Concerns over Guess? Agreement," *California Apparel News,* 2 to 8 October 1992, p. 2.

28. Lax, interview.

29. Meeting between Gerald Hall, district director, Department of Labor and members of the Coalition for Garment Workers, Los Angeles, 9 July 1998.

30. Ibid. Nationwide, the number of investigators working for the Department of Labor dropped from about 950 in 1987 to 780 in 1996, before being boosted to 900 in 1997 (most of the additional investigators were assigned to apparel). These agents are responsible for 120 million workers in 6.5 million workplaces, a daunting task, to say the least. See statement before hearings of the House Committee on Education and the Workforce Subcommittee on Oversight and Investigations, Suzanne B. Seiden, acting deputy administrator, Wage and Hour division, Department of Labor, in Los Angeles, 18 May 1998.

31. Joe Rodriguez, testimony, Los Angeles Jewish Commission on Sweatshops, 23 April 1998.

32. Richard Reinis, testimony, Los Angeles Jewish Commission on Sweatshops, 2 December 1997 and 2 April 1998.

33. Stuart Silverstein, "Self-Regulatory Group to Police Clothes Markers' Work Conditions," *Los Angeles Times,* 20 June 1995, sec. D, p. 1; Kristi Ellis, "Los Angeles Manufacturers to Form Alliance," *California Apparel News,* 2 to 8 June 1995, p. 4; Michael Marlow, "Los Angeles Contractors: A New Set of Rules," *Women's Wear Daily,* 22 June 1995, p. 9.

34. "Apparel Industry Official Blasts Self-Regulatory Group," *Los Angeles Times,* 22 June 1995, sec. D, p. 2.

35. Reinis, testimony, 2 April 1998.

36. Steven Greenhouse, "Sweatshop Raids Cast Doubt on Ability of Garment Makers to Police Factories," *New York Times,* 18 July 1997, sec. A, p. 8; see also Edna Bonacich, "Sweatshops Won't End til Workers have Power," *Los Angeles Times,* 4 August 1997, sec. B, p. 5.

37. "Labor Department Survey: No Change since '96 on Compliance," *California Apparel News,* 29 May to 4 June 1998, p. 1.

38. "Effectively monitored" shops were those with at least six of the following seven components of monitoring in place: review of payroll records, review of timecards, interviews with employees, provision of compliance information, advice regarding compliance problems, recommendation of corrective actions, and subjection to unannounced visits. Shops that were merely "monitored" had at least one of the seven components in place.

39. United States Department of Labor, Wage and Hour division, "Los Angeles 1998 Compliance Survey" (fact sheet).

40. "Labor Department Survey."

41. House Committee on Education.

42. The topic of monitoring in the garment industry is being thoroughly studied by Jill Esbenshade, in the Ethnic Studies Department at the University of California at Berkeley, for her dissertation. She has written a report, "The 'Social Accountability Contract': Monitoring and Labor Relations in the Global Apparel Industry" (Chicano/Latino Policy Project, University of California at Berkeley, 1999).

43. Hall, meeting.

44. Idem, telephone conversation with authors, 12 June 1998.

45. Unless otherwise stated, the discussion of TIPP is based on the Fourth Annual Report, 1996.

46. TIPP, Second Annual Report, 1994.

47. Ibid., p. 9.

48. Quoted in Silverstein, "Self-Regulatory Group."

49. Julie McElwain, "Uncommon Ground: Despite Common Interest in the Apparel Industry, the State and Federal Labor Departments often Appear to Work at Odds," *California Apparel News,* 7 to 13 June 1996, p. 10.

50. Don Lee, "Task Force in Tatters: State-Federal Tensions Hinder Garment Industry Crackdown," *Los Angeles Times,* 4 August 1996, sec. D, p. 1.

51. "Labor Dept Set to Go after Stores Selling Garments from Sweatshops," *Los Angeles Times,* 9 September 1994, sec. D, p. 1; Kristi Ellis, "DOL Targets Retailers," *California Apparel News,* 16 to 22 September 1994, p. 6; Joanna Ramey, "Reich Seeks Retailers' Aid in Nailing Sweatshops," *Women's Wear Daily,* 12 September 1994.

52. Joanna Ramey, "Reich, Retail Execs Meet on Role of Stores in Sweatshop Crackdown," *Women's Wear Daily,* 19 October 1994, p. 2.

53. Joanna Ramey, "Labor's Good Guy List: Limited Leads 31 names," *Women's Wear Daily,* 5 December 1995, p. 2.

54. Joanna Ramey, "Unlisted Retailers Score Labor's List," *Women's Wear Daily,* 6 December 1995, p. 2; Stuart Silverstein and George White, " 'Good Guy' Labor List Gets a Bad Rap: Some Garment Industry Leaders Say the Roster of Firms Fighting Sweatshop Conditions Is Far too Short," *Los Angeles Times,* 6 December 1995, sec. D, p. 1.

55. Ramey, "Unlisted Retailers."

56. Kristi Ellis, "Labor's Good-Guy List Criticized at Meeting in L.A.," *Women's Wear Daily,* 8 December 1995, p. 11.

57. Joanna Ramey, "U.S. Department of Labor Releases Its First List of Sewing Shop Abuses," *Women's Wear Daily,* 3 May 1996, p. 2.

58. Don Lee, "U.S. Cites Labor Law Violators in Garment Industry: New York and California Businesses Dominate the List of 330 Firms, Prepared at the Request of Retailers," *Los Angeles Times,* 6 May 1996, sec. D, p. 1.

59. Ramey, "U.S. Department of Labor."

60. Joanna Ramey, "Reich Sees Summit as the 'Turning Point' in Sweatshop Wars," *Women's Wear Daily,* 17 July 1996, p. 1.

61. Joanna Ramey, "Labor Secretary Alexis Herman: A New Anti-Sweatshop Strategy," *Women's Wear Daily,* 4 September 1997, p. 14.

62. Joanna Ramey, "Labor's Alexis Herman Aims to Enlist Youth; Survey Slams Makers," *Women's Wear Daily,* 20 October 1997, p. 1.

63. Mary McCaig, "The CFA Asks the DOL to Get a Clue," *Apparel Industry Magazine,* April 1998, p. 15.

64. Joanna Ramey, "Labor Urges Lenders to Join Anti-Sweatshop Crusades," *Women's Wear Daily,* 20 July 1998, p. 22.

65. Joanna Ramey, "10 Makers, Retailers Sign On for Clinton's Anti-Sweatshop Panel," *Women's Wear Daily,* 5 August 1996, p. 1.

66. Joanna Ramey, "Sweatshop Task Force, at Impasse, Called by White House for Meeting," *Women's Wear Daily,* 28 March 1997, p. 9.

67. Joanna Ramey, "Anti-Sweatshop Task Force Reaches Agreement on Recommendations," *Women's Wear Daily,* 9 April 1997, p. 2.

68. Joanna Ramey, "Clinton Urges Industry to Enlist in the War against Sweatshops," *Women's Wear Daily,* 15 April 1997, p. 1.

69. Medea Benjamin, "No Sweat for Companies to Agree: The Presidential Commission Accord on Sweatshops Doesn't Go Far Enough to Protect Workers," *Los Angeles Times,* 17 April 1997, sec. B, p. 9.

70. Joanna Ramey, "Karen Kane Is 2nd Company to Quit Anti-Sweatshop Unit," *Women's Wear Daily,* 20 June 1997, p. 14.

71. Joanna Ramey, "U.S.-E.U. Sweatshop Meeting Scheduled for Today in Brussels," *Women's Wear Daily,* 20 February 1998, p. 13; "U.S.-Europe Sweatshop Summit Called Useful, Worth Repeating," *Women's Wear Daily,* 23 February 1998, p. 8.

72. H.R. 90, 106th Cong., 1st sess. The Senate version differs slightly from the House version in that it specifically defines retailers (in their private-label production) as manufacturers. All Congressional legislation can be easily accessed at the Congressional website (http://thomas.loc.gov/). See also Joyce Barrett, "Sweatshop Bill Would Make Vendors, Retailers Liable for Contractor Violations," *Women's Wear Daily,* 26 September 1996, p. 2.

73. Eric Wilson, "N.Y. Sweatshop Law: Vendors Jointly Liable, Stores Seem off Hook," *Women's Wear Daily,* 11 August 1998, p. 1.

74. Julie Su of the Asian Pacific American Legal Center has set forth a number of legislative proposals and we borrow heavily from her suggestions. See also, Lora Jo Foo, "The Vulnerable and Exploitable Immigrant Workforce and the Need for Strengthening Worker Protective Legislation," *Yale Law Journal* 103 (June 1994): 2179–212; Lora Jo Foo, Laura Ho, and Thomas M. Kim, "Worker Protection Compromised: The Fair Labor Standards Act Meets the Bankruptcy Code," *Asian Pacific American Law Journal* 2 (Fall 1994): 38–59.

75. Karre Lynn, "Home Field Advantage: The L.A. Business Team Is Doing Its Best to Ensure That the Garment Industry Remains in Los Angeles," *California Apparel News,* 9 to 15 January 1998, pp. 6–7; Lee Romney, "Riordan Names Director of L.A. Business Team," *Los Angeles Times,* 30 June 1998, sec. D, p. 2; Howard Fine, "Business Team Achieves String of Successes," *Los Angeles Business Journal* 29 June 1998, p. 3.

76. Laura Sainz, assistant director, Los Angeles Business Team, interview by authors, 2 May 1997.

77. Robert J. Lopez, "$100,000,000 Vote: A Federally Funded Empowerment Zone Is Good News for L.A., but Its Limited Size Will Exclude Many Needy Areas," *Los Angeles Times,* 7 November 1993, sec. B, p. 14.

78. Efrain Hernandez, "Exclusion from Funds Stuns Local Activists," *Los Angeles Times,* 25 December 1994, sec. B, p. 3; Rich Connell, "Delays, Lack of Focus Dogged L.A.'s Grant Bid," *Los Angeles Times,* 25 December 1994, sec. A, p. 1.

79. Lopez, "$100,000,000 Vote"; Hernandez, "Exclusion." The proposals that were eventually funded came from New York City, Chicago, Baltimore, Atlanta, Detroit, and the Philadelphia-Camden, N.J., area. The U.S. Department of Housing and Urban Development also planned to select sixty-five urban enterprise communities, each of which would receive $3 million in federal assistance.

80. The initial federal offer was for $250 million; the city eventually obtained an additional $180 million, including the right to invest the additional money in any community in which 20 percent or more of the residents fell below the poverty line (John Schwada and Jean Merl, "L.A. to Get Infusion of Federal Funding Aid: In Lieu of 'Empowerment Zone' Status; U.S. Will Award $400 Million for a Nonprofit Community Development Bank," *Los Angeles Times,* 10 May 1995, sec. B, p. 1).

81. According to federal requirements, at least one job must result from every $35,000 that is loaned by the bank. The community development bank is to provide subsidies for interest rates and loan fees, as well as loan guarantees, for participating private banks. The bank will also make a limited number of direct grants and provide technical assistance. The program is not without some risks: Future federal community development block grants for social services, economic development, and housing will serve as collateral to guarantee the banks loans (Jean Merl, "Ambitious Bank Plan Would Aid Poor Areas," *Los Angeles Times,* 10 May 1995, sec. B, p. 1).

82. J. L. Sullivan, "Growing Respect for Apparel in L.A.," *California Apparel News,* 21 to 27 August 1998, p. 1; "Bank Wants to Empower Industry Entrepreneurs," *California Apparel News,* 21–27 August 1998, p. 4; Lee Romney, "Banking on a New Strategy: Community Lender Looks to Strengthen Industries as Whole," *Los Angeles Times,* 15 August 1998, sec. D, p. 1.

83. Schwada and Merl, "L.A. to Get Infusion"; "Riordan, Group to Lobby for U.S. Funds: Redevelopment: Mayor Will Lead Delegation to Washington Seeking Anti-Crime Money and Business Tax Credits for Inner-City Revitalization Plan," *Los Angeles Times,* 21 January 1995, sec. B, p. 16.

84. "Mayor to Industry: 'Get Mad at Me.' " *California Apparel News,* 23 to 29 January 1998, p. 6. Sullivan, "Growing Respect."

85. Quoted in Sullivan, "Growing Respect."

86. George White and Nancy Rivera Brooks, "Carole Little Is Moving—to a Bigger L.A. Site," *Los Angeles Times,* 20 May 1995, sec. D, p. 1; James Rainey and Nancy Rivera Brooks, "Riordan's Personal Efforts Warm the Business Climate," *Los Angeles Times,* 30 September 1994, sec. A, p. 1; Donna K. H. Walters, "Carole Little Sews Up Deal with Mayor Riordan," *Los Angeles Times,* 16 July 1993, sec. D, p. 2.

87. Lynn, "Home Field."

88. This section is co-authored with Goetz Wolff, of Resources for Economic Development, who also teaches in the Department of Urban Planning at the University of California at Los Angeles, is a member of the Apparel

Roundtable Educational Consortia, a participant in the California Fashion Association Technology and Education Council, and the Apparel Project Director of the North American Integration and Development Center at the University of California at Los Angeles. Wolff has conducted research and written extensively on the question of industry upgrading as a method of dealing with both the raising of labor standards and the retention of the apparel industry in southern California. Wolff directed and coauthored a study for the California Policy Seminar, "State Policies to Promote Industrial Upgrading for Low Wage Manufacturers," by Jean Gilbert, William Kramer, Daniel J. B. Mitchell, and Goetz Wolff (Berkeley, Calif., 1997). He received a grant from the John Randolph Haynes and Dora Haynes Foundation to study ways to combat low wages in manufacturing industries in Los Angeles. See Goetz Wolff and Carol Zabin, "Manufacturing Matters: A Sectoral Approach to Combating Low Wages in Los Angeles" (University of California at Los Angeles, Lewis Center, 1997), Chapter 4.

89. Ian Taplin, "Segmentation and Organization of Work in the Italian Apparel Industry," *Social Science Quarterly* 70 (1989): 408–424; "Strategic Reorientations of U.S. Apparel Firms," pp. 205–233 in Gary Gereffi and Miguel Korzeniewicz, eds., *Commodity Chains and Global Capitalism* (Westport, Conn.: Praeger, 1994); Roger Waldinger, *Through the Eye of the Needle: Immigrants and Enterprise in New York's Garment Trades* (New York: New York University Press, 1986); Peter Dicken, *Global Shift: The Internationalization of Economic Activity,* 2d ed. (New York: Guilford Press, 1992), chap. 8.

90. Southern California Edison Company and DRI/McGraw-Hill, *Southern California's Apparel Industry: Building a Path to Prosperity* (Los Angeles, Calif.: Southern California Edison Company, 1995). Goetz Wolff served as a consultant for this project.

91. AB 3662, Legislative Counsel's Digest; see also Southern California Edison, *Southern California's Apparel Industry,* appendix C.

92. These ideas are adapted from materials prepared for the Los Angeles Jewish Commission on Sweatshops by Steve Kaplan, a labor attorney.

93. Emerald Yeh and Christine McMurry, "No Need to Trade in Conscience for Affordable Clothing: Some Say Stamping Out Sweatshops Will Drive Garment-Makers to Other Countries. But a San Francisco Project Is Proving That Manufacturers, Workers and Consumers Can All Win," *San Francisco Chronicle,* 21 July 1996.

94. "DOL Comes Down Hard on New York." *California Apparel News,* 24 to 30 October 1997, p. 6.

95. The Garment Industry Development Corporation, "Keeping Jobs in Fashion: Annual Report 1995–96." (New York: Garment Industry Development Corporation, 1996).

96. For a review, see Stephen M. Mitchell, *Delivering Integrated Services: Models for Facilitating Change in Small and Mid-Sized Firms* (Annapolis Junction, Md.: National Alliance of Business, 1997), 79–91.

97. *GDIC News,* spring and summer 1997.

98. Mitchell, *Delivering Integrated Services.*

99. Rodriguez, interview.

100. This section is based on research and interviews conducted by Goetz Wolff and his collaborators.

Notes for Chapter 9. Worker Empowerment

1. For example, see Michael Piore, "The Economics of the Sweatshop," pp. 135–142 in *No Sweat: Fashion, Free Trade, and the Rights of Garment Workers,* ed. Andrew Ross (New York: Verso, 1997).

2. Cited in Stephen I. Schlossberg and Judith A. Scott, *Organizing and the Law,* 4th ed. (Washington, D.C.: Bureau of National Affairs, 1991), vii.

3. Kate Bronfenbrenner, et al., eds., *Organizing to Win: New Research on Union Strategies* (Ithaca, N.Y.: ILR Press, 1997).

4. United States Departments of Labor and Commerce, *Commisions on the Future of Worker-Management Relations: Fact Finding Report* (Washington, D.C.: May 1994); and *Report and Recommendations* (Washington, D.C.: December 1994).

5. Kate Bronfenbrenner, "The Effects of Plant Closing or Threat of Plant Closing on the Right of Workers to Organize: Final Report" (report submitted to the Labor Secretariat of the North American Commission for Labor Cooperation, 1996).

6. Sheldon Friedman, et al., eds., *Restoring the Promise of American Labor Law* (Ithaca, N. Y.: ILR Press, 1994); Richard W. Hurd, "Assault on Workers' Rights," Industrial Union Department, AFL-CIO, Washington, D.C., 1994; Martin Jay Levitt, *Confessions of a Union Buster* (New York: Crown, 1993).

7. Bronfenbrenner et al., *Organizing to Win,* p. 5.

8. Industrial Union Department, AFL-CIO, *Insurmountable Obstacles: An International Comparison of the Path to Union Recognition between the U.S. and the Industrialized Democracies* (Washington, D.C.: AFL-CIO, 1995).

9. Bronfenbrenner, et al., *Organizing to Win,* pp. 2–3.

10. Clementina Duron, "Mexican Women and Labor Conflict in Los Angeles: The ILGWU's Dressmakers' strike of 1933," *Aztlan* 15 (1984): 145–61; Juan Gomez-Quinones, *Mexican American Labor, 1790–1990* (Albuquerque, N.M.: University of New Mexico Press, 1994); John Laslett and Mary Tyler, *The ILGWU in Los Angeles, 1907–1988* (Inglewood, Calif.: Ten Star Press, 1989); Douglas Monroy, "La costura en Los Angeles, 1933–1939: The ILGWU and the Politics of Domination," pp. 171–78 in *Mexican Women in the United States: Struggles Past and Present,* ed. Magdalena Mora and Adelaida R. Del Castello (Chicano Studies Research Center, University of California at Los Angeles, 1980); Rose Pesotta, *Bread Upon the Waters* (1944; reprint, Ithaca, N. Y.: ILR Press, 1987).

11. Laslett and Tyler, *The ILGWU,* p. 92.

12. For a comparison between organizing problems in the apparel and other immigrant-employing industries, and for a discussion of the difficulties in organizing garment workers in Los Angeles as contrasted with other United States cities, see Edna Bonacich, "Intense Challenges, Tentative Possibilities: Organizing Immigrant Garment Workers in Los Angeles" (paper presented at the conference on Immigrants and Union Organizing in California, University of Cali-

fornia at Los Angeles, 15 May 1998). This chapter draws some sections from that paper.

13. Schlossberg and Scott, *Organizing,* p. 391.

14. This story was told by David Young, who was director of organizing for the ILGWU at the time.

15. Nancy Montweiler, "ULP Remedies Should Not Be Limited for Illegal Aliens, Board Concludes," *Bureau of National Affairs,* 16 February 1996, p. AA-1. The decision is: National Labor Relations Board, "Supplemental Decision and Order, A.P.R.A. Fuel Oil Buyers Group, et al.," 320 NLRB no. 53, 21 December 1995.

16. "ULP Remedies."

17. In a related, more recent case, a California Superior Court judge awarded $47,000 in back wages to an undocumented domestic worker and nanny from Indonesia. The judge, a Republican appointee of Governor Pete Wilson, rejected as a "non-issue" the worker's immigration status. "Whether or not a person is in the United States legally or not does not impact upon their ability to seek minimum wage for services performed." This was not a union organizing case, but it does suggest that the courts can decide to give precedence to basic workers' rights over their immigration status (Patrick J. McDonnell, "Domestic Workers Given Back Pay in Rare Win," *Los Angeles Times,* 1 June 1997, p. 1).

18. Especially noteworthy is SEIU's success in organizing immigrant janitorial workers in its Justice for Janitors campaign, and HERE Local 11's success in organizing immigrant hotel and restaurant workers.

19. The Landrum-Griffin Act's original sponsors included the Republican senators, Jacob Javits of New York and Barry Goldwater of Arizona.

20. Vicki Young, "Congress Seeks Data on Claiborne Payments to Union," *Women's Wear Daily,* 26 March 1998, p. 14; Joanna Ramey, "Rep. Hoekstra's Letter Swipes Feds, UNITE," *Women's Wear Daily,* 27 March 1998, p. 25; Eric Wilson, "Liquidated Damages: Cost of Doing Business or Windfall for UNITE? UNITE's Formula under Fire," *Women's Wear Daily,* 16 June 1998, p. 1.

21. Steven Greenhouse, 18 July 1997, sec. A, p. 8.

22. *Los Angeles Times,* 4 August 1997, sec. B, p. 5.

23. This was a precursor to the Los Angeles Jewish Commission on Sweatshops, which will be discussed in Chapter 10. Rich continued as an active member of the commission; Edna stepped down under pressure from Stan Levy, who threatened to discredit the commission if she became a member.

24. Studies of Asian garment workers in Los Angeles include: Edna Bonacich, "Asians in the Los Angeles Garment Industry," pp. 137–63 in *The New Asian Immigration in Los Angeles and Global Restructuring,* ed. Paul Ong, Edna Bonacich, and Lucie Cheng (Philadelphia: Temple University Press, 1994); Richard Kim, Kane K. Nakamura, and Gisele Fong, "Asian Immigrant Women Garment Workers in Los Angeles: A Preliminary Investigation," *Amerasia Journal* 18 (1992): 69–82; Peggy Li, Buck Wong, and Fong Kwan, *Garment Industry in Los Angeles Chinatown, 1973–74.* Asian American Studies Center, working papers no. 5 (University of California at Los Angeles, 1974).

25. The ILGWU was successful in organizing undocumented workers in a waterbed manufacturing plant in 1985, before the passage of the Immigration Re-

form and Control Act, as described in Hector L. Delgado, *New Immigrants, Old Unions: Organizing Undocumented Workers in Los Angeles* (Philadelphia: Temple University Press, 1993).

26. Ruth Milkman and Kent Wong of the University of California at Los Angeles are conducting a study of the Guess campaign as part of a larger study of organizing immigrant workers in Los Angeles. Robert Ross is planning to study it as part of a new study of sweatshops.

27. Ralph Armbruster, "Cross-National Labor Organizing Strategies," *Critical Sociology* 21 (1995): 77–91; "Cross-Border Labor Organizing in the Garment and Automobile Industries: The Phillips Van Heusen and Ford Cuautitlan Cases," *Journal of World-Systems Research* 4 (1998): 20–51; "Globalization and Cross-Border Labor Organizing in the Garment and Automobile Industries" (Ph.D. diss., University of California at Riverside, 1998); Ralph Armbruster-Sandoval, "Globalization and Cross-Border Labor Organizing: The Guatemalan Maquiladora Industry and the Phillips Van Heusen Workers Movement," *Latin American Perspectives* 26, no. 2 (1999): 108–28.

28. Teresa Carillo, "Women, Trade Unions, and New Social Movements in Mexico: The Case of Nineteenth September Garment Workers' Union" (Ph.D. diss., Stanford University, 1990).

29. Armbruster, "Globalization and Cross-Border Organizing," 1998, pp. 185–89.

30. Asian immigrants are overrepresented in the contractor population so the definition of the struggle of Asian garment workers as an "Asian community issue" is made somewhat more difficult because it raises more intracommunity contradictions. Nevertheless, Asian community activists have plunged ahead.

31. The influence of Paulo Freire, *The Pedagogy of the Oppressed* (New York: Continuum, 1981), should be evident in these ideas. Indeed, Paulo Freire himself once visited the Los Angeles Garment Workers' Justice Center and engaged in an inspiring dialogue with its members.

32. Jeff Hermanson, "Organizing for Justice: ILGWU Returns to Social Unionism to Organize Immigrant Workers," *Labor Research Review* 20 (1993): 53–61.

Notes for Chapter 10. The Antisweatshop Movement

1. Center for Ethical Concerns, "Garment Workers Study" (Marymount University, November 1995 and 1996).

2. Visit the Sweatshop Watch website at www.sweatshopwatch.org, for a description of the organization and its members and activities, for its newsletter, in which some of the developments in the movement are reported, and for links to other antisweatshop organizations. The coalition also maintains a list for regular updates about antisweatshop activities.

3. Indeed, there are signs that religious leaders are becoming more involved with labor issues, joining forces with the labor movement in an attempt to win greater equality for oppressed workers. See Danny Feingold, "Putting Faith in Labor: In a New Trend, a Motley Coalition of Southland Clergy Is Taking Up the Workers' Cause—and Winning," *Los Angeles Times,* 28 August 1998, sec. E, p. 1.

4. See Kitty Krupat, "From War Zone to Free Trade Zone: A History of the National Labor Committee," pp. 51–78 in *No Sweat: Fashion, Free Trade, and the Rights of Garment Workers,* ed. Andrew Ross (New York: Verso, 1997).

5. Janice McCoart, ed., "An Academic Search for Sweatshop Solutions: Conference Proceedings," Marymount University, Arlington, Va., 30 May 1997.

6. Andrew Ross, ed., *No Sweat: Fashion, Free Trade, and the Rights of Garment Workers* (New York: Verso, 1997).

7. For a review of the history and activities of AIWA, see Miriam Ching Louie, "Immigrant Asian Women in Bay Area Garment Sweatshops: 'After sewing, laundry, cleaning and cooking, I have no breath left to sing,' " *Amerasia Journal* 18 (1992): 1–26.

8. John Anner, "Sweatshop Workers Win Long Fight with Jessica McClintock," *Labor Notes,* May 1996, p. 2.

9. "Are Your Clothes Clean?" (pamphlet) City of Bangor, Maine, n.d.

10. Krupat, "From War Zone," p. 58.

11. Ibid., pp. 59–62.

12. Joanna Ramey, "Kernaghan to Press Wal-Mart on Sourcing," *Women's Wear Daily,* 30 July 1998, p. 11; Valerie Seckler, "NLC Wants Wal-Mart Source Info," *Women's Wear Daily,* 31 July 1998, p. 2.

13. Julie Su, "El Monte Thai Garment Workers: Slave Sweatshops," pp. 143–49 in *No Sweat, Fashion, Free Trade, and the Rights of Garment Workers,* ed. Andrew Ross (New York: Verso, 1997).

14. George White and Patrick McDonnell, "Sweatshop Workers to Get $2 Million," *Los Angeles Times,* 24 October 1997, sec. D, p. 1.

15. Cited in "El Monte Workers Win $2 Million Settlement," *Apparel Industry Magazine,* December 1997, p. 8.

16. Kristin Young, "Class-Action Suit Points Finger at U.S. Retailers," *California Apparel News,* 15 to 21 January 1999, p. 4; George White, "Law Firm Targets Retailers over Alleged Garment Labor Abuse," *Los Angeles Times,* 8 January 1999, p. C3; Eric Wilson, "$1B in Lawsuits Filed Charging Major Firms in Saipan Labor Abuse," *Women's Wear Daily,* 14 January 1999, p. 1.

17. John Zarocostas, "Clinton to WTO: Focus More on Labor Standards," *Women's Wear Daily,* 20 May 1998, p. 6.

18. Edna Bonacich has been active in Common Threads and the Coalition for Garment Workers; Richard Appelbaum has been active in the Jewish Commission.

19. See "Common Threads in Struggle: An Interview with Edna Bonacich," *Against the Current,* March/April 1998, pp. 13–14. Among the activists in Common Threads were Mizue Aizeki, Heather Archer, Roxane Auer, Carolina Bank, Edna Bonacich, Judy Branfman, Karen Brodkin, Eva Cockcroft, Susan Conrad, Jessica Goodheart, Suzi Hoffman, Mary-Linn Hughes, Michelle Mascarenhas, Becky Mead, Alessandra Moctezuma, Sheila Pinkel, Julia Stein, and Carol Zabin.

20. Quoted in Larry Kanter, "Public Art Project Irks Apparel Leaders," *Los Angeles Business Journal,* 28 April 1997, p. 3.

21. This section is adapted from materials prepared for the Los Angeles Jewish Commission on Sweatshops by David Waskow, American Jewish Congress regional program director, and Evely Laser Shlensky, immediate past national chair of the Commission on Social Action of Reform Judaism.

22. Other commission members include Steve Kaplan, past president, American Jewish Congress, Pacific Southwest Region and current commission co-chair; Jack Fine, vice president for legislation, American Jewish Committee, Los Angeles chapter; Laura Lake, president, National Council of Jewish Women, Los Angeles; Rick Chertoff, executive director, Jewish Labor Committee, Western Region; Rabbi Steve Carr Reuben, Kehillath Israel and vice president of Social Action for the Southern California Board of Rabbis; Rabbi Alice Dubinsky, assistant director, Union of American Hebrew Congregations, Pacific Southwest Council; Rabbi Steve Jacobs, Kol Tikvah; Rabbi Perry Netter, Temple Beth Am; and the former state senator, Alan Sieroty. Ben Bycel, the president of the University of West Los Angeles (and former head of the Los Angeles Ethics Commission) serves as the commission's legal counsel, and David Waskow, the regional program director of the American Jewish Congress, provided staff assistance through the summer of 1998. Richard Appelbaum serves as the commission's chief consultant. Carol Levy is no longer a member of the commission.

Note for Afterword

1. Sizing up the U.S. Apparel Market, "Apparel Industry Trends: Economic Newsletter of the AAMA," March 1998.

Bibliographic Note

Apart from a few studies of the location of the industry by Allen Scott ("Industrial Organization and the Logic of Intra-Metropolitan Location, III: A Case Study of the Women's Dress industry in the Greater Los Angeles Region," *Economic Geography* 60 [1984]: 3–27; and *Metropolis: From the Division of Labor to Urban Form*, pp. 91–118 [Berkeley: University of California Press, 1988]), following on the earlier work of Charles Goodman (*The Location of Fashion Industries, with Special Reference to the California Apparel Market* [Ann Arbor: University of Michigan Press, 1948]), few academic works about the upper end of the apparel industry in Los Angeles have been published. More recently, Allen Scott and David Rigby, both from the Geography Department of the University of California at Los Angeles, have written about the "cultural products" industries of Los Angeles, including crafts and fashion (David L. Rigby, "The Apparel Industry in Southern California," Dept. of Geography, University of California at Los Angeles, 1995; Allen J. Scott, "The Craft, Fashion, and Cultural-Products Industries of Los Angeles: Competitive Dynamics and Policy Dilemmas in a Multisectoral Image-Producing Complex," *Annals of the Association of American Geographers* 86 [1996]: 306–323; Allen J. Scott and David L. Rigby, "The Craft Industries of Los Angeles: Prospects for Economic Growth and Development," *CPS Brief* 8 [July 1996]). In addition, a study of the Jewish role in the industry, published by the Southern California Jewish Historical Society, provides a brief history of the development of the industry in Los Angeles ("Two Pair Pants Come with This Coat—A Perfect Fit: History of Jews in the Southern California Apparel Business," *Legacy: Journal of the Southern California Jewish Historical Society* 1 [spring, 1988]). The major Los Angeles jeans manufacturer, Guess? Inc., has been the subject of a book that covered its legal battles with New York jeans maker Jordache Enterprises (Christopher Byron, *Skin Tight: The Bizarre Story of Guess v. Jordache—Glamour, Greed and Dirty Tricks in the Fashion Industry* [New York: Simon and Schuster, 1992].

Despite this limited academic coverage, a great deal is written about the business end of the industry in newspapers and magazines, government reports, and so on. One finds articles on particular firms or designers, on the economic health of the industry, on style changes, on the social activities of leading figures of the industry, and so forth. The *Los Angeles Times* and the *California Apparel News,* as well as national trade newspapers and magazines such as *Women's Wear Daily, Bobbin,* and *Apparel Industry Magazine* continually discuss what is going on at the upper end of the industry.

Studies of the lower end have tended to focus on a few themes. Of special interest has been the fact that the majority of workers in the Los Angeles industry have been women and people of color, especially Latinos or Latinas and Asians. Thus studies of gender and ethnicity abound.

Studies of Latino and Latina workers include a dissertation based on participant observation and interviews by Maria Angelina Soldatenko ("The Everyday Lives of Latina Garment Workers in Los Angeles: The Convergence of Gender, Race, Class and Immigration" [Ph.D. diss., University of California at Los Angeles, 1992]), a study of homeworkers by Rosa Martha Fregoso ("The Invisible Workforce: Immigrant Home Workers in the Garment Industry of Los Angeles" [master's thesis, University of California at Berkeley, 1992]), and two contributions by Gregory Scott, ("The Everyday Politics of Domination and Resistance: An Ethnographic Inquiry into the Local Production of Garments for the Global Market" [master's thesis, University of California at Santa Barbara, 1992]; and "Sewing with Dignity: Class Struggle and Ethnic Conflict in the Los Angeles Garment Industry" [Ph.D. diss., University of California at Santa Barbara, 1997]). M. Patricia Fernandez-Kelly, together with her coauthors, Anna M. Garcia and Saskia Sassen, has studied homework and informalization in apparel and electronics, in Los Angeles and elsewhere (M. Patricia Fernandez-Kelly and Anna M. Garcia, "Hispanic Women and Homework: Women in the Informal Economy of Miami and Los Angeles," pp. 165–79 in *Homework: Historical and Contemporary Perspectives on Paid Labor at Home,* ed. Eileen Boris and Cynthia R. Daniels [Urbana, Ill.: University of Illinois Press, 1989]; and "Informalization at the Core: Hispanic Women, Homework, and the Advanced Capitalist State," pp. 247–64 in *The Informal Economy: Studies in Advanced and Less Developed Countries,* ed. Alejandro Portes, Manuel Castells, and Lauren A. Benton [Baltimore, Md.: Johns Hopkins University Press, 1989]; M. Patricia Fernandez-Kelly and Saskia Sassen, "A Collaborative Study of Hispanic Women in Garment and Electronics Industry" [report to the Ford, Revson, and Tinker Foundations, May 1991]; and M. Patricia Fernandez-Kelly and Anna M. Garcia, "Power Surrendered, Power Restored: The Politics of Work and Family among Hispanic Garment Workers in California and Florida," pp. 215–28 in *Challenging Fronteras: Structuring Latina and Latino Lives in the U.S.,* ed. Mary Romero, Pierrette Hondagneu-Sotelo, and Vilma Ortiz [New York: Routledge, 1997]).

A topic of special interest that has been studied in connection with Latino garment workers has been immigration status. Sheldon L. Maram and Stewart Long conducted a survey of workers that resulted in several analyses of the effect of undocumented status (Sheldon L. Maram, "Hispanic Workers in the Garment and Restaurant Industries in Los Angeles County: A Social and Economic Profile," Working Papers in U.S.–Mexican Studies, no. 12 [University of California at San Diego, 1980], Sheldon L. Maram and Stewart Long, "The Labor Market Impact of Hispanic Undocumented Workers: An Exploratory Case Study of the Garment Industry in Los Angeles County," [report to United States Department of Labor, Employment and Training Administration, 1981]; Stewart Long, "Undocumented Immigrants in the Los Angeles Garment Industry: Displacement or Dual Labor market?" *Journal of Borderland Studies* 2 [1987]: 1–11; Andrew Gill and Stewart Long, "Is There an Immigration Status Wage Differential between Legal and Undocumented Workers? Evidence from the Los Angeles Garment Industry," *Social Science Quarterly* 70 [March 1989]: 164–73). More recently, James Loucky and colleagues examined the effect of the Immigration Reform and Control Act (IRCA) on garment workers and workers in other industries (James Loucky, Nora Hamilton, and Norma Chinchilla, "The Effects of IRCA on Selected Industries in Los Angeles," report prepared for Ford Foundation, Los Angeles, 1989).

Asian immigrants have also been studied, though more as contractors than as workers. Peggy Li and her colleagues studied the industry in Chinatown, focusing primarily on workers, but also interviewing contractors (Peggy Li, Buck Wong, and Fong Kwan, "Garment Industry in Los Angeles Chinatown, 1973–74," Asian American Studies Center working papers, no. 5 [University of California at Los Angeles, 1974]). Richard Kim and colleagues updated a study of Asian garment workers and expanded the study to cover other Asian groups (Richard Kim, Kane K. Nakamura, and Gisele Fong, "Asian Immigrant Women Garment Workers in Los Angeles: A Preliminary Investigation," *Amerasia Journal* 18 [1992]: 69–82). Hyung-ki Jin and Darrel Hess each conducted surveys of Korean garment contractors (Hyung-ki Jin, "A Survey on the Economic and Managerial Status of Sewing Factories Owned and Operated by Korean Contractors in the Los Angeles Area," Industrial Research Institute for Pacific Nations, California State Polytechnic University, Pomona, Calif., 1981); Darrel Eugene Hess, "Korean Immigrant Entrepreneurs in the Los Angeles Garment Industry" [master's thesis, University of California, Los Angeles, 1990]). Edward Park, partly working with our project, examined contracting and other roles played by Korean Americans (Edward J. W. Park, "From Entry to Entrenchment: Korean Americans and the Los Angeles Garment Industry, 1970–1995" [paper presented at the conference of the Pacific Sociological Association, Seattle, 1996]).

A few studies have attempted to examine the relationship between Asian contractors and Latino workers; Edna Bonacich has written several ("Alienation among Asian and Latino Immigrants in the Los Angeles Garment Industry: The Need for New Forms of Class Struggle," pp. 155–80 in *Alienation, Society and the Individual,* ed. Felix Geyer and Walter R. Heinz [New Brunswick, N.J.: Transaction, 1992]; "Asian and Latino Immigrants in the Los Angeles Garment Industry: An Exploration of the Relationship between Capitalism and Racial Oppression," pp. 51–73 in *Immigration and Entrepreneurship: Culture, Capital and Ethnic Networks,* ed. Ivan Light and Parminder Bhachu [New Brunswick, N.J.: Transaction, 1993]; "Asian Immigrants in the Los Angeles Garment Industry" pp. 137–63 in *The New Asian Immigration in Los Angeles and Global Restructuring,* ed. Paul Ong, Edna Bonacich, and Lucie Cheng [Philadelphia: Temple University Press, 1994]). Ku-Sup Chin surveyed Korean contractors and Latino workers (Ku-Sup

Chin, Socorro T. Sarmiento, and David A. Smith, "Exploiting Migrants: The L.A. Garment Industry and Global Restructuring" [Program in Social Relations, University of California at Irvine, May 1997]). He served as a research assistant on this project, and we report some of the results of his survey of Korean contractors in this volume.

Unionization has been a significant theme in the sociological literature. Douglas Monroy and Clementina Duron wrote articles on Mexican women's participation in dressmakers' strikes in the 1930s (Douglas Monroy, "La Costura en Los Angeles: 1933–1939: The ILGWU and the Politics of Domination," pp. 171–78 in *Mexican Women in the United States: Struggles Past and Present,* ed. Magdalena Mora and Adelaida R. del Castello [Los Angeles, Calif.: University of California at Los Angeles, Chicano Studies Center, 1980]; Clementina Duron, "Mexican Women and Labor Conflict in Los Angeles: The ILGWU Dressmakers' Strike of 1933," *Aztlan* 15 [spring 1984]: 145–61). Rose Pesotta, a union leader at the time, wrote her own memoirs that include her tour of duty in Los Angeles. (*Bread Upon the Waters* [1944; reprint, Ithaca, N.Y.: ILR Press, 1987]). John Laslett and Mary Tyler have written a history of the International Ladies Garment Workers Union (ILGWU) in Los Angeles, and Laslett, raising issues of race and gender, wrote about Rose Pesotta's relationship with the union (John Laslett and Mary Tyler, *The ILGWU in Los Angeles, 1907–1988* [Inglewood, Calif.: Ten Star Press, 1989]); John H. M. Laslett, "Gender, Class, or Ethno-Cultural Struggle? The Problematic Relationship between Rose Pesotta and the Los Angeles ILGWU," *California History* 72 [spring 1993]: 20–39). Hector Delgado wrote a book about an organizing campaign among undocumented workers by the ILGWU, albeit not in a garment factory (*New Immigrants, Old Unions: Organizing Undocumented Workers in Los Angeles* [Philadelphia: Temple University Press, 1993]).

Apart from the two major themes of capital and labor, a third genre of literature exists, namely, unpublished studies instigated to urge the industry or the government to pursue certain policies. These studies include several works emanating from the Urban Planning program at the University of California at Los Angeles (before it was folded into the School of Public Policy and Social Research), among them, Bullock et al., ("Manufacturing L.A.'s Future: An Industrial Policy Proposal for the City of Los Angeles" [master's thesis, University of California, Los Angeles, 1993]); Jean Gilbert, "Restyling the Los Angeles Apparel Industry: Models, Options and Resources for Industry Revitalization" [report prepared for Southern California Edison and the Apparel Industry Roundtable, Los Angeles, 1994); Sumanta Ray, "Transformation of Labor-Intensive Production: The Los Angeles Garment Industry" [master's thesis, University of California at Los Angeles, 1990]). The Southern California Edison Company helped to convene the Apparel Industry Roundtable that resulted in several documents describing and recommending changes for the industry (Southern California Edison Company and DRI/McGraw Hill, *Southern California's Apparel Industry: Building a Path to Prosperity.* [Los Angeles, Calif.: Southern California Edison, 1995]; Goetz Wolff, "The Apparel Industry and Regional Restructuring: Opportunities for Continued Growth" [pamphlet prepared for the California Community College Fashion Symposium, CaliforniaMart, Los Angeles, 1995]). These last two sources overlap somewhat.

Several policy studies have been written more recently, including a study conducted for the California Policy Seminar by Jean Gilbert et al. ("State Policies to Promote Industrial Upgrading for Low Wage Manufacturers" [report, California Policy Seminar, Berkeley, Calif., 1997]), a report for the Haynes Foundation by Goetz Wolff and Carol Zabin ("Manufacturing Matters: A Sectoral Approach to Combating Low Wages in Los Angeles" [Lewis Center, University of California at Los Angeles, 1997]), especially chapter four on the apparel industry, by Wolff, and a report by Goetz Wolff that was delivered at a fashion symposium in 1997 ("The Apparel Cluster: A Regional Growth Industry" [pamphlet prepared for the California Community College Fashion Symposium, CaliforniaMart, Los Angeles, April 1997]). The authors of these policy studies tend to be much more aware of the workers' problems than are the authors of most industry studies, and generally propose ways for the industry to eliminate sweatshops by upgrading itself while remaining competitive.

Index

Bahrain, Investcorp Bank based in, 87
BancBoston Financial, 32
Bangladesh, offshore production, 58, 59, 60
Bank of Boston, 32
Bank of New York, 32
bankruptcies: contractor, 301–2; manufacturer, 42, 45, 46, 47, 59, 101; retailer, 84–89, 102
banks: commercial, 31, 32, 76; Federal Reserve, 20–21; loans to, 247; Los Angeles Community Development Bank, 259, 260, 353n81. *See also* Union Bank
Barbara Lesser label, 70
Barclay's Commercial, 32
Barnard, Harry, 130–31
Barnes and Noble, 93
basics, 10–11; buying offices and, 98; "fashion basics," 29, 59; offshore production for, 71, 79; retailer consolidation and, 90–91. *See also* sportswear
B.A.T. (British American Tobacco) Industries, 87
Baum, Tracy, 114
BCBG Max Azria, 42, 48, 168; Francine Browner, Inc. bought by, 34, 48, 332n46; retail store operation, 29, 101; specializing in women's wear, 34; Vernon, 37–39
Beach Patrol Inc., 34
Bebop Clothing, 71, 168
Beerman, Rabbi Leonard, 311
Beit Tzedek, 313
benefits. *See* fringe benefits
Benjamin, Medea, 299
Bergdorf Goodman, 86
Berman, Harry, 46
Bernstein, Jonathan, 114, 115–16, 117, 121–22
Between a Rock and a Hard Place: A History of American Sweatshops, 1820–Present, Smithsonian Institution, 119–20, 123, 310
BID (Business Improvement District), 109–10, 248
Big Bisou Inc., 168
Bisou Bisou label, 34, 168
Bloomingdale's, 87
Bluestone, Barry, 81
BNY Financial Corporation, 32

Bobbin, 257
Bonacich, Edna, 115, 116, 123, 276–78, 356n24, 358n18
Bongo brand, 34, 168
Bon Marché, 87
bonuses, 185, 211
bootstrap ideology, 121–23. *See also* upward mobility
boycotts: by community antisweatshop groups, 300, 301–2. *See also* strikes
Bradley, Ellen, 95, 98
Bradley, Tom, 117, 126, 129, 132
Bradshaw, Victoria, 238
Brasking Inc., 168
Brazil, Korean manufacturers from, 44–45
Bregman, Ruth, 106, 110, 115
Bregman and Associates, 98–99, 106
Bregman Clinic, 98
Breton, Neal/Breton Industries, 324n8
Britain: Ethical Trade Initiative, 244; Labour Party, 8; Pakistani contractors and workers, 141
British American Tobacco (B.A.T.) Industries, 87
Broadway Stores, 86, 87, 211
Broadway Trade Center, 128–29
Brown, Bernard, 225–26
Bugle Boy Industries, 58–59, 67, 70, 101, 111, 126
Bullock's, 85, 87, 89, 90
B.U.M. Equipment, 59, 132
B.U.M. International, 46, 167, 308
Burdines, 87
Bureau of Field Enforcement, California, 224
Bureau of the Census, United States, 4, 169, 325n23; *County Business Patterns,* 18, 143, 325n23, 342n18
Burma, offshore production, 55
Business Improvement District (BID), 109–10, 248
buying offices, 33, 35, 96–99, 105, 106
Bycel, Ben, 278
Byer California, 168

CAIC. *See* Coalition of Apparel Industries of California
California: antiimmigrant movements, 19, 25, 165, 197–98, 273, 281; apparel industry beginnings, 32–35; Apparel Industry Revitalization Act (1994), 254;

135–36, 140–58, 162–63, 196; upward mobility ideology and, 22, 79, 121, 136, 196. *See also* contractors; manufacturers; ownership
environmental impact, apparel industry, 201, 318
equality. *See* egalitarianism
equipment and tools: workers paying for, 184, 185–86. *See also* sewing machines; technology
Equitable Life Assurance Society, 76, 106, 133
ethnicity: California law enforcement agents', 223; CaliforniaMart tenants' revolt and, 130; contractors', 20, 136, 140–58, 145*table*, 146*table*, 163, 291, 342n7; and contractor-worker alliance, 290; discrimination based on, 154, 194; homeworkers', 185; manufacturers', 39–41, 43–45, 196, 326n38; middleman minority role, 20, 140–42, 153, 154, 163, 291; UNITE, 282; wage differences by, 181; workers', 20, 140–42, 153, 169*table*, 171–74, 181, 185, 194, 280–81, 290, 341n4. *See also* African Americans; immigrants; Jews
Europe: Eastern, 141; high fashion, 33; offshore production, 59; tariffs, 56. *See also* Britain; European Union; Netherlands
European Americans: contractors, 145, 147; garment workers, 171, 172; manufacturers, 40, 43, 44; at top of industry hierarchy, 20. *See also* Jews; whites
European Union, 244, 319
executives: perks, 212–13; salaries, 22, 79, 103, 105, 122, 210–19, 216*table*. *See also* managers; professionals
exports: "corporatist" solution and, 256; by manufacturers surveyed, 43; manufacturing for, 4, 7, 9. *See also* offshore production; trade
eye strain, workers', 177, 179

factoring, 31–32
Failures and Promises of the Garment Industry, 274
Fair Labor Association (FLA), 244, 304, 305
Fair Labor Standards Act (FLSA), 166, 227–29, 237, 244, 264

Famous-Barr/L. S. Ayres/The Jones Store, 87
Farrell, David, 210
fashion: apparel industry driven by, 9–11, 14, 17–18, 28–29, 33–34; buying offices and, 97, 98; entertainment industry and, 17, 33, 34, 73, 77; environmental impact of promoting, 201, 318; high fashion, 33, 326n27; and image, 287–88; in industries other than apparel, 13–14; as lifestyle, 217–19; Los Angeles as center of, 17–18, 28–29, 33–35, 73–74, 77. *See also* apparel industry; basics; design
"fashion basics," 29, 59
Fashion District, Los Angeles downtown, 35, 37, 38*fig*, 74; BID, 109–10, 248; "Clean and Safe" project, 109; contractors' locations and, 145, 146–47; ethnicity of manufacturers in, 41; expansion proposal (1992), 129; factory structures, 176; Korean contractors, 41, 151; manufacturers' locations and, 37–39, 41, 52, 326n31; property owners, 105–6, 109–10, 128–33; Santee Alley, 30, 156; Street Beautification Banner Campaign, 110; supportive services near, 74, 76–78. *See also* CaliforniaMart
Fashion Headquarters, Inc., 231
Fashion Industries Guild, 98, 114, 115, 117, 118, 324n10, 338n17
Fashion Industry Alliance, 260
Fashion Industry Forum, 241
Fashion Industry Group, 106
Fashion Industry Modernization Center, New York City, 256
Fashion Institute of Design and Merchandising, 77, 105, 106, 112, 132, 333–34n72
Fashion Resources Inc., 182–83
fashion shows, 10, 248. *See also* showrooms
federal government. *See* United States
Federal Reserve Bank, 20–21
Federated Department Stores, 85–89, 98, 211, 240
Feinstein, Dianne, 125
female workers, 170–71; clothing consumption, 82; community antisweatshop groups and, 309–10; for contractors, 152–53; homeworkers, 185; interviewees, 175–76; managers, 173; striking, 266; wages (1990), 181; white garment workers in South, 171; young proletarianized, 7

Immigration Reform and Control Act
(IRCA), 170, 193, 271, 272–73, 281,
356–57n25
imports: department store reliance on, 91;
NAFTA and, 53, 157; United States rise
in apparel imports, 9, 10fig, 14, 16, 54–
57, 63, 329n11. *See also* consumption;
offshore production; trade
income, 19–25, 122, 202–3; executives', 22,
79, 103, 105, 122, 210–19, 216table; Korean
contractors', 154–55, 217, 343n26; retail
shoppers', 82, 83. *See also* distribution
of income; poverty; profits; wages
incubator projects, 254
India: offshore production, 55, 59, 60;
workers in Africa from, 141
Indians, American, Los Angeles garment
workers, 172
Indonesia, offshore production, 55, 58, 60
Industrial Wage Commission, California,
21–22, 158
industries: compliance consultancy, 234,
305; "cultural-products," 72–73; deindustrialization in developed countries,
4; polarization along race and class
lines, 19–25. *See also* apparel industry;
entertainment industry; management;
manufacturing; production; workers
inflation, 21
informal sector. *See* underground economy
INS. *See* Immigration and Naturalization
Service
inspections: law enforcement, 223–24,
226–27, 239–40. *See also* monitoring;
raids; sweeps
Interfaith Center for Corporate Responsibility, 244
International Ladies' Garment Workers'
Union (ILGWU), 11, 267; industry
collaboration, 25; Jewish participants,
311; jobber's agreements, 284; and joint
liability, 225; merger with ACTWU, 11,
265, 282, 283; organizing directors of,
283, 291; organizing through NLRB
elections, 269; strike against Good
Times/Song of California (1995), 123;
and undocumented workers, 272,
356–57n25
International Mass Retail Association, 211
Internet, 93, 301, 304, 336n43
interviews, worker, 175–76

Introspect brand, 42
inventories: electronic point-of-sale, 83,
90, 92–93, 198, 251; turnover, 91–93, 257,
317–18
Investcorp Bank, 87
ironing, male specialty, 153, 170
IRS, 176, 179, 223, 239
Israel, offshore production, 60

Jaclyn Smith label, 99
Jacobs, Larry, 40, 167–68
Jag brand, 34
Jalate, Ltd., Inc., 31, 34, 49–50, 168, 234
Janis-Aparicio, Madeline, 250
Japan: apparel consumption, 9; offshore
production, 54, 56
J. C. Penney Co., 50, 81, 88; homeworkers,
185; and law enforcement, 240, 308; as
mass merchandiser, 334n5; Monarch
Knits and Sportswear, 167; private-label,
64, 90, 99, 101, 165
J. Crew Group Inc., 308
jeans, 34; Guess, 51, 67; Jordache, 51;
Levi's, 67, 100–101; Wrangler, 215
Jeans Plus, 235
Jessica McClintock, antisweatshop
campaign, 299, 301–2
Jewish Coalition on Sweatshops, 276–77,
278, 356n23
Jewish Commission on Sweatshops, 299,
311–13, 356n23, 358n18, 359n22
Jewish Federation Council of Greater Los
Angeles, 113
Jewish Relief Fund, 116
Jews: charities, 114, 115, 116, 117; community antisweatshop groups, 299, 311–
13; contractors, 145, 147, 148; Eastern
Europe, 141; garment workers, 171;
immigrants, 121, 123; manufacturers, 31,
39–40, 41, 43, 44; power elite, 104, 114,
115, 116, 117, 119, 142; property owners,
151; vertical integration, 144
J. H. Snyder Company, 132
Jin, Hyung-Ki, 150, 152
J. Michelle of California, 68
JNCO label, 34, 165, 168
jobbers, 28, 144
jobbers' agreements, 284–87, 291, 292
jobs. *See* labor
job security, 176, 183, 265; for contractors'
workers, 137, 188; decrease in, 4, 5, 8, 21

locations. *See* districts, garment; geography; globalization; offshore production
Logan, Karl, 78
Lola, Inc., 34, 39, 168
"look": California, 33–35; in collections, 28
Lopez, Luis, 147–48
Lord & Taylor, 87
Los Angeles, 322n6; antisweatshop community groups, 309–15; apparel industry retention efforts by, 246–49; attractions of, 17, 33–35, 72–79; Community Development Bank, 259, 260, 353n81; Community Redevelopment Agency, 105, 126, 132, 250, 310; "cultural products," 72–73; Department of Water and Power, 249; earthquake (1994), 109; East, 39; Economic Development Corporation, 36, 68, 106–7, 122, 333–34n72; employment patterns, 16, 17*fig,* 35, 36–37, 53, 54, 65, 68–69, 72, 169, 169*table;* enterprise zones, 246–48, 249, 353nn80,81; entertainment industry, 17, 33–35, 39, 73, 77, 213; ethnic forms in apparel industry, 141; as fashion center, 16–18, 28–29, 33–35, 73–74, 77; garment contractors (population), 142–47, 145*table;* garment manufacturers (population), 35–36, 142–43, 325n24; garment production locations, 37–39, 41, 52, 145–46; garment/textile percentage of county economy, 36; Garment Workers Justice Center, 164, 175, 176, 182, 293–94, 313, 357n31; garment workers (population), 16, 36, 65, 122–23, 143, 169–70, 169*table,* 171, 187, 342n18; at global crossroads, 58; income distribution, 19, 25; living wage ordinance (1997), 21, 120, 159, 322n5, 324n25; as national manufacturing center, 16, 35; Office of Economic Development, 110, 248, 250; polarization of race/immigrant status and class, 19–25; population (1900–1940), 32–33; school system, 197; sweatshops, 2–3, 4, 19, 21, 48, 66, 78–79, 120, 221. *See also* apparel industry; districts, garment; government; riots, Los Angeles (April 1992)
Los Angeles Alliance for a New Economy (LAANE), 250
Los Angeles Business Journal, 133, 213–14
Los Angeles Business Team, 246, 248, 249

Los Angeles County Bar Association, 51
Los Angeles Glo, Inc., 167
Los Angeles Manufacturing Networks Initiative, 122
Los Angeles Times, 71, 106, 124–27, 215, 276, 277
Los Angeles Trade-Technical College, 77, 78, 260–61; in CFA, 112; Tate of, 106, 108, 111, 254
Louis Bernard Inc., 107
Lucero, Isaura, 294
Lucky Brand Dungarees, 34, 39
Lucky Sewing Company, 301–2
Lumer, Jack, 105, 132

Macy's, 81, 85–87, 90, 91, 211, 215, 334n5
Macy's East, 86–87
Macy's West, 86–87
Magnin, I., 85
mail-order catalogue houses, 81, 87, 99
Malaysia, offshore production, 55, 58
male workers: garment workers, 152–53, 170–71, 173; managers, 173; wages (1990), 181
malls: department store anchors, 83; sweatshops connected with, 167. *See also* shopping centers
management: and piece-rate system, 180–81; "social contract" with unions, 6, 264–65; sweatshop labor for, 167. *See also* capital; contractors; executives; managers; manufacturers; ownership; retailers
managers, 81, 105, 169; ethnicity, 171, 172, 173; floor, 191–93; gender, 173; power elite, 24, 105, 106; share in distribution of proceeds, 20, 215–17. *See also* executives; management
Manatt, Phelps, and Phillips, 106
Mandarin International, 306
manufacturers, 27–52, 198; advertising costs, 215; codes of conduct, 303–7; collegiate licensing by, 304–5; community antisweatshop groups pressuring, 307; competition, 23, 52, 339n23; compliance programs/monitoring, 3, 52, 69, 229–36, 276, 305–6, 314, 350n38; contracting advantages for, 12, 30, 49–50, 136–40, 266, 285; contractor alliances with, 260–61; contractor relationships' stability, 188, 285; contractors lumped

Text and Display:	Galliard
Composition:	Integrated Compositions Systems, Inc.
Printing and binding:	Haddon Craftsmen
Illustrations:	Bill Nelson
Index:	Barbara Roos